D1179056

'THE BLUE BEAST'

'THE BLUE BEAST'

Power & Passion
IN THE GREAT WAR

JONATHAN WALKER

The
History
Press

First published 2012

The History Press
The Mill, Brimscombe Port
Stroud, Gloucestershire, GL5 2QG
www.thehistorypress.co.uk

British Library Cataloguing in Publication Data.
A catalogue record for this book is available from the British Library.

ISBN 978 0 7524 6597 5

Typesetting and origination by The History Press
Printed in Great Britain
Manufacturing managed by Jellyfish Print Solutions Ltd

Contents

Acknowledgements   6
Introduction   9

PART I   Winifred Bennett

1   A Romanian Cradle   15
2   'To Die Would Be an Awfully Big Adventure'   30
3   Afternoon Delights   50
4   Elysium   64

PART II   Emilie Grigsby

5   Southern Belle   73
6   Mascot of High Command   90
7   Salons and Cabals   107
8   Reputations   124

PART III   Sylvia Henley

9   A Liberal Heritage   129
10   'One Half of a Pair of Scissors'   140
11   Betrayal   156
12   A Changing World   177
     Afterword: 'The Human Soul on Fire'   183

Notes   186
Bibliography   208
Index   219

Acknowledgements

While the last of the main characters in these pages died in the 1980s, their families can still provide a direct link. It was my good fortune to come into contact with the descendants of two of these extraordinary women. My sincere thanks to sculptress and gardener Camilla Shivarg for her kind hospitality and generous help in allowing me access to the papers and albums of her great-grandmother Winifred 'Wendy' Bennett, and for her permission to quote from the papers and reproduce photographic images. Similar thanks to her father, Alexander Shivarg, for unravelling some of the complexities of Winifred's family connections.

Anthony Pitt-Rivers extended the same kind hospitality and allowed me to examine his amazing collection of Stanley family photograph albums. He gave me valuable insights into the world of his grandmother, the Hon. Sylvia Henley, and I acknowledge his kind permission to reproduce photographs of Sylvia, her family and friends. As the senior member of his family, he kindly granted permission to quote from Sylvia's correspondence, held in the Bodleian Library, Oxford. Anna Mathias was similarly gracious in granting permission for me to quote from the correspondence of her grandmother, Venetia Montagu.

My thanks to Helen Langley, the Curator of Modern Political Papers at the Bodleian Library, Oxford University, for her assistance and my thanks to the Trustees of the Bodleian Library for their permission to quote from letters in the Sylvia Henley collection. I am also grateful to the Bonham Carter Trustees for their permission to quote from the letters written by Herbert Henry Asquith.

I acknowledge the help of Tony Richards and the Department of Documents, at the Imperial War Museum, for their assistance in accessing Lord French's correspondence and my thanks to the Trustees of the Imperial War Museum for their permission to quote from the letters of Field Marshal Lord French and to reproduce his image from their photographic collection. His impenetrable handwriting is a huge challenge to any researcher, and must have gone some way to allaying fears about the consequences of his letters falling into enemy hands. Deciphering the entire collection was certainly a labour of love for me. We do not know the effect it had on his mistress, but in certain photographs, 'Wendy' does look slightly 'boss-eyed'.

My thanks to the staff of the Liddell Hart Centre for Military Archives for helping me access records and to the Trustees of the LHCMA for granting me permission to quote from the diary of Lady Hamilton, contained in the papers of her husband, Sir Ian Hamilton. I am grateful to fellow author Celia Lee, for originally drawing my attention to the value of the Hamilton Papers and for providing me with background material on Charles Repington.

The late Professor Richard Holmes, who wrote a colourful and informative study of Field Marshal Lord French, gave me the benefit of his considerable knowledge of the Commander-in-Chief. Richard's humour and spirit in the face of failing health was an inspiration to all. (The publishers would also like to take this opportunity to express their admiration and gratitude to a great historian and a generous man, always ready with advice and help with Spellmount titles, happy to lend his own authority and reputation won over many years to the work of other authors.) I also appreciate the help and support of fellow researchers and medal experts, Keith Northover and John Arnold, while Professor Donald Thomas, Michael Walker, Chrissie Parrot and Mike Read all helped me to locate sources. Jasper Humphries, Director of External Affairs at the Marjan Centre for the Study of Conflict and Conservation was always a constant reference for historical accuracy. My thanks to my good friends Mark and Geraldine Talbot, Derek and Jo Lamb and Peter and Sue Hansen for their generous hospitality while I was researching.

I have made every effort to obtain the necessary permission to reproduce copyright material in this work, though in some cases it has been impossible to trace the current copyright holders. Any omissions are entirely unintentional and if any are brought to my notice, I will be most happy to include the appropriate acknowledgements in any future re-printing. I acknowledge permission to quote passages from the following: the novelist Francis Wyndham, and his agents Rogers, Coleridge & White for passages from his novel, *The Other Garden*; Little, Brown Book Group for *Dawn Chorus* by Joan Wyndham; Oxford University Press for *The War in the Air, Vol. III* by H.A. Jones; Penguin Group for *Sex and the British* by Paul Ferris; Constable & Robinson for *Thanks for the Memory* by Mary Repington; the extract from *The Autobiography of Margot Asquith*, edited by Mark Bonham Carter, is by kind permission of the Trustees of the Bonham Carter/Asquith Papers held in the Bodleian Library; United Agents Limited for permission to quote from *Diana Cooper* by Philip Ziegler; Orion Publishing and John Julius Norwich for kind permission to use extracts from his edition of his father's diaries, *The Duff Cooper Diaries;* Professor Nicholas Deakin for permission to quote from the correspondence of Henry Havelock Ellis.

While the concept of 'service' in most walks of life is fast disappearing, archivists and their assistants manage to maintain a dedication and helpfulness that is so useful to authors and researchers; my thanks to the staff of the Mary Evans Picture Library in Blackheath, London; Elen Wyn Simpson of the Archives and Special Collections,

Bangor University; Dr Caroline Corbeau-Parsons of the de Laszlo Archive Trust; Ilaria Della Monica, Director of the Berenson Archive at the Harvard University Center for Italian Renaissance Studies, Florence, and to Annabel Sayers, my very competent researcher in that beautiful city. My mother, Lady Walker, gave me useful advice on the history of fashion, while the antiquarian booksellers, Jarndyce, were most helpful in locating past auction records. My friends at Sidmouth Library, Gill Spence, Meriel Santer, Victoria Luxton and Sylvia Werb, did a marvellous job keeping me supplied with numerous out-of-print titles.

Whilst some of the great houses that feature in these stories no longer exist, there remain a number that are lovingly maintained by their current owners. Special thanks to Quentin Plant for his kind hospitality at his beautiful home; similarly, my thanks to Dr Michael Peagram for sharing his archive at his home, Bletchingdon Park, Oxford, and to Andrew Whittaker for his help and generous hospitality concerning 80 Brook Street in Mayfair.

I wish to express gratitude to Barbara Briggs-Anderson, Curator of the Julian P. Graham Historical Photographic Collection for her help with the portrait of George Gordon Moore. Her work on behalf of Loon Hill Studios in Santa Barbara, helps preserve the legacy of Moore's post-war creation, The Santa Lucia Preserve in Carmel. The Anders Zorn painting of Emilie Grigsby appears by courtesy of Sotheby's Picture Library, while Sir John Cowans appears by kind permission of the National Library of Scotland. The National Monuments Register kindly gave permission to reproduce their image of 'Old Meadows.' Emilie Grigsby's couture collection is housed in the Victoria & Albert Museum and the image of her original Poiret mantle is reproduced by courtesy of the Trustees of the Victoria & Albert Museum and the Design and Artists' Copyright Society. The Library of Congress in Washington is a rich source of photographic material, not only concerning US history, but also Edwardian Britain. Images from the library's collections from the Bain News Service, Carl van Vechten and the Moffett Studio are reproduced in this book.

Finally, I have appreciated the help and advice of Shaun Barrington of Spellmount and The History Press. As always, I am indebted to my wife Gill, who has endured three years of my immersion in Edwardian England and has supported me all the way along this project. It has been a fascinating journey.

Jonathan Walker, 2012

Introduction

This is the true story of three intriguing Edwardian women who became mistresses or close confidantes of some of the most powerful men in the British Empire. These women reached the zenith of their influence as Britain embarked on the greatest war that the world had ever seen. Yet their names are hardly known today, eclipsed by the dazzling profiles of their lovers and relegated to the 'footnotes of history'. Winifred Bennett, Emilie Grigsby and Sylvia Henley were three very different characters from diverse backgrounds. Winifred had an exotic upbringing in Romania, Emilie was the essence of a seductive American adventuress, while Sylvia enjoyed the privileged life of an aristocrat. The first two were certainly mistresses while the latter could be described as a 'very close companion' to her suitor. They were not the stereotype of the young 'kept' mistress, but were women in their thirties, who were financially independent of their admirers – both Winifred and Sylvia were married, while Emilie was hugely wealthy in her own right.

In fact, most Edwardian women discovered that marriage gave them independence for the first time in their lives. Single girls, especially before the war, were subject to extraordinary protection. Their reputation had to be spotless and their lives were constantly monitored and chaperoned. Their one release was marriage, though the success of a marriage was thought to depend more upon mutual love and friendship than upon a woman's sexual fulfilment. Yet that idea was already under attack by enlightened women, and Winifred Bennett was one who had lost patience with a sterile marriage. Once she had discovered the power of her allure, the temptation to test it became irresistible.[1]

Many members of London 'society' knew about these affairs, but because these women were discreet, they found they were accepted by many society hostesses. Other women might be curious, while most men were captivated by their company. After all, they epitomised the 'blue beast' – Edwardian upper class slang for sexual passion – a subject most women would only whisper about in mixed company. Conversation amongst their girlfriends was another matter.[2]

If sex was still largely a taboo subject for polite conversations on the Home Front, what was happening on the Western Front? The Great War poets concentrated relentlessly on the horror and pity of trench warfare, the vision that overarches every interpretation of the war. But few soldiers at the time spent their days thinking about the ghastliness of the Western Front. Their diaries and letters reveal that when they were not enduring periodic terror, they were exhausted from constant labouring duties, or if in reserve, they were kept busy with repeated training and exercise sessions. When they did relax, they thought about home, or more personal, physical needs. Charles Carrington, author of the hugely successful memoir, *A Subaltern's War*, and a soldier who had seen as much action as the poet Siegfried Sassoon, had no truck with Sassoon's 'precious and gloomy' view of the soldier's lot. 'What most young soldiers talked and wrote letters about,' he countered, 'were girls, football, food and drink.'[3] Indeed, it is no surprise that contemporary marching songs confirmed that girls, and the possibility of sex, dominated the thoughts of these young men. As they marched up to the front, singing to the tune of 'Tipperary,' the soldiers usually substituted the familiar words we know today, with their own robust lyrics:

That's the wrong way to tickle Marie,
That's the wrong way to kiss:
Don't you know that over here, lad,
They like it better like this.
Hooray *pour la France!*
Farewell, *Angleterre!*
We didn't know the way to tickle Marie,
But now we've learnt how.[4]

They certainly had. The bill for tickling Marie during the war was over 150,000 hospital admissions for venereal disease, in France alone. Some soldiers even visited brothels because they wanted to deliberately catch VD and be invalided out of action. While the ranks would join brothel queues – and according to one participating soldier, they often exceeded 300 men – some officers enjoyed the services of more discreet prostitutes.[5]

If most soldiers had sex on the brain, the common conception was that their superior officers and the senior politicians running the war were somehow devoid of sexual impulses. There remained a conspiracy of silence about their private lives and if there was any whiff of scandal, it was ignored or denied by a compliant press. The overriding concern was that 'the lower orders' should not be exposed to bad behaviour by senior military commanders, or indeed politicians. Consequently, this security from exposure only helped to encourage some leading figures, so that their sex lives exploded out of control and their public life came to grief. There had been sex scandals in the late Victorian period. Everyone in political circles knew about Charles Parnell and his mistress Kitty O'Shea; but when he eventually married her, the saga became public and helped destroy his political career and undermine the Irish Party. Sir Charles Dilke followed a similar path, and following the Cleveland Street brothel raid, Britain's 'respectable' society suddenly began to reassert itself. By 1895, with the trial and conviction of Oscar Wilde, decadence appeared to be back in its box. But after the turn of the century, inspired by the lifestyle of King Edward VII, promiscuity had returned, and as long as affairs were conducted in a discreet manner, society could tolerate it. Such discretion was mandatory, for the ruling class feared that a succession of scandals would pollute the lower classes who, it was believed, would be ill-equipped to handle it. Furthermore, a resulting lack of confidence in the upper class's destiny to rule could strengthen the hand of the socialists and even threaten revolution.[6]

For Britain, at least, revolution never came. The First World War brought huge convulsion to Europe and Russia but it was business as usual in Britain's 'corridors of power', and sex was part of the deal. The first wartime Prime Minister, Herbert Henry Asquith, enjoyed a succession of female confidantes and surrounded himself with colleagues such as Lord Curzon, who was only too ready, as the popular ditty went, to 'sin with Elinor Glyn, on a tiger skin.' Cabinet Minister Lord Milner dallied with the exotic Cécile, while Lloyd George famously bedded any number of secretaries before meeting Frances Stevenson at the Welsh Chapel near Oxford Circus. He appointed her as both his Personal Secretary and mistress (he eventually married her). Batting for the opposite team, Lord Esher had a penchant for young boys, while the appalling Lewis Harcourt attacked anything on two legs.[7]

Many senior military figures took mistresses as a matter of course, especially if they were seemingly beyond reproach. Sir John French, as Commander-in-Chief, only answered to the Chief of the Imperial General Staff, who in turn took his orders from the Government (HMG) in the shape of the Secretary of State for War. Sir John Cowens was the Quartermaster-General throughout the war, and along with the Adjutant General, was one of the most senior commanders who sat on the Army Council. Both these men enjoyed a varied sex life outside their marriages. This lifestyle was no less popular in the Navy. Admiral Beatty enjoyed a passionate and lengthy affair with Eugénie Godfrey-Faussett, wife of the aide-de-camp (ADC) to the King. Taking mistresses was also de rigueur amongst allied military commanders. In the early days of the Battle of Verdun, the notable French commander, Philippe Pétain, had to be extracted from the clutches of his mistress, the aptly named Eugénie Hardon, while General 'Black Jack' Pershing, the Commander-in-Chief of the American Expeditionary Force, found solace in the arms of his exotic French-Romanian mistress, Micheline Resco.[8]

It is important to remember that power and influence in post-Edwardian Britain still remained within a very small coterie. Politics, the legal profession and the Officer Corps of the Army drew most of their members from 'society', a prescribed group who lived in country estates and maintained a foothold within the 20 square miles of central London. The Upper Class formed the bedrock of 'society', a class that has been estimated to contain some 60,000 souls at the outbreak of the First World War.[9] Society could accept the artistic, the amusing and the clever, as long as they knew the form. Its members could also be tempted by an injection of wealth or beauty, often in the shape of an American heiress. But society remained suspicious of anyone whose family was not recognised, and they felt secure as long as they could exclude the increasingly confident middle classes. Sex, of course, crossed all boundaries and it was a good thing that there were injections of new blood. After all, in such a small social group the gene pool was limited. Nothing illustrates the circumscribed, not to say incestuous nature of these relationships better than the case of Patsy Cornwallis-West. In 1874 she enjoyed a spell as a mistress of the priapic Edward, Prince of Wales, and gave birth later that year to a son, George. When he came of age, George married Lady Randolph Churchill (Jennie), who was 20 years his senior, but who also had been a mistress of the Prince of Wales.

The medium for passion and confidences was, of course, the letter. Postal services were remarkable compared to today. The 'penny post' had been in force for decades and the fixed price would only come to an end in 1918. In London, collections took place from pillar boxes every hour up to midnight, and deliveries were made every hour up to 9.00pm at night. So lovers could write a letter to their *amour* and receive a reply that same day – an impressive system, considering it was 100 years before emails. The onset of war affected the postal service, with large numbers of postmen enlisting in the services, but this shortage was partially alleviated by the enrolment of women. What may surprise the modern reader is the volume of letter writing that went on. Lady Cynthia Asquith, married to Herbert, one of the Prime Minister's sons, observed that in one typical morning's post she received, apart from letters from her husband and various girlfriends, letters from male friends 'Ego, Lawrence, Aubrey and Bluetooth'.[10] All were full of joy, sorrow and gossip which would be dutifully answered. Yet there were glaring cases where people did not write. The Prime Minister H.H. Asquith, for example, was a prolific correspondent with all his 'harem' but inexplicably never wrote to his son Raymond during Raymond's ten-month service at the front. It was a mistake that Asquith never had a chance to rectify before his son's death.

Another enthusiastic man of letters was Field Marshal Sir John French. If the researcher has the patience to decipher French's appalling handwriting and decode his hidden messages, his letters to his mistress Winifred Bennett are a treasure trove of political and military gossip.[11] When the Imperial War Museum purchased this collection of 99 letters at auction in 1975, they did so primarily for the valuable insight they gave into the mind of, and pressures on, the Commander-in-Chief. The letters provide some fascinating insights into his views and opinions of his French allies, as well as his own colleagues.[12] Fortunately for this study, they also provide marvellous glimpses into the world of wartime London society as well as illuminating the real passion of French's relationship with Winifred. This society may have been frivolous, vain and full of excess but its members included some of the most influential and powerful people in the country and as a social group, they deserve to be studied.

Sylvia Henley's correspondence, particularly her letters to her husband, fulfil much the same promise. They include valuable comments on the political leaders of the day, especially H.H. Asquith, to whom Sylvia was emotionally tied. There is fascinating social comment as well as gossip and it must be remembered that gossip was not just confined to women. The politicians thrived on it and their wives and mistresses acted as conduits for every titbit of military or political news. This proved too much for the more taciturn commanders, such as Haig or Kitchener. The latter, especially, blamed his own reticence on his Cabinet colleagues, whom he maintained could keep nothing from their women – except for Asquith, who told other people's wives. 'If they will only divorce their wives,' Kitchener growled, 'I will tell them everything.'[13]

Considering their world was so small – geographically and socially – it is surprising that Winifred, Emilie and Sylvia rarely met. They certainly knew of each other's existence from society gossip. When Emilie visited an art exhibition, she was struck by the beautiful portrait of 'Mrs Bennett', whose dark, penetrating eyes mesmerised the room. And when Sylvia was holidaying in Homburg with her sister before the war, she spied the renowned beauty 'Mrs Bennett' across the town square. Sylvia even photographed Winifred in her white dress and parasol, as you might snap a celebrity, and when she returned home, pasted the image in her personal photo album.[14] Beauty and mystery were appreciated in this age, as in any other.

The Edwardian period, followed by the tumult of the First World War, brought huge change to women's lives, but the extent of that change depended on class, age, and martial status. Nevertheless, Winifred, Emilie and Sylvia were all extraordinary women who carved out their own destinies as mistresses or confidantes. They would never again enjoy such influence or indeed, have so much excitement. But it was always a dangerous game.

PART I

WINIFRED BENNETT

1

A Romanian Cradle

Winifred Bennett always had the air of an exotic English beauty. She was tall, slim and elegant, but her demeanour and her heart belonged to another, more untamed and Latin culture. Although she was of British extraction, Romania owned her soul.

Her family, the Youells, originated in East Anglia, where they had been established for generations around the town of Southdown on the Norfolk/Suffolk borders. Winifred's grandfather was a Great Yarmouth banker and her father Edward became a shipping agent. But Edward Youell had his eyes set on wider horizons. He married Mary Watson, whose family had business interests in Romania – a country largely unknown in Victorian Britain. Nevertheless, the couple emigrated in 1874 and Edward joined the family shipping agency, Watson's, based in the Romanian port of Galatz. He swiftly prospered, becoming a partner in the new business of Watson & Youell. With a successful enterprise behind them, Edward and Mary produced three girls. Winifred, the eldest, was born in 1875, Sybil in 1879 and Gladys followed in 1882.

Winifred's granddaughter, Joan Wyndham, recalled her grandmother's exotic upbringing in Romania 'in a family that still greeted incoming guests with bread, salt and a five-gun salute'. According to Joan, Winifred 'had been cared for by a gypsy wet-nurse and had a tame bear that walked up and down on her back if she was ill'.[15] Such superstitious practices were widely followed in Romania amongst all social classes and the 'bear treatment' was a staple cure for all sorts of maladies. In the event of an illness, a gipsy would be summoned, arriving with a small bear on a leash with a ring through its nose. The patients lay on their front and the bear climbed on their back and danced up and down while the gypsy thumped a tambourine. At least Winifred never resorted to calling in the local *baba,* or woman witch-doctor, relied upon by so many rural Romanians.

Romania also had its sophisticated side. The Youell's home town of Galatz was the largest port on the Danube and a gateway to the vast Black Sea, some 80 miles to the east.[16] It had its own vibrant expatriate community and had connections to Britain – General Gordon, the hero of Khartoum was a past inhabitant. The town's social life was dictated by its climate. Winters in Galatz were harsh and when the snow arrived, it was driven in across the plains by the bitter easterly wind, or *viscol.* Still, urban life was more hospitable than the freezing countryside where entertaining ceased between November and February. As winter gave way to spring, so social activities picked up in the town, and by summer, the hectic round of balls, receptions and parties got under way. In Galatz, one of the social rituals during the summer was the evening promenading that took place around the *Strada Domneascâ* and Public Gardens. With the heady scent of acacias and lime trees in bloom, pedestrians enjoyed the balmy evening air and would be joined by a succession of 'victoria' carriages, pulled by sleek, beautifully groomed horses, driven by grooms in full livery. Like most of the town's wealthy elite, Edward Youell hired both his carriage and the Russian coachmen by the month, enabling Winifred and her sisters to take full advantage of this piece of theatre. They draped themselves across the carriage seats, parasols in hand, to be admired by a procession of young men. Always clothed in the latest Paris fashions, the girls would smile and nod at the passing young army officers, strutting about in tight scarlet tunics.[17]

One hundred and fifty miles away lay the capital, Bucharest, which offered more interesting social opportunities for the girls, and there was a lively young court surrounding the Romanian royal family. Romania was a comparatively new country, formed in 1861 from the Principalities of Walachia and Moldavia, and from the beginning the new state was always subject to the whims of the neighbouring empires of Russia, Austria and Turkey. Choosing a monarch for the new state was not easy. There was too much in-fighting for a Romanian to be selected for the throne, and the first local candidate was ousted within a few years. He was replaced by the unimaginative but dutiful Prince Carol, a scion of the Prussian royal family. While he successfully managed the basics of the state apparatus, Carol walked a tightrope in the handling of foreign affairs. Because of his family connections he was pro-Prussian, while his people were decidedly pro-French – a position that was sorely tested during the Franco-Prussian War in 1870.[18] At last, in 1881, Romania was elevated to the rank of a Kingdom and Prince Carol was proclaimed King Carol I.

Carol's marriage to his wife Elizabeth was not a happy one, and their hopes for the future lay in their son, Prince Ferdinand. In 1893 the timid Prince married eighteen-year-old Princess Marie of Edinburgh, granddaughter of Queen Victoria and a niece of the Russian Tsar. Princess Marie's mother was very concerned, not so much about the marital match, but more about the state of the country her daughter had adopted. 'Very insecure,' she warned, 'and the immorality of the society in Bucharest *quite awful.*' And that sharp observer of court life, Lady Geraldine Somerset, was similarly unimpressed. 'Disgusted to see the announcement' she groaned, 'of the marriage of poor pretty nice P. Marie of Edinburgh to the P. of Roumania! It does seem too cruel a shame to cart that nice pretty girl off to semi-barbaric Roumania.' The early days of their marriage were not promising. Ferdinand was attentive enough but his awkward physical advances failed to register with his home-sick bride, who yearned for more passion and a mature romance. Furthermore, her new home was hardly welcoming. The *Palatul Victorei* was a solid, sombre place with heavy furniture, no flowers and few comforts. However, the Princess soon found support and friendship from amongst the English members of Romanian society – particularly Winifred and her gregarious sisters.[19]

Barely four years into her marriage, Princess Marie, or 'Missy' as she was known, began an affair with her ADC, Lieutenant Zizi Cantacuzèe. While her husband was ill, Marie spent long hours in the saddle with her riding partner Zizi, and even an enforced separation in Nice and Villefranche failed to cool the Princess's obsession. She returned to find that Zizi had been 'moved sideways' but to her delight, was now leaping about the royal court as a 'gymnastics instructor' to the King. Marie was producing babies at an alarming rate, which pleased her in-laws, but her public displays of affection with her athletic lover were dynamite to the Romanian Royal Family. However, while her family disapproved, Romanian society indulged her extra-marital activities and even applauded her affairs, which included a later friendship with the hugely wealthy Waldorf Astor, as well as a passionate affair with the Romanian aristocrat, Prince Barbo Stirby. Hearing of her tangled and arguably neurotic love life, the British Royal Family were relieved that her earlier possible match with Prince George (later George V) never materialised. Meanwhile, not to be left out, Crown Prince Ferdinand embarked on a number of extra-marital relationships, but was careful to be more discreet.

Princess Marie's affairs were closely dissected by the Romanian court and the expatriate community. Indeed, the three Youell sisters were avid admirers of the errant Princess, who had evolved into a style icon – her newly decorated boudoir and Byzantine tastes were quickly adopted by those in her social circle. Winifred and her sisters were soon sporting this exotic fashion; with their dark eyes and their command of French and Greek, they were soon assimilated into smart society.[20] Another close friend of the girls was Héléne Chrissoveloni, the beautiful daughter of an extremely wealthy Greek banker.[21] Parties at the Chrissoveloni villa in Galatz were glamorous and boisterous affairs, hosted by Héléne's brothers Zanni and Dimitriu with the Youell sisters as regular guests. During these evenings, mellow music and dances soon gave way to fast, traditional Romanian dances such as the *Galaonul De La Birca*, fuelled by copious quantities of *tzwica* plum brandy. Dancing was, after all, something akin to a national pastime in Romania and it was not surprising that romantic liaisons flourished in this atmosphere. Sybil Youell became close to Zanni Chrissoveloni, while the statuesque Winifred dallied with Prince Ghika and other young blades. Winifred found these young army officers very seductive. With their Romanian swagger and flashes of wit and anger, these men could drink heavily and display violence towards their women, yet maintain an extraordinary hold over them. Winifred's friend, Ethel Pantazzi observed the species in its natural habitat:

> The men stand in the middle of the ballroom deciding on their future partners. The masculine attire deserves as much notice as that of the fair sex. For one black-coated civilian there are ten officers. Most of the military contingent glitter with gold braid and medals. Some uniforms are red, some brown, some black, the collars and sleeves slashed with yellow, pale blue or pink; all are fashioned to show a slender waist to the best advantage. Patent-leather boots, moulded to fit foot and ankle without a wrinkle; perfectly cut white gloves, every shining perfumed hair in place, an occasional monocle fixed immovably to the eye – this is the ensemble presented before the music strikes up. Then each rapidly approaches the lady of his choice, smartly clicks the heels together and bows.[22]

In this testosterone-fuelled atmosphere, Winifred's suitors were romantic but totally faithless and in the end she settled for less exotic fare in the shape of a British diplomat. Percy Bennett was an ambitious mandarin who had recently arrived at the British Consulate in Galatz, one of sixteen international consulates that had sprung up around the city's thriving grain and timber trade. He was also attached to the European Commission of the Danube, an international body briefed to control and develop trade along the great river. This organisation had a large entertaining budget, which provided lavish parties at its headquarters in a palace in Galatz, or on board its boat, the *Carolus Primus*. And it was on board this pretty steam yacht that Winifred first encountered Percy. In 1896, after a short romance, Percy proposed to her, and in the Romanian tradition, offered her diamond earrings rather than a conventional engagement ring. Some months later, the couple married, but it was hardly a *grande affaire* and friends thought the match was surprising. Winfred was taller than her spouse, more vivacious and outgoing and at 21, was ten years younger than her rather solid and humourless husband. That was a problem, but one that Winfred was prepared to overlook, since Percy had ambition and looked set for a successful career that could take the couple all over the world. It was evident from an early stage that Percy was single-minded.

Born in 1866, Andrew Percy Bennett was raised in the quiet town of St Leonard's, in Sussex. His father, the Reverend Augustus Bennett had hoped that a career in the church might suit the young Percy but instead the boy finished Cambridge and chose to head straight into the diplomatic service. In 1890 he was posted to Government House in Hong Kong, a territory only ceded to Britain less than 50 years before, but one that had nonetheless become a flourishing commercial centre, bursting with energetic traders and entrepreneurs. The island was already overcrowded, having risen from a population of 4000 in 1841 to a quarter of a million souls when Percy arrived. In addition there was a boat population of 32,000 immigrants, who helped drive the thriving economy. Hong Kong enjoyed a free port status and there were no customs duties on its imports of rice, flour, opium and tea. But there remained an ever-present threat to its trade – piracy. Instances of this capital crime had fallen with the rise of the faster steamships, but a notorious band still operated in the region, who attacked and looted a passenger ship, *Namoa,* in December 1890. This sort of incident was disastrous for Hong Kong trade and Percy was determined to see justice carried out. The pirates were captured by the Chinese, swiftly tried and then executed the following year by traditional but brutal Chinese means. As a trade official, Percy was on hand to witness this ghastly spectacle on Kowloon beach when 34 prisoners in two batches were beheaded in front of a crowd of Chinese and European spectators, some of whom posed afterwards for photographers besides the decapitated pirates.[23] Such grim displays did not put Percy off his job and he continued to impress his superiors with his crisp and business-like demeanour, which resulted in his promotion to Vice-Consul in 1893. He was briefly posted to Manila, before returning to Galatz the following year.[24]

The Bennetts did not have long to wait before yet another new posting was offered to Percy – this time in New York. As HM Consul, he and his new glamorous wife arrived there on board SS *Campania* at the end of 1896 and he remained there for three years, while Winifred travelled backwards and forwards to visit her family in Romania. Winifred became pregnant and in 1900, the couple returned to Europe, with Percy's new appointment as commercial attaché to the British Embassy in Rome. On 26 April 1900, Winifred gave birth to their only daughter, Iris. She was not confined for long and soon entered into Rome's hectic social life.

The Edwardians and post-Edwardians loved to dress up and they lived in an age when there was an abundance of rich, well-made fabrics and talented seamstresses who could create glorious costumes for all occasions. They also adored the stage and one way of combining both passions was to perform in *Tableaux Vivants* (living pictures). Winifred was an enthusiastic player and lost no time in appearing before the King and Queen of Italy in a series of these *tableaux.* The theatrical performances had originated in Italy and the craze spread to the rest of Europe. They involved the cast dressing up in period costume and arranging themselves in a rigid pose to recreate a classical tale or painting. The curtain would be pulled back and the audience would gasp and then applaud as they surveyed the exotic and colourful scene. No-one in the cast moved, which was quite an achievement, given that the scene might be 'Diana the Huntress' involving diaphanous costumes in a draughty theatre or country house drawing room.

Winifred's statuesque beauty was not just confined to the stage; she stood out on the diplomatic circuit and her presence at social or embassy events was often noted in the European newspaper columns. Percy's subsequent appointment as Commercial Secretary and Principal Attaché at the British Embassy in Vienna provided further opportunities for Winifred to shine on the society circuit. She took great delight in helping to arrange the marriage of her younger sister, Gladys, to Captain Alexander Hood, in a splendid Viennese ceremony. Winifred was still a much photographed beauty and in a pre-celebrity age, professional or amateur photographers would relish the chance to capture her image. She also had her portrait painted by the celebrated artist Philip de László, who was working out of his studio in Vienna. According to his friend, Otto von Schleinitz, de László's portrait of Winifred 'created a happy combination of classical and modern elements'. Whatever the merits of its execution, the portrait found favour with the sitter and when de László moved to London after 1907, she lent it to him for his exhibitions in the capital.[25]

The striking 'Mrs Bennett' could be glimpsed at all the right parties or balls and whenever the British Monarch, Edward VII, visited his favourite spa resort of Marienbad in Bohemia, Winifred would leave Vienna and join the throng following the royal visitor. In fact the King visited the spa town's Hotel Weimer virtually every year, to take the waters and vainly attempt to diet. After nine years of this treatment he was still universally known as 'Tum Tum'. However, he did try some gentle exercise and could play a respectable round at the Marienbad Golf Club, where Percy happened to be secretary. Introductions to the royal personage abounded and Percy and Winifred found they were often in illustrious company.

In 1905, just as Percy was growing accustomed to the grand life, he was moved off the central European stage and back to Romania. Winifred was delighted because she could catch up with family and friends, but Percy's new brief was very pedestrian. He was to promote Britain's trade interests at the impending Bucharest International Exhibition. It was to be held in a newly designed park in the centre of the capital. With its own lake and landscaped gardens, the event was supposed to showcase Romania's emerging commercial interests. But as planning got under way, Percy was distracted by another, more dramatic international event.

On 2 July 1905 the Russian battleship *Potemkin* suddenly appeared without warning, just off the main Romanian sea port of Constanţa. The crew had mutinied in the Black Sea, killing seven officers, and then called at Odessa to incite revolution. Finally, *Potemkin* steamed down the west side of the Sea towards Constanţa with the Russian navy in pursuit. Percy, who was a keen photographer, happened to be in the port at the time and rushed down to the main harbour to snap the vessel offshore. For the moment that was as close as he got, for the Romanian authorities refused to re-supply the ship and fearful that their pursuers would catch up with them, the mutineers sailed away. They then tried to access the Russian port of Theodosia, but failed and so returned to Constanţa on 8 July, flying the Romanian flag. The mutineers entered negotiations with the Romanian authorities, in the hope that asylum might be granted, and the crew surrendered the *Potemkin*, half-scuttling her in the process. As the sullen mutineers entered the town, they were surprised to receive a rapturous welcome from many of the local Romanians. Amongst the crowd that thronged the quay was Percy Bennett, who joined in the lively but stilted discussions with some of the mutineers, one of whom cut off his sailor's 'Potemkin' hat band and gave it to the diplomat.[26] Some of those who gave themselves up to Russian representatives in the town were subsequently executed but hundreds of other mutineers managed to escape into Romania's interior.[27]

As the excitement of revolutionary events died away, Percy had to return to the more mundane business of Bucharest's International Exhibition. When it finally opened, it was a disaster from the very beginning. King Carol's overlong opening address was delivered in his monotonous German accent, which few could understand and the unbearable heat caused many of the frock-coated delegates to collapse. Interest was only revived when one of the organisers brought forward a parade of Roman soldiers in full armour and scarlet cloaks to wander through the exhausted crowd.[28] For all its pretensions to European modernity, Romania was still a backward country. There were no railways and few good roads, and although the capital, Bucharest, had acquired some solid European architecture and smart central avenues, many of its side streets were muddy and shabby. Serfdom had only been abolished in 1848 and the largely peasant population had yet to benefit from any government oil revenues. The country did possess a wealthy landowning class known as *boyars,* as well as a small and increasingly influential middle class of merchants and professionals. Short and dark, unlike their Slav neighbours, they spoke French and saw themselves as a 'Latin island in a sea of Slavdom'. Their reputation as lovers owed something to their Roman origins.

For those who could afford to escape the stifling heat of the summer in Bucharest, the delights of nearby Sinaia awaited. This was a pretty resort with its own Casino, high up in the Carpathian Mountains where Winifred and Percy were often invited to stay in some of the luxurious villas that dotted the mountainside. It was here that Winifred witnessed at first hand the liberal attitudes of the society. Many male Romanian aristocrats, married or not, considered it was constant open season for romantic conquests. Single Romanian girls though, were under far tighter control than their European counterparts, for not only did they share the restrictions of constant chaperoning but were also often confined to their homes. However, the fortunes of Romanian women often changed dramatically on marriage. Then, freedom was extensive and the taking of lovers was indulged. Even divorce was far easier than in any other European country. For despite being a devoutly religious country, the Romanian Orthodox Church allowed a person to marry and divorce up to three times – each time in church – without any apparent loss of social standing. When a large number of extra-marital lovers were added to the mix, members of the small Romanian high society had a very intimate knowledge of one another.[29]

The comfortably off seemed immune to mounting grievances amongst the wider Romanian population and in 1907 the country erupted. Ironically, it was in Winifred's home town of Galatz that the upheaval was most dramatic. The peasants revolted over the failure of land reform and attacked government buildings. The weak government collapsed, and an intimidated King Carol stepped in, using the army to brutally crush the uprising. It was also the very year that Winifred's younger sister, Sybil married her long-time lover Zanni Chrissoveloni in Galatz, and despite the bridegroom's enormous wealth, the celebrations were decidedly low-key. The mood had changed in the country, especially since Romanian soldiers had killed thousands of protestors and razed whole villages in the countryside. Any sense of national unity would not return until the country was threatened by the Central Powers in the First World War.

As unrest swept Romania, Percy was moved back to Western Europe and appointed a Royal Commissioner, with the brief to support a series of international exhibitions held in London, Brussels, Rome and Turin. The first show, in 1908 in West London, also celebrated the recent 1904 *Entente Cordiale* between Britain and France.[30] This brought the Bennetts into more civilised territory, yet although Winifred originally saw Percy's career as rather glamorous, after a while the endless new postings and repetitive round of embassy and consulate parties started to pall. He was wedded to his career and was totally oblivious to Winifred's desire for attention and for her sexual needs. He took himself extremely seriously and engaged a number of photographers to capture, for posterity, the image of the austere diplomat. Instead of taking him seriously, Winifred began to see her husband as a figure of fun and was much amused by his nickname on the diplomatic circuit, of 'Pompous Percy'.[31] Still, for all his tedious habits, Percy's latest appointments meant that Winifred was in easy reach of London and Paris; and to facilitate her regular jaunts to the cities, in 1910 Percy purchased a base in London. Number 5 Devonshire Terrace was a three-storey house in a quiet street between the expanding Paddington Station and Kensington Gardens. It would prove an ideal base for Winifred, not only for shopping and meeting friends, but also for pleasures of a more sensual kind.

Winifred had already seen that the diplomatic world was full of irregular relationships and London was no exception. She befriended Henriette Niven, the wife of a landowner and mistress of diplomat Thomas Comyn-Platt. Henriette, or 'Etta', was a flamboyant personality and had little interest in covering up her relationship with Comyn-Platt, who was later reported to have fathered her son, the actor David Niven.[32] Winifred had been brought up in a sexually liberated world in Romania and although she had enjoyed dalliances, she was about to enjoy her first true passion. By 1910, her marriage to Percy was moribund and, like an increasing number of Edwardian women, she did not feel bound by society's expectations. Typical of these tenets was the idea that women should not enjoy sex. 'A modest woman seldom desires any sexual gratification for herself,' one eminent doctor wrote. 'She submits to her husband, but only to please him; and, but for the desire of maternity, would far rather be relieved from his attention.' This was definitely not her creed, for she had done with pleasing Percy and at 35, time was running out for her.[33]

She soon found pleasure in Captain Jack Annesley. They first met at an embassy party, while the old Etonian was on leave from his regiment, stationed in India. Winifred was immediately struck by his charm, gentle humour and perfect manners. He was five years younger than her. He was sporty, had an illustrious military record and was interested in Winifred from their first meeting – in short, he was everything that Percy was not.[34] For one thing, cavalry officers still enjoyed the greatest social cachet and Jack's regiment, the 10th (Prince of Wales's Own Royal) Hussars, or 'The Shiny Tenth' as it was known, was considered the smartest of the cavalry regiments.[35] Indeed, they were the first cavalry unit to be converted to Hussars, years before Waterloo, and counted that great battle, as well as Sevastopol and Afghanistan, amongst their honours. Such a fine regiment required its officers to be well turned out and well equipped, and Captain Annesley would be expected to provide not only his own uniforms and kit but also three horses, one of which had to be a cavalry charger.[36] Everything had to be from a prescribed source. His sporting tailors had to be Studd & Millington in Conduit Street, and his shirt makers were to be found in Savile Row. His hatter would be Lincoln Bennett in Sackville Street and Kammon & Co. in New Bond Street would supply his boots. There was no doubt that in his parade dress uniform of plumed busby, blue tunic and breeches, knee boots and jack spurs, coupled with a flash of arrogance, he looked every inch the dashing cavalryman.

Jack Annesley was also very eligible. He was the eldest son and heir of the 11th Viscount Valentia, lately MP for Oxford, Master of the Bicester Hunt and the owner of several fine estates. It was true that the family title was an Irish creation and there was therefore no seat in the House of Lords, but the Annesley family were a collateral branch of the Earls of Annesley and maintained their substantial seat at Bletchingdon Park, north of Oxford. They also held other estates in Norfolk, Northamptonshire and Ireland.[37] But it was to Bletchingdon that Jack and Winifred retreated. Since Percy Bennett was constantly away on consulate business, Winifred and Jack's affair flourished and this beautiful 60-room Georgian house, set in its own 3000 acres of grounds, was the setting for many weekend trysts. There were known as Saturday-to-Monday house parties, which often included Jack's brother Caryl, or any of his six sisters, while for shorter spells together, the lovers would visit the Annesley's London house in Lincoln's Inn Fields, or Winifred's own new house in Devonshire Terrace.[38]

Jack had previously enjoyed a numerous succession of 'sweethearts' and showed little inclination to manage a steady relationship. No doubt Lord Annesley thought that Winifred was at least a stabilising influence on his heir, and there is no doubt that Winifred and Jack were deeply in love. Their relationship may well have been an open secret, but Winifred was certainly not ostracised for it. An illicit affair was perfectly acceptable in some quarters, as long as the lovers were discreet and did not flaunt their activities.[39] It also relied on taciturn servants – who recognised all the signs of an affair – as well as the couple's observance of the strict etiquette for calling on each other. In London, men would normally attend their clubs after four o'clock in the afternoon, always being careful never to arrive home before seven in the evening. This period was then reserved for calling and was often the convenient time for wives to receive their lovers. Visiting cards were a necessary part of the ritual. Women visitors were required to leave two of their husband's cards and one of their own, or combinations depending on who was in and who was out. It was a complicated and dated etiquette but, as Lawrence Jones recalled, it would remain mandatory during the Edwardian period and for some years after:

> For every dinner eaten, a visit must be paid to your dinner-hostess. In the season when dinner-parties before dances were frequent, several Sunday afternoons had to be given up to these visits. If you were lucky and your hostess was not at home you left two small cards, with the corners turned up to indicate that they had been 'dropped' by yourself and not by a servant. If your hostess was at home, you must carry your silk hat, stick and gloves upstairs into the drawing-room, as a sign that your visit would not be unduly drawn out.[40]

Unlike women, men would have their address on their cards and while etiquette had relaxed in the last decade, it was still not permissible for women to call on a man alone. She would have to take a female friend or chaperone. Even as the Edwardian era was coming to a close, the rules of chaperonage were still strict and a single woman had to be escorted home from parties by a married woman, while hotels, with the exception of the Ritz, were definitely out of bounds. Yet, despite these rigid codes of etiquette, there were places where lovers could mingle, out of the public gaze and even without chaperones. In the immediate years before 1914, 'night clubs' were expanding and competing with each other to become the most fashionable venue. Ragtime had come over from America and Negro bands were 'simply to die for'. Night-clubs were opening up everywhere and the tango and fox-trot were even increasingly popular at more formal evenings.[41]

Night-clubs were simply not Percy's 'thing' and Winifred's increasing disappearances in the evening at last raised an eyebrow from her husband. There was a furious row when Percy extracted the truth from Winifred. She pleaded with him to keep her lover and he threatened to throw her out. Their nanny had secured young Iris away at the top of the house, but the shouting must have been heard by most of Devonshire Terrace. The situation only quietened down when Winifred told the puce-faced Percy that her lover was shortly returning with his regiment to India and the affair would probably not survive.

So Jack 'Pick' Annesley, the celebrated 'beau sabreur', left London in 1911 and resumed his life in Rawalpindi. During the later years of his regiment's ten-year posting to India, he had fulfilled the roll of regimental Adjutant, a job only interrupted by his constant round of polo chukkas. This time, together with team-mates 'Gibblet' Fielden, Billie Palmes and 'Pedlar' Palmer, he won the much coveted Inter-Regimental Polo Cup. He was also on parade for the Delhi Durbar in the same year, when George V was crowned Emperor of India. However, this life of ceremonial and sport ended in November 1912.[42] While 'The Tenth' were deployed to South Africa, Jack was appointed Aide-de-Camp (ADC) to Major-General Hon. Julian Byng, a senior officer of the 10th Hussars. Winifred was delighted, since Jack would be returning to England. Percy sulked.

Jack, as an ADC, would spend occasional weekends at Major-General Byng's country house, Newton Hall, which was situated on the Easton Estate at Great Dunmow, in Essex. The interesting thing about this house was that it was leased from the legendary Daisy Brooke, Countess of Warwick, ex-mistress of the late King Edward VII. Not known for her discretion – she was called 'The Babbling Brooke' – she was still in circulation, though rather desperate to keep the flame alive. She had also recently become an unlikely convert to socialism and the estate had become home to fellow Fabians such as H. G. Wells. This was not quite the company the Byngs normally kept, but Lady Byng was more concerned with keeping the 'blue beast' at bay:

> Our landlady was the famous and beautiful Lady Warwick, by then grown quite stout though her features remained lovely and her desire to charm every man was as strong as ever … I laughed, having watched the performance as she placed herself with one hand on the top of a wicket gate, her beautiful head thrown back at its best angle; she gazed into Julian's eyes, and thought she had him fascinated. Such a waste of time, for when I told him, he laughed and said he couldn't tolerate 'well-fed ewes who aped skittish lambs'.[43]

Jack was similarly unimpressed and managed to steal occasional meetings with the more alluring Winifred. But his time in England was limited. For where Byng went, Jack, as ADC, was sure to follow, and promotion soon took Byng to Egypt, as GOC, British Force in Egypt.[44] The British presence in Egypt was rather bizarre. The country was, in theory, still part of the Turkish Empire, though Britain had been her 'protector' for the last 50 years. No formal written agreements confirmed Britain's occupation but the Egyptian Army was British-trained and a large number of British civil servants held together the country's administration. After trade, the prime asset to be protected was the Suez Canal, and this role absorbed most of the 5000-strong British garrison.

When Byng and his entourage arrived in Cairo, they had no accommodation and Jack Annesley found himself billeted along with his Commanding Officer in Lord Kitchener's house (curiously the German Legation abutted the house). Everyone in the house handled 'K' with great delicacy, treading carefully lest the slightest breach in the established order resulted in a blast from the formidable Consul-General of Egypt. The only living thing that avoided his wrath was his pet dove, upon which he lavished inordinate attention, while his sole recreation seemed to be growing orchids. The only woman in the house, Lady Byng, remembered 'a strange and certainly not a lovable man, an odd mixture of greatness and petty meanness'.[45] Consequently, whenever they could, the occupants of the house made off for visits to some of the city museums, which contained treasures from the Valley of the Kings. The city's skyline was then dominated by Saladin's great mosque, which topped Citadel Hill. Beyond lay the Sphinx, its paws still buried in the sand, in front of the Pyramids. Dhows plied the Nile while endless caravans of camels trudged along the high canal banks and shepherd boys herded flocks of sheep or goats around the narrow streets. It was a picturesque, though poverty-stricken landscape.

As well as his regimental duties, Jack Annesly, as an ADC was also required to attend the endless round of Cairo dinners and receptions. Byng's wife Evelyn, being a fluent French speaker, became Kitchener's unofficial hostess, as well as the leader of Cairo society.[46] They hosted visits from numerous cosmopolitan businessmen and Suez Canal magnates, but arranging banquets was always a problem. There were never enough eligible single women to partner the numerous staff officers or legation officials. For while single daughters from local British families could be wheeled out, it was unacceptable for the daughters of well-to-do Muslim families to make up numbers. There was often severe retribution for western-educated Egyptian girls who abandoned the veil and mixed too enthusiastically with British bachelors.

While Jack was engaged in duties in Egypt, Winifred kept up the round of social engagements in London, partnering the reluctant Percy to official and private dinners. He had recently been appointed a CMG, known in the Civil Service as a 'Call Me God' – highly appropriate in Percy's case – and it had made him even more unbearable.[47] In January 1914, the couple accepted an invitation for dinner from their near neighbour, a Canadian-born entrepreneur and adventurer, George Gordon Moore. An intriguing and mysterious figure, prominent in both London and international circles, Moore had recently acquired the lease of 94 Lancaster Gate. It was a vast and imposing building forming the terrace end of one rank of colonnaded houses overlooking Kensington Gardens.[48] George Gordon Moore (not to be confused with the Irish poet and philanderer, George Moore) had taken the house in part to provide a base for his good friend Field Marshal Sir John French. Moore, who had left a wife and child at home in Detroit, was used to entertaining on a lavish scale, but was seen by many as an *arriviste*. Born in Ontario, Canada, in 1876, he moved to Michigan where he enjoyed a short career as a barrister before embarking on a hugely successful business career as a company promoter. He developed the Michigan electric transportation system as well as controlling public utilities across the US, Canada, Brazil and some German states.[49] He was able to retire in 1912 but his connections with German businessmen would later come to haunt him and damage his reputation as a patriot and supporter of Britain.

For the moment though, Moore was fêted in London for his extravagant and legendary parties. One dinner he gave at the Ritz in 1912 boasted flowers that cost £2000, gold jewellery for all the women guests, and a troupe of Negro singers. He made huge efforts to court Asquith as well as his wife, Margot and son, Raymond.

Other regular recipients of his hospitality were General Sir John French, Lord Elcho, Lady Cunard and the constant object of his affections, Lady Diana Manners. The generosity was not all one-way. On 13 July 1912, Asquith hosted a large family dinner party and one of the few outsiders invited was George Gordon Moore. He made sure to maintain his currency as an influential figure who 'knew the right people' in New York as well as London, and this necessitated frequent transatlantic trips aboard SS *Mauritania*.[50] In 1912 he was also engaged in setting up a game reserve in the Smokey Mountains, on the borders of Tennessee and North Carolina, where he introduced elk, buffalo, bear and the Russian Blue Boar into the rugged landscape. He clearly relished the role of 'frontiersman': 'The biggest boar we ever killed was 9 [feet] from tip to tip. The skin on his neck was three inches thick; eleven bullets were found, which over the years had been embedded in the fat.'[51] Unfair jibes may have hinted at the similarity with Moore's own physique, but when in Britain, he could entertain his young, sophisticated companions with tales of the wild. He was a particular favourite amongst the inhabitants of England's country houses, such as the Charteris family, whose Gloucestershire country house, Stanway, was the meeting place for the socially exclusive set known as the 'Corrupt Coterie'.[52]

Moore's dinner party in January 1914, to which the Bennetts were invited, was an altogether more solid affair. He had invited an interesting mix of soldiers, diplomats and adventurers, together with their wives. Late in the evening, just after the ladies had withdrawn and the men were settling into their ruby port under a cloud of cigar smoke, Moore's house companion, Sir John French, arrived home. He had just returned from his club, where his foul mood had been tempered by copious quantities of alcohol. The recently elevated Field Marshal's mood was further lifted when he encountered the ladies chatting in the drawing room. He loved women, but at that time he was still an emotional wreck, having been unceremoniously dumped by a recent lover. As he made his way into the room he saw the glorious, statuesque figure of Winifred standing in front of one of the large sash windows overlooking Kensington Gardens. Sir John nodded to the other ladies and made his way towards her, holding himself up to his full 5'2" before introducing himself. Her deliciously warm smile and witty conversation soon melted the stern Field-Marshal and, as he later recalled, worked 'miracles' for his state of mind. The spell was broken as the men returned from the dining room to join the ladies. Pompous Percy introduced himself to French with a few platitudes, but the conversation flagged and French decided to retire to bed, carrying with him an image of the beauty by the window.[53]

Despite Winifred's love for Jack Annesley, she found her encounter with Sir John was tantalizing. He was, after all, one of the most senior army commanders and he had a very engaging manner – other top commanders she had met, such as General Sir William Robertson, were gruff and had little time for social chat.[54] Winifred found her brief conversation with French was delightful. When he talked to her, he made her feel that she was the most important person in the room. Physically he was no match for her athletic lover Jack, yet French had an extraordinary charisma and he exuded power. After all, he had enjoyed a very successful military career. A short stint in the Royal Navy had been followed by a commission in the 19th Hussars in 1874. After fifteen years he rose to the command of his cavalry regiment and by the start of the Second Boer War in 1899, he was GOC the Cavalry Division. His successes in commanding the cavalry in South Africa, notably at the Battle of Paardeberg and in operations to stem the Boer invasion of Cape Colony, earned him promotion to Major-General. On his return to England he was appointed to the Aldershot Command and by 1911, French, at 59, was a full General and Inspector-General of Forces. However, his domestic life was a mess. He had been married to Eleonora Selby-Lowndes for some 30 years, with two surviving sons and a daughter, but he had drifted away from his wife and family. [55] He had since pinballed through a succession of lovers and had settled into a bachelor existence. Eleonora had been a steadying influence during the early years of their marriage and although she remained in love with her husband and showed him extraordinary loyalty, his passion for her was clearly spent.

Since 1912, French had mingled with a fast set in London, which included the 37-year-old George Gordon Moore. French also became smitten with an Irish peeress from this circle and the following year the pair embarked on a passionate affair. It ended in disaster for French, who was left reeling with 'a great deal of bitterness caused by selfish deceit'.[56] Given his position as an ADC to King George V, as well as Chief of the Imperial General Staff, French's amorous adventures during this period seemed almost reckless. His elevation to Field-Marshal in 1913 did little to curb his enthusiasm for casual relationships, though the souring of a recent affair had slowed him down. His brief encounter with Winifred had soothed his inner demons but they did not meet again that year; and throughout the summer of 1914, French became consumed with threatening events across the Channel and the likelihood of war.

Meanwhile, George Gordon Moore was still enthusiastic about his famous parties, especially if they could be designed around the young, vivacious socialite, Diana Manners. She was the 22-year-old daughter of the Duke of Rutland, though she bore a striking resemblance to her mother's lover, the rampant Harry Cust. Diana played the Rutland card for all it was worth, and the 65,000 acres owned by the Duke, together with access to the family's impossibly grand London house at 16 Arlington Street, gave the young Diana considerable clout in social circles. Moore became besotted with the feisty party-girl and she became a regular at the Lancaster Gate soirées. However, while the attraction was not mutual, Diana soon realised the pull she had on Moore and the mysterious influence he, in turn, exerted on Sir John French. Despite her revulsion at Moore's physical appearance, Diana decided the connection was worth pursuing.[57]

As the international situation deteriorated in July, Winifred worried that Jack might soon find himself in action. However, it was not the prospect of death that worried Jack, but the arrival of the bailiffs. His expensive tastes and high mess bills had pushed him into debt and his father had bailed him out by selling Eydon Hall, a family estate in Northamptonshire. The sale made £33,000, of which £14,464 was settled on Jack to provide him with an annuity. This was not a small sum, equivalent to £2 million in today's money and would have provided a good income even by the standards of a cavalry officer. So, financially secure, Jack returned from Egypt with General Byng on 12 August to report to his regimental depot and await the return of the Hussar squadrons from their posting in South Africa. Back in London, Jack managed to secure a day's leave to spend time with Winifred and took her to the jewellers Garrard and then to Cartier, in New Bond Street. He bought her a beautiful ring and necklace before he left for an uncertain fate at the front. Winifred wrote to him soon after he left. She also wrote a note to Sir John French, wishing him 'God Speed' on his new mission as Commander of the British Expeditionary Force (BEF). It was a patriotic gesture that was made by a number of other women, but Winifred's letter meant more to French than she could imagine.

'To Die will be an Awfully Big Adventure'

It was the end of a Bank Holiday when the outbreak of war was announced. The crowds of Londoners who were in the centre of the city for the holiday flocked to Buckingham Palace; but their mood was not one of celebration. Most people were curious to hear what would happen next and there was tension in the air. The government's declaration of war was noble enough and, in moral terms, 'it was a war against unprovoked aggression and the violation of international treaties.' Britain was a signatory to those treaties, and for most people, that was sufficient cause.[58]

Men and women all reacted differently to the outbreak of war and women's views were as varied as men's. Ethel Bilborough, perhaps reflecting contemporary newspaper reports, wrote in her diary that 'poor little Belgium was drawn in' and that Germany had shown her 'fangs'. Vera Brittain was stirred by the 'stupendous events' but was awed by the scale of the impending war, fearing the news was 'unparalled in the history of the world'. Asta Nielsen though, spoke for all women, when she witnessed their personal anguish at seeing husbands, sons or lovers departing for the front. 'They would not let go of their hand even for a moment,' she noted, 'nor would they stop staring through their tears at the beloved, embarrassed face, perhaps for the very last time.' This was Berlin, but it could have been London or Paris. Whatever grand strategies were being played out, the war would be deeply personal.[59]

While there was great apprehension amongst those left behind, women were universally proud of their soldiers going off to the front, and it was not just patriotic sentiment. Uniforms gave even the puniest man the look of a warrior, and a hand-tailored officer's uniform could make the most awkward ex-public-schoolboy into a hero from *Deeds That Thrill the Empire*. Even the not-so-young soldiers had a romantic aura about them, especially if they were cavalrymen. The Commander-in-Chief, Field Marshal Sir John French, was a 'thruster' and the thought that even he might be charging into the abyss, created a flutter amongst the more mature women. Margot Asquith, the equine wife of the Prime Minister, was rather smitten with French's strutting about. The Commander-in-Chief was fond of telling friends that when war was declared, he found himself alone with her. According to French, she gave him a medallion engraved with a saint's head, which he had to promise to wear. Margot then flung her arms around his neck and started kissing him. 'What can one do under such circumstances,' he reasoned, as Margot pleaded 'Do, do give me something you have worn yourself – anything, and send it to me.' Eventually French sent her something that had been very close to his person – part of his saddle. She dutifully hung it above her bed, until she heard of his other amorous adventures, and down it came.[60]

Infantry and cavalry units had to be recalled for action from across the British Empire. Captain Jack Annesley had arrived in Britain ahead of his regiment, the 10th Hussars, who were being hastily shipped home from Cape Town. Arriving at Southampton, they moved up to Salisbury Plain to join the 6th Cavalry Brigade gathering for training. Jack joined them at their camp and on 8 October men and horses were all shipped across to Ostend for deployment in the British line. Winifred Bennett tried to keep track of the fast-moving events across the Channel, but was disturbed to hear some of the wilder stories circulating about the cavalry clashes:

> A certain Sergeant-Major Grant decapitated a heavy German trooper who was shouting, 'Kamerad, kamarad! I vas a vaiter at ze Ritz', as both rode hell for leather over a fence into a cottage garden. The unfortunate German's head fell into a chicken run.[61]

Such grim encounters were rarely repeated, for although the 10th Hussars were initially used in a mounted role, skirmishing briefly with some Uhlan cavalry, they were soon ordered forward as dismounted troops to take part in the First Battle of Ypres.[62] Jack knew many of the early cavalry casualties, especially those he had played polo against. 'Poor young Leatham,' the *Tatler* magazine lamented, 'blown to bits by a direct shell hit,' while 'poor Victor Brooke, who was a very pretty horseman and also a soldier of the brainy order' was also killed.[63] Both were formidable polo players, and they would not be the last of the pre-war polo heroes to die. The 10th Hussars lost some notable casualties in the early days at Ypres. On 12 November, Jack's old friend from Boer War days, Major the Hon. Willie Cadogan, was hit in the groin and died instantly. Three days later, as the 6th Cavalry Brigade moved up to support the 4th Guards Brigade between Hooge and Zillebeke, Captain Jack Annesley was shot dead by an enemy sniper at Klein Zillebeke.[64]

The local telegram boy cycled up the long drive to Bletchingdon Park to deliver the telegram. Lord Valentia's butler received it and carried it through the vast hall to his master's study, knocked and entered. Valentia was at his desk answering correspondence and looked up to see the butler's grim face. Nothing was said between the two as the buff envelope was placed on the desk. Valentia gestured his butler away and carefully opened what he knew was bad news. 'I regret to inform you ...'

After the sudden, convulsing shock, Valentia broke the news to his wife. Knowing that Jack's lover, Winifred, would not be formally notified, he immediately wrote to tell her of his death. Until he received a letter from his son's commanding officer and his fellow officers, Valentia would have no way of knowing the details of his son's death. The blow was only slightly softened by the numerous letters the family received, reminding them that Jack was 'the best sort', 'a brave fellow who always looked after his men' and 'a chap who was always in the pink and will be sadly missed.'[65]

Winifred was inconsolable and her husband, on hearing of Jack's death, had no wish to comfort her. Support, however, was forthcoming from an unlikely source. The Commander-in-Chief of the British Expeditionary Force, Field Marshal Sir John French perused the daily casualty lists and noticed Jack Annesley's death. It was well known in London society that Winifred and Jack were lovers and French had fond memories of his first meeting with Winifred at 94 Lancaster Gate before the war. He had also met Jack on several occasions during his military service. French felt impelled to contact her and after returning to his headquarters at St Omer, on the evening of 19 November, he wrote a short note:[66]

My dear Mrs Bennett

This is only a line to say I know you must be terribly sad. I am so sorry. Indeed I feel for you and always will.

FM French

Then, he added a brief postscript to his letter, 'You wrote me such a nice letter. I wonder if I ever answered it. Thank you for thinking of me.'[67]

Jack Annesley's memorial service was held on 23 November 1914 at Bletchingdon Church, which lay several hundred yards from the main house. The packed congregation included family and friends and towards the back sat a tall, hunched figure swathed in black. Winifred was overtaken by grief, but she had no grave to mourn and no official family connection to hold onto. While he had lived, Jack's relationship with Winifred was almost sanctioned by his family; but ex-mistresses had no claim on anything – not even keepsakes. Winifred certainly had no need of financial support because of the compliant Percy, but Jack's finances were in a mess. He had failed to make a will and died intestate. Only months before, his father had sold a prime estate to help him and now that was immediately liable to death duties. It was a bitter pill for Lord Valentia to swallow and sending in his cheque to his solicitor to settle the tax bill, he wrote, 'I enclose a cheque for Lloyd George and I wish it would choke him.'[68]

It was a miserable Christmas at 5 Devonshire Terrace. Luckily, Percy was away but Winifred wanted to be alone. Elsewhere in London, the first Christmas of the war was extraordinary. People were not quite sure whether they should be celebrating or keeping quiet in deference to the men at the front. The scenery in the capital was definitely changing, largely because of the threat from enemy 'Zeppelin' airships. A defensive perimeter was set up covering Buckingham Palace to Charing Cross, defended by three pairs of guns and searchlights, with a large command gun position at Admiralty Arch. Should an airship or Zeppelin appear, a flight of naval aeroplanes would be scrambled from Hendon aerodrome. If the aircraft came off worse, emergency landing strips were prepared in Regent's Park, Kensington Gardens, Battersea Park and even in the gardens of Buckingham Palace. Following complaints from the Lord Mayor and the City of London that this was insufficient, more guns and searchlights were installed, especially on the bridges over the Thames. From Hampstead to Highgate, the city could still be distinguished, but only just. Street lights were dimmed and odd ones taken out to break up long lines of lights that might assist Zeppelins with their bearings. By the following year, all streetlights were turned off and lights in offices and shops were dimmed. The fierce and brilliant blaze that had illuminated Edwardian London was now reduced to a weak glow.[69]

The festival was greeted quite differently on the Western Front, as one young British officer observed:

> On Xmas Day we heard the words Happy Xmas being called out, whereupon we wrote on a board 'Gluchliches Weihnachten' and stuck it up. There was no firing so by degrees each side began showing more of themselves and then two of them came halfway and called out for an officer. I went out and found that they were willing to have an armistice … Both sides came out, met in the middle, shook hands and wished each other the compliments of the season and had a chat.[70]

In other parts of the frontline, there were spontaneous actions that saw men from the Lancashire Fusiliers take on Saxons in a game of football in No Man's Land. Units from the London Rifle Brigade openly chatted with Würtembergers, exchanging tobacco and showing each other family photographs. As the sound of *Good King Wenceslas* and *Stille Nacht* wafted across the frozen mud, news reached the British Commander-in-Chief. French was incandescent with rage, incredulous that he had been informed of 'unarmed men running from the German trenches across to ours, holding Christmas trees above their heads'.[71]

Meanwhile, Winifred had heard more news from her relatives in Romania. In October 1914, Ferdinand had been crowned King of Romania and despite his German roots was now leaning towards the Triple Entente, or 'Allies' as they had become known.[72] He was encouraged in this move towards the Allies by his half-British wife, Queen Marie and her 'official' lover, Prince Stirby. But the poorly armed Romanians, bereft of stocks of ammunition, feared their belligerent neighbour Bulgaria, who had yet to declare for either side. Consequently, for the moment, Romania was not prepared to side openly with the Allies and risk antagonising Bulgaria.

In January 1915, French briefly returned to London for several meetings at the War Office in Whitehall, staying overnight at 94 Lancaster Gate. He had heard

that Percy Bennett was still away on business and took the opportunity to visit 5
Devonshire Terrace and offer his sympathies to Winifred in person. French exuded
charm and concern and lifted her spirits. He did not stay long, but she was touched
by his kindness and as he was driven away by his chauffeur her thoughts at last
shifted from Jack. After a very rough Channel crossing on 15 January, the C-in-C
arrived back in France and was driven along the *pavé* road towards GHQ. It was not
a stately progress. As the staff car negotiated the last few miles to the headquarters,
the road narrowed and they were met with an unending stream of oncoming cavalry,
ambulances and wagons. French's motor jolted along with one wheel off the road
in deep mud until, eventually, they pulled into the drive of the headquarters, and
headed towards French's office. The courtyard in front was full of activity and littered
with staff cars, servicing the officers who worked in the coach houses and servants'
quarters adjoining the main chateau. French stepped out of his motor and everyone
nearby straightened themselves and saluted as he passed.

At once, French set about his routines, including the inspection of the Indian
Cavalry Corps 'looking splendid in spite of the cold and snow'. The sight of these
serried ranks of Empire cavalry stirred French and reminded him of his days in South
Africa. No doubt, once the winter was over and the front began to move again,
these mounted forces would take up their customary roles of reconnaissance and
exploiting breakthroughs in the enemy lines. Terrible weather and battle casualties
would in fact soon take their toll on the Indians. Conditions in Flanders proved to be
wholly alien to such troops and their nightmare would weigh heavily on French.[73]

French soon wrote to Winifred, asking whether there was any service he could
render regarding her recent loss. She replied, quicker than he expected, and asked
him to find out what had happened to Jack Annesley's possessions after he was killed.
Winifred knew his parents, as next of kin, had received a small quantity of personal
effects but there were alarming stories in *The Times* of the theft of officers' swords
after their death. While regiments took care to organise the return of their fallen
officers' effects, quantities of kit had disappeared in transit and Winifred was alarmed
that her letters to her former lover might have fallen into the wrong hands. She was
also desperate to know what had happened to the letters she sent just before his
death, which would have arrived in Belgium after the tragedy. After making enquiries
on her behalf, French was able to reassure Winifred that all her letters had been
burnt: 'Everything was destroyed – those which were found and those which arrived
afterwards.' French was particularly thorough in the business of covering tracks. He
had, after all, some experience in the business.[74]

Winifred was very relieved that details of her past affair could not now leak out. But
she remained anxious about the danger of living in central London. The Zeppelin
threat was very real and although her daughter Iris was away at boarding school for
much of the year, she still returned for the school holidays. It seemed that Londoners
talked of little else but the Zeppelin menace, and with good reason. In the airship
sheds at Friedrichshafen and Nordholz, production had continued at a furious rate

and by January 1915, the German Navy were able to launch airship raids on towns along the Norfolk coast. High-explosive and incendiary bombs were dropped and although there were only 20 casualties, there was widespread alarm at this assault on the British mainland. Over the next few months, Zeppelins appeared in the night skies in increasing numbers and in a shift in policy, the Kaiser finally sanctioned bombing attacks on London. Improvements in airship design had increased the range and bombing capability of the new Zeppelins, so the City of London, with the exception of historic buildings such as St Paul's, was now a priority target.

French could do little to physically protect Winifred in London, but he could help her emotionally. It did not disturb her to read in his letters that, barely three months after her bereavement, French was describing her as 'darling' and his 'beautiful valentine'. He genuinely helped her cope with grief: 'Try to think there is no such thing as Death; that the spirit – the real being – is always there. Cold comfort to a sorrowing heart but time, the great healer, will show this to you.'[75] For her part, Winifred felt their meeting at Devonshire Terrace in January was fate, and that their discussions were 'sacred'. Indeed, they both seemed to ascribe a spiritual dimension to their growing relationship.[76] Spiritualism was very much in vogue and Winifred's early contact with mysticism in Romania allowed her to explore such ideas. London society was awash with clairvoyants and séances – some more serious than others – and French certainly pursued notions of a spiritual power connecting the living, the dead and the universe. He believed the soul was immortal and, as he once told Winston Churchill, 'If you looked over the parapet and got a bullet through your head, all that happened was that you could no longer communicate with your comrades. This would be a worry to you, so long as you were interested in worldly affairs and after a while your centre of interest shifted.'[77] While such belief might reassure French in hazardous situations at the front, it was a belief that carried its own dangers in his relationship with Winifred:

I start for battle early tomorrow and I might not get another letter off for three or four days or even for a long time then. It is the most wonderful experience I have ever known because these long days have known such reality – and it is really this vast mutual love between us which could horribly give me the occult power of detachment. You are so near and cling close, passing up through dense clouds till we get beyond & see those <u>blinding</u> visions of light & sun. It makes me sad and depressed having to come back here.[78]

French's interest in 'the occult power of detachment' was a step too far for Winifred. She relied as much as he did on the growing intimacy of their relationship, yet he now appeared to be advocating a very high kind of spiritual adventure where, in order to acquire something physical, you first had to give up any emotional attachment to it; only then were you well positioned and in control and could thus go about achieving your quest. This removal of sentiment would indeed allow a military commander to achieve his objectives with a single minded, if frightening, sense of purpose. But this was not the stuff of passionate affairs, and such talk in his letters only served to increase Winifred's insecurity. To bring French down to earth, she sent him a photograph of herself in a silver lamé dress, draped over a chaise longue. It seemed to work:

> What a lovely picture! And thank you. Thank you a thousand times. How I shall treasure it. I shall tell them to hand it back to George [Moore] if a shell happens to catch me – just now they are dropping bombs all around. Yesterday 12 fell near my 'Poste de Command' at Bailleul.[79]

While most soldiers hid their 'near misses' from their wives or lovers, French seemed to relish telling Winifred that he was in the thick of the action. Although the proper place for a Commander-in-Chief was in a chateau to the rear, where he could pull together all the strands of command and control, French was always keen to go forward. Despite popular legend, the higher levels of command were not immune to risk and death on a regular basis and some 78 generals were to be killed or die of wounds during the First World War. By early 1915, many of French's more junior colleagues had already perished. February saw the death of one of the most able staff officers, Brigadier-General Johnnie Gough VC. French told Winifred that he was haunted by the loss:[80]

> Alas, alas! Another friend of mine died. The Chief of Staff of the 1st Army, Gen. Gough was caught by a stray bullet and died of his wounds, Sunday last. My mansion is becoming thick with the spirits of my friends. God bless and keep them all. One gets to think of death a lot.[81]

Despite a nasty bout of flu in February, Winifred continued to write regularly to French, with her letters arriving only two days later at GHQ. She was a passionate woman but also adored the doting and fussing that French employed in his wooing. While her marriage to Pompous Percy provided some financial stability, her husband still clearly failed to provide the romance and attention she craved. French could provide that, as well as considerable stamina in the bedroom – but he also supplied that other ingredient of Edwardian love, spirituality. In their letters, most Edwardian women would complement the physical act with copious quantities of literary or spiritual allusions. Indeed, some women survived just on the spiritual, much to the frustration of their husbands. One thwarted Lieutenant-Colonel wrote, 'My wife considered all bodily desire to be nothing less than animal passion, and that true love between husband and wife should be purely mental and not physical.'[82] French was equipped for both possibilities, for he was well read and could employ numerous literary quotes or romantic images to describe his love. Such tactics left the taciturn Percy seriously wanting.

While Winifred's role as a wife and mistress inevitably made some women wary, attitudes to women's sexuality were rapidly changing. The old role models of the virtuous, but passionless married woman versus the sexual (and therefore immoral) woman, were fast disappearing. In many circles, the sexual married woman was becoming the desired model, rather than the sexless spinster. This was a profound change, and one that Winifred was only too happy to embrace.[83] French too, was used to women who were bold and prepared to challenge established views. He had, after all, tolerated a very extreme example of the 'new woman' in his sister, Charlotte Despard. From the very early days, she had espoused radical causes; she had formed the Women's Freedom League, a militant offshoot of the Suffragette movement, and during the war she became a founder of the pacifist 'Women's' Peace Crusade'. French was sorely tested by her anti-war platform, but for the moment he remained loyal to his sister.[84]

For all the spiritual investigation and expression, Winifred and French were very much physical lovers, their lust heightened by their letters, full of sensual imagery. The couple however still needed a reliable courier system, as well as a safe postal address. George Gordon Moore, ever keen to be in French's confidence, proved to be the answer. He acted as a trusty and regular personal courier service as well as relaying first-hand news between the pair. In London, Winifred often lunched with Moore at French's insistence, and Moore would then travel across to France, armed with her latest letters and tantalising news of what she was wearing, or whom she had seen. On Moore's arrival at GHQ, the Field Marshal would devour the American's titbits and gossip about Winifred, as well as lurid tales from the hedonistic life at Lancaster Gate. French would then allocate his friend some quasi-military task – necessary to cover his increasingly frequent visits to Headquarters. When Moore wasn't available for a courier trip, French sent his love letters to his own address, 94 Lancaster Gate. Winifred lived only a few streets away and would call to collect them from French's valet, John Frost. It was simply too hazardous for French to send his letters direct to Winifred's home at 5 Devonshire Terrace, where they might be intercepted by Percy on his periodic visits home, or by an inquisitive maid. While French's correspondence was secure in transit, Winifred's letters were more likely to go astray, though postal censorship did not yet operate so rigorously for mail leaving Britain.

For all his sentimental musings, French had some frightening mood swings and his sudden rages became legendary at GHQ. Although he was apt to erupt at the slightest irritation, Winifred would write him soothing messages and with her 'rest, peace and impish joy', she was usually able to calm him down. At other times, he could be very affable and relaxed with his men, as Christopher Baker-Carr discovered when he had a rare and bizarre encounter with his Commander-in-Chief when staying overnight at GHQ:

Brooke told me to go upstairs and have a wash in his bedroom before breakfast. In the middle of my toilet, in walked Sir John, in a blue dressing-gown, whistling cheerfully. He asked me if I had everything I wanted, and wished to know where I had been and what I had seen. Then, remarking that it was time for him to dress, he walked off to his own room, whistling cheerfully once more.[85]

There was no doubt that his happy demeanour resulted from his joy over his relationship with Winifred and by the end of February 1915, French was declaring in Arthurian tones:

> You have made me a thousand times better man than I was three months ago. This process goes on to become more powerful every day. With your gage in my hand and your love in my heart there is no knightly thing I cannot do.'[86]

For French, with his rhetorical sword in hand, visor clamped shut and clutching his lover's 'gage', or pledge, it seemed he was invincible. He certainly felt a world away from his 'gay' life of wild parties at Lancaster Gate in London. Yet, this social whirl was still going on. The first six months of the war had failed to curb the activities of London society, though eligible men were fast evaporating as volunteers left for the front. George Gordon Moore's parties at Lancaster Gate, far from receding, seemed to gather pace and intensity, and were dominated by members of the 'Coterie' set. Diana Cooper remembered 'uproarious parties behind barred doors, which were called by our enemies the "Dances of Death".' Exotic jazz bands, torrents of champagne and wildly expensive imported flowers were Moore trademarks and of course, a plentiful supply of glossy actresses and girls about town; more than enough to satisfy the mix of hungry young army officers as well as more mature generals Moore sought to impress. For these girls, the war brought a vibrancy and urgency to their relationships, as one partygoer recalled:

> Life was very gay. It was only when someone you knew well or with whom you were in love was killed that you minded dreadfully. Men used to come to dine and dance one night, and go out the next morning and be killed. And someone used to say, 'Did you see poor Bobbie was killed?' It went on all the time you see. [87]

The restaurants and night clubs were full of officers on leave, who continued to patronise the clubs even after the 1915 ban by the London District Authority. Who could deny those who were about to return to face death the glories of an 'Apache Night' or a 'Bacchanalian Revel'? There were young officers, barely out of school, who would spend all their money on expensive hotels, with girls only too happy to help them do it.[88]

Unusual drinks for the time, such as absinthe or vodka, were consumed in large quantities and American delicacies – soft-shell crabs and avocados – were hungrily devoured. Many outsiders felt such excess was obscene at a time of national emergency, but for many of the young officers on leave from the front, such frenzied parties 'combated any pause that would let death conquer their morale'. For Moore, the parties helped cement his influence in society – but they were always an excuse to be close to the elusive Diana Manners. No Moore party was complete without her. Indeed, the party was usually over whenever Diana left, and Moore would promptly close down the evening, much to the dismay of the legion of partygoers.[89] He had become obsessed with her, ever since their first meeting at 'Stanway', where she showed off the intellectual brilliance of her 'Coterie' set. He proceeded to shower her with expensive presents but she was less than impressed. 'A most unusual man of thirty-six,' she later recalled, 'Red Indian in appearance with straight black hair, flattened face and atomic energy.'[90] Moore was never a man to be put off a mission. He believed that his tremendous wealth would be a bait to catch her, but neither she nor her family had need of his fortune – though she was perfectly happy to help him spend it.

Moore had his uses, and Diana and her mother wanted to secure a safer staff job for Diana's brother, Lord John Granby, who was serving on the Western Front. So she set about persuading Moore to 'see what he could do' with his close friend Sir John French. It worked, and Granby was saved from the trenches. Diana called in further favours from Moore, including passes and chauffeurs for the family of Edward Horner, desperate to visit him as he lay wounded in a French hospital. The family was hugely grateful – but Diana always stopped short of showing just how grateful she was. Ever hopeful, Moore continued to deluge her with presents and on one occasion at Lancaster Gate, forced himself on her. She extracted herself from the man who she described as a 'squat and podgy Red Indian' and ran from the house. She would always return nevertheless, to tease him, to extract dinners and presents; and still claiming to be repelled by him.[91]

In his off-duty hours, French was becoming rather tired of hearing from Moore about Diana Manners' exploits. They were so trivial compared to his task in hand. As the frosts of winter thawed, he prepared the next round of military operations. In his letters to Winifred, French was careful to omit details of operations but he was happy to impart news that certain offensives were about to begin, albeit with cautions of 'this is the calm before the storm (this is for you only)' or 'this is only for your private ear.'[92] These comments alluded to the forthcoming Battle of Neuve Chapelle, which French hoped would be the prelude to driving the Germans back from the Lille-Douai Plain. On the eve of the battle, French wrote to Winifred with news of the preparations:

I am hoping for great things from the 15 inchers [guns] – known throughout the 1st Army as 'Grand Mamas'. The first 9.2 inch gun was called 'Mother' and the 4.6 inch guns as 'Babies'. Winston Churchill is sending a few ships to bombard the coast around Ostend – I want them to distract the enemy's attention and keep him from sending reserves south.[93]

As he geared himself up for battle, French announced to his lover 'Tomorrow I shall go forward with my war cry of "Winifred", though if mounted on a white charger, he would not have gone very far on a Western Front battlefield.[94] The battle, under the control of Haig's First Army, commenced on 10 March and saw British troops advance to a depth of 1200 yards into enemy positions. Despite a massive preliminary barrage, the Indian Corps and IV Corps failed to make further headway. It was a clear example of how British forces could break into enemy lines but could not then exploit that advantage by a subsequent breakout. For the duration of the battle, French had been at his forward command post at Hazebrouck, some fifteen miles from the frontline but within easy reach of Haig's headquarters. On the morning of Saturday 13 March, while British troops were digging in to consolidate their small gains, French was calculating his next move. His thoughts were interrupted by the arrival of George Moore, bearing the latest letter from Winifred. French warmly greeted his old friend and spent the next two hours discussing news and gossip from home, as well as the state of current military operations, before driving Moore over to the main HQ offices at St Omer. There, Moore was given wide access both to facilities and personnel and French relished his company, telling Winifred 'I love seeing dear old George for he always talks to me of you.'[95]

French was clearly besotted by Winifred and despite their difference in ages – by this time he was 63 and she was 40 years old – it was an extremely passionate affair. Though short and stout, French was still fit and moved around in a jaunty manner. His white moustache was full and bushy, in line with King's Regulations that ordered that the upper lip should not be shaved.[96] Major-General Sir Edward Spears, who worked closely with French, recalled:

> He was a shortish man, very burly with a big toned step; he always made me think of a wild boar. He stuck out his chin very much and had quite a drooping moustache. He gave the impression of being very much the soldier.[97]

Everything about French's mien was military, but underneath the gruff exterior he was an extremely sentimental man, especially when it came to women. Winifred was something of a hypochondriac and clearly enjoyed French's fussing over her health. Writing on 8 April 1915, after Winifred had gone outside with a sore throat, French pandered: 'I hope your beautiful throat behaved. It was very naughty of you Darling, for you might have caught a horrible cold in this weather.'[98] It was a good thing that none of the hundreds of thousands of troops, shivering in sodden trenches, could hear their Commander-in-Chief's concern for his mistress.

George Gordon Moore came out to see French again on 21 April 1915, bringing more letters from Winifred. In these letters, Winifred lamented the death, five months earlier, of Jack Annesley, telling French how much she had loved him and how his death still tormented her. She remained emotionally fragile, thankful for French's touching support but fearful that he might let her down – that she might risk loving and losing again. For his part, French believed the affair had released some extraordinary ardour in him and he relished Winifred's vulnerability, for it enabled him to be both a passionate lover as well as an emotional rock. He was only too happy to send her flowers from 'John' or to organise brief forays back to London for meetings with the Secretary of State for War, Lord Kitchener, which presented opportunities to see her. If he could not get away, he could occasionally telephone her, though the switchboard operator might eavesdrop on their conversation, and the line was usually so crackly that they could barely hear each other.[99] And then there was 'dear old George', though Moore was getting rather restless about being a mere courier and was now expanding his brief during his visits to GHQ. Using his knowledge of construction and current scientific research, Moore was able to assist French in his quest to upgrade the potency and reliability of British high-explosives, mortar bombs and hand-grenades. During the spring of 1915, he spent considerable time in the reserve areas of the British lines, testing these new ideas and introducing his American contacts.[100]

The Commander-in-Chief and his aides were not just confined to one chateau at GHQ. Even in 1915, the General Headquarters was a very large enterprise, which comprised numerous offices in buildings and chateaux in and around St Omer. French found it necessary to have separate quarters set apart from his work and installed himself together with a small staff in the nearby Chateau de Blendecque. It was always a long day. A colleague observed that French rose at 6.00am and usually had discussions with some of his General Staff before breakfast. Then there would be overnight reports to digest before he visited his Army Commanders and sometimes his French Army counterparts. Over a working lunch he would entertain visiting dignitaries and then in the afternoons he would visit formations in reserve or carry out post mortems on military operations.[101] Dinner was once again an opportunity to discuss the direction of the war, particularly with visiting politicians, (or 'frocks' as they were known), such as Arthur Balfour and Winston Churchill. French did not always keep back behind the lines and made a point of visiting forward positions at Ypres. He clearly wished Winifred to see him in the dashing role of Henry V rallying the troops (with echoes of 'once more unto the breach'), rather than a shuffler of paper:

> It bucks them all to see me and I get a much better idea of the actual situation. When things are going well it doesn't matter but at times like we have been going through lately, I am obliged to be a good deal at the front. Don't fear my precious love. I wear my helmet always and I don't think God will want me yet.[102]

Soldiers crave tales of normality from home and French was no exception. Now that summer was approaching, he loved to hear about Winifred's picnics with her fifteen-year-old daughter, Iris, whom French had recently met:

> I loved to read of your picnic in the wood darling, with that most delightful child of yours – I am so glad I know her now – she has your nature and disposition

exactly and promises to be beautiful like her lovely mother. I was so charmed by
her beautiful natural manners – really like you.[103]

Winifred briefed French on the usual social gossip doing the rounds amongst their
friends in London, but her beloved Romania was never very far from her thoughts.
In Galatz, her sister Sybil's in-laws, the Chrissovelonis gave large donations to
Romanian field ambulances but drew the line at allowing their properties to be
used as billets for the recently arrived Russians. They were supposed to be protectors
but most local *Galatziotes* viewed them with alarm, even to the extent of pouring
away the town's supplies of wine to deny it to their 'allies'. Prime Minister Asquith
had again pressed the Romanian Envoy in London as to when Britain could expect
Romania's entry into the war. Clearly playing for time, the Romanians replied that
they could only do so when Italy entered and even then they would need a massive
contribution of artillery shells from Britain. This would prove to be embarrassing, for
Britain itself was suffering from a shell shortage. The deadly bargaining continued,
Germany courting Italy with offers of the border region of Trentino, while Britain
offered her more influence in the Balkans. However, even if Romania stayed neutral
for the moment it still helped the Allies, by depriving the Central Powers of access to
Romania's valuable oil deposits.

    Despite the exhausting nature of his job, French always had reserves of energy and
craved physical contact with Winifred. He would return to London at any excuse:

> I could tell you all you are to me. How deeply, fondly and intensely <u>I love</u>
> You, with all my heart through and through. Darling I am sending these few lines
> today because I rather hope to get over on Wednesday or early on Thursday and
> return here on Thursday afternoon. There are a few things I must see 'K' [Kitchener]
> about.[104]

After a while, even the cover of business was dispensed with, as French engineered
secret trips to London. 'I have arranged that no-one shall know,' he confided in one
letter, 'that I am in London, so that I am absolutely free to be with you as much as
you can let me.' The idea that a very powerful man, trusted with the pursuit of a war,
should suddenly put aside his responsibilities to be with his sweetheart must have
been very seductive to Winifred. However, the war would not wait for French and he
was soon compelled to return to GHQ. A week later, on 8 May 1915, George Moore
arrived at the Headquarters, bearing more of Winifred's letters as well as news of his
latest lunch with her. Moore, a self-confessed atheist, was so enthusiastic about the
affair that he confessed to French that it was the 'first thing in his life that made him
believe in the possibility of a God'.[105] Indeed, the following day, French would have
need of his Maker, as the Battle of Festubert commenced. The Commander-in-Chief
observed the operations from the tower of a ruined church, with his ever-faithful
friend Moore alongside him. In his later memoirs of the period, *1914*, French recalled:

A friend was standing by my side on the tower, and to him I poured out my doubts and fears and announced my determination. He warned me that the politicians would never forgive the action I proposed, and that it meant my certain recall from the command in France. But my decision was made and I immediately started for my Headquarters, fully determined on my course of action.[106]

That course of action was to publicise the chronic shortage of British shells – a situation that was endangering the lives of British soldiers. But French's action was not quite as spontaneous as he would wish his readers to believe, for he had already arranged for another friend, Colonel Charles Repington, Military Correspondent for The Times, to be on hand, to witness the poor performance of British artillery. It was Repington who would be the vital conduit of the news and despite French's undoubted input, The Times correspondent always maintained that the words were his own, and were not suggested by French.[107] Once Repington's copy was relayed to The Times it only remained to plan the timing of the public exposé. During the evening of 13 May 1915, the conspirators dined together in London. Freddy Guest MP, also ADC to Sir John French, arrived late, having just returned from France clutching a bundle of memos and letters from his superior. Those around the table included Thomas Marlowe, Editor of the Daily Mail, Sir James Dalziel MP, owner of the Pall Mall Gazette, and T.P. O'Connor MP, Irish Nationalist and Editor of The Sun. One notable absentee was Geoffrey Robinson, Editor of The Times. Although he was heavily occupied in running Repington's disclosure for the following morning's newspaper, Robinson lacked the spirit for a sustained press campaign – that would be placed in the hands of Thomas Marlowe at the Daily Mail, who was spoiling for a fight with the Government.[108] T.P. O'Connor, one of the main architects of the dramatic disclosure, had mixed motives, but the promotion of Lloyd George was certainly one of them. He would later write an article in the Strand Magazine about 'the beauty of D's [David's] family life', which enraged Lloyd George's mistress, Frances Stevenson.[109]

The 'Great Shell Scandal' as the headlines screamed, erupted on 14 May 1915 and in the days following, Asquith's Liberal Government started to unravel. French was besieged by those demanding to know the extent of his involvement in the drama. He kept his head down, but his wish to be left in peace was prompted by more personal reasons. On the same day that the shell story broke, he learned of the death in action of his two cousins, both close to him. Arthur French, Lord Frayne, and his half-brother, Lieutenant George French, were killed in the Battle of Aubers Ridge on 9 May. There were other friends amongst the casualties, including Lieutenant-Colonel Bertie Paget, whom French and Winfred knew from the London party circuit before the war.[110]

A week later, George Moore arrived back at GHQ and his effect on French was cathartic. The two dined together that night and Moore left in the morning, but not before he had tackled French on the matter of his ongoing squabble with Lord

Kitchener. They discussed Kitchener's vulnerability and his isolation within the Cabinet. 'Nothing will go right while he's there,' French barked.[111] In fact, Moore only served to stoke up his friend's hatred of Kitchener, reminding him, if he needed reminding, that the shortage of artillery ammunition was severely hampering operations. There was only one man to blame and French vented his spleen by writing to Winifred:

> It is simply maddening. The whole line has advanced a good way, but in two days I shall have to stop and stand still for a week – simply to accumulate enough ammunition to get on. And we know this infernal man [Kitchener] wouldn't listen to what was told him and thought he knew what we wanted better than we knew ourselves.[112]

French had some allies within the Cabinet. One member thought Kitchener, 'works hard, is outspoken and hates red tape, but he does not really know WO [War Office] requirements'.[113] While Kitchener managed to cling onto power, there were numerous accusations of incompetence at the War Office, with Sir James Dalziel, prompted by Lloyd George, launching a blistering attack in the House of Commons on the department's handling of supplies.

While French could not abide Kitchener, as far as the country was concerned, the 'tall, grim, silent figure' could do no wrong.[114] So, it seemed for the moment that Kitchener's position was impregnable; not so those of his trusted lieutenants, such as General Sir Horace Smith-Dorrien. The GOC Second Army was one of Kitchener's favoured subordinates and had served under him in Egypt, South Africa and India. He was already out of favour with French.[115] News of the smouldering enmity had even reached King George V, who was anxious to know what was going on at GHQ. Luckily for the King, his son the Prince of Wales was attached to the headquarters staff. 'I want to know privately,' the King wrote to Prince Edward, 'if the C-in-C has had a row with General Smith-Dorrien. You might find out and let me know.' It was quite probable that the Prince gave his father a biassed report about French, for he thought him 'an odd little man and far from clever'. For his part, French was glad to get rid of the Prince whenever he could and was happy to grant him leave in the first winter of the war to return to Sandringham for part of the shooting season. By 6 May, the speculation was over and French 'degommed' Smith-Dorrien.[116]

The absence of censorship in neutral America allowed a lively debate about the rift between French and Kitchener and its effect on British morale. *The New York Times* was particularly cutting in its observations. Tracing their feud back to the Boer War, the newspaper cited the removal of General Sir Horace Smith-Dorrien and disagreements with the French Government as evidence of Sir John French's abrasive style of command. Warming to the task, the US journalists attacked French for 'losing his grip' and for preferring officers for their aristocratic pedigree rather than military flair.[117] Indeed, French's unpopularity appeared to be fairly widespread and one politician visiting the front was told that the men 'would greatly prefer Gen. Haig as C-in-C to Sir John French'.[118] Winifred did her best to remind French of Kitchener's hold over the nation, as well as tempering her lover's fury over other senior figures he held responsible for Britain's predicament.[119] Admiral Jackie Fisher had just resigned in protest at the allocation of naval resources and Asquith's Liberal Government had lost its credibility. French fumed that Winston Churchill had pushed through the Dardanelles Expedition, and though he remained a fervent admirer of the man himself, he knew that Churchill's chancy venture would make further demands on the nation's meagre supplies of artillery shells. Still, one thought of Winifred in her silver lamé dress seemed to dispel the Commander-in-Chief's ire. Having recently spied his lover in the shimmering silver number, French christened Winifred, his 'Silver Girl'. At the same time, he made sure that he was granted a suitable pet name, and re-branded himself in his letters as 'Sir Lancelot'.[120] Both were trapped, they maintained, in loveless marriages and such was the passion between the two that Winifred constantly lamented the fact they had not met before those unions.[121]

In June 1915, the lovers had to survive without the help of their go-between, George Gordon Moore. He was on a mission to America, not only to check on his business interests but to escape his complicated love life. According to French, Moore believed he was in love with several women, including Lady Diana Manners, and it was making him 'sad and distraught'. Yet, when he arrived in New York and was immediately besieged by the press, it was not his love life that was in the spotlight but his relationship with French.

The Commander-in-Chief stood accused again of preferring aristocratic officers – and allowing women to visit GHQ. The journalists knew that Moore was a regular visitor to the headquarters and they wanted answers. There was also the question of the breakdown in relations between French and Kitchener. Moore launched into a spirited rebuttal of all the allegations against his friend, as well as issuing a denial about the bitterness between the two Field Marshals. Moore tried to deflect attention away from GHQ by lauding the performance of the Canadian troops at Ypres, but the pressmen continued their questioning. He admitted that he was 'almost continuously' at GHQ on military business, though he omitted the fact that the primary reason for his visits was to facilitate the affair between Winifred and French. The secret appeared to be safe for the moment, even from the notoriously intrusive American pressmen.[122]

However, Moore could not keep out of the limelight – even in America. In August, he was back on the stage again, this time in Detroit, to trumpet the Allied cause. In a passionate address before the annual convention of 'Veterans of Foreign Wars', he alleged that in the US there were potentially over 2½ million German and Austrian reservists – foreign nationals who were capable of creating havoc in the country. And with only a paltry regular US Army of 200,000 to defend vital installations, any enemy invasion of the US mainland would be swift and successful. As Moore hammered home his points, the audience of veterans were warned of an immediate crisis and that war with Germany was imminent.[123] While Moore's speeches no doubt helped the British cause on the international stage, he seemed insensitive to the raft of opposition building against him in Britain. Many were jealous of Moore's hold over French and objected to his intrusions at GHQ. Charles Whibley, a confidant and 'literary mentor' of Lady Cynthia Asquith, thought that Moore's spell was cast even wider than French. For the adventurer had also charmed Lord Northcliffe and was able, so Whibley believed, to influence the press baron to promote French's cause. This in turn irritated Kitchener and fanned the flames of their bitter rivalry.[124] There was talk in London that Moore was a spy, but it was more likely that he had become obsessed with his own influence amongst the powerful, and that was an end in itself. Moore was careful to cultivate his pre-war relationship with Asquith, sending the Prime Minister a present of a box of very large cigars as well as an expensive book, *Remarkable Women*, for his daughter Violet.[125]

While Moore was in the US during the summer of 1915, Winifred headed out of London with Iris and took a holiday cottage at Beachy Head. They were joined at the house by Winifred's sister, Gladys, who was also relieved to be clear of London and the suburbs. Civilians still lived in fear of further Zeppelin raids, even though the airships had so far failed to penetrate the heart of the city. A combination of bad weather and poor navigation saw most airships dumping their bombs outside the capital, or into the Thames estuary. However, on 8 September 1915, *Kapitänleutnant* Mathy in the airship *L13* crossed the Wash and headed for the capital. At 10.40pm the massive airship dropped its remaining water ballast in an attempt to rise above shell-fire from the ground. Operating a wire leading from the ship's control cabin, her watch officer then opened the shutters along her belly and unlocked the safety catches holding the 'eggs'.

The first bombs fell on Golders Green, and then at a cruising height of 9000 feet, the airship flew along a course from Euston Station towards Smithfield Market and Moorgate Street. Civilians on the ground were aghast and it was not long before wild stories circulated, with one observer claiming 'The Zepp was so low that I saw their horrid German faces in the searchlight.' Nonetheless, the attack was real enough. Incendiary and high-explosive bombs continued to tumble from the airship, blasting craters and burning buildings. The airship's crew even found time to drop a ham-bone on a parachute, with the inscription 'a memento from starved-out Germany', before returning unscathed to Germany. It was the final insult to the feeble British defence, whose guns were ineffective and whose aircraft crash-landed in the dark before even sighting the target.[126]

As Britain was the junior partner in the coalition with France, much time was taken up with liaison between the two headquarters. French's mastery of the foreign language was far from assured, so he often left the detail of weekly meetings to his staff. There was, however, a regular round of medal exchanging between the commanders of the two countries, which always amused French. Writing to Winifred, he was tickled by the sight of the normally gruff, Sir William 'Wullie' Robertson, submitting to Gallic overtures:

> At Chantilly this morning, Robertson, my Chief of Staff was presented with the Legion of Honour and Joffre kissed him on both cheeks: it doesn't sound very funny if you don't know him, but if you did, it would make you laugh.[127]

In September there was further news to cheer French, for he heard that the Duchess of Rutland and her daughter, Lady Diana Manners, had abandoned their hospital. French had been constantly pestered by the pair, who set up the infirmary behind the lines in a château near Boulogne. They had secured private funding, but now it had failed, French asked Winifred, 'I wonder what they've done with all the money! What an ass, dear old George is, to be taken in by these people.' Moore had indeed financed most of the operation with support from several wealthy Americans, including Gordon Selfridge, the founder of the Oxford Street department store. All the equipment for this hospital was purchased and staff employed, when the Red Cross suddenly refused to endorse it, which killed off the enterprise.[128]

Diana Manners surmised that the Red Cross pulled out because of Moore's involvement, but the organisation may have clashed with the formidable Duchess. In any event, French was tiring of the antics of Diana and her mother and only tolerated them because of George Moore's infatuation with Diana. Yet while French felt qualified to warn Moore about the dangers of the powerful 'Rutland–Cunard gang' and other 'female influences', French himself remained distinctly bewildered by the opposite sex. His letters to Winifred also betray a certain cynicism about his past relationships: [129]

> I have always found women so different – so exacting, inclined to be selfish, dominating and self-serving – you are the exact opposite to all this! When I think of you in your spiritual loveliness, my perfect Princess, I feel that I am only fit to be allowed to worship at your shrine.[130]

The forceful women who dominated the London social scene clearly frightened French, who sought sanctuary in Winifred's comforting and safe embrace. For although Winifred was at ease in their social circles, she was never quite one of them. French may have been accepted by society because of his military rank and his undoubted charm with women, but Winifred rather unsettled the arbitrators of who should be accepted into society. Her exotic upbringing in Romania, coupled with the fact that 'her people' were not widely known in English society, excluded her from the inner aristocratic circle. The fact that she was a mistress might have made some hostesses wary of her sexual allure but morally, it was of little consequence to them.

A Commander-in-Chief was subject to other distractions. French was also responsible for the safety of the King during his visits to the Western Front and in October he was called upon to attend on George V. All went well during the visit, until the King finished his mounted review of First Army troops and as he moved away, something spooked his horse. The animal suddenly reared up, threw the King and rolled on him. Battered and bruised, he was hastily carried away to a Dressing Station and then on to heavily guarded private quarters. The King was not a strong man and was badly shaken by the experience, but French's main concern was that the enemy would hear of the incident and attempt to bomb his quarters. French immediately instructed anti-aircraft guns to be placed around the house. They were not needed and after several days, the King was sent back across the Channel, much to French's relief.[131]

Meanwhile, the home front was having its own problems with defence. The British press were outraged at London's vulnerability to Zeppelin attacks and demanded action. Winifred was now back in London and though Iris had been dispatched to boarding school, Winifred was concerned at the proximity of her house to the potential bombing target of Paddington Station. There were moves to improve security. An Admiralty Flag Officer was appointed to oversee the defence of London and over 100 new anti-aircraft guns and 50 powerful new searchlights were diverted from the Fleet and installed around the city. Further cover was provided by new observer posts around the south-east coast, though these were barely installed by the time of the next raid on London. During the evening of 13 October, proceedings in the House of Commons were suddenly interrupted by cries of 'Zeppelins, Zeppelins', followed by distant explosions. The Chamber emptied as the Honourable Members poured out into the darkened New Palace Yard, followed by some of the less infirm members of the Lords. Big Ben was not illuminated and exuberant shouts and wild gesticulating from the MPs pointed out the extraordinary sight over the Thames. Sailing serenely through the night, Zeppelin *L15* could be clearly seen, with searchlights playing across its silver body. A large gun erupted in Green Park and shells exploded beneath the airship. She turned and passed directly over the Palace of Westminster before moving on to drop several bombs in the neighbourhood of Charing Cross. She passed on above the Strand to Lincoln's Inn, Chancery Lane, and Hatton Garden, dropping more bombs as she went. Curiosity from crowds gathering in the gloomy streets soon gave way to panic as explosions rocked the façade of the offices of *The Morning Post* near the Lyceum Theatre. Passers-by were thrown off their feet and showered with glass and falling masonry. A gas main erupted and blazed furiously as survivors staggered away from the large crater in the road, which was strewn with limbs. As the smoke cleared, 38 people lay dead or seriously injured. A moment later, another explosion could be heard in Aldwych and a column of smoke billowed up near the Strand Theatre. The theatre was crowded for a performance of *The Scarlet Pimpernel* and miraculously there were no serious casualties. But people were not so fortunate in Chancery Lane, where a passing omnibus took the full force of an explosion, killing the driver and conductor outright. A trail of destruction extended across Aldgate and Limehouse as the searchlights lost the enemy ship and 'pom–pom' guns fired wildly into the night sky. Having dropped all her bombs, *L. 15* moved out into the Thames estuary and disappeared into the night.[132]

After the latest Zeppelin attacks, there was a level of fury on the streets of London that had not been seen before. People were outraged that their homes were vulnerable, though this was a state of affairs that the Belgians and French had become used to. Ironically, Londoners 'were now more and more charged with that hatred, which became less and less amongst the soldiers at the front'.[133] Meanwhile, in France, there was some optimism that the worst might be over. Even after the disaster at Loos at the end of September, French remained extraordinarily upbeat, predicting to Winifred, 'We ought to be able to bring off a very decisive attack and victory in the early spring, which should finish this war.'[134] But the suffering was a long way from ending.

On 14 November 1915, French wrote to Winifred on the anniversary of Jack Annesley's death. It was a poignant letter, in which French dwelt on the nature of grief and sorrow. He heard from Winifred that she had visited Jack's family church at Bletchingdon. Alone, she knelt in the draughty church and prayed for his soul – an image that touched French deeply. She could only imagine where her former lover's grave was; luckily she would not see the terrible state of the Ypres cemetery where he lay. It was enough to haunt even the formidable Margot Asquith, wife of the Prime Minister, who visited the graveyard just weeks after Jack was buried:

The Ypres cemetery will haunt me forever. No hospital of wounded or dying men could have given me a greater insight into the waste of war than that dripping, gaunt and crowded churchyard. There were broken bits of wood stuck in the grass at the head of hundreds of huddled graves, with English names scrawled upon them in pencil. Where the names had been washed off, forage caps were hanging, and they were all placed one against the other, as closely as possible. [135]

Afternoon Delights

In the autumn of 1915, as Winifred was lamenting the death of her former lover, her new suitor was not in the best of health. Whether it was the exertions of his passionate love life or the stress of his command, French suffered what appeared to be a heart attack and was briefly confined to bed. Haig coolly noted in his diary that this was the second heart attack that the C-in-C had suffered within a year.[136] French was also battling to save his career, for there was mounting criticism over his tenure as Commander-in-Chief, aggravated by the increasing, unimaginable casualties – 995,000 were killed, wounded or missing in 1914, while the tally for 1915, including the recent disastrous Battle of Loos in September, exceeded 1,430,000.[137] In fact, according to Haig, it was French's poor allocation of reserves at Loos that spectacularly prevented him from achieving a breakout. Such a failure was critical and enabled senior military figures like Kitchener, Robertson and Haig to put together a case for French's removal. It only remained for the Cabinet to be persuaded and plans were already afoot to deal the political blow.

On 15 November, the Minister of Munitions, David Lloyd George, orchestrated a stealth attack on French. Lord St Davids, a prominent Liberal and close ally of Lloyd George, launched a blistering attack on the conduct of the British Headquarters' Staff in France. In a House of Lords debate, he cited testimony from regimental officers and reports from fourteen national newspapers that some appointments to the Staff were only made if an officer could offer good racing tips or play a sound rubber of bridge. Warming to his cause, Lord St Davids also repeated the earlier newspaper allegations of 'ladies visiting at British Headquarters'. *The Tatler* reported that eyebrows were raised when 'the bachelor Lord Haldane sweetly refuted the allegations', claiming that if ladies had appeared at GHQ 'it was in spite of a great many difficulties put in their way'.[138]

St Davids was a prominent Liberal, and both his brothers were also Liberal MPs. One was the recently promoted Major-General Ivor Philipps (38th Welsh Division), who was attached to Lloyd George's Ministry of Munitions. Philipps had visited GHQ the previous month to seek out material for his brother's cause but French had got wind of the visit and kept out of his way. Later that day in Amiens, when Philipps happened to see French again, the C-in-C froze him out. He had little joy elsewhere. In his mission to investigate defects in British gun barrels, he sought out nearby units of the French Army. But as he confided to Charles Hobhouse, 'I know nothing of metals or shells, and can't speak or understand French.' Undeterred by the lack of hard data from his brother, St Davids nevertheless caused a mighty rumpus with his allegations. While he praised Sir Douglas Haig and his First Army Staff, it was obvious that his attacks on an overmanned GHQ Staff were really aimed at the Commander-in-Chief, Sir John French.[139]

When French heard about St Davids' comments in the House of Lords, he was furious. Again, he vented his anger in his letters to Winifred. 'A fellow calling himself St Davids … I don't know what his original name was before he bought himself a peerage, but it does seem rather hard that an institution like the House of Lords can allow people to tell such barefaced lies.' French, clearly depressed by the whole affair and now chain-smoking, concluded, 'The Germans are nothing compared to our own people.'

Was there any truth in the allegations? Despite his love of female company French had, on recorded occasions, actually refused to allow women into GHQ. In 1914, Margot Asquith was invited to visit the King of Belgium in his headquarters and also attempted to call on French at British GHQ. Hardly alluring in her leather breeches and waistcoat, the Prime Minister's wife was refused entry by French, who claimed he was 'too busy'.[140] French knew his enemies were circling and confided to Winifred:

> There have been a lot of intrigues. That's why I told you that you mustn't be surprised at anything happening. I've heard a good deal about it all. They may get rid of me now, but I am more doubtful of it than I was, as I have a lot of good friends in the Cabinet … but I truly don't much care.

French would fight his corner and he could rely on old friends, such as Lord Grenfell, to refute St. Davids' allegations; but clearly the old bull was tiring. As far as French was concerned, removal from the Western Front would mean the loss of his old love, the Army, but more time could be spent with his new love, Winifred. 'The politicians may throw me over,' he warned her, 'as a last chance to save themselves. But Darling, I want you to remember that I shan't care one jot about all this. It is only you that matters.' His career and everything that he fought for appeared to be falling away, yet he had the huge consolation of Winifred's love. Nonetheless, he was an angry man, and during November, French spent the last weeks of his command railing at both Kitchener and the politicians whom he believed contributed to his downfall, branding them 'infernal humbugs and liars'.[141]

Haig was in line to succeed French as C-in-C and there was little love lost between the two commanders. Despite his undoubted military qualities, the taciturn Haig had little of French's charisma and socially, he scored few marks amongst the formidable female hostesses of the day. Mabell, Countess of Airlie, remembered him from his Aldershot posting when he was Brigade Major to French. 'In those days, she noted, Haig 'was not universally popular, for in spite of his charming manners, he was thought opinionated and conceited. He used to take charge of General French and move him about like a policeman.'[142]

French's correspondence with Winifred over the next few weeks make it clear that he knew his days at St Omer were numbered. On 2 December 1915, he decamped to the Ritz in Paris, where he met General 'Papa' Joffre and confided to the portly French C-in-C that he was leaving his command in France and returning to England. He also dined with the courtier Lord Esher and his wife over several evenings, during which Esher tried to soothe the feelings of the Field Marshal. The private worlds of Esher and French could not have been more different. Esher was a predatory homosexual, yet they remained the oldest and best of friends. However, writing to Lord Stamfordham, Esher was under no illusions about the difficulties of working with French:

> Your diagnosis of the little Field Marshal [French] is quite accurate. He is not an intriguer, but just a passionate little man with, as you say, a hot temper and uncontrolled feelings. Anyone can work him up into a sort of mad suspicion, so that he falls an easy prey to the people about him. It was impossible to get him to see D.H. [Haig] or accept an invitation to visit our lines. He was angry with me because I tried to soothe his lacerated feelings, lacerated by his own vain imagining, as the idea incrusted in his mind that D.H. ousted him from command is, as you well know, false.[143]

Whoever dealt the 'Brutus' blow, French was informed by Prime Minister Asquith that his position as Commander-in-Chief was no longer tenable and he resigned on 6 December 1915.

By the end of the month, French was back in the familiar surroundings of 94 Lancaster Gate. On New Year's Eve he went out with some old friends to celebrate at the Carlton and he was delighted, at first, to be joined by George Moore, who had recently returned from America. 'I am very glad that old George is now home,' he told Winifred. 'He has an excellent head and is very sound about most things.' But French soon found that the excesses of their pre-war parties no longer held the same appeal and his friend's antics were becoming boring. The New Year's party turned out to be an anti-climax. It was French's first visit to a restaurant in over a year but the evening degenerated and, as he observed, 'George got rather drunk (such as he always is – no worse) and made Dorothy furious.' All French could think about was his 'Darling Silver Girl', and now that he was back in London with the position of Commander-in-Chief Home Forces, there would be ample opportunities for the lovers to meet.

Percy Bennett, however, was not about to surrender his wife. He certainly did not agree with the late Lord Cardigan, who remarked to one who came to apologise for running off with his wife, 'My dear sir, you have done me the greatest service that one man can render another.' It was a quote that French was fond of repeating to friends, especially those who readily accepted his amorous arrangements. On a grander scale, it had been the same with Edward VII and his lover Alice Keppel, who, with the exception of three premier peers, were entertained and accepted as a couple by smart society.[144]

French was pleased to be back in London, near his old haunts, but he was still smarting over his removal, though keeping a brave face on it. 'French's recall has been beautifully covered up,' observed Lady Hamilton, 'he has firmly seen to that.'[145]

In early January, Percy Bennett insisted that Winifred accompany him to Egypt, at least for the first month of his new posting. She agreed to go with him, leaving French smouldering at home. Yet French had enough to keep himself busy. There were the rounds of hospitals to be made, and visiting the wounded and disabled soldiers had a strong effect on French's emotions. 'I've spent this afternoon going around hospitals,' he wrote to Winifred, 'and have found some old friends amongst the officers – what a lot of these poor fellows have lost a limb or were infirmed for life – oh this war, I hate it all so.'[146] Several days later he was back:

I'm busy this afternoon going around hospitals again. There is a big one in The New King's Road, Chelsea, called The Marsden. There is a ward in it for all the men whose wounds have blinded them. I've spoken to several who had lost both eyes and many who were blind. It was terribly sad and very pathetic to see how good and cheery and practical these dear fellows were. One poor chap had the top of his head from the nose upwards blown into a shapeless mess.[147]

French had seen such tragic sights before, but they were in South Africa or on the Western Front. Seeing these casualties in civilian hospitals at home was somehow more shocking to him. It made the concerns of his friends seem even more trivial. Writing to Winifred, he despaired of George Moore's female companions:

George insisted on having Mrs Dunlop and Diana [Manners] to lunch. He asked me as a special kindness to come back and meet them here. I did – they talked all the time about their infernal hospital and their presence bored me to tears! I think they are beginning to bore old G also.[148]

French was now based at the War Office, just opposite the entrance to Horseguards Parade in Whitehall. But he made sure that any contentious political discussions took place at his home at Lancaster Gate. On 22 January 1916, *The Times* military correspondent, Charles Repington, visited the house to talk with French and George Moore about the reasons for French's dismissal. French was guarded and maintained that Asquith needed him more at home to reorganise the shambles in the Home Forces, than out in France. It was perhaps, a weak, if tactful line for French to take, but Repington then tackled Moore, who was clearly relishing his year of influence and was eager to talk of his own bitterness towards Lord Kitchener.

French's house was directly opposite the Lancaster Gate entrance to Kensington Gardens and the parkland was a delightful haven for lovers such as French and Winifred. A fashionable pastime was to promenade beside part of the lake known as the 'Long Water'. This lake was shallower than in the nearby Serpentine and in winter, after several days' frost, the ice was thick enough to attract hoards of young skaters. In spring, the Italian Gardens burst into colour and the beds were full of forsythia in bloom.[149] Leafy glades beside the water provided not only shade but also privacy for lovers, except that one area had become the centre of attention in recent years. On 1 May 1912, a statue of Peter Pan had appeared, as if by magic. J.M. Barrie, who had created the character some years earlier, secretly commissioned Sir George Frampton to sculpt the figure and quietly place it on the spot where Peter Pan had landed after flying out of the nursery. Barrie placed a surprise announcement in *The Times* that the statue had arrived and both the young and the old flocked to see it. French admired the story of the boy who never grew up and who would lead his gang of 'lost boys' to 'Neverland'. The proximity of Kensington Gardens added an extra frisson for French, for it was the real-life meeting place of J.M. Barrie and the Llewelyn Davies family on who the 'lost boys' were based. French and Winifred were absorbed by the characters in the story and soon adopted pet-names. He became 'Peter Pan' and Winifred became 'Wendy Darling', Peter Pan's friend and guardian. French had bestowed a unique name on his lover, as Barrie had invented the name 'Wendy' for the Peter Pan story. Until then, no-one in the world had been called by that name, so 'Wendy' Bennett was unique.[150]

When darkness fell, Kensington Gardens, along with other parks in London, took on a less innocent air. Units of the newly formed 'Women's Patrols' were out in force, combing the thickets and bushes, looking for fornicators. Their mission, which was carried out by pairs of doughty, middle-aged women with armbands and lanterns, was to preserve public morals and stamp out 'gross indecency'. Quite how the copulating couples were moved on is not recorded, but there were increasing complaints from the residents of Park Lane that young people who had been pushed out of the parks were now engaging in sex in 'dark corners' of Mayfair. Not surprisingly, sex-related crime increased dramatically during the war, and if even a sedate northern town such as Grantham could record 383 cases of prostitution in one year, the Women's Police Service in the metropolis must have been kept extremely busy.[151]

Not all 'afternoon delights' were taken in the open air. Certain hotels had earned a reputation for a very relaxed attitude to soldiers on leave. 'The Cavendish' was one establishment that encouraged visits from army officers and where the owner, Rosa Lewis, was happy to provide them with 'a nice clean tart and a parcel of luxuries'. There was even talk of erecting a commemorative plaque on the wall of the hotel, 'To all the women who fell here during the Great War'. Even the humble tea-shop failed to be immune from the 'wave of immoral behaviour' sweeping the capital. A *salon-de-thé* in Copthall Avenue was the scene of 'riotous behaviour' when customers moved on from a cup of tea and a bun to fondling the scantily clad waitresses. According to the subsequent court report, further menu choices appeared to be a glass of milk or a tumble with the head waitress. Magistrates were informed that such activities were not isolated in London and one case concluded with the Justice of the Peace admonishing, 'It is a pity in these dark days that young men should have time to waste in such frivolities.'[152] He rather missed the point.

On 29 February 1916, French was mollified by his elevation to the peerage, as Viscount Ypres, and there followed a steady round of social as well as military appointments. Amongst others, he called on Lady Hamilton, whose husband Sir Ian was still out of favour as a result of the Gallipoli debacle. French had climbed the slippery career ladder alongside Hamilton but the latter's devoted wife was suspicious of French's motives:

> I flew home to get into my red tea gown as Lord French was coming to have tea with me. He was shy at first, but thawed gradually, and quite enjoyed himself. He was charming about Ian, and said he thought he was being treated with great injustice … I wonder if he is genuine – he has always been jealous of Ian and is probably glad in his heart he is out of the way, though possibly still nervous about his re-employment.[153]

Winifred returned from Egypt, without Percy, and into the arms of her newly ennobled lover. She immediately commissioned a new photograph of herself in the silver dress so beloved by French. The photographer, Yevonde Cumbers, known as 'Madame Yevonde', operated from studios in Victoria and produced racier, flamboyant studies, and it was not long before an enticing Winifred stared out of the pages of *Tatler* and *Sphere* magazines. Perhaps owing more to the silver screen than 'polite circles', Winifred's photograph was sometimes accompanied by accounts of her arrivals at parties or recitals, and in common with other ladies, the colour and style of her dresses were faithfully reported. For while her role as a mistress might exclude her from the tables of the more rigid hostesses, she remained a married woman, and that, together with her style and elegance, ensured her entry to most houses. Winifred was also involved in the constant round of charity bazaars, concerts and 'at homes' in aid of the troops, which mushroomed in response to growing casualties. She helped out with Lady Lansdowne's Officers' Families Fund that looked after bereaved families of fallen officers, or she might take part in a *matinée musicale* at Claridge's, in aid of French Hospitals. The 'Cape to Cairo' fair was a week-long event that saw Winifred and her friends battling to purchase African products such as ostrich feathers and animal skins, all in aid of the Red Cross. No serious concert was complete without an appearance by Sir Thomas Beecham. The libidinous conductor was always a great favourite amongst the ladies, with his dramatic range change from 'languid' to 'furioso', which required a change of clothing half way through the performance. He was equally adept at removing his clothing for more private performances.[154]

Winifred enjoyed visits from her exotic sister, Sybil, who would arrive from Paris with her white Pomeranian dog, which had been smuggled through Customs in her fur muff. Sybil was very wealthy through her marriage into the Chrissoveloni banking dynasty and divided her time between Bucharest and Paris. She moved in influential and artistic circles and counted her sister-in-law, the legendary beauty Princess Hélène Soutzo, amongst her closest confidantes. Hélène kept a luxury apartment in the Ritz in Paris and hosted a fashionable salon, which attracted artists and writers such as Marcel Proust and Paul Morand.[155]

Veiled attacks on French and Moore had escalated and rumours of Moore being a spy had crystallised into newspaper allegations that he had passed secrets to the enemy. His detractors simply could not understand how the Commander-in-Chief's most trusted confidant could be a Michigan promoter. Indeed, it was hard to understand French's fascination for the naturalised American, beyond a mutual love of women and parties. Moore's later use as a courier for the affair with Winifred complicated the friendship, for French could not now risk deserting Moore. The London newspaper *The World* informed its readers that Moore's co-partner in his London-based Investment Registry Company was a German businessman by the name of Loewenfeld. Moore's supposed enemy contacts also included the German Ambassador to the United States, Count von Bernstorff, whom Moore was alleged to have met on a recent trip to America. Furthermore, the libel asserted that all information that was 'passed on' to the Germans had been acquired during Moore's frequent visits to GHQ – visits at the behest of French. The story soon spread and the allegations were picked up and repeated in the *Manchester Evening Chronicle*. By now, Moore had heard enough and sued the proprietor of the *Chronicle* for libel. The sensational case came to court in March 1916. The packed court room, which Winifred did not attend in case her name was mentioned, was amazed to see Lord French take the witness stand in defence of his friend – and his own reputation. The prosecution threw in the old claim of women at GHQ, to which Moore replied that the only woman he had ever seen entertained there was the rather venerable Lady Eileen Roberts. Furthermore, he refuted the accusation that he had met Count von Bernstorff in America by producing the alibi of his meeting with Colonel and Mrs Roosevelt. The defence collapsed and on 9 March, Moore won his case against the *Chronicle* and received a subsequent published apology in *The World*.[156]

No doubt Moore's case would have been seriously compromised if his role as courier for French's affair had been exposed in court. It was always a possibility and French was relieved when the case was over and Moore left for a spell in America. Even Winifred, with her reserves of tact and wisdom, could not dispel French's anger. He was consumed with his mission to expose the perpetrator of the stories about GHQ, as well as those behind his removal from France. For the latter, he blamed his successor Field Marshal Sir Douglas Haig. In fact, Haig was not directly involved in French's fall but he certainly benefited from it, and it was this fact that French converted into motive. The hatred between these two erstwhile friends was mutual.

'I would not receive Viscount French in my house,' Haig growled, 'I despise him too much.'[157] French's obsession with this intractable feud was also driving away his erstwhile allies, such as Lord Esher. 'I have a pathetic letter from Lord French,' he wrote, 'very embittered but rather noble in its simplicity. He is grievously disappointed.' And then by way of compensation, 'The little man is a lovable fellow and I am very sorry for him. But war is ruthless.'[158]

French had failed to remove Kitchener in the 'Shell Scandal', and kept up his enmity with the Secretary of State for War, both at work and in social engagements. This proved an embarrassment to all concerned. Society hostesses such as Jean Hamilton found their lunch or dinner party could be ruined by French and Kitchener glaring at each other across the dining table: 'Lord French rang me twice to-day, and spoke to me himself – the first time to ask me if Lord Kitchener was dining with us, and that if he was, he (Lord French) would be unable to come.'[159]

French had no such inhibitions when he was entertaining at Lancaster Gate. Even during his enforced absence, George Gordon Moore continued to allow French full use of the house, staff and dining budget, which he used with great regularity.[160] With her husband away, hopefully for some time, on Foreign Office business, Winifred was now free to play the hostess for her lover. It was a role for which she was eminently suited, as one relative recalled, 'she had the hedonist's magic power of dignifying the most tentative sortie with the excitement of an outing and of transforming the tamest indulgence into a special treat.'[161] Winifred continued to energise French, while his wife Eleanora maintained a dignified silence, raising their children, Richard, Gerald and Essex, at home in Hertfordshire. Divorce in such circumstances never really appeared an option. After all, it was only some 50 years before that it was still necessary to obtain a private Act of Parliament to secure a divorce, with the result that only about 300 cases had ever occurred. Then the 1857 Matrimonial Causes Act allowed women to divorce through the courts on the grounds of their husband's adultery, subject to additional conditions. In the years leading up to 1914, there were approximately 700 divorces each year. A wife's adultery on its own was sufficient grounds for a divorce petitioned by her husband. Not only would a wife be pilloried in court, but the case would be salaciously reported in the national press and she would be ostracised from society, perhaps never to see her children again. Conversely, a wronged wife would have to prove not only her husband's adultery but also his cruelty or desertion for over three years. While Eleanora did not wish to immerse her family in the bitterness that divorce proceedings would bring, French certainly had no wish to push her in that direction. He remembered only too well the scandal that erupted 20 years before, when serving in India. He had embarked on an affair with a brother-officer's wife and was named as the co-respondent in the subsequent divorce proceedings.[162]

However, even if these traumas could be surmounted, it was the fear of the indignity caused by the public court hearings and uncensored press reports that really prevented most divorces. If spouses remained oblivious to those consequences cases would then be heard by the Probate, Divorce and Admiralty Division of the High

Court and although the wigged and monocled figure of Sir Francis Jeune was no longer present, the reputation of his divorce hearings was still very much alive. Even though it was women who suffered under the divorce laws, it was predominantly women who flocked to hear the vivid details of marital breakdown in weekly court hearings. Such events had become something of a public spectacle, in the same way that earlier generations had thronged to public executions. As the war progressed and couples spent longer apart and mixed more freely with the opposite sex, the annual divorce rate more than doubled. Such increased opportunities for adultery provided good copy for national newspapers engaged in their own circulation war. Most editors still longed for a repeat of the celebrated pre-war Lady Colin Campbell case, with allegations of her adultery with a duke, a general, a doctor and a fire chief. For the moment, though, there remained a consensus amongst the newspaper proprietors and senior political and military figures that exposing each other's mistresses would 'not be in the public interest', not to mention their careers.[163]

Abroad, divorce appeared an easier matter. In France the 1907 revisions to the old Code Napoleon allowed divorce by mutual consent, while in the United States, laxer divorce laws had resulted in 72,000 petitions in 1906 alone. However, in Edwardian and 'Georgian' Britain, reputation was everything. If Lady French wished to divorce her husband, intimate details of his affair with Winifred would be aired in the public press and it would demolish his standing in society and destroy his career as a professional soldier. Unlike many women, Eleanora French did not have to worry about the financial consequences of such a downfall, for she had her own substantial family wealth to fall back on. It was more the point that she had become almost resigned to her husband's antics. Since the early 1900s he had embarked on a number of affairs before Winifred, all of which must have caused Lady French terrible hurt but, as other historians have surmised, despite it all, she still loved her husband.[164] In Winifred Bennett's case, becoming divorced from Percy would probably leave her penniless, with an undesirable reputation and tenuous contact with her daughter Iris. 'Pompous' Percy might have considered filing for divorce, but to become a public cuckold would take some handling. There was also the concept of 'class solidarity'. The upper middle and upper class felt they had to preserve their image in the face of the 'lower orders' and even if Percy had found Winifred in bed with French, he would have considered it vulgar to display his feelings, at least in public.[165]

On 27 August 1916, Romania finally entered the war on the side of the Allies. Winifred was initially delighted when she heard the news that her country had invaded Austria-Hungary and brought another 600,000 troops into the war. After a year of stagnation on the Western Front, it looked like this could be a knock-out blow to the Central Powers, and Hungary, with its large Romanian population, now faced the real possibility of annexation. But optimism was short-lived. After the Romanian Army's cautious advance into enemy territory, they were suddenly thrown back by a German-led Bulgarian force and were routed. By November, the Central Powers had pushed the Romanians even farther back across the Danube and were closing on the capital, Bucharest. The city was in dire straits. Already packed with refugees fleeing the German advance, the outlying districts saw outbreaks of typhus, and in the coldest winter in living memory, many froze to death or died of disease.[166] Such military and civilian losses were worsened by Russia's delay in transferring large forces to the Romanian front. Recriminations now flowed between London and Paris for having encouraged the Romanians to enter the war in the first place.

Meanwhile in Galatz, Winifred's parents, Edward and Mary Youell, prepared themselves for the country's German occupation and their probable internment. For the moment, their house became a focal point for expatriates in the city, desperate to hear news about the Western Front – news which the Youells had gleaned from their daughter's letters.[167] Time was running out for Romania but now it was the Allies that dithered. Because of his past experience of the country, Percy Bennett now found himself the Foreign Office representative at the Inter-Allied conference on Romania, and he saw at first hand the lack of consensus amongst the Allies about how to treat their new partner. Such disagreements were mirrored in the British capital, where a fierce row erupted between David Lloyd George and the Chief of the Imperial General Staff, General Sir William Robertson, over whether British forces and supplies should be diverted to Romania. While the bickering went on between the 'frocks and the brass hats' in London, news came in on 6 December that Bucharest had fallen to the Austro–German forces. This latest disaster was, according to the War Council member, Maurice Hankey, used by Lloyd George as a stick to beat the floundering Asquith. 'It is all an intolerable nuisance,' he noted, 'and is precipitated by the tragedy of the Romanian collapse.' With the imminent fall of his political coalition, Asquith resigned.[168]

As Asquith entered the political backwaters, French received another setback to his hopes of rehabilitation. Much to Winifred's distress, his name was mentioned in the breaking scandal involving Patsy Cornwallis-West and her undue influence in the upper echelons of the British Army. The ageing siren, once the lover of Edward VII, was in court over allegations that she had 'called in favours' from senior army officers, such as General Sir John Cowens, in her plan to transfer a young officer from his unit. The officer had not reacted to her sexual advances and she was retaliating; but not before she had insisted on the removal of an obstructive Brigadier-General. French, as the former Commander-in-Chief, was duly criticised by the Inquiry for failing to detect Patsy's 'sinister influence' in correspondence, but there was little evidence to prove that she was calling in any past favours from the libidinous C-in-C.[169]

Duly chastised, French carried on as Commander-in-Chief Home Forces, and his position, if anything, looked stronger. This was largely the result of the demise of his old adversary, Lord Kitchener, who had been lost at sea the previous June. French's brief included control of forces in Ireland and his biggest headache was the continuing problem of Irish rebellion. He was therefore spending increasing time in Dublin, and in 1917, he found reason to purchase a small country house at Drumdoe, in Roscommon. Ever mindful of his need to be near his lover, he also took over the lease of 94 Lancaster Gate from the absent George Moore, who had left Britain and returned home to Michigan, to indulge his passion for horses and stud farms. Meanwhile, Winifred busied herself running a stall in the Grafton Galleries, which doubled as a hall for picture exhibitions in the day and a night-club in the evenings. She spent some evenings with Romanian friends enjoying nostalgic folk poetry or music, and mixed in dances at the Hyde Park Hotel, Prince's Club, or the more risqué Buzz Buzz club. Despite the strictures of wartime Britain, these meeting places continued to be patronised, albeit out of the public gaze. Society columns in magazines still needed portraits of those 'about town' to fill their reports of parties or fashionable events. Winifred was keen to launch Iris into society and one step was to commission some portraits of her, taken by the exclusive Madame Lallie Charles studio, in Curzon Street. Ironically, at about the same time, French's wife Eleonora decided to have her photographic portrait taken by Bassano and have it published, defiantly, in the same magazines as the pictures of Winfred and Iris. It was a small gesture from a dignified woman who, remarkably, had still not quite given up on her husband.

News from Romania continued to be depressing. The fall of the Russian Provisional Government in November 1917 had removed a vital prop to Romania's attempts to stay in the war. There was also the problem of revolutionary fervour spreading from Russia and Bolshevik troops stationed alongside Romanian forces attempted to coerce them and establish soldiers' soviets. King Ferdinand, while not a man of intellect, nevertheless grasped the urgency of the situation and conceded land and electoral reforms, which seemed to stem mass desertions amongst the Romanian Army. However, the Romanians were still powerless to stop the advance of German and Hungarian forces into sizable chunks of their territory. With only the Bessarabia region left under their control, they were forced to surrender to the Central Powers. The Treaty of Bucharest, signed on 7 May 1918, gave the occupying Powers full control over the country's agricultural and oil production and Winifred lost contact with her parents.[170]

During late 1917 Percy Bennett was appointed Consul-General in Zurich and made sure that Winifred and Iris would accompany him. Although Percy was well aware of his wife's continuing affair, he still wanted her with him. Neutral Switzerland was an important posting and the office of Consul-General required a spouse to help host the numerous official functions. Although this removed Winifred temporarily from French's orbit, the lovers still kept up their correspondence, though they now had to evolve another plan for the delivery of letters. While Percy had been away and Winifred was living alone in London, it was a simple solution for French to correspond. But now that the Bennetts were 'together' in the same address in Zurich, it was impossible for streams of the Field Marshal's letters to be sent to the consulate in Zurich. So French devised a new plan. Using the willing services of Winifred's younger sister Gladys, who lived in Woking, Surrey, French sent his love letters to her home. Gladys would then send a covering letter to her sister in Zurich, with French's correspondence tucked inside.[171] Such covert operations seemed to add a frisson of excitement to the affair and French remained extremely grateful to Gladys for her connivance in the deception.

Trapped in Zurich, Winfred's spirits were lifted by the arrival of her lover's letters, but she increasingly found light relief amongst Zurich's bohemian set. The country's neutrality ensured a constant passage of artists and writers eager to escape the war and Winifred delighted in the company of such *avant-garde* performers. This only acted to distance her even more from her straitlaced husband who buried himself in official business. Even the appearance of the incomparable Irish novelist and poet James Joyce failed to stir him. In fact it only served to irritate him, for when Joyce tackled the Consul-General in April 1918 over his dispute with a Consulate employee, Percy steadfastly refused to consider the merits of Joyce's case. The incident involved a touring group of actors, known as 'The English Players', who were managed by Joyce and who were putting on Oscar Wilde's play *The Importance of Being Earnest* in Zurich that summer. An employee of the Consulate, who was an amateur thespian, helped fill one of the roles, only to fall out with Joyce over his expenses. There ensued a furious row between the two at the Consulate where, according to one of Joyce's biographers, the employee threatened to 'wring Joyce's bloody neck and chuck him down the stairs'. Not surprisingly, Joyce took great exception, pursuing not only the employee but also his superior, Percy, and the affair rapidly escalated. Percy took a dim view of the Irish writer, especially as he had failed to offer his services as a soldier to the Crown. Percy even went so far as to send Joyce a registered letter requesting that he report for military service. This feeling of disgust was entirely mutual.[172]

Winifred, who had just enjoyed a fortnight in London, returned to Zurich right in the middle of the diplomatic row and was amused to hear that Percy was 'on the ropes' in his fight with the Irish writer. Joyce, meanwhile, had picked up that Percy's nickname at the Consulate was 'Pompous Percy', and with his creative juices flowing, penned a wounding limerick in honour of the diplomat:

> There's an anthropoid consul called Bennett
> With the jowl of a jackass or jennet
> He must muzzle or mask it
> In the waste paper basket
> When he rises to bray in the Senate.

Not satisfied with mere poetry, Joyce decided to immortalise Percy in his literature and barely disguised him as the boxer, 'Pucking Percy', in his novel, *Ulysses*.[173]

Such satire failed to impact on the Consul General who had more pressing matters in hand. Switzerland during the First World War was a hive of activity and both Zurich and Berne were bristling with spies and undercover activity. The British Consulate had to keep a close eye on events, which were rapidly running out of control. The winter had seen serious rioting in Zurich and in the early months of

1918, socialists and Bolshevik sympathisers were emboldened by events in Russia. While a general strike throughout Switzerland would not be mounted until the end of the year, the authorities and British diplomats were clearly worried:

> There is much excitement here about the attempts at a Russian Revolution in Zurich. It is shameful that the Boches should have done all in their power to start a revolution here with the help of Russian Bolsheviks. The idea was of course that it would spread to Allied countries. One leader, Platten, a German, was naturalised in 1912, another later still. There are two women, Rosa Bloch and a Russian, Balabaroff. The latter arrived in Zurich some weeks ago with ten million roubles to ferment revolution. They poured money into a People's Bank and gave their word they would not engage in propaganda. Needless to say, this so-called mission has done nothing else but propagate Bolshevism.[174]

The spring of 1918 did not look good for the Allies. The sudden onslaught of the German *Michael* Offensive had taken the enemy to within sight of Amiens, and they were jubilant. Nights out in Zurich were difficult to stomach:

> The Germans and Austrians have been distinguishing themselves this Easter and it appears the members of both Legations came in motor-cars from Berne on Good Friday to the Palace Hotel. They dined together in the evening, a real debauch evidently, in the big dining room. A telephone call had come from Berne announcing the fall of Amiens, so the women put on lovely evening frocks, covered themselves in jewels, and the champagne flowed in rivers. Some nice Swiss people came also to the hotel for the Easter holidays and said the Boches were indescribably bestial. One of the German party leaped to his feet and yelled 'Hoche dem Kaiser.' All the other Boches rose as one and 'hoched' until the roof nearly blew off. It was all too much for the Swiss who left in protest.[175]

In April 1918, Winifred left Zurich and returned to the Bennett house in Devonshire Terrace with her daughter, who was delighted to return to her friends and her burgeoning social life in London. Both mother and daughter immediately launched themselves into charity events and revues designed to raise money for the Red Cross or hospitals for the wounded. They both joined Ivor Novello and a talented cast in a matinee held at the Charing Cross Hospital. Iris went on to work as a volunteer at the American Officers Inn in Cavendish Square.

The following month, the 65-year-old Lord French was appointed Lord Lieutenant of Ireland and took up residence at Vice Regal Lodge, Dublin. Unlike Percy Bennett, he did not insist on his spouse accompanying him, so Winifred was able to follow at a discreet distance. French's role, as he was keen to remind everyone, went way beyond the ceremonial. He was in effect the military Governor of Ireland who enjoyed a seat in the British Cabinet and was mindful of the threat posed to British rule by the militant nationalists, Sinn Fein. To this end, he immediately approved the arrest of a dozen of the principal Sinn Fein leaders. He also had to contend with the prospect of enforcing conscription in Ireland if the war continued into 1919 – a move which would inflame an already volatile situation.

While her lover busied himself with new ways to defeat the nationalists, Winifred was more interested in the domestic arrangements at Vice Regal Lodge. Whenever she could, she brought Iris over to Dublin, where there were a good number of dashing young officers on French's Staff, including his ADC, Captain Dick Wyndham, who could be counted on to give Iris their undivided attention. Meanwhile, Winifred had to return to London in the autumn of 1918, where she found a subdued city. Although the war would end in weeks, any feelings of triumph amongst the population were muted by the ravages of the flu epidemic. Despite a peak in the previous July, the virus had returned with a vengeance in the first week of November and fatalities exceeded the earlier surge. By the time the epidemic was spent in Britain several months later, the scourge had killed 151,446 troops and civilians.[176]

Not surprisingly, even a virulent epidemic could not dampen spirits in the capital when the eleventh hour of the eleventh month finally arrived. Crowds flocked to the Mall and Trafalgar Square, and there was joyous singing and dancing. Here and there, along all the numerous little alleyways and courtyards that traversed central London, Londoners held their own celebrations, as one reveller recalled:

> I went through the Temple, which was deserted, and up one of those little streets near Charing Cross, and there under an archway were two old women in prehistoric-looking bonnets and capes dancing stiffly and slowly to a barrel organ, the kind which has one leg and which you hardly ever see nowadays, played by a man so ancient that he looked as if he should have held a scythe rather than a hurdy-gurdy. In the Mall crowds had come to look at the German guns, and there were people standing and gazing at Buckingham Palace.[177]

The war had ended, but Lord French's war in Ireland was not over. As 1919 dawned, the Anglo-Irish War started in earnest and Michael Collins, the Intelligence Chief of the IRA, began selecting his targets from amongst the British establishment. French, as Viceroy and Lord Lieutenant of Ireland, was included on his list of candidates for assassination.

4

Elysium

In the immediate aftermath of the war, senior military and political figures descended on Paris for the Peace Conference. On 18 January 1919, statesmen convened for the purposes of winding up the defeated German, Austro-Hungarian and Ottoman Empires and drafting new treaties and borders. Winifred was looking forward to visiting Paris with Lord French, who was due to attend in his capacity as the *de facto* Governor of Ireland, but a nasty bout of pneumonia laid him low. Winifred's daughter Iris was constantly at his bedside in London and entries in her diary disclose her fears for his life. He slowly recovered, but Winifred seems to have carried on with her busy social life, especially as it concerned launching her – sometimes resistant – daughter into society. In March she hosted a reception with her sister, Sybil, for the Queen of Romania, held at the Hyde Park Hotel. It was followed by a ball at the Duke of Rutland's house in Arlington Street, where much to Winifred's delight, Iris danced with the Prince of Wales. Everyone watched the dance, smiling as they always do in the immediate presence of royalty, and Iris carried the glow for weeks afterwards.[178]

On Monday 2 June 1919, London saw one of its most celebrated weddings when Diana Manners married Lieutenant Duff Cooper at St Margaret's, Westminster. Lady Hamilton observed that the bride 'looked radiantly happy, but her mother looked forlorn, plain and carelessly dressed – she is furious Diana makes such a poor marriage.'[179] Winifred and Iris attended the glittering occasion and although Lord French was committed in Ireland, George Gordon Moore was waiting in the wings, ready to offer the couple financial help. In fact there would be no shortage of invitations, financial or otherwise, for the glittering couple during their married life. Each had their diversions and Diana maintained her charisma well into her later years. During the Second World War Lord Moran observed her charming the Prime Minister, Winston Churchill. 'There,' he whispered to Jock Colville, 'you have the historic spectacle of a professional siren vamping an elder statesman.'[180]

Soon after the wedding, Winifred and Iris left for a spell in Paris, where they stayed with Winifred's sister Sybil and her husband, Zanni. The Peace Conference was still in full flow, and the Treaty of Versailles with Germany had just been signed on 28 June 1919. They witnessed a magnificent parade of Allied troops, against a backdrop of an illuminated Eiffel Tower and while bands played and fireworks erupted, Iris was swept up in the carnival atmosphere to dance with French soldiers, or *poilus,* in front of the Opera House. Then there were trips to the great French cathedrals and tours of the chateaux in the Loire. Back at the conference, there was uplifting news for Winifred. She knew her beloved Romania had paid a very heavy price for her engagement in the war – over 400,000 Romanians were killed – but it was a sacrifice that made few headlines in the newspapers in western Europe. Nonetheless, at the Paris conference, and after much lobbying from Queen Marie, Romania was rewarded with a sizeable increase in her borders to include Transylvania and Bukovina.

In July 1919, Winifred and Iris left Paris for Ireland to spend the summer with Lord French. While he was dealing with business in Dublin, they had the use of the country house at Drumdoe, near the shore of Lough Arrow, Roscommon, a day's drive from the city. It was a bolt-hole for French and Winifred and also something of a playground for Iris who loved 'the little place with an old ruin in the grounds and a glorious lake with a motor boat and five puppies in the stables'. Winifred often bathed with Iris in the lake, swimming out to a little island they called 'Wendy Island.' There were hills to climb, which when conquered gave fabulous views out across the Atlantic.[181] In August Winifred and Iris decamped to Vice Regal Lodge to enjoy the more sophisticated delights of the city. It was difficult to believe there was an armed rebellion going on. There were races at Phoenix Park or Leopardstown and army polo matches to watch. Fancy dress parties were a regular feature and exotic Indian princes came to stay, including the Rajah of Kashmir. Then there was the Servants' Ball, which, according to Iris, was enlivened when 'Peter Pan danced with the house keeper, while I danced with the butler.'[182] But Iris really wanted to dance with one of French's staff officers, Captain Dickie Wyndham, who was taking a keen interest in the willowy vision. On 29 August 1919, Iris recorded in her diary, 'Captain Dickie Wyndham very persistent' and the following day, 'Dickie Wyndham very attentive again.' Winifred was also enjoying the prospect of a love match for her daughter, especially as Wyndham appeared to have all the accoutrements for keeping Iris in some style – notably he was heir to 'Clouds', the Wiltshire country house that had been the meeting-place of the legendary 'Souls' social set. However, the lovers were to be parted in September, when Iris had to return with her mother to London, leaving French to deal with the deteriorating situation in Ireland.

Without his love by his side, French spent a dour autumn in Ireland. It was also a daunting military situation, for the IRA had been stepping up their attacks and British intelligence was failing to keep pace. It was not helped by the number of British agents who had been eliminated. Michael Collins and his nationalist colleagues had cancelled a number of operations against British Cabinet members and in the winter of 1919, plans were crystallising for an attack on Lord French. Collins learned from the son of a railway worker that French was due to travel back on the train on 18 December from his country house to Dublin. An IRA ambush was set up near Ashtown railway station, where French was due to alight for the short car drive to Vice Regal Lodge in Dublin's Phoenix Park. French failed to show that day and the

ambush was postponed to the following day. At 11.40am on 19 December, French's
train pulled into Ashtown Station, where he was met by an armed convoy of three
cars, together with outriders, ready to take him into the city. The IRA believed he
would be travelling in the second car of the convoy and so prepared to drag a farm
wagon across the road to act as a blockade, while hiding a number of gunmen with
grenades behind a hedge. French was quicker off the mark than the rebels thought,
and by the time they had arranged the wagon properly, the first car of the convoy
had already sped past. French had swapped cars and was, in fact, in this first vehicle.
The rebels, however, caught the second car with a grenade which landed on the seat,
blasting it across the road. The third car, containing the armed escort, swiftly caught up
with the ambush and retaliated with blazing guns, ripping into the rebel ranks. A rebel
grenadier was shot through the throat and killed, while several of the British forces
were wounded. The shaken Viceroy arrived at Vice Regal Lodge shortly afterwards, his
car punctured by shrapnel, but he was unharmed. It was an extremely close call and
the next time the IRA would be more successful against British targets. It failed to
divert French from his strategy, though the publicity surrounding the attack gave the
IRA much notoriety. It was enough to completely destroy French's relationship with
his irascible sister, Charlotte, who had now taken up active support of the IRA.[183]

Iris became engaged to Dickie Wyndham, but before her marriage, she had
undertaken to visit her father Percy, who was now Ambassador to Panama. Biting her
lip, Winifred agreed to accompany Iris on the long trip and the pair set off in January
1920. It was a grim cruise, Iris observed, unrelieved by the company on board:

> Horrible small boat, smelly and badly painted. Tiny cabin. Felt thoroughly miserable
> – and to think that only last night I was dining with Dickie at the Ritz! The other
> passengers are an extraordinary assortment, but very friendly. There is Madame
> Galinet – divorcée; Miss Ashton – sour spinster; Mr Mackay – drunken Scottie;
> Miss Moraes – Jamaican Jewess; Major Seymour – young man with decided but
> narrow views; Mr Fraser – Chi-chi? Miss Andrews – nice girl; Major Tulloch –
> verbose idiot; Lord Williams – very posh.[184]

When the ladies eventually arrived in Panama they were greeted by an ebullient
Percy, preparing for a visit from the Prince of Wales. A dance in his honour was
held at Government House and Winifred managed to put aside her enmity for her
husband, especially as there would be a chance for Iris to enjoy another dance with
the Prince. And he did not disappoint. As the band struck up, he ignored his arranged
dance 'menu' and swiftly took to the floor with Iris. As they spun around the floor,
the Prince scanned the room for further suitable dance partners and spied a pretty,
petite girl swathed in ostrich plumes. When Iris's dance finished, the Prince launched
himself at the girl and proceeded to whirl her around the floor for dance after
dance. Meanwhile, the formidable ball organiser, keen to spread the Prince's favours
amongst the eligible girls, tried to break up the partnership. Her subtle methods

failed, so she whispered loudly in his ear that his dance partner 'was a boilermaker's daughter and had not been invited'. The Prince finally took the hint.

By May the girls were back in England, where Iris was delighted to be re-united with her fiancée, and plans were made for an autumn wedding. Just before the great day, Iris consulted her mother about what to expect in the bedroom. 'What do I have to do to please a man?' she enquired. Winifred for once did not draw on a lifetime of experience. 'Well, darling,' she replied, 'remember to always use lots of scent and never let him see you brush your teeth.' Armed with such sound advice, Iris ventured forth and the couple married on 20 October 1920, with Winifred and Lord French in attendance, the latter 'wearing a top hat that made him look considerably taller'.[185] Winifred's surprisingly coy advice for the wedding night was no use to her daughter. According to Joan Wyndham, it was a disaster:

> Dick, although he was now twenty-six, was also still a virgin and hadn't the slightest idea how It was done. In his desperate attempts to find out, he caused Iris terrible pain, but achieved nothing. My mother, who once described her experience to me, said that it had been quite terrifying: she had felt as if she was being torn apart. When they woke in the morning, they could hardly bear to look at each other – Iris full of pain and frustration, Dick crippled by embarrassment and shame. Sadly as they felt there was no point in trying again, they drove to the nearest doctor, who penetrated her hymen with a surgical instrument. As a result, my mother was frigid for life. 'Did you know,' she once asked a friend, 'that women also have their moments, just like men do? I wonder what it feels like.' But my poor mother was never to find out.[186]

Winifred was now free of any responsibilities, though the situation in Ireland was not conducive to regular social visits to see French. In the autumn of 1920, the pair enjoyed a week together in Paris with Winifred's sister, Sybil and her husband Zanni Chrissoveloni. Winifred, at 45, was still at her sexual peak, but her lover was 68 and clearly tiring after a gruelling military career that was almost over. Indeed, the following May, French was compelled to retire as Lord Lieutenant of Ireland and on 5 June 1922, he was created Earl of Ypres.[187] By this time French's ardour seemed to have cooled and writing from the Hotel de Crillon in Paris, he had already demoted Winifred from the role of 'Wendy Darling.' She was now known, rather confusingly as 'Michael Darling' (the youngest of J.M. Barrie's three fictional Darling children, and brother of Wendy). In the summer of 1922, French and Winifred both attended a ball in St James's, London, but they were in separate parties and although French told Winifred she looked 'most spiffing', he left early without saying goodbye. That year, he surrendered the lease on 94 Lancaster Gate and it must have been about that time that the passion and yearning of their relationship petered out. French was hard pressed financially, yet still had expensive tastes, with trips to Paris to stay in the best hotels. When invitations came from Winifred's sister Sybil, who still lived in the capital, French eagerly snapped them up. But he still hankered after living in Ireland and even purchased another country house, Hollybrook, near Boyle. But French was warned to keep away from both this property and his other country house, Drumdoe, for fear of attacks by nationalists. Such warnings were not made lightly, and in 1923, Drumdoe was raided by rebels and much of the contents and furniture were carried off.[188] In 1923, French was appointed Captain of Deal Castle, a post that was not salaried, but gave him a base in England. In May 1925, he fell seriously ill and as he lay in the draughty confines of the castle, he faced death with the stoicism which had marked his professional life. While his alter ego, Peter Pan, viewed death as 'an awfully big adventure', French felt he had experienced enough adventures in life. Worn out and riddled with cancer, he died on 22 May 1925.

George Gordon Moore, the man who had given so much to both French and Winifred and who had enabled their affair to ripen, had already left Britain. In 1923 he bought the Rancho San Carlos in Carmel, California and set about creating a vast wildlife reserve, which was later developed into the Santa Lucia Preserve. He was able to indulge his love of ranching and polo, creating superb facilities on the estate and living the life of a playboy. He was reputed to be the inspiration for F. Scott Fitzgerald's *The Great Gatsby*, but his gilded life was not to last. The financial crash of 1929 wiped out his business empire and he lost his beloved animal reserves. In 1940, he met up again with the object of his obsessive love, Diana Cooper. While Moore remained a huge fan of the socialite, she still witheringly described him as 'a mammoth truffle, black and of no known shape'. Moore may not have been a success with women, (or this woman in particular) but his triumphs were to be found elsewhere. When he died in 1970, his true legacies were the Santa Lucia Preserve in California and the descendants of his beloved Russian blue boars, who still roam Tennessee's Smokey Mountains.[189]

'Pompous Percy' continued to play a part in Winifred's life during the 1920s. He remained a financial lifeline for her while they stayed married, since most of her private capital was lost in Romanian railway stock. But she could hardly bear to be near him. Unfortunately, there were occasions when they had to meet for the sake of Iris, and their daughter's new home, 'Clouds', was usually the venue. The ghosts of 'The Souls' who used to meet there, such as Arthur Balfour, George Curzon or Margot Tennant, clearly did not have a benign effect on the Bennetts, who spent most of their time cruelly taunting each other. Mercifully for Winifred, Percy's next Ambassador's post after Panama was Venezuela.[190] That kept him out of the country until 1925, when he finally retired. Despite their long years of separation, neither Winifred nor Percy had pushed for a divorce, because of the unsavoury publicity. In the 1920s, divorce became immeasurably easier because of two changes in the law. The Matrimonial Causes Act of 1923, dispensed with additional grounds such as cruelty and allowed a husband or wife to petition for divorce proceedings purely on the grounds of their spouse's adultery. The other change involved press reporting. In 1926, the Judicial Proceedings (Regulation of Reports) Act prohibited newspapers from reporting the details of divorce cases, and at a stroke, salacious and humiliating details were removed from the public gaze. This restriction was not designed to shield the wounded parties, but more to preserve public decorum and maintain respect for the professional and upper classes. By this time though, Winifred had lost her only love and divorce would achieve little. Percy, however, had met a woman he wished to marry – the improbably named Edith Mustard – and was impatient to divorce Winifred. Making use of the new legislation, in 1927 he set up the necessary farce to provide 'evidence' of his adultery and thereby secure his divorce.[191]

In the time-honoured way, Percy organised a prostitute to meet him in a hotel bedroom. The practice allowed a tame waiter to burst into the bedroom, catch Percy *in flagrante* and then later swear that he saw the couple naked in bed together – sufficient evidence for the courts to accept adultery and grant a divorce. The inherently buttoned-up Percy was 'too embarrassed to undress, sat up all night fully clothed and only dived beneath the sheets at the last moment.' It was enough to grant him a divorce and in 1928 Percy married his rich widow, moved to Hove, and much to his granddaughter's amusement, became president of the local bowls association.[192] Percy proceeded to live up to his nickname of 'Pompous Percy', by publishing a book about himself titled, *Reminiscences Connected with my Official Career 1893–1927*. It was not a best-seller and Percy died, disappointed, in 1943.

Iris Bennett's marriage to Captain Wyndham was not a success, but much to everyone's surprise, they produced a daughter, Joan. They divorced in 1925, but not before he discovered sex and found love in the arms of the Marchioness of Queensbury. According to his friend Cyril Connolly, he also discovered that he enjoyed a sound whipping, becoming known as 'Whips Wyndham'. But whatever his personal preferences, he was not lacking in courage and met a tragic end when he was later shot dead in Palestine while covering the 1948 Arab-Israeli War for *The Sunday Times*.[193] Iris meanwhile, found platonic love in the company of the artistic Sidonie 'Sid' Houselander and later with her friend 'Marilyn', both of whom in turn became her companions. The extended family, which now included Iris's daughter Joan, was joined by Winifred, who after French's death had become rather a lost soul. The unusual family moved around London during the 1930s, first at Elm Park Gardens, then The Boltons and latterly at 7 Palace Gate, Kensington. Winifred's last address was ironically very close to her beloved Kensington Gardens, where as 'Wendy' she had spent so many happy times with her 'Peter Pan'.[194] Although she was by now in her early 60s, 'the beautiful Mrs Bennett' had kept her allure. Francis Wyndham who knew her in the autumn of her life, captured her essence in his sublime novel, *The Other Garden*:

> Her beauty still blazed; buttercup hair; long eyes that seemed as soft as purple pansies; generously curving lips that never quite ceased to smile. These features were often partly hidden by the wide brim of a picture hat, which she wore at a slant to cover one side of her face and around which an admirer had to peer to

enjoy an uninterrupted view. She had lost her figure decades ago, but it didn't really matter; that mysterious deep bosom, with no visible cleft, which vaguely and not ungracefully merged into a comfortable stomach and rolling hips, only added to her womanly glamour. She was indeed womanliness incarnate, in the sense that her Edwardian contemporaries had given to the word: sweet and warm as a bower, apparently slightly scatter-brained yet assumed to be essentially wise.[195]

Winifred kept a portrait of Lord French over her bed. One day, her forthright granddaughter Joan came into the bedroom and spying the picture of the Field Marshal in full dress uniform, demanded to know 'Who's that old geezer?' Winifred snapped back, 'How dare you talk about your godfather like that.'[196] Joan, it appeared, had little sentimentality and recalled that the only possession that she inherited from Winifred was 'a saggy green divan' on which the lovers had consummated their passion. As time went on, it was not the only thing that sagged. Joan observed her grandmother maintaining all the rituals of keeping age at bay:

> Granny was lying in all her anti-ageing paraphernalia – cold-cream on her face, pipe-cleaner curlers in her hair, a chin strap tied on top of her head and a little tin circle stuck between her eyebrows to keep out the wrinkles – gazing wistfully at a portrait of Peter Pan on the wall opposite.[197]

In 1938, Winifred's health started to deteriorate. She was only 63 years old, but had never been physically robust. Iris watched her sad end:

> She is helpless as a child and weeps at the slightest thing. Her mind wanders, taking her back to her Romanian childhood wandering through the woods and paddling through the streams. She speaks only in Romanian, calling for her *mamoushka* for help. I think she is going to die … strangely enough her face has regained some of its early beauty. It has lost that terrible haunted look and now at last, she seems peaceful and happy.[198]

Winifred slipped in and out of consciousness. Her mind turned to her dashing former lover, Jack Annesley, and her later champion, 'Peter Pan.' It was thirteen years since French had died and no-one had come close to replacing him. Her thoughts drifted through the meadows near Galatz and through the glades in Kensington Gardens, and finally, she found herself in the Elysian Fields. It was 15 March 1938 and she had died of heart failure, with her family around her. Even her outspoken granddaughter Joan could hardly take it in:

> It has taken me quite a long time to realise that I shall never see Granny again. What an extraordinary thought, and how mysterious and unreal this death seems, like something out of a book of old magic – a genie who takes people out of this

world and makes them vanish. When I come home next, she will have left London. She will not have gone to Panama, Paris or Romania; she will have gone on to another place – a strata of space and spirit. If I say, 'Where is Granny?' they will say she has gone to Elysium, Nirvana, or Heaven – what you will. She knows now all that has happened from the beginning of time, she understands how there can be 'Three in One'. How wrong it seems connected with someone so prosaic and worldly as one's grandmother, last seen staggering out of a shop in Kensington laden with purchases – potted hyacinths and marron glacés – wearing galoshes and a fur coat.[199]

In her prime, Winifred's brand of passion had always been soft and enveloping – reassuring even, as French would testify. She could seduce a man with her dark, intense stare, yet she never sought to mentally control her lover. She brought peace and tranquillity to French, whose manic moods always threatened to skew his judgements, which were crucial to the well-being of millions of men. In the end, she embraced 'the blue beast' and enjoyed the sexual passion that many Edwardian women were only beginning to discover.

PART II

EMILIE GRIGSBY

5

Southern Belle

The Waldorf-Astoria on Fifth Avenue was one of the largest hotels in the world. In 1901 it was barely ten years old and had already become one of New York society's premier venues. On a warm summer's evening the dining room was packed as Admiral Sigsbee, Commander of USS *Maine* and a great raconteur, hosted a small party, including Captain Richmond Hobson, hero of the recent Spanish-American War, the elegant Susan Grigsby and her beautiful daughter, Emilie. The ladies tilted their heads and laughed politely at their host's jokes – at the similarity of their surname and how, but for a shaky hand on the register, they could be related. It was all going so well. Sensing his charm was having some effect, the Admiral moved slightly closer to Susan. She was similarly buoyant, believing that the Grigsbys had claimed another social conquest and in her efforts to launch Emilie into New York society, she thought the Admiral would make a useful contact. It was time to toast their good fortune. But some way off, in the bar area, there was a disturbance. A group of race goers were celebrating a successful day at the nearby Saratoga Race Course and one man in particular was drunk and making a lot of noise. The Kentucky horse trainer looked respectable enough, but he was swaying about and starting to shout and berate the barman. He acted as if he owned the hotel and with his hat perched on the back of his head he swaggered off around the hotel corridors, singing out of tune. The diners could hear this spectacle coming towards them and then, before any staff could intervene, the drunk had launched himself through the dining room doors. Everyone turned around as the Kentuckian steadied himself, before gazing around at the sea of faces. Before Susan Grigsby could shield her face, the inebriate had locked on to her and with a startled expression, he shouted, 'Hullo, Sue! What in the hell are you doing here?' Sue Grigsby turned crimson and spluttered. Before she could recover her composure, the Kentuckian had reversed and was announcing to anyone who would listen, and there were plenty of those, what a coincidence it was that he should bump into his old *Madame* from Cincinnati. He didn't realise that brothel keepers were entertained at the Waldorf–Astoria.[200]

It was an event that would have finished off most social mountaineers, but not Sue and Emilie Grigsby. After the ghastly exposure of her mother's background, Emilie decided she would escape and keep re-inventing herself, moving on every time her own or her family's past caught up with her.

Yet, in the very beginning, it had all looked so promising for the 'Kentucky Beauty'. Emilie (or Emily as she was originally known) Busbey Grigsby was apparently born in 1876, but as the state of Kentucky did not keep comprehensive birth records before 1911, this cannot be confirmed.[201] However, there was no doubt about her parentage. Her father was Colonel Lewis Braxton Grigsby, a veteran of the Union cause during the American Civil War, while her paternal grandfather was a slave owner on a large scale, with farms in Mississippi and Kentucky. Emilie would also later claim a blood-tie to Carter Braxton, a signatory to the American Declaration of Independence. Her mother, Susan Burbridge, was also well connected, with an uncle who was another Union General, S.E. Burbridge, and a grandfather, James Fisher Robinson, who was briefly Governor of Kentucky. So, with a rich southern pedigree, Emilie looked set to become a genuine 'Southern Belle'. But some time in the late 1870s, the family fortunes plunged. After fathering Emilie and her brother Braxton, Lewis Grigsby died prematurely, leaving Susan to bring up her children in Lexington with very little money. The young and vivacious Sue nevertheless became very popular amongst the local racing fraternity, and possibly with the help of a 'benefactor', her situation improved enough to send her two children to boarding schools – Emilie to the Ursuline convent in Brown County, and Braxton to St Mary's Seminary in Ohio.

Sue Grigsby clearly had a talent for relieving men of their money, but her next venture proved a step too far. In the early 1890s, she opened a brothel in Elm Street, Cincinnati and soon the dollars were rolling in. According to contemporary reports, her son Braxton knew exactly what was going on at 'home', but his sister Emile remained unaware until the nuns at her secluded convent informed her that she had 'a cross to bear'. Despite the warnings of the nuns about the dangers of material wealth and sins of the flesh, Emilie emerged from her Catholic education as a beautiful, confident, ferociously ambitious young woman. Still mindful of her vows and her spiritual mission to 'reclaim' her mother, Emilie persuaded Sue to convert to Catholicism, even going so far as to make a pilgrimage to Rome to receive a blessing from the Pope.[202] While religion would always remain a constant in her life, the dangers of this world soon became Emilie's prime concern. The Cincinnati police were becoming increasingly interested in the activities at the Grigsby's and prospects for the future of the brothel looked bleak. Luckily, Emilie would soon find another source of support, this time from one of America's most controversial and colourful business magnates, 55-year-old Charles Tyson Yerkes.

Yerkes had made a fortune in Philadelphia, lost it, was imprisoned, then made another fortune as the 'Traction King' of Chicago in the 1880s. Using his expertise in urban transport and knowledge of electrification, the ruthless 'robber baron' transformed Chicago's overland transport system and in doing so, accumulated vast personal wealth. He ploughed this into a variety of corrupt deals, but also used it to finance his expensive lifestyle and mistresses. By 1895, he had decided to leave the 'Windy City', driven out by irate business competitors and prosecutors. He remained the financier of one local project, which took several more years to complete. The Yerkes Observatory, at Williams Bay, Wisconsin, was finally handed over to the University of Chicago in 1897. It housed the world's largest refracting telescope and remained the one project of which Yerkes was inordinately proud. However, he was now determined to move on and build a base in New York.[203] He started by constructing a palatial brownstone mansion at 864 Fifth Avenue, which cost over $2m, and he filled it with his valuable collection of art and antiques. Collecting art was a great passion for Yerkes, though some critics sneered at his taste. Amongst the more questionable artists in his hoard was the Belgian painter, Jan van Beers, whose 'oily charm' worked well with some of the more mature sitters, including Yerkes' long-suffering wife. Yerkes himself had his portrait painted by the artist, seated by his desk with spectacles in hand – a splendid and typical example of the new American entrepreneur. Yet this façade of propriety hid a darker side. The 58-year-old Yerkes had met Sue Grigsby several years before and was very taken with her young daughter, Emilie. He commissioned van Beers to produce a portrait of Emilie, barely into her teens, but with a coquettish tilt of the head that promised much. Indeed, Yerkes now decided that Emilie should become a permanent part of both his personal and financial future.[204]

So Emilie knew where her future lay; and it was not back in Cincinnati. In 1897, the Elm Street 'red-plush citadel of illicit frolic' was finally closed down by the police and Yerkes moved Sue Grigsby, Emile and her brother Braxton to New York. He then installed the whole family in a suite in the Hotel Grenoble, complete with servants and the use of a carriage and horses. He employed Braxton as his secretary, while the ravishing Emilie was allowed to waft around the fringes of 'polite society', probing for any entrée. Next, Yerkes decided she should have the necessary means to entertain and showcase herself on a lavish scale and in 1898 installed her in a sumptuous mansion at 660 Park Avenue, not far from his own house. Furnished with a Steinway grand piano, antique French Empire furniture, paintings and other works of art, it was by any measure, a palace. It consisted of five floors with half a block of frontage on the exclusive Park Avenue, though only measured 20 feet deep. Inside, the rooms were an extraordinary mix of objects from Yerkes' travels together with Emilie's eclectic tastes. Native Indian costumes and medieval clerical vestments vied for space with oriental ivories and a vast library of over 6000 books. Stunning Aubusson tapestries adorned the marble walls; an old velvet cloak strewn across a table had reputedly belonged to a knight of the Golden Fleece. As a temple to Emilie, any visitor ascending the stairs would be faced with a huge, seductive portrait by François Coppée of the 'lady of mystery'. Emilie's *grand salon,* the scene of some extravagant entertaining, was a bizarre mix. The floor was covered in bear, tiger and leopard rugs, with suits of armour and battle-axes tilting precariously over old masters. At one end was a large organ, behind which lay a small room, akin to a nun's cell. It contained a single iron bed and sparse, almost monastic, furniture as well as a little chapel recess. This, visitors were solemnly advised, was Emilie's room of contemplation. They may have spied false doors and mysterious passageways beyond, but it was as far as any guest ventured. 'The House of Mystery' as it became locally known, contained a secret. A concealed lift was in operation that would take Yerkes up from the basement to Emilie's real bedroom on the top floor.[205]

To the outside world Emilie was Yerkes' ward, and she explained away her apparent wealth with a fictitious Kentucky inheritance. The fact that she was his mistress, 40 years his junior, only came to the notice of his estranged wife the following year. Nevertheless, Yerkes was careful to maintain the public image of a married man and on occasions his wife was wheeled out of the family mansion at 864 Fifth Avenue to appear alongside the financier. It was an arrangement that suited Yerkes admirably, who was able to call on Emilie at 660 Park Avenue at will.[206] She in turn kept up the pretence of being his docile ward, while harbouring her own hopes of social conquest. With his support, she set out to cultivate New York society – a vaulting ambition.

Emilie soon appeared at one or two fringe society events and became friendly with the Spencer Trasks of Saratoga Springs. Trask was the hugely wealthy financier behind Thomas Edison and his light bulbs and their 'adoption' of Emilie was seen by her as a great step forward. But Mrs Trask heard of Sue Grigsby's blighted background and no end of 'Kentucky Belle' posing or talk of Civil War heritage could save Emilie. She was instantly dropped. Undeterred, she moved on, and in 1901 met a young naval hero from the Spanish-American War. Richmond Pearson Hobson was known as 'the most kissed man in America' when he became a legend after his mission to scuttle the collier *Merrimac,* in order to obstruct the shipping in Santiago Harbour. Emilie became close to him, attended functions with him and there was even talk of an engagement. But then the whispers started about Emilie's background and Hobson's furious father insisted that a denial of the engagement be placed in the New York press. Yerkes sheepishly obeyed and under the alias 'Captain Grigsby' duly placed the announcement.[207]

By the turn of the century, Charles Yerkes had amassed an estimated fortune of $20 million from the sale of shares and stocks in his railroad and tramway companies. His vast wealth had resulted from a mixture of energy, cunning and corruption and by

1900 he was looking beyond the shores of America to new investment opportunities in London. More importantly, Emilie was ready to venture out of New York, where she was having little social success, and conquer new territory.[208]

Emilie visited London, possibly for the first time, early in 1902. It was arranged that she would visit the city at the time of Edward VII's coronation and she was chaperoned by Mrs Ellen Dunlap Hopkins, a 'well-to-do painter' and founder of the New York School of Applied Design for Women. Ellen Hopkins thought Emilie 'the most beautiful woman I ever saw. Her eyes were brown. Her hair had the reddish gleam of gold. Her face, sad in expression. Her complexion like alabaster. Her form was beautiful.'[209] A visit to London was seen as essential for social advancement, for New Yorkers perceived social life in London as the height of taste and fashion. The old anti-British patriotism that existed in the early years of the nineteenth century had long since gone, to be replaced with an admiration for the way the British aristocracy lived. Polo, yachting, racing and hunting were all vigorously pursued by East Coast Americans, determined to acquire the trappings of 'the old country'.[210]

In 1900, London was the largest city in the world and the financial hub of a vast empire. Yet in transport terms, it was fractured and under-funded. Trams were horse-drawn and there were some sixteen railway companies controlling largely steam-driven underground trains. There were only three electrified tubes in the city and this was the area that Yerkes targeted, setting his sights on financing the Charing Cross tube as well as the electrification of the District Line. First he took over the bankrupt Baker Street-Waterloo Line, which became known as the 'Bakerloo' Line.[211]

Not only was the underground railway a huge novelty, it was also a much cleaner alternative to over-ground steam-driven trains. Railway window ledges were always smothered in black grease, and passengers' shirt cuffs and the hems of dresses were constantly grubby. Travelling above ground in London in the autumn was also a test of navigation. Smog, that grim combination of fog and smoke from thousands of belching chimneys, usually shrouded the capital for days at a time and visibility could be reduced to yards. As daylight faded, feeble gas lighting guided commuters and shoppers home.[212]

While he established himself in London, Yerkes travelled backwards and forwards to New York in some style on the latest steamships. He was sometimes accompanied by his long-suffering wife, but Emilie never travelled on the same ship.[213] She, too, was busy splitting her time between Britain and America, where she had become involved in publishing. She developed a taste for beautifully bound vellum books, produced by small presses, and she collaborated with Thomas Bird Mosher, a publisher working in this field. No doubt Bird was keen to secure Emilie's financial support for some of his more unprofitable ventures, but she had literary pretensions of her own. She wrote a novel, based on her own experiences and concerning the rise and development of a young woman. The tortuous title *I: In Which a Woman Tells the Truth About Herself* was published in 1904 by Appleton's of New York and received a lukewarm reception from critics. There was much lingering over the seductive body of the heroine, Sidney, as she advances beyond the reach of her worthy but dull husband and falls into the hands of that standard Victorian villain – the millionaire. He lavishes presents on her and installs her in a tower, only for her to turn on him. There is much sorrow but eventually Sidney regrets her greed and her inherent virtue is duly rewarded. It was a moral tale in which the autobiographical melded with fantasy and wish fulfillment. The heroine's musings and high opinion of herself certainly had a familiar ring to it:

> I could draw out as much attention and admiration from men as I knew what to do with. I think in fact, a slight contempt arose within me as I first found what an easy prey they were. Birth and breeding, together with my dancing, my gaiety, my high spirits, and the refinement of person and speech which were my heritage, seemed sufficient. It was the part of the men I met to find me charming, and of my friend to make my path easy … I can see that self- and sex-consciousness became fully awakened in me, and the craving for the admiration of men grew by what it fed on.[214]

It is thought that Yerkes never purchased any residential property in England. While in London he rented a house in Savoy Court and Emilie was installed in a house in Mayfair, as well as having the use of a riverside cottage in Taplow near Maidenhead called 'The Chalet'. This made Emilie a near neighbour of Lord and Lady Desborough, who lived in some style and splendour at Taplow Court. The Desboroughs were that marital union which worked so well in the upper echelons of society. Lord Desborough was an ex-Conservative MP who was elevated to the peerage in 1905. While he was 'handsome, noble and extremely boring', his wife Ettie was lively, intelligent and blessed with a wicked wit.[215] Her parties at Taplow Court often included leading politicians and soldiers. They could be either delightful or daunting, depending on a guest's current political fortunes. Lady Hamilton, wife of General Sir Ian Hamilton, suffered a particularly humiliating house party, or 'Saturday to Monday', as such parties were known. Her husband had accepted command of the Mediterranean Force, which had upset Lord Kitchener. As Jean Hamilton recorded in her diary, many of Kitchener's supporters were fellow guests who wasted no time in freezing out the Hamiltons:

> 7pm. No wonder I was frightened but it was much worse than anything I expected. I feel as if I had the plague – everyone flies at my approach and all conversation immediately stops. I have now flown to take refuge in my own room … All those people are so political and are furious with Ian for helping the Liberal Government out of a hole by taking Malta when Lord Kitchener had refused it.[216]

Although Emilie and the Desboroughs were neighbours, given Ettie Desborough's dislike of Americans – let alone new arrivals with a distinctly dubious past – there was little chance of any social exchange. Nonetheless, Emilie entertained in some style at Taplow, though always reserved the right to shock her guests. During one evening, she put on an impromptu solo dance routine, 'holding her soft, clinging dress', she sashayed around in a circle, lost in some sensual thoughts, but oblivious to the dropped jaws of her party. Self-doubt was never a problem for Emilie. In the spring of 1903, she attended a tea party in London. By chance, Henry James, the American-born writer who had lived in England for over 40 years, was also present and soon became the object of Emilie's attention. His novel, *The Wings of the Dove* had recently been published and Emilie fancied her similarity to one of the heroines. Gliding over to him, she asked 'Oh, Mr James, everyone says I'm like Milly Theale. Do you think so?' James's reply is not recorded but initially he may have been flattered by her knowledge of his book about a Titian-haired beauty who uses her wealth to storm the gates of society. But he could not have based the heroine on Emilie, as she supposed, because his book was published before she ever met him. Four chance meetings between the 'Master' and his pursuer failed to secure a relationship for Emilie, who in desperation sent the confirmed bachelor a Christmas ham, cooked in champagne. She failed to realise that James had been fending off women for years, probably due to repressed homosexuality, or simply a fear of physical intimacy. Undaunted, Emilie cautiously fed stories to journalists that the couple were in love and that an engagement might be expected. When Henry James was confronted with this news, he became extremely irritated, 'She must have put about the rumour,' he snapped, 'which though I thought her silly, I didn't suppose her silly enough for.' His inspiration for his fictional character was really a cousin, Minny Temple.[217]

In 1904 Emilie set off from New York bound for Paris on board the steamship *Kron Prinz Wilhelm*. She had one of the best suites on the ship and it was a fortunate coincidence that Mrs Kernochan, one of New York's leading socialites, should be in an adjacent suite. They met while promenading on the deck, where, it was reported, 'Emilie ventured a modest bow.' The formidable lady had not heard of Emilie before but it was not long before the Grigsby charm started to work, with tales of her Kentucky aunt's legacy. Mrs Kernochan was impressed and extended an invitation to Emilie to visit Newport, Rhode Island, on their return. The friendship continued in Paris, where Emilie was introduced to further reputable New York names, including the redoubtable Mrs Stuyvesant Fish. But while Emilie might be whooping at her success behind her apartment doors, her plans were about to fall apart. One evening, a dinner was arranged at the Ritz and as the party, including Emilie, made their way through the hotel lobby, she suddenly spied some strawberries on display. It was midwinter and the Ritz price was exorbitant, but unperturbed she insisted on buying all the stock and threw 1800 francs at the startled stallholder, announcing that everyone was invited to a champagne and strawberry party at her rooms in the Hotel Bristol. This overt display of wealth did not go down well with the party, who began to make enquiries about Emilie's origins. As soon as the New York socialites arrived back in their home city, they were met at the docks by their agents, keen to confirm that there was no Kentucky inheritance and that Emilie's money had all come from Yerkes. According to witnesses, Mrs Kernochan was 'almost prostrated' at the news that she was duped; when a Cincinnati police captain appeared with the timely news that Emilie's mother had kept a brothel, the dowager turned puce. Before she left the docks, Emilie's invitation to Newport was withdrawn.[218] Social disgrace did not deter the 'Southern Belle', especially as she was about to inherit a sizable fortune.

On 29 December 1905, Emilie's 68-year-old benefactor, Charles Yerkes, died in a suite in the Waldorf-Astoria Hotel. It was not a tranquil deathbed scene. As Yerkes lay critically ill, Emilie kept up a constant vigil beside his bed. When he suddenly deteriorated, his wife appeared. Emilie heard the arrival and as she attempted to leave the suite by a side door, Mrs Yerkes cut off her exit. There was a furious row in the corridor and fellow guests rushed out of their rooms to witness the spectacle. Nurses were called and Emilie was swiftly evacuated to a waiting carriage.[219] Minutes later it was all over. For a mistress, Emile had done well, for it is estimated that even before his death Yerkes had given her a fortune of between $2m and $4m, including the 'House of Mystery' in New York. Nevertheless, newspaper headlines screamed, 'Yerkes Cut off his Protégées – No Provision for Emilie Grigsby and Gladys Unger.'[220]

Unger, another pretty favourite of Yerkes, was indeed left out of his fortune, but Emilie, while not a beneficiary of the Yerkes Will, still had considerable sums settled on her during his life, including some fabulous diamonds and pearls. This did not prevent her extracting more money from his business deals, even after his death. Two years later, she successfully sued the Central Trust Company and obtained 47,000 shares in promotional bonds in the London Underground Railway. In Yerkes' last months, Emilie had established a close relationship with his personal doctor, Henry Loomis. The friendship had blossomed after Yerkes' death, much to the chagrin of Loomis's wife Julia, who followed her husband on one of his trips to Europe. She was dismayed to find that he disembarked at Hamburg instead of the expected destination of Cherbourg. It was enough for Julia Loomis to commence divorce proceedings, citing Emilie, who promptly scuttled off on the next available liner to escape the scandal. [221]

Even though Emilie had to keep ahead of her detractors, she was still a free and extremely wealthy woman. She was also in her prime and the perfect specimen of an Edwardian woman. The dominant female Edwardian fashion tended to follow 'The Gibson Girl' look, with hour-glass figure and bouffant hair. But Emilie was not just a follower of fashion. A contemporary report in 1905 described her as:

> ... a girl whom any person in the street would turn and stare at. An ideal figure, she had a wonderful alabaster-like complexion which any woman might envy. Her reddish hair was a striking feature. She had the carriage and style to which men apply the admiring word 'thoroughbred.' She dressed in perfect taste, with an

individuality of style that made whatever fashion she adopted seem to be the last triumph of art in clothes. She was a woman of the stamp which made everyone who saw her ask, 'who is she?'[222]

She only had to mask one physical defect, and full-length Edwardian dresses certainly helped. Some time after 1905, during a dinner in London, she suffered a blood clot in her right leg, which was apparently only remedied by breaking her leg above the knee and re-setting it. This drastic treatment resulted in her becoming slightly lame on her right side, yet the incident seems to have had little effect on her mobility, or indeed her sex life.[223] It certainly didn't curtail her travels to America or Paris, which she visited frequently in order to patronise the fashion houses of Worth and Paul Poiret. There, she would select the latest couture fashions, including sumptuous tea gowns, ball gowns and underwear. It was an exciting time for fashion-conscious women, who were invited by designers to ditch their corsets and adopt the new bodices, which would shortly evolve into the bra. It meant freedom to move easily, to cycle, to play sports – in short, to be comfortable. This fashion trend was tied into the whole 'new woman' idea, and it was a trend that Emilie heartily endorsed. It was enthusiastically promoted by Poiret, who had originally worked for the conservative House of Worth before establishing his own fashion house in 1903.[224] He then made his name with the 'kimono coat' and made it his mission to free women from the corset. In 1909, Margot Asquith, the wife of the British Prime Minister, invited him to put on a fashion show at 10 Downing Street, which he was delighted to do, and even the Prime Minister looked in to see the latest creations. Asquith received some bad press for allowing a foreign designer, rather than a British one, into Downing Street, and Margot promptly severed the connection. Emilie always remained one of Poiret's most devoted clients.[225]

Emilie loved 'names', whether it was in the fashion world or the arts. In New York, she had commissioned the rising German artist Wilhelm Funk to paint a full-length portrait of her but she was now looking for a more celebrated artist. In the summer of 1907, the Swedish portrait painter Anders Zorn was in London to execute a portrait of Sir Ernest Cassel, the banker and friend of Edward VII. Emilie knew about Zorn's work, and of course that his latest subject was close to the monarchy, and immediately commissioned him to paint her portrait.[226] The Swedish painter was also well known for his nude studies and Emilie was painted lying half-naked in bed. She made a fine subject for Zorn, with her head tilted back, lips parted and the suggestion of her fabulous curves beneath the cotton sheets. The portrait was soon hanging above the stairs of her house – a delicious promise for any suitor.[227]

Her patronage of the arts did not stop there. Opera was another route to 'society' and although she could not obtain a box at the Metropolitan Opera House in New York, as these tended to be inherited by certain families, no-one could stop her becoming a subscriber and being named alongside many of the 'Four Hundred', the families who headed New York society. America's love affair with the super-rich was boosted by the coverage they received in the quality press, enhanced by the widespread access photographers enjoyed to the smarter events. Invariably it was the Astors or Vanderbilts who topped the bill, and there were attempts to copy the court circular that appeared in the London *Times*, but tailored to New York's 'aristocracy'.[228] And that aristocracy guarded its membership fiercely. Intruders into this club of 400, however wealthy, were not welcome and the society matrons made sure that contenders such as Emilie would be ostracised. This was all good sport for the newspapers, as their circulation increased by advertising the doings of wealthy *arrivistes,* which in turn resulted in outraged responses from the inner circle. Corrections would be printed in subsequent newspapers, bringing further derision on the unfortunate players.

New Yorkers loved a list and, rather like the seats in the Opera House, even personal tax assessments were publicly listed in newspapers. Risers and fallers were mostly familiar names, including Emilie Grigsby, who in 1906 was assessed for tax on New York property worth $500,000 (worth approximately $50 million today). Income tax did not exist in America, and would not become a reality for another eight years, so apart from the asset tax, Americans kept what they earned. Such a liberal tax regime allowed Emilie's wealth to accumulate and the value of her personal realty placed her just below the Carnegies, Rockefellers and Vanderbilts.[229] She was easily wealthy enough to buy a 'cottage' in the achingly fashionable Newport, Rhode Island. However, owning one of these vast country houses would not gain Emilie access to the Newport season of parties, balls and dinners held by some of the Four Hundred. It was all too closely monitored to allow interlopers, but there was hope. After 1906, Mrs Astor, the last of the proclaimed heads of New York society, began to withdraw from hosting events and society split into 'sets'. Younger New York women were increasingly looking beyond – either to the new causes of social injustice or women's rights, or to new social capitals in America such as Washington and Los Angeles; or even to Europe, and particularly London. Emilie was ahead of the game.[230]

She increasingly sought the company of literary critics as well as editors and journalists, working for fringe or investigative journals. She enjoyed a short commercial partnership with the publisher Thomas Mosher, who produced beautiful short-run editions of the classics and she co-published with him a vellum edition of the *Rubaiyat*. Cash-strapped publishers were only too ready to accept financial help, regardless of its origins, and Emilie became popular in the publishing world. When in New York, she was regularly entertained by Jack Cosgrave, the socialist editor of *Everybody's Magazine*, a monthly New York journal that combined investigative stories with fiction. Although Cosgrave's brief was promoting social justice, he was well known for his entertaining and lively dinner parties, with guests drawn from the world of the arts and politics. Many were well-travelled and, like Emilie, constantly moved between New York and London, Paris or Rome.

In May 1911, Emilie declared that she was finally giving up on New York and moving to London, announcing 'Fifth and Madison Avenue may be closed to me, but I'm young, pretty and there are other worlds to conquer.'[231] She soon leased a house in Hertford Street, Mayfair, with a retinue of seven black American servants, a family tradition that she was loath to surrender. While houses in Edwardian London with black servants were not unusual, Emilie appeared to be surprised at the level of prejudice. When she crossed from New York to Europe in 1909 on board SS *Lapland*, she was accompanied by her black maid and valet. The ship stopped at Antwerp before coming into the port of Dover. Her arrival would prove un-newsworthy on its own, but she cabled the *New York Times* to file a story about racial attitudes that she knew would interest the press. She had left her two black servants to eat in the servants' quarters on board ship, but a chauffeur, also dining in the same area, refused to eat with the black couple and there was quite a disturbance. The *New York Times* duly published the story, which announced not only Emilie's enlightened views on racial matters but also news of her arrival in Europe.[232]

The house in Hertford Street was lavishly furnished and in the drawing room, strategically placed, were photographs of the Prince of Wales and Princess Mary, inscribed, in not wholly realistic handwriting, 'dearest friend Emilie'. She was desperate to be known as a friend of royalty but she was also keen to be known in artistic circles and had made some headway with the fringes of theatre land. Of particular interest to her was a tight-knit group of theatrical writers and performers that included the author Edith Havelock Ellis, wife of the sexologist, Henry. Edith was a powerful woman. She was a feminist, socialist and author of seven books and despite her marriage, was a practising lesbian, or as Henry described things when he woke up to the situation, 'a practitioner of sexual inversion'. Edith, who styled herself 'Edith Lees', surrounded herself with kindred spirits such as the feminist Olive Schreiner and homosexual writer Edward Carpenter, and she encouraged a succession of 'dear friends'. Indeed, she wasted no time in describing the details of her relationships to her bewildered husband. For a time, Emilie flirted with this circle, relishing a certain excitement and danger in their company and she was intrigued by their bohemian lifestyle and their dalliance with the socialism of George Bernard Shaw. Emilie was also experimenting with her sexuality and found amongst her new friends a very liberal attitude towards Sapphic relationships. She had certainly witnessed some very intimate acts during her visits to Paris, where lesbianism, unhindered by the Napoleonic Code, flourished in the private salons of wealthy and aristocratic Parisians.[233] Open lesbian relationships were tolerated in artistic circles and although they were not illegal, they were taboo in society at large. Such relationships might not always be physical, especially as traditionally 'decent women were expected to have no sexual feelings.'[234]

Another young woman who enjoyed this risqué company was Belle da Costa Greene, the exotic librarian and confidante of J.P. Morgan.[235] Emilie had met her several years before in New York at one of Jack Cosgrave's dinners, but Belle also spent a lot of her time in London, searching out finds for her employer's extraordinary book collection. It appears that she was also in London during 1910 to terminate a pregnancy arising from her affair with the married American art historian, Bernard Berenson.[236] Shattered from the experience, Belle threw herself into her work, which invariably meant further contact with dealers and collectors in the city and, according to her letters to Berenson, she was the subject of both male and female sexual attention. The latter was not a new phenomenon for Belle, who had in the past enjoyed the company of lesbians, such as the singer Lillie Lawlor and the theatre producer Bessie Marbury. One of Belle's new, more persistent admirers was Emilie Grigsby, who engineered a number of encounters with the librarian, to discuss more than just the art of bookbinding. Belle teased and taunted her lover Berenson with an account of one evening with Emilie. 'I just lay back and studied her,' Belle wrote, 'such an exquisite, angelic looking creature.' Bizarrely, Emilie tried to give Belle one of her couture gowns – a Fortuny creation, very similar to one that Berenson had recently sent her from Paris. As the evening progressed, it seemed that Emilie was increasingly interested in, as Belle put it, 'Topic No. 2', which was her code for lesbian approaches. Belle claimed they had 'an affair', though it is not clear whether she was teasing Berenson or whether they actually engaged in 'tipping the velvet'. Whether there was physical contact or not, the dark, exquisite Belle was clearly fascinated by Emilie and there was no doubt that their paths would cross again.[237]

Amongst the more liberal elements in Edwardian society, lesbianism was tolerated and indulged and seen as something daring. Even the strictly heterosexual Lady Diana Manners thought it rather audacious and fun to be photographed in the nude by the buxom wife of the German Ambassador in London, who was a well-known lesbian. Meanwhile, Edith Havelock-Ellis was welcoming Emilie into her more-than-ample bosom. She took a liking to this fresh, sensuous American, giving her a signed copy of her book, *My Cornish Neighbours*. But Edith had other favourites and was also taking a keen interest in the actress, Beryl Faber, who was appearing in one of Edith's plays. Edith was delighted when Beryl asked her to visit her home in the village of West Drayton, some fourteen miles outside central London. Edith was taken with the village, but more so with the possibilities involving the actress, and when the lease of a nearby property, Woodpecker Farm, became available in August 1912, she swiftly acquired it. Husband Henry was appalled but had little say in the matter and busied his mind with matters of spiritual sexuality, stimulated on occasions by the drug mescaline. Bizarrely, although he was feted as a sexual expert, Henry Havelock-Ellis would remain a virgin until he was 60. In the meantime, Edith was certainly not going to change his status and it was only a devoted lover who would eventually come to Henry's rescue.[238]

Although Woodpecker Farm was a pretty Elizabethan cottage, it was distinctly unloved, being 'out of repair, infested with vermin, and lately discovered as a suitable abode by convicts and vagabonds'. Nonetheless, Edith, with her usual vigour and love for the idea of farming took on the lease and assaulted the building, throwing large sums of money at the project, while Henry glowered in the background. No sooner had she started the renovations than the prime object of her affections in West Drayton, Beryl, announced she was moving. Beryl publicly announced that she had fallen out with her landlord but more cynical friends claimed that it was the prospect of having Edith as a near neighbour that prompted the move.[239]

Edith was perplexed to find that without Beryl she would increasingly rely on her husband for company at Woodpecker. This went against the tenets of their strange relationship, founded on a lack of sexual relations and the agreement that they would not live together. After two years working on the cottage, debts mounted, and Edith started to look for someone to take on the liability. Fortunately, she did not have long to wait. Her friend Emilie had paid several visits to the cottage and delighted not only in its history but also in its position, for it lay on a direct line between central London and Windsor Castle. Should her social ambitions be realised, she would be well placed for royal invitations. She swiftly took on the lease, changed the name to 'Old Meadows' and set about converting the farm to a small English country estate, complete with rose garden.[240]

Emilie was now ready to sell up all her assets in New York and make a complete break with the US. But she was still embroiled with the Yerkes estate over various financial settlements and some of the legal fights had become bitter. Taking time out one day from meetings with her attorneys in New York, she attended a lunch at Jack Cosgrave's house. Emilie found herself the only woman at the party, but lost no time in homing in on one particular man, by the name of Max. She monopolised him, telling him about her 'blameless life' and how some people had the wrong idea about her. He responded with wry smiles and let her continue her monologue, which ended with a request for his visiting card and an invitation for him to see her before she left for London. He had no card on him and as they left after lunch, he turned down her invitation of a lift in her motor car. Emilie became intrigued, even desperate to meet the young man again. She telephoned Cosgrave the following morning, enquiring 'Who was that tremendously interesting man I met last night and what is his address?' Cosgrave replied, 'Max Pam'.' There was a deathly silence on the other end of the telephone. Pam was the main attorney for the Yerkes estate and the very man engaged in fighting the legal battle with Emilie.[241]

In June 1911 Emilie came closer to realising her ambition of meeting royalty. She had a chance meeting with a Mlle Dussau, who was Princess Mary's French governess, and this gave Emilie the way-in she was looking for. She cultivated the friendship and the French girl was soon inviting her, via the staff entrance, into Buckingham Palace. There, on occasions Emilie encountered the fourteen-year-old Princess and worked her charm. It was not long before she secured an invitation to Windsor Castle where the French governess was employed. It was an extraordinary coup for Emilie, but one she could not keep secret for long. She soon committed the cardinal sin of talking to the press and cabled the *New York Times,* saying how much she was liked by the young Princess and that after staying at Windsor Castle she had been invited to the forthcoming coronation of George V. Warming to her theme, she also announced that she would join an official party travelling to India to witness the coronation of the King as Emperor of India, a ceremony known as the Dehli Durbar. It was a colossal faux pas, and those who had to listen to Emilie's stories about her 'close friendship' with Princess Mary were determined to verify her story with the Palace.[242]

She relished what these headlines would do to those who had tried to destroy her social ambitions in New York but she did not understand that talking to the press about any royal invitations or connections would signal the end of that association. However, she had only just begun her campaign. On 8 July 1911, she again cabled her contact at *The New York Times*, listing a host of aristocrats and statesmen who were supposed to be queuing up to entertain her. The headline declared 'Society Leaders at Miss Grigsby's' and proceeded to announce her social conquest of London. She held a reception at her house for Mlle Dassau and claimed that it was attended by such luminaries as the Earl and Countess Fitzwilliam, Lord and Lady Clifford, Sir Edward and Lady Ward as well as many others. Furthermore, she claimed that such was the stampede to launch her into society that Lord and Lady St Davids gave a garden party in her honour. Having secured a seat at His Majesty's Theatre next to the Duchess of Marlborough, Emilie announced that her list of engagements was to be topped by an invitation to the Duke of Marlborough's seat at Blenheim Palace.[243]

On 9 July, when copies of the *New York Times* were opened in the smartest morning rooms across New York, jaws dropped and faces darkened. The newspaper editor was inundated with complaints not only from the hostesses of New York, but from indignant English and Irish peers who had never even heard of Emilie. It appeared that no-one had held parties in her honour and even her admittance to Buckingham Palace was unauthorised. A caustic denunciation of Emilie's attempts at social mountaineering was published several days later. However, although she disappeared with the now unemployed Mlle Dassau to Paris for a week, she was determined to return to London and continue her campaign.[244]

On 26 August, she travelled to New York to organise the sale of her house and contents on Fifth Avenue. She sailed on the White Star liner RMS *Olympic*, sister ship of RMS *Titanic* and settled into the finest suite on board, with three Chow dogs and her black maid and manservant in attendance. When she stepped off the liner in New York, conspicuously dressed in black, waiting pressmen thrust the recent newspaper columns at her. She 'looked wearily at the clippings but said not a word'. But of far more interest to the waiting pressmen was the huge train of luggage that followed her off the ship. Inside the fourteen trunks and eleven bags were over 60 expensive gowns and jewellery valued at $800,000. This collection of emeralds, diamonds, rubies and pearls was examined at the Customs House on the harbour pier in full view of the disembarking passengers. It was a spectacle that Emilie enjoyed, for the passing throng could clearly hear the long list of valuables shouted out by the inspecting officers.[245]

Emilie's affairs usually had some spin-off benefit and none more so than her relationship with the publisher Mitchell Kennerley. The libidinous bookman had set himself up in a rather grand building in New York, where his top floor office had become a love-nest. Even the receptionist was a former mistress. He also employed Braxton Grigsby, Emilie's now 'broken-down' brother. Kennerley had commissioned a bronze sculpture of Emilie, by Jo Davidson, but pride of place on his desk was a photograph of her – totally naked. She must have retained her affection for him, for she used him to negotiate the sale of her house contents with the Anderson Auction Company on nearby Madison Avenue. Andersons, of course, were keen to handle a sale of such public interest, which included a large and diverse collection of exquisite paintings, sculptures, jade, tapestries, furniture and books, as well as a Steinway piano. There were paintings by Claude Monet and Camille Pissarro; carbon prints by Titian, Van Dyck and Botticelli; signed limited edition volumes by Charles Dickens (including his personal correspondence), Thomas Hardy and Henry James as well as exquisite, rare volumes from William Morris's Kelmscott Press. Characteristically, there were also two gold boxes each containing delicate feathered birds, which would appear and trill on a timer before disappearing back into their containers. Some of her collection was inherited from Yerkes or donated by subsequent lovers.[246]

The sale of Emilie's contents at 660 Fifth Avenue took place in January 1912.[247] Before the contents were removed to the Anderson auction house, the auctioneers opened up the house to show their provenance. There was a rush of inquisitive ladies to view the interior, especially those who had ostracised Emilie, as well as newspaper reporters, who scrambled over each other to examine the 'House of Mystery'. One reporter who entered the building was overcome. 'It makes you feel religious,' he confessed, 'and serene thoughts exude. The atmosphere is deliciously solemn.' This religious feel was enhanced by a presentation portrait of the late Pope Leo XIII, whom Emilie claimed to have met on her pilgrimage with her mother.[248] She reported that she was selling the contents, not for the large income that she would derive, but out of revenge – she wanted to sell all the gifts that had been showered on her by male lovers and they in turn would have to bid to buy them back. In the event, they paid handsomely for the privilege, with Emilie realising nearly $200,000 from the sale – probably double the normal auction value of such items. She meant her departure to be permanent and kept only her semi-naked portrait by Anders Zorn and a few other pieces. The house was taken over by P.J. Bartlett, a wealthy New York lawyer, and such was Emilie's desperation to be out of the city that she even backed out of a contract for the purchase of an electric landau, leaving her outraged supplier chasing her with a lawsuit. However, she told reporters after the sale, 'I will take my nine servants with me and spend my summers in England and my winters in the Riviera. After all, I am treated better in London.'[249] That remained to be seen.

During the winter of 1911–12, Emilie met 67-year-old Sir Sidney Colvin in London, recently knighted for services to the arts. Colvin was an influential figure in the art and literary world and knew an extraordinary number of writers, counting

Henry James, J.M. Barrie, George Meredith and Rudyard Kipling amongst his friends. Furthermore, he was Robert Louis Stevenson's literary advisor, a past Slade professor of fine art, and Keeper of Prints and Drawings at the British Museum. He could offer Emilie more than enough knowledge about objects she wished to collect, such as Japanese woodcuts or early editions of Keats or R.L. Stevenson. Married in 1903, Colvin was captivated by Emilie, who showed a student's ready worship of her tutor, as well as radiating great beauty at his side. They began an affair, which may have only lasted for months, but through Colvin Emilie met many of her literary heroes, some for the second time around. George Meredith had been a one-time lover of Emilie's and she was keen to remind Colvin that she had been the inspiration for one of his fictional characters, Lucy Feverel in *The Ordeal of Richard Feverel: A History of Father and Son*, an avant-garde and slightly scandalous work concerning attitudes to sexuality.[250]

Just before the start of the society season on 1 May 1912, there was frantic last-minute booking of London hotels. Floods of American visitors were arriving in England, undeterred by the recent *Titanic* disaster in the Atlantic. Because of the catastrophe, the White Star Line decided to withdraw RMS *Olympic* from service and put her in dry-dock in Belfast, stranding hundreds of her passengers. Emilie went to a chaotic Euston station to see off some friends and decided to make an entrance by arriving in an authentic Red Indian outfit with matching headdress.[251]

She spent much of that year organising improvements to Old Meadows and the surrounding grounds, which bordered the old village green in West Drayton. It was a perfect retreat for Emilie from her hectic life in Mayfair, yet was so accessible. The village had its own station and a population of about 1500, and importantly for a committed Catholic, it had its own Catholic church serving a large Irish immigrant congregation.[252] Yet Emilie still could not settle. In January 1913, after spending several weeks in Paris – mainly consumed with trips to her couturiers – she left for India on a trip to visit the Yogi philosophers of Hindustan.[253] It is hard to imagine a more extreme change, from a life of conspicuous consumption to spiritual contemplation. Still, spirituality was a popular preoccupation of the time, and Emilie was always keen to keep abreast of any fashion. Predictably, her expedition had something of a royal progress about it, with luggage trains and servants following in her wake. However, the pull of the London 'season' was too strong and by early summer she was back amongst her old haunts.

This time, rather than the arts scene, she was looking at the British Army – but only one general at a time. Through the international promoter and socialite, George Gordon Moore, she met his close friend, the Chief of the Imperial General Staff, General Sir John French. At the time, French was careering in and out of disastrous affairs, having separated from his wife some years earlier, and despite his elevated position was always keen for new assignations. Emilie gave the General an open invitation to Old Meadows, with the prospect of 'afternoon delights'. One afternoon in June 1913, he appeared at the cottage. While his driver sat in his motor car outside, the jaunty General explained to Emilie that he had been in Hounslow that morning and could not pass without calling to see her. He was also proud of his recent promotion and showed her the new cross-baton tabs on his tunic; there was much sexual banter as he talked of his new Field Marshal's baton. He told her of the time when, as a young Captain, he was stationed at Hounslow and used to walk all the way into London to meet a lover and walk all the way back.[254]

French, like so many hot-blooded men, was captivated by Emilie. She simply exuded sensuality. One contemporary writer, who later based a fictional character on Emilie, was awestruck:

> Her form was beautiful. She was not more than five feet five inches tall but she wore, usually, clinging soft white robes that seemed to give her height. I remember distinctly once seeing her in long white robes adorned with ropes of faint pink coral and I thought her the most beautiful creature I had ever seen.[255]

Her allure continued to ignite both sexes. Belle da Costa Greene, who was constantly travelling back and forth across the Atlantic in search of valuable volumes to add to the J.P. Morgan Library, was still enamoured with Emilie. The pair met again in New York, where Belle was still flirting with the bohemian set. Writing to her lover Bernard Berenson, Belle reported that most of the women she met in this group seemed to be living with other women, and again teased Berenson about her crush on Emilie. 'Emilie Grigsby has just left and I had a very amusing and very interesting "affair" with her.'[256]

As a 36-year-old glamorous, wealthy and single American woman, Emilie continued to fascinate every man, and many women that she encountered. Wives were understandably wary but by constantly changing her friends and lovers, she masked her colourful background. After several years based in London, she was starting to feel more secure and decided to acquire a more permanent home in the capital. It had to be Mayfair, and she was always rather taken with Brook Street, a thoroughfare in the heart of the Grosvenor Estate. It had always been the home of celebrated generals, eminent surgeons and composers, so when in 1913 *Country Life* magazine advertised a newly refurbished apartment block on the corner of Brook Street and Gilbert Street, she snapped up the lease. 80 Brook Street was a very large house, near the Grosvenor Square end of Mayfair, with the requisite number of professional neighbours including surgeons, dentists, physicians and chemists, as well as a number of well-heeled Americans.[257] Mary Burns, niece of J.P. Morgan and married to the Cabinet Minister 'Loulou' Harcourt, owned two adjacent houses just across the street, while Lady Randolph Churchill (now Mrs Cornwallis-West) lived at no. 72.[258]

Early visitors to her home included Auguste Rodin and W.B. Yeats. With her extraordinary wealth, Emilie could afford to be a patron of the arts – but she was moving on. She had already impressed one of the most senior commanders in the Army, Sir John French, and now, with a splendid new house not far from the War Office, Emilie was poised to become 'the official mascot of High Command'.

Mascot of High Command

In response to Germany's invasion of Belgium, Britain declared war at 2300 hours on 4 August 1914. The announcement was greeted in America with resignation and little enthusiasm. Although Emilie was decidedly pro-British, there was an isolationist core running through the American people, and it was a mood appreciated by President Woodrow Wilson. Consequently, he declared a policy of strict neutrality for America on 19 August.[259] Although many Americans had strong British (or French) ties, there were still sizable minorities of first- and second-generation Germans and immigrants from the Austro-Hungarian Empire to consider. The Irish also had an influential lobby in America and ultimately, it would take the expansion of German submarine warfare and the consequent death of American nationals to jolt the people into outrage.

Emilie treasured anything English, especially literature and poetry. During the long, hot summer of 1914 she had immersed herself in volumes of verse by Wordsworth, Southey and Browning. Increasingly however, she was drawn to a new style of poetry, called the 'Georgian' temper, which had been in vogue since George V's accession to the throne in 1910. While it never scaled the literary heights of Wordsworth or Keats, this spirited and patriotic verse chimed with the heady days of 1914–15, when death on the battlefield still seemed a heroic ambition. Rupert Brooke, with his fine, clean looks embodied this ideal. His first volume, *Poems,* published in December 1911, had only received mild acclaim, but since then, his fame and following had multiplied. He attracted a dedicated group of disciples and despite his sexual ambiguity, this included a good many female admirers. Brooke had made a journey from Fabian socialism to 'ultra patriotism', and his lines in 'Peace' and 'The Soldier' reflected the mood of fierce patriotism across the country during the early months of war.[260] By the time Emilie met him, the priapic poet was already embroiled with four other women – Cathleen Nesbitt, Lady Eileen Wellesley, Kathleen 'Ka' Cox and most recently, Violet Asquith. His poetry certainly moved Emilie, who was proud to relate that the poet had spent his last night in England with her at Old Meadows, before leaving for the ill-fated Dardanelles expedition in 1915. According to Emilie, when he left in the morning, Brooke penned some eloquent lines in her visitors' book, which she then had engraved on a bronze plate above the cottage porch. Quite when he stayed in West Drayton cannot be established, but it was not on his last night in England. Brooke had joined the Hood Battalion, Royal Naval Division, and prior to embarkation in February 1915, he spent the last two weeks at the battalion's training camp at Blandford in Dorset. He occupied himself in the bleak and muddy station by endless kit inspections, weapons training and brushing up on his Greek, before embarking on the *Gratuity Castle,* via Avonmouth Docks, bound for the Mediterranean. His friend, 'Oc' Asquith, the Prime Minister's son, remembers being told by Brooke that 'he was quite certain he would never come back, but would be killed.' His death from septicaemia on 23 April shocked Emilie and his wide circle of friends and admirers.[261]

All received a further shock several weeks later, when they heard the news that RMS *Lusitania,* after leaving New York, was sunk by a German submarine on 7 May 1915 near Ireland, with the loss of 1198 lives. While she was not an American ship, 128 Americans perished, and US newspapers trumpeted 'Washington believes that a grave crisis is at hand.'[262] Even so, Americans were hardly rushing to the recruiting sergeant. Although some 'Ivy League' boys from the smartest East Coast universities might join the dashing airmen of the 'Lafayette Escadrille' or other adventurers might sign up with the French Foreign Legion, the American people remained only mildly supportive of the cause. However, in London, Emilie noticed a gearing-up of American activity amongst the host of Anglo-American charities and friendship circles, tempered by the muttering Irish contingent. In her local Catholic Church community, the Irish element remained resolutely cool towards British policy. Emilie's friend, Sir Shane Leslie, the Irish diplomat and cousin of Winston Churchill, knew only too well the influence of Irish Americans on American public opinion. 'There was,' he said, 'growing anger of the Irish in America at the continued postponement of Home Rule.'[263] The thorny issue of Asquith's refusal to allow Irish independence would not go away.

Such irritants barely affected the *grand dames* – those beautiful American heiresses who had married into the British aristocracy, such as Consuelo Marlborough, Adèle Essex, Eloïse Ancaster and more famously, Jennie Churchill. The presence of Americans in the English social scene did cause some pontificating from their English cousins. The novelist Hugh Walpole lamented, 'I wish Lewis [Sinclair Lewis] would learn to talk instead of orate – but that's what no American will ever learn.' The English socialite Lady Desborough even took a dislike to Canadians, branding them 'utterly obvious and yet full of shoddy sentimentality, just like the Yanks'.[264] Still, American women found favour with the most sought after lover in the land. Edward VII said of American women, 'I like them because they are original and bring a little fresh air into society. They are not so squeamish as their English sisters and they are better able to take care of themselves.'[265] The British feelings of superiority were misplaced – there was much they could learn from their American cousins. Many Americans possessed a dynamism born of a rising industrial nation that seemed to have evaporated from many British family dynasties. And on a slightly more pedestrian level, Americans were often the last word in personal hygiene. Grooming mattered to them and their teeth were always immaculate, compared to the yellowing plugs and 'wet dog' aromas of some English gentlemen. Cleanliness was so important to Emilie that she increased the number of bathrooms when she purchased 80 Brook Street to make sure there was at least one on each floor. Before any excursion or 'at home', she would marinade herself in perfumed water and then apply some subtle scent. Like other wealthy post-Edwardian women, she would never buy a ready-made scent, but would have her favourite formula, which might contain over 50 ingredients, kept by a local perfumer and made up on request.

So, suitably dressed, scented and coiffured, Emilie ventured forth, determined to snare a high-ranking officer. There had been her dalliance with Sir John French, but he was now fully occupied running both military operations and a new mistress. So it was by good fortune that she re-encountered Lieutenant-General Sir John Cowans. Some years before the war, Emilie had briefly met him through her contact at the War Office with a Permanent Under Secretary, Sir Edward Ward. It was Ward who had mentioned the possibility of her watching King George V's coronation procession from one of the War Office balconies, and Cowans, never one to pass up the chance of meeting a pretty woman, introduced himself on the balcony. At the time, he was Director-General of the Territorial Forces and one of the Army's rising stars, a fact not lost on Emilie. As a 48-year-old Major-General, he had been appointed Quartermaster-General in 1912 and promoted Lieutenant-General in 1915. Now, as a member of the Army Council, he was one of the most important and influential officers in the army and, remarkably, had risen entirely through his own talents. Without the customary help from a 'patron' and no wealth to speak of, nor titled or landed family to ease him through the corridors of power, he had forged ahead using his keen brain and undoubted charisma.[266] Emilie and Cowans shared a quick wit; more importantly, they shared a vigorous commitment to sex. Cowans was married but had enjoyed a string of affairs and had managed to remain on good terms with his ex-mistresses and remarkably, with their husbands.

Emilie very rarely fell into a relationship, however brief. Liaisons were strictly on her terms and usually she had tracked and seized her man, either for sex or because his wealth or talents would gain her entry into a new social set. Invariably, her well-honed allure would haul in her man with little effort. Cowans, however, was different. His magnetism disarmed even a well-practised girl like Emilie and when they began an affair in 1915, it was largely on his terms. Standing six feet tall, Cowans was taller and more imposing than his colleagues, but his appeal went much further than his physical appearance, as one female admirer recalled:

I should say his great attraction for women was that he really loved them all – and understood them – their little ways and weaknesses – and that he couldn't bear to hurt them. He *did* of course, but one felt that he never did it deliberately. His tenderness as well as his sense of humour was irresistible. There was an 'Oh, but I love you too' attitude about him always, which melted the stoniest, and yet with it all he was big and strong and had such a wonderful brain. A man's strength and woman's intuition combined I should say. He was so lovable that you had to forgive him – and he had 'ways' – I shall never forget him buttoning his coat with me inside when I'd helped him on with it, about the second time we had met. As he put in the second arm he turned facing me as one does, opened both sides of the coat wide, buttoned me up inside it, roaring with laughter! In anyone else, I should have thought it an awful cheek, but there are people who can do these things and be liked for them and others who most certainly cannot do them.[267]

Cowans could seduce his women with laughter, but once they had succumbed to 'Jolly Jack', what were the consequences for them? After all, he may have been a considerate lover but precautions were probably not high on his agenda and they would be left to the woman. Despite the image often projected by romantic novels of the delicate and sheltered female, many Edwardian woman were actually well versed in birth control methods; but it did depend on background and education. For women such as Emilie Grigsby, sexual knowledge was a vital part of their armoury. Sexual habits were changing rapidly in the earliest decades of the twentieth century and East Coast Americans were open to discussing or analysing attitudes to sex. But for the ignorant, poor or illiterate, the only source of enlightenment was the chemist's catalogue. Even for the educated, such as Emilie, there was always a risk of pregnancy or contraction of a sexually transmitted disease. A single woman, however wealthy, did not have the cover of a family for any child conceived outside the matrimonial bed. Emilie could use the time-honoured natural methods of contraception. Withdrawal was an option but this was unreliable and many found it unsatisfying, while using the rhythm method, or 'safe period', was similarly haphazard – even doctors did not know how to calculate fertility dates accurately. However, such basic methods were widely used, as they were sanctioned by both Protestant and Catholic churches, whereas barrier methods were not.[268] Nonetheless, from the turn of the century, there was quite an array of barrier contraceptive devices available in Britain, though most remained illegal in America. Prevalent amongst these was the cap. Actually using it presented problems; it was hardly conducive to a romantic atmosphere if the woman had to insert it in front of her lover. However, if the home was prosperous, she could disappear to the bathroom. For the poor, there was only an outside lavatory, enough to cool the ardour, particularly in a harsh winter. So the cap proved to be very much the choice of the better off. Douches were used after intercourse, as it was believed that internal washing after sex not only prevented unwanted pregnancy but also guarded against sexually transmitted diseases. One commercial application of this idea was the painful-sounding 'irrigator' machine – a device that proved unreliable in inexperienced hands. Emilie's former lover, the poet Rupert Brooke, suffered anxiety after a night of passion with Katherine Cox after they 'mismanaged the machine', and as an abortion or illegitimate child was out of the question for Cox, Brooke went into a panic. The soldier-poet rather unheroically even contemplated suicide when the prospect of marriage was offered as a solution to the crisis.[269] If all else failed, pamphlets recommended 'coughing, sneezing or jumping' as the answer, or the even more unconvincing advice for women to, 'sit bolt upright immediately upon ejaculation' – a method which would surely have resulted in some very startled lovers.[270]

During the late Victorian and Edwardian periods, there were plenty of false dawns in the development of contraceptives. In the 1890s, the specialist rubber company Lamberts believed they had developed the ultimate device by launching the new 'Combined Pessarie and Sheath' for use by both men and women. Not for the squeamish, the rubber sheath had a steel coil rim at the base, which when rolled up, produced a cap-type device for the woman, or when fully unrolled, a sheath for the man. Adverts for the product proudly boasted, 'can be used again and again'. This was not as ludicrous as it seems, for good quality sheaths were expensive – four shillings each in 1912 (equivalent to £18 today) – and consequently there was quite a demand for a repeat performance. By the time of the First World War, rubber sheaths had become more attractive to couples, for although they still had a drawstring to tighten at the base, they no longer had seams, being manufactured by glass moulds dipped into liquid rubber. The London Rubber Company was established in 1915 and soon became a market leader for sheaths, although during the war, most of their raw materials had to be imported from America. To persuade most men to don a sheath, they first had to be persuaded that sheaths might also prevent sexually transmitted diseases, and in Edwardian England, rates were shockingly high. Christabel Pankhurst claimed that 75–80 per cent of all men were infected with gonorrhoea and a 'considerable percentage' with syphilis. While this was certainly a fanciful claim, there is no doubt that in this pre-penicillin age, syphilis was certainly rife in certain parts of the population.[271] Respectable families could be infected either by a straying husband or by inherited genes (when symptoms often presented as early blindness). At least the Edwardian medical establishment had finally accepted that a syphilitic parent could produce an infected newborn. Nonetheless, the social forces preventing men and women going for treatment were considerable. 'Respectability' was highly prized in society and any woman rumoured to have the disease would be instantly shunned.

Considering the scale of sexual diseases amongst the general population, the British Army (unlike the French) was very slow to offer prophylactic advice to its troops. There was no policy of distributing sheaths or even discussing how they could be used, for fear of actually encouraging promiscuity. Later measures included the provision of pots of calomel cream and buckets of permanganate of potash to reduce infection. Given that the cream contained mercury, its regular use cannot have improved the health of the errant member. In the early years of the war, soldiers had to trust in the basic detection methods employed by the brothel, including, as one private noted, 'the old lady cock examiner'.[272]

Because there was such squeamishness, women could find it difficult to acquire contraceptives. Although by 1914 London had a host of barbers shops who would sell gentlemen 'something for the weekend', 'surgical stores' selling contraceptives for both sexes were usually in the grim parts of the city. Alternatively, devices could be obtained by post, after answering coyly worded adverts for 'French novelties', though one unscrupulous seller dispatched fleur de lys party hats to disappointed lovers.

These contraceptive devices can and did fail, so what happened when a woman found she had an unwanted pregnancy? If she was single, like Emilie, it was out of the question to have a normal pregnancy and birth – she would be completely ostracised. Emilie could travel back to New York and have an illegal abortion performed by a sympathetic doctor, but risk blackmail or exposure. However, it was more likely that she could afford to employ a discreet doctor in London. Abortion had been illegal in Britain since 1803 but the laws on abortions were never as rigorously enforced as in America. If she could not face a surgical procedure in London, 'liver pills' or lead pills were available that might induce a miscarriage, or the explosive combination of gin and gunpowder.

The war years had seen fewer chaperones on the streets, though it was still considered 'bad form' for a woman to receive a man alone in her house. Even if the opportunity presented itself, being alone together did not necessarily result in intercourse. For many, intimacy stopped short of this and 'technical' virginity was extremely important for unmarried women. Duff Cooper recalled his girlfriend, Lady Dianna Manners. 'How I adored her,' he purred. 'I don't suppose there is any more beautiful thing in the world than she, naked to the waist.' However, while he professed to an obsession with Diana, he could still be diverted by chance encounters. In October 1916, he met a chorus girl, Babs Walter, who had recently married. He admitted he quite liked her and he 'rapidly had her, which was very agreeable,' rather as he might have enjoyed a good wine.[273]

It seemed that General Sir John Cowans was yet to be caught out but it was quite probable that nurseries in the smartest households across London possessed babies with the same eyes as 'Jolly Jack'. Like many seducers, he always took great care over his appearance and though not blessed with dark and dangerous looks, he made the most of what he had been given. He sported a moustache, like all officers and most gentlemen, in keeping with King's Regulations. Whether women found this attractive on all men is questionable, though etiquette manuals did warn men 'not to caress the moustache incessantly, however delicate or robust its growth', in the presence of women.[274] His thinning hair was a sensitive issue and when one fellow house guest, Rosie Boot of music hall fame, hid his hair brush in his bed as a practical joke, the General was appalled. How could he brush his hair before going to bed? When he played practical jokes, such as telephoning his friends at 3.00am in the morning and playing a cigar-box tune loudly down the mouthpiece, it was always hilarious as far as he was concerned.[275] In such high jinks he was different to his largely reserved and formal colleagues. An old friend from Darjeeling, Sir Edward Denison Ross, related that Cowans was known as 'the finest Quartermaster-General since Moses', and that 'he was so full of high spirits and banter, so fond of the lighter side of life.' It was also Cowans' confidence that made this highly charged man so successful with women. 'They all loved him,' Ross recalled. 'His charm was irresistible; the compliments he paid them were outrageous.'[276] Yet, despite his constant wandering, Cowans remained married to Eva, a vicar's daughter, for over 30 years, and though there were no children, she was wearily resigned to his attraction to and for other women. He had a gift for making women feel very comfortable and however ill-informed Emilie might be about some war topic, or indeed any social issue, he would make her feel his equal. In short, he made women feel good about themselves and in his contemporary military world, inhabited by some huge and strutting egos, that talent made a welcome change. Sonia Keppel was always delighted when he came to visit her mother, Alice, the former mistress of Edward VII. 'Things seemed brightest when Sir John Cowans was present,' she recalled. His energy was legendary. He rose early in his house at 72 Curzon Street and was at his desk in the War Office by 8.00am. Completely in command of his brief, he was one of the very few men who were unafraid of the Secretary of State for War, Lord Kitchener. As Quartermaster-General, Cowans was ultimately responsible for organising the vast number of army camps and billets, as well as the provision of uniforms, blankets, mess utensils and most importantly, food.[277] He was a believer in the maxim that not only does an army march on its stomach, but it also fights on its stomach. For such a senior commander, Cowans was famously accessible and managed to handle a constant succession of lobbyists who besieged him for help with their particular campaigns. He was even accessible to formidable women, such as the Marchioness of Londonderry, who bullied him into allowing the newly formed Women's Legion to provide cooks for convalescent hospitals. Cowans so admired Edith Londonderry and her quest to introduce women into jobs and support roles for the war effort that he gave her 'a beautiful little Colt revolver' to defend herself during her forays across the Channel.[278]

With such an all-consuming job, and the problem of pleasing so many women at the same time, Cowans had little time for other activities. He was no sportsman and neither was he fond of riding. A man of simple tastes, he read little and appreciated art even less, though he befriended the artist William Orpen and arranged for him to receive a commission in the Army Service Corps. In fact, Orpen was one of a tight-knit group of Cowans' friends who met every Wednesday to relax and have fun at Londonderry House. Known as 'The Ark', this informal grouping of soldiers, artists, writers and politicians was a very low-key alternative to the 'Souls' or 'Coterie' sets and had no artistic ambitions. All the members were given names, so that Cowans became 'Merry John the Mandrill', Winston Churchill was 'the Warlock'. Even the venerable statesman Arthur Balfour was known as 'Arthur the Albatross'. Everyone competed at the silliest party games. It was all a vent for their stressful work and for the relentless keeping up of appearances at the War Office or House of Commons – and it was not a world Cowans introduced to Emilie.[279] He kept her separate, in the way that he kept all his loves. But she was the same and there seemed to be an unspoken rule that each could keep to their own circles, to meet only for uncomplicated, passionate lovemaking at 80 Brook Street.

While Emilie and Cowans revelled in each other, many couples were desperate for help. Until 1918, when Dr Marie Stopes published her groundbreaking book, *Married Love*, sexual advice was very limited. Her correspondence to worried couples predated the book's publication and although Dr Stopes offered an important service about a much misunderstood subject, she was a Doctor of Science rather than Medicine and much of her wisdom was suspect. One concerned woman wrote to her seeking help to overcome the impotence of her hard-working husband. Stopes' reply must have left 'worried of London' completely baffled, for she prescribed a daily diet of oranges, oysters and stout, to be taken with copious amounts of Swiss mountain air.[280]

However, the tone of Stopes' advice was right for the time. While prepared to describe the sexual act, it was couched in the language that her readers could feel happy with. Although there was no talk of 'the blue beast' in describing sexual passion, a vagina might be 'the portals of her body', while sexual intercourse was 'the union'. A query concerning masturbation, or 'the secret vice' from one young worried woman prompted the prescription of two sessions per month, as exceeding this limit was 'dangerous'. Rather like Havelock-Ellis, who described and advised on lovemaking and sexual intercourse while still a virgin, Stopes wrote much of the material for *Married Love* while remaining *intacta,* as her marriage was never consummated. 'I paid such a terrible price for sex-ignorance,' she confessed, 'that I feel that knowledge gained at such a cost should be placed at the service of humanity.' Her advice that men engage in foreplay and prolong intercourse was revelatory. [281] Even French authors and hygienists, popularly thought to be more liberal, concentrated more on childbirth rather than preparing women for their wedding night. Sadly, Stopes had to advise young brides 'not to expect romance' on their first night – an understatement in the light of the 'savage rutting' experienced by some startled girls.[282] Indeed, if the experiences of Lady Emily Lutyens were commonplace, the marital bed was a pretty unattractive place to inhabit. The famous architect's wife yearned 'for a sexually satisfying love-match, and failing to get it, brought her physical relations with her husband to an end when the children were born.' Sir Edwin's habitual pipe smoking hardly helped. 'Don't take your pipe out of your mouth and then ask me to kiss you,' she quite reasonably demanded. Ultimately, Emily Lutyens believed 'that a woman has the right over her own body' and this thinking was increasingly adopted by frustrated wives.[283] Sigmund Freud stimulated the debate and journals such as the *Freewoman* during its brief life took up the challenge of advancing sexual knowledge. From this journal's letters page, it is clear that there was a growing demand from women for more information about the enjoyment of sex – rather than just the mechanics of birth control or prevention of disease.[284]

Some time during the summer of 1915, Emilie and Cowans finally became sated with each other, and although there were still occasional trysts, both started to look elsewhere. In Emilie's case, she was keen to extend her influence into the political and press arena, and saw her chance with the continuing crises surrounding the Prime Minister, H.H. Asquith. She decided to lend her support to Lord Northcliffe, a newspaper proprietor of some standing and a man who had a roving eye, who could appreciate a heaving bosom and breathless flattery. Northcliffe was extremely influential, controlling some 40 per cent of the British morning and evening newspapers, including *The Times* and *Daily Mail*. Although he was very wealthy and had been ennobled in 1906, he was ill-at-ease in the drawing rooms of the establishment and his raw ambition rankled with those to whom power was assumed by birthright. Northcliffe was more openly disliked by his political opponents, especially the Liberal Party and its leader H.H. Asquith, who would readily admit to his close *confidante* Venetia Stanley, 'I hate and distrust the fellow and all his works.'[285] He had good reason, for Northcliffe was determined to be rid of Asquith as Prime Minister. The press baron had already helped to demolish the old Liberal Government in May 1915, through his press campaign about the shell shortages. However, Asquith had remained at his post, albeit presiding over a Coalition Cabinet. The debacle at Gallipoli continued to rumble on through 1915 and Northcliffe's ire was further fuelled by his close friend, the Australian journalist Keith Murdoch, who had ignited the controversy in the press.

Emilie made herself useful by allowing the press baron to use 80 Brook Street as a 'safe house'. He could hold meetings and pursue intrigues against his opponents, on neutral ground and away from prying eyes, while the chatelaine of the house provided comfort and refreshments. Northcliffe was too consumed with his own illicit activities to become romantically involved with Emilie. He had embarked on a number of affairs himself and had sired illegitimate children, the first when he was sixteen. Not to be outdone, his wife had been caught *in flagrante* with the manager of *The Times* newspaper. After that drama there was a determination to keep indiscretions within the family; when the wife of Northcliffe's brother, Harold Lord Rothermere embarked on an affair, it was with their younger brother, St John.[286] Northcliffe's private life may have been chaotic, but in his public life he was focussed – not only on his newspaper empire but on a number of vendettas against those he felt were failing to prosecute the war effectively, notably H.H. Asquith.

It was during one of Northcliffe's conspiratorial meetings at Brook Street in the autumn of 1915 that Emilie first encountered Colonel Charles à Court Repington. There was an instant mutual attraction. The 58-year-old former Military Attaché was now Military Correspondent for *The Times,* with one of the best address books in London. An influential, if controversial, figure in military circles, he was a close friend of Sir John French and was involved in breaking the recent 'Shell Scandal' story.[287] In his private life, 'Thruster' Repington was an accomplished rider. He also possessed a legendary sex drive and had a complete inability to remain faithful to one woman. While his long-time common-law wife, Molly, remained knitting at their home, Maryon Hall in Hampstead, Repington would wine and dine officers and politicians in pursuit of a good story. He would also make sure he was surrounded in his haunts by some of society's most glamorous women.[288] At first, Emilie was just another girl about town, but Repington found her intriguing and sensual and she was also wealthy – an atrribute not lost on the impecunious writer. Lady Hamilton, a close friend of Molly, who also knew Repington well, rated Repington's mind and ingenuity but was appalled at his sexual profligacy. 'I shudder when I think,' she wrote, 'of all the women he pursues with his evil passions – poor little Molly tied now to a sex maniac.' There was no secret about Emilie's affair with Repington and during the autumn of 1915 they regularly lunched together at fashionable restaurants such as Prince's or Ciro's, which, despite the war, managed to maintain an imaginative menu. Sometimes they would be joined by Emilie's friend, the actress Doris Keane, who would amuse them with tales from the theatre world. Doris, with her 'dark, magnetic eyes' found Repington's endless contacts most useful and frequently pestered him to arrange a meeting with a certain married man, who was 'the only man left in England' who interested her.[289] Emilie had to share Repington's favours and even pay for his extravagant lifestyle and in return he promised further society introductions, and perhaps more importantly, offered her a satisfying sexual relationship. She certainly did everything to make herself enticing, as she confessed in her thinly disguised memoir:

> I had learned by this time a lot of fine lady ways. I was still athletic and never, I
> think, effeminate or precisely voluptuous, but I went in for all things fragrant, dainty
> and alluring about my personal belongings. I detested strong perfumes, directly
> and obviously applied, but I considered scented baths a necessity. My wardrobe
> was never extravagant or over-fashionable, but I cared much for the luxury of
> underclothing of silk, or of cotton of cobweb fineness of texture and perfection of
> handiwork; I delighted in sumptuous and delicate negligée. On my dressing table
> I never could endure the heavy tinny wares of the silversmith. All my brushes and
> boxes were of the smoothest ivory.[290]

When Emilie and Repington wanted to escape out of town, Old Meadows provided the perfect sanctuary. The cottage was deep inside its own grounds. It was also a safe place for conspiracies and Emilie's great friend Shane Leslie recalled that French, Repington and Northcliffe met at Old Meadows to hatch the plot to remove Asquith, though his report that Kitchener had earlier dined there with French must be inaccurate, as there was no social contact between such sworn enemies.[291] Back in Mayfair, Repington continued to conduct meetings at 80 Brook Street, largely involving post-mortems on the removal of his friend, Sir John French. Rumours about plots circulated widely and his scheming was the talk of society. Molly Repington's friend, Jean Hamilton, met the philanderer on frequent occasions, but could never quite corner him about his activities. 'I longed to mention Miss Grigsby to him,' she noted in her diary. 'Adèle Essex told me that the intrigues of the Northcliffe Press are mostly conducted at her house now.[292]

During the second winter of the war, few social activities were interrupted and serious sacrifices were still to be made in London:

> Here in London, you know, the question does still arise sometimes to one's mind –
> is there really a war? People are going racing again, some are even dancing, there's
> a new revue every week, our drawing-rooms with their blue-painted, spring-like

ceilings are as full as ever of flowers. The new 'semi-evening' frocks are not made
of sack-cloth, and ... we're not living entirely on chops and cheese, nor doing our
own washing and sewing either.[293]

Night clubs flourished, especially in Soho, where a large number had sprung up by
the winter of 1915, though they had recently been ordered to close at night at the
same time as restaurants. The area also boasted a large number of restaurants, opened
to cater for the flocks of smart young women brought in to work in the nearby
government offices, while the network of lanes and narrow streets also hosted new
dress shops catering for the emerging dancing craze. Magazines were full of military-
inspired ideas for Christmas presents. Debenham and Freebody in Wigmore Street
could provide regimental scarves for either officers or their wives or sweethearts.
For children, Gamages of Holborn were selling a boy's Royal Flying Corps uniform
or a miniature nurse's outfit for girls. There were regimental brooches, watches and
bracelets for those at home, or similarly embossed 'comfort kits', of razors and soaps
to send to the men at the front. Meanwhile the spirit of teetotalism that had recently
crept in, fell away when the King admitted that he had succumbed to a few drinks
when ill, and after all, 'it was Christmas.' The drinks cabinet and wine cellar at 80
Brook Street remained resolutely open for business.

Emilie still had some outstanding disputes over Yerkes' estate and on 30 January
1916 she left England for New York on SS *Rotterdam*. There was some convoy
protection from British destroyers as the passenger liner left Falmouth but those
aboard were still concerned. Since the outrage over the sinking of the *Lusitania*,
German U-boats had been ordered to refrain from attacking liners but over-
enthusiastic submarine commanders were always a worry.

Emilie stayed in New York and took the opportunity of meeting up with some
old friends in the smart quarters of Manhattan. She flirted with the bohemian, artistic
women in Greenwich Village and although she was no artist and her literary talents
were limited, she shared their hedonistic attitudes. She sympathised with their ideas
of sexual freedom, though the sexual excesses of women such as the wealthy Mabel
Dodge made even Emilie's activities appear restrained. Mabel was very happy to
openly discuss both her heterosexual and lesbian relationships as well as debating
the glories of orgasm. She cut a formidable figure, organising influential salons of
feminists and socialists to which she dragged along her dog called Climax. Belle da
Costa Greene, that great observer of the urban 'new woman', declared these women
to be free of responsibilities, with an independence that only personal wealth could
allow. They did not have to earn a living through marriage and consequently had a
masculine outlook. A typical member of this tribe, 'took her pleasures as a man does,
and wearies of them and casts them aside as a man does.'[294]

Emilie may have tired of this company, or more likely, she was keen to return to
Britain before the German U-boat policy was reversed and six weeks later she was
back on board SS *Rotterdam*, bound for Plymouth. Once she had landed, she returned

to London and found the capital was alive with 'Zeppy' rumours and fears of new attacks. Most people returned home quickly from work – and stayed there. If word of a Zeppelin 'blowin' in' reached the city, lights went out, fire engines were readied and special constables prepared for a busy night. As long as there were no actual attacks, some married women were pleased with this turn of events, as it severely curtailed wandering husbands and visits to their club, or possibly their mistress, were out of the question.[295] The threat of enemy attacks, together with the increasingly long casualty lists, seemed to usher in a new mood. Society women, such as Lady Adèle Essex, were now keen to project self-sacrifice as the norm. The former Adela Grant of New York had married the widower Earl of Essex and successfully blended into the English landscape, acquiring not only a title but also the estate of Cassiobury Park in Hertfordshire. When interviewed by The New York Times at the beginning of 1916, she was keen to play down any mention of excess:

> There are no longer any such things as dinner parties. We've quite put them out of our minds. Eight or ten people meet, perhaps several times a week, and happen to dine together; but there is no thought of dress and little of the dinner – except to keep it simple and sufficient. A dinner used to begin with soup and fish, there was an entrée – but now! Now it is soup or fish, there is a meat course and a pudding; that is all.[296]

Despite Lady Essex's earnest protestations about cutting back, life for the upper classes went on much as before, at least in private. Women were still keen to be seen in the latest fashion, and food, although subject to periodic 'thrift' campaigns, was still in plentiful supply and could be supplemented by provision from a family estate. The supply of meat was erratic but rationing and the attendant queues would not be seen in the capital until the last year of the war. Alcohol was not restricted. Indeed, consumption rose during wartime and sparkling wine, champagne and port were quaffed in ever increasing quantities. If guilt was attached, it could be overcome. 'I was shocked to death,' admitted Lady Scott after a dinner party, 'seeing the extravagance of the women's dresses – and we eat foie gras, I eat it too with a feeling of disgust.' The end of the year would see restaurants restricted to two courses at lunch and three for dinner, though ways could be found to outwit the regulators. In the world of entertainment, theatre performances were encouraged as a means to maintain morale, even if shows might be interrupted by bombing raids.[297]

It is a myth that all the incoming Americans had a loyalty to each other and formed some type of sorority. Those American women who considered themselves 'old money' or who had married into the British aristocracy, such as Adèle Essex, saw themselves as a class apart from the racy Emilie. This was certainly true of the impecunious Jennie, Lady Randolph Churchill. As near neighbours in Brook Street – and fellow Americans – she and Emilie might acknowledge each other if they passed in the street but there was no social interaction. No doubt Jennie took a dim view of

Emilie's social ambitions and sexual adventures, despite some overlapping friendships, such as Charles Repington. She must have known the origins of Emilie's wealth. Yet Jennie's own relationships had hardly been conventional. Following the death of her first husband, Lord Randolph Churchill, there had been a number of affairs, culminating in her marriage at the age of 46 to the 26-year-old George Cornwallis-West, the suave, good-looking son of Patsy. This marriage had fallen apart and the couple divorced in 1914. Since then, Jennie, who had now returned via deed poll to the name of Lady Randolph Churchill, had fallen in love with Montagu Porch, another man nearly half her age and even younger than her son, Winston.[298]

While her love life was a maze, Jennie Churchill was entirely organised when it came to supporting the war effort. She arranged recitals and fundraising events in London, while working tirelessly at the American Women's Hospital. She also supported the American Red Cross and regularly appeared at a war canteen at London Bridge Station. An acquaintance, Lady Hamilton, thought her 'full of doughty deeds and a restless longing to be happy', and such deeds included support for the Society of American Women in London, another organisation that excluded Emilie. The Society had famously helped equip the hospital ship *Maine* during the Boer War. Now in the latest emergency it had enlisted the support of other prominent American women in London, such as Lady Astor, the Duchess of Marlborough, Mrs Selfridge and Mrs Herbert Hoover, in worthy schemes.[299] The organisation asked Emilie's friend, Belle da Costa Greene, to speak at one of their meetings about her work as librarian of the J.P. Morgan Collection. The committee obviously knew nothing of Belle's exotic private life, yet they must have known all about Emilie's antics, for despite her great wealth, she continued to be excluded from the society's events.[300]

Apart from sexual adventures, Emilie's other great passion in life was clothes. She made forays for everyday wear to the established London shops of Debenham & Freebody, Dickens & Jones or Harvey Nichols. Although the dress code had somewhat relaxed during the war, in Mayfair formality was still strictly observed. Every gentleman that passed along Brook Street was clad in a frock-coat and there was no departure from these social rules, as a young barrister, L.E. Jones, observed:

> When not working, a young gentleman was allowed to walk through parts of London in a dark suit and a bowler hat, provided gloves were worn or carried; but never in Pall Mall, St James' Street, Piccadilly, Bond Street or Mayfair. Here full morning-dress was expected, for might you not meet a lady of your acquaintance? As for smoking a pipe, even when bowler-hatted in Holborn or Baker Street, that was not to be thought of.[301]

Although there were tight restrictions on travel in wartime, as the citizen of a neutral country, Emilie could still make visits to Paris. There were passport clearances to be dealt with and she had to call in a few favours to ensure an easy passage through checkpoints. The journey now took at least eighteen hours, travelling via Newhaven and Dieppe, as Folkestone was reserved for military personnel. And she would not be travelling in her customary style. Ostentatious baggage trains were out and the only passenger boats not requisitioned by the Navy were a motley collection of 'wobbly cockleshells'. Still, when she reached Paris, she found enough vestiges of the pre-war city. The fashionable restaurants and cafes, though depleted, were open in the evenings. Art galleries functioned and her apartment was still available. So she set off to her favourite couturiers in search of new 'tea gowns' and evening dresses. Her slim waist, large bust and curved hips were well suited to the fashions of the day, and since smart women had to have a different ball gown for every occasion, regular fittings were required. She called on Maison Worth, then on to Callot Soeurs, the fashion house run by four sisters in the Avenue Matignon. She also patronised another well-known couturier in the wartime city, Jeanne-Marie Lanvin, who operated from a boutique on the Rue du Faubourg Saint-Honoré. She left an account of a typical visit to one of her couturiers:

> Two demure, respectful French girls in black silk gowns came forward. One of them carried a slip of white silk for me to try on. It would be fitted and form the foundation of the gown, which itself would not require fitting. It could not be completed under a month. Monsieur had said. *Ca m'est égal.* It would be sent quite safely and well packed in *une trés grande boite.* All this explanation was given as I removed my dress. The slip was then put on and skilfully fastened. A running fire of low-voiced exclamation in French all the while, 'what superb lines! A torso for a sculptor, *n'est-ce pas?* It was not often one had the joy to work on such a figure. Then the corsage was swiftly cut in a curve around the shoulder line with scissors. I stood before a cheval-glass. As the severed strip of silk rippled down to the carpet, I explained with a frown that Madame had made the neck quite low … I heard her murmur to her assistant in French, rapidly, under her breath, 'with a bust divine, which it were a crime to conceal.'[302]

Emilie sported the new calf-length dresses, a daring height which had never been reached before. It was a fashion, perhaps inspired by a shortage of material, which was eagerly adopted by women war workers who found the new lengths very practical. But the shift was not entirely for sensible reasons. After all, when legs had always been swathed in yards of voluminous material, even the suspicion of an ankle or calf descending from a motor, was enough to set temperatures rising.[303] There was little else to raise the spirits, for Paris was not the bright city that Emilie remembered before the war. It was true that the government had returned to the capital in early 1915 after its temporary withdrawal to Bordeaux and martial law had been rescinded in the spring, so moving around the city was easier. But by the end of the year, nearly half the French coal mines were still under German occupation and domestic fuel was in short supply. Food prices had risen dramatically and the supply of fabrics was restricted. It was not such shortages that persuaded Emilie's friend, the designer Paul Poiret, to close his couture business in Rue du Faubourg Saint-Honoré. He and his cutters had reluctantly joined the 3rd Rouen Corps of the French Army. Poiret certainly lacked martial spirit, but once the Army realised who they had in their ranks, he was moved to the Quartermaster's Department with the task of checking the quality of army uniforms.[304] His was not the only shuttered shop in the city and the streets were subdued – far more than London – with large numbers of women veiled in black from head to foot, mourning the loss of a son or husband. By the end of 1915, the French Army had been terribly mauled, suffering 1.4 million casualties out of 5.5 million mobilised men. And the long, costly years of attrition had barely begun. If Emilie was more or less detached from this suffering, it was because this was still not America's war. At least, not yet.[305]

Emilie left Paris and returned to London, leaving her new dresses to be made and sent on to her several months later. Whether she was entertaining at Brook Street or visiting an exhibition, Emilie was always extremely self-aware, and when she came into a room, she knew that every man would notice her hour-glass figure, while the women would sense a threat. 'Always I was at my best in the evening,' she confessed, 'although my skin was startlingly white, its tints were firm and warm and there was deep color in my lips and luster in my eyes.'[306] She was always ready for an assignation and it wasn't long before she contacted Charles Repington, who needed little persuasion to join her for lunch at a restaurant, followed by the promise of 'afternoon delights' at 80 Brook Street. They enjoyed a light lunch, catching up on all the gossip while Emilie had been away. Then, as it was raining, they hailed a taxi and were soon delivered to her house. Entering the hall, they swiftly handed their coats to a maid and Repington followed Emilie as she slowly climbed the stone stairs to her bedroom. Repington was a connoisseur of the female form and knew exactly how to please a woman, but he was never too impatient. He would have found her voluptuous curves no longer restrained by the corsets that had given her such a tiny waist in pre-war days. A local surgeon had told her that banishing the corset was a marvellous achievement, since the device was not only bad for circulation but its compression generated 'fervent spasms, inducing female sexual desire'. She felt the reverse was true and she was liberated by her new soft silk Parisian lingerie that was embroidered with her name. Her modern 'brassiere' was to be unhooked to reveal her hourglass figure.[307]

There were many such afternoon delights for the couple, for Repington rarely stayed the night at Brook Street, unless he went through the ritual with Molly that he was staying in town for a dinner at his club. Emilie's servants, of course, saw it all, and kept their silence. They had remained in her service for years and since they were American nationals, they would not be required for military service until their country entered the war. Other households with local staff had lost their domestic servants in large numbers, with many joining the services as well as the better paid munitions industry. Valets, and coachmen had already decided to do their patriotic duty by enlisting and in January 1916 conscription scooped up all remaining single males and widowers without children under the age of 41.[308] In large London houses, masters and mistresses now had to carry out their own household chores. No longer would the young ladies of the house lie in bed until 10.00am, dally over breakfast, rest between telephone calls and then be dressed for lunch. Lack of manpower forced this change, yet there was also growing peer pressure amongst well-to-do young women that they should do something – or be seen to do something – for the war effort.

Hard physical work or committees were not Emilie's style. She saw herself as a political hostess and in particular as a supporter of her lover's intrigues. She mirrored Repington's attitudes, supported his friends and criticised his enemies, though she was never very thorough with her research, as Jean Hamilton noted in her diary:

> She, Miss Grigsby, met Lady Haig somewhere the other day, and not knowing who she was, began abusing Sir Douglas Haig, quoting Col. Repington's opinions about him to his wife! Col. R. is a great enemy of Sir Douglas Haig's, because after the article he wrote in 'The Times' last year about the good German position, our lines were shelled, and Douglas Haig said it was R's fault, and abused him for it.[309]

Molly Repington knew that 'Charley' was always 'wandering' but because she adored him, she refused to confront him, especially over his relationship with Emilie. Molly and Repington barely went out together and she spent many evenings alone in Hampstead, while Repington pursued his intrigues, with Emilie in support. The Southern Belle was everything that Molly was not – socially engaging, beautiful and, most of all, a splendid hostess. She could charm and flatter those at The Times or the War Office, those whom Repington sought to influence. However, there were women, such as Maud Cunard, who could not tolerate Repington's treatment of his common-law wife, demanding 'This must be put right.'[310]

Molly in fact knew more than Maud about how mistresses operated. After all, she had been one herself during Repington's first marriage, before graduating to the more permanent role of common-law wife. She may have felt that if she confronted Repington with an ultimatum, he might leave her. In her memoirs, she conceded that in Repington's life 'from time to time some beautiful lady's star would be in the ascendant, but never for very long.'[311] She knew that 'the old badger' had a limited attention span and that before long, he would be moving on from Emilie. Molly's friend, Jean Hamilton, knew that he was already casting around. 'R. [Repington] is a great supporter of Sir John French,' she wrote, 'Molly tells me they are boon companions, and share each other's orgies.[312]

Although Emilie's earlier affair with Sir John Cowans had now been supplanted by the Repington liaison, she retained an extraordinary hold on him – as she had always done with ex-lovers – even to the extent of occasional sex. She saw Cowans from time to time and realised that he had moved on, but was still surprised to learn of the depth of his sexual deceit. It transpired that as early as 1913 Cowans had become the lover of Dorothy Dennistoun, wife of another officer. Even in the gossip hothouse of London society, he had managed to keep this affair secret, despite regular trips from his house in Curzon Street to Dorothy's nearby apartment. But this was no ordinary affair. Since his wife's relationship with the Quartermaster-General, Lieutenant-Colonel Ian Dennistoun had swiftly risen from the rank of Captain and had started to secure some interesting staff jobs, beyond his modest abilities. In 1915, Dennistoun received a choice appointment in Gibraltar, followed by the post of Secretary to the Governor of Jamaica.

The Quartermaster-General appeared to be offering the weak-willed Dennistoun some good career prospects in return for his ignoring the affair. Furthermore, Dennistoun was entering into the arrangement with some enthusiasm. In the spring of 1916, he arrived at the Ritz Hotel in Paris ahead of Dorothy and Cowans to make sure the bedroom he had booked for them was sufficiently grand. Dennistoun, who was once known as 'Tiger' for his sexual prowess, had apparently evolved into a pussycat – a pimp, trading his wife for his own advancement.[313] Although Cowans had always proved to be such a brilliant administrator in his military career, he was certainly lowering the bar in his private life. Emilie wondered how long his two worlds could co-exist.

Salons and Cabals

On 23 May 1916, Emilie took Charles Repington to the Royal Horticultural Society Great Spring Show, held in the gardens of the Royal Hospital in Chelsea. They lunched there with a Naval contact of Repington's, who supplied the journalist with aeroplane statistics for one of his military articles in *The Times*. The show had survived the war cutbacks, but it was becoming increasingly difficult to staff properly and many of the sites had been turned over to vegetables. Nonetheless, the 1916 display was a blaze of colour and Emilie took particular delight in the rose exhibits – she was becoming something of an expert in their cultivation, and her rose garden at Old Meadows was a glorious sight.[314] In fact, it was her roses that enticed the recently ennobled Lord French to visit the cottage shortly afterwards. However, his old friend Repington happened to be in residence at the time and, fearing some competition for Emilie's attentions, took exception to the Field Marshal's appearance. According to a friend of Emilie's, there was an argument between the two on the terrace outside and Emilie tried to separate the warring factions. As she did so, her pearl necklace was broken in the scuffle and all the pearls scattered across the paving. A truce was then declared and French and Repington were both to be seen scrambling around the terrace on all fours, picking the pearls out of the crevices.[315]

Barely two weeks later, the country was shocked by the death of the legendary Lord Kitchener, who was drowned when HMS *Hampshire*, which was carrying him to Russia, struck a mine and sunk off the Orkney Islands. While Repington was moved to describe him as 'a firm rock which stood out amidst the raging tempest', the shock of his death did not last very long amongst society. Several days later, large numbers of people, including Emilie, flocked to the wartime Epsom Derby race. Three years earlier the Derby had been the scene of high drama when the suffragette Emily Davison was killed under the King's horse. Even now, in 1916, there was some debate about whether horse racing should take place at all at a time of national emergency and just after the death of a national hero. It was agreed to move the famous race to the Suffolk course of Newmarket and rename it the 'New Derby Stakes'. In the event, it was a great success and an enthusiastic throng cheered on the popular winner, the filly Fifinella owned by Sir Edward Hulton, the north-country newspaper owner and publisher of the popular picture papers.[316] The consciences of those attending were certainly eased by the appearance of a large crowd of wounded soldiers, brought in from nearby hospitals, who mingled with other spectators. It was in such circumstances that civilians could hear first-hand about conditions on the Western Front from men who had been in the thick of the fight. Few of the wounded would actually talk of their personal terrors however and made light of the deprivations of trench life. They would mention the continuous, infernal noise of war, calling it 'a bit of a racket', for all other senses were secondary. Pain, danger, fatigue and cold came a long way behind the shattering roar at the front that made men continually shout at each other to be heard. Often, because of their deafness, those in the front trenches could only tell when the guns had stopped by the lack of concussion, rather than the reduction in noise. For such men, the roar that greeted the Derby winner seemed a mere whisper.

Although Emilie's Elizabethan cottage at West Drayton fulfilled a role as a country retreat, with its intimate beamed and panelled rooms, it was not the best location for a 'salon'. Such a meeting place for artists and writers, or indeed soldiers and politicians, needed to be in the heart of London, near Parliament, the War Office, or the smart galleries and clubs. 80 Brook Street fitted the bill admirably. The street was named after the Tyburn Brook that used to run under the thoroughfare. Grosvenor Square lay barely 100 yards to the east, while a minute's stroll to the west took you into New Bond Street and Hanover Square beyond. Claridge's, was just across the street, which boasted the latest in interior design and fine dining. The old hotel had been demolished after Mr Claridge died in 1895, and a new one was erected at the turn of the century. Since the war began, it had become a regular haunt for senior military figures, including Marshal Foch, who was a familiar face in Brook Street during his visits to London. However, while Brook Street was extremely fashionable, Emilie had an uphill struggle competing with other, more well-established salons in London. Sonia Keppel recalled the reputable gatherings run by her mother, Alice:

> Mamma opened her house at luncheon time, once or twice a week to a miscellaneous collection of politicians, service-chiefs, diplomats, soldiers home on leave, war correspondents and such of her women friends and Violet's girlfriends as were available to amuse them ... Mamma dominated the big table, where usually it was tacitly understood that the conversation should remain on a light level with the darker shades of war excluded from it.[317]

Alice Keppel still had currency from her love affair with 'Kingy', as her children knew the late monarch. And the 47-year-old paramour still maintained the glorious husky voice, the lustrous hair and the wicked sense of humour that had so captivated the King. She was equally at home discussing the splits within her beloved Liberal Party, or the problems in Romania, though most men were mesmerised more by her still proud *embonpoint* and their thoughts of her past experiences and the secrets she held. Privately she fretted over the future of her other daughter, Violet, who, between bouts of crushes on other girls, was fired from working at the Grosvenor Gardens canteen for 'confusing cleaning powder and cocoa'.[318]

Even if Emilie's salon could not quite attract the grandees who frequented Alice Keppel's drawing-room, her house could certainly equal any other in Mayfair. 80 Brook Street was a fine example of late Edwardian architecture and stood on the corner of Brook Street and Gilbert Street. Emilie was able to entertain in rooms that were light, airy and bright – so different from the sombre atmosphere in her previous Victorian homes.[319] Much of this light could be attributed to the new domestic electricity, which was gradually taking over from gas. Gas had been ten times lighter than candlelight but it was dirty and its fumes could ruin books and paintings. It also killed most house plants with the exception of the aspidistra, which accounts for the plant's widespread appearance in many Victorian houses (and music hall songs). Electricity was cleaner, more efficient and could be switched on and off easily. Interestingly, the advent of electric light changed room colours, so that Victorian deep blues and greens, which had looked muted under yellow gaslight, appeared lurid under electric light. Consequently, room colours changed to lighter and more neutral shades. But electricity was more expensive than gas and although Emilie could easily afford its running costs, many households could not, and its installation became something of a class demarcation.[320]

When visitors entered 80 Brooke Street they would be shown into the morning room by a maid and would then be greeted by the hostess in the drawing room, overlooking the adjacent Gilbert Street. The rooms were beautifully proportioned and Emilie had incorporated a number of architectural antiques, including some splendid chimney pieces, into her new post-Edwardian home, making it appear older and grander than its provenance. The only concession to wartime regulations was the placing of the mandatory buckets of sand and sinister-looking respirators within easy reach, in the event of enemy bombing.[321] The basement below housed a warren of rooms such as pantries, washrooms, the kitchen and stores, incorporating all sorts of new domestic appliances. There were electric kettles, irons, and vacuum cleaners that no longer had to be dragged by horses to the house and operated through a window. Steam-driven washing machines had appeared, though refrigerators would not be commercially available until the 1920s, so the 'ice man' still called each day to deliver a top-up for the ice-box.[322]

Returning to the hall, guests would climb the stone staircase to the first floor where they would be entertained in the dining room or several other reception rooms. The second and third floors contained eight bedrooms, including Emilie's suite and her dressing-room and had the luxury of several well appointed bathrooms and separate lavatories (always housed apart in Edwardian houses). Since the advent of running water in the 1870s, bathrooms had evolved. Washbasins, hip-baths and showers were large and resembled laboratory equipment. However, the bath itself had just experienced a revolution in design, and Emilie could now slip into a porcelain enamel creation and soak in a tub that retained its brilliant white lustre.[323] Ascending to the top of the house, the fourth floor contained the servants' quarters, rather dimly lit and only brightened by the central skylight. Still, it provided accommodation for her reduced American staff – now comprising a housekeeper, ladies maid, scullery maid, cook and chauffeur – the envy of her British neighbours, who, as mentioned, all suffered a shortage of servants.[324]

The house was full of antiques and increasingly, English pieces. The straitened times had squeezed the fortunes of many of the great houses and furniture had flooded into the market. Rather than depressing prices, the abundance of good quality pieces merely fuelled the excitement of buyers and none more so than American collectors. Emilie personally attended most of the Christie's sales and found herself bidding mainly against agents of American collectors or the smaller band of English munitions millionaires – the only ones who could afford the rocketing prices.

Guests at Brook Street were often treated to a roll-call of Emilie's political connections, and she loved to drop the names of artists with whom she had become acquainted. She later told Shane Leslie, a self-confessed admirer, that she had many connections with the art and literary world and that she was the inspiration for several remarkable sculptures. She believed she was the likeness behind Paul Bartlett's statue representing 'Religion', one of six huge Georgian marble figures that he installed in the attic portico above the entrance to New York City Public Library. Bartlett completed these figures in 1916 and there may well have been a connection with Emilie. The bond with religion fitted well with her projected image of piety and religious observance. Bartlett had studied sculpture in Paris and had worked with Rodin, whom Emilie also claimed to have known. In fact she contended that she was the inspiration behind Rodin's sculpture *Le Baiser* (The Kiss), a work that has since been widely replicated. This was a claim too far, since the beautiful piece was originally commissioned in 1887 when Emilie was not even into her teens.[325]

Although Emilie looked upon herself as a 'mascot of the High Command', she was also drawn to soldier adventurers, regardless of rank – and if they were 'outsiders', such as the Canadian Joseph Boyle, so much the better. Repington was good sex, with a great address book, but he was no swashbuckling adventurer. Boyle, by comparison, was an 'exaggeration of a man', and had a massive physical presence, having been a prize-fighter and gold prospector in the Klondike Gold Rush of the 1890s. As a result, he became hugely wealthy and during the First World War he was determined to assist the Allies, crossing to England in the summer of 1916 to offer his services. Arriving in London, he immediately approached the Canadian Army headquarters and British War Office, but they failed to appreciate his organising abilities. He booked into the Savoy Hotel, where he would remain for the nine months of his stay in England. Despite this prestigious address and his influential contacts, he failed to be adopted by the Canadian Expeditionary Force. He pursued all other avenues, including a chance meeting with Emilie, who rushed to provide him with more contacts. For the moment he remained her friend rather than her lover, but Boyle was a driven man, whose horizons were always changing.

While Emilie garnered support for the Canadian, she continued to offer Repington encouragement in his campaigns, including his zealous mission to advertise the

Army's manpower shortage. There was always some meeting being held in London's club land to debate the course of the war or argue over current controversies and Repington was determined to attend, or speak at, as many of these meetings as possible. Emilie often accompanied him. On 19 October 1916 they both went to the Bull Dog Club, a debating and patriotic institution in Edgware Road, where Repington appeared on the stage to rouse an excited crowd that included raucous Australian and Canadian troops.

As a single, independent woman, Emilie was always seen as a threat by other married women. She was in her thirties, and to be attractive and unmarried in a society that expected women to be married by their early twenties was a constant source of intrigue to most men. But there were other like-minded spirits, and in London at the time, there were a number of single American-born women. Emilie chose as her close friends Doris Keane and Gladys Unger, two Americans who had also been mistresses of her former lover, Charles Yerkes. All three women had first met in Paris before the war, where Emilie maintained an apartment and held a regular salon for artists and their admirers. The 'three bucaneers' then gravitated to London, but it was Emilie who had really gained financially from the association with Yerkes. The actress Doris Keane had arrived in London in the autumn of 1915 to take the romantic lead in a new theatre production of *Romance*. In her early years in Illinois, it was reported that Yerkes had funded her acting ambitions by putting her through drama school in New York and then Paris. While she was a favourite of the 'Traction King' for a period, he failed to make provision for her in his will, but she had since made a creditable living from appearances at the Garrick Theatre in New York, as well as the Lyric in London. Now, the 34-year-old dark-eyed beauty was enjoying huge popularity playing to packed houses at the Duke of York's Theatre.[326]

The other member of the inseparable trio of ex-mistresses was the writer and artist, Gladys Unger. Born in California in 1884, she moved to England when she was three and was later educated at South Hampstead School. Following the example of her father, she showed early promise as an artist and spent some time in Paris studying techniques at the Académie Julien and it was during her stay in the French capital that she encountered Charles Yerkes. Before his death in 1905, Yerkes appears to have funded the promising young artist but when she returned to England, her career took off in another direction. Realising a long-held ambition to become a writer, she made constant trips to the British Museum Reading Room, and armed with bundles of research material, she started to produce large numbers of historical romances. Her first play, *Edmund Kean* was penned in 1903, to critical acclaim, but it was her increasing social prominence and display of wealth that was attracting attention. She lived for a time in an exquisite house in Charles Street, Mayfair, crammed full of valuable paintings and works of art – almost a repository for Yerkes' London collection. But this did not check her desire to succeed in the world of theatre and by the time of the outbreak of war, she had written eight more plays, comedies and musicals.[327]

The three friends would meet at either Emilie's house in Brook Street, or Gladys's house at 18 Park Village West, in Regent's Park, which had become the rendezvous for a bohemian set. The American girls all had motor 'broughams' and would be seen scooting around Mayfair and the West End – Gladys in her Vauxhall and Doris in her Napier. Gladys might take the posse to see behind the scenes of the musical *Betty*, which was recently adapted from her book, or they might crowd into a box to watch the play *The 13th Chair*, starring Mrs Patrick Campbell. If Emilie wanted a more lively and undemanding evening, she would contact her lover Repington and the pair would visit a music hall. These halls were noisy, colourful and often filled with soldiers on leave, looking for a good night out. Perhaps predictably, the halls attracted the condemnation of some high-profile figures, such as General Smith-Dorrien, who was an able commander but one who had plenty of time on his hands following his dismissal from the Western Front. He campaigned against the sexual innuendo of some of the performances and how the evening was spoiled by 'a lot of wriggling girls with extremely few clothes on'. He refused to believe that the troops were being entertained by these shows, claiming that in their hearts they would prefer acts that 'appealed to the best side of their patriotic natures.'[328] Part of the problem with the music hall was its reputation for prostitutes. Certain theatres such as The Empire came under attack for allowing these 'trollops' to loiter in the promenade areas of the theatre. Business was obviously brisk, for the music-halls were alleged to have earned large sums from 'commission'.[329] Even without the distraction of these women, wartime shows could be difficult for the performers. London audiences were so sensitive to the threat of enemy airship raids that any exterior noise would cause some excitable theatregoer to jump up and shout 'Zeppelins. Quick, get down.' The dramatic moment on stage was lost, as everyone in the audience either tried to scuttle under their seats, or stampede towards the exits. Inevitably, false alarms in theatre land were soon replaced by the real thing.

At the end of the summer, German High Command decided to launch their largest and most daring assault yet on London. In the late afternoon of 2 September, sixteen airships slipped their moorings at their base in Germany, crossed the Belgian coast and approached the south-east of England. The Admiralty picked up their approach and duly warned Naval vessels in the Channel and North Sea, while aircraft from No. 39 Home Defence took off to engage the enemy. Twenty-one-year-old Lieutenant William Leefe Robinson lifted off in his converted BE2c fighter from Suttons Farm airfield, near Hornchurch, at 2300 hours and, after several abortive searches, finally spotted one of the airships. As the *Shütte-Lanz*, *SL.13* Zeppelin, a veteran of earlier missions, headed towards the city, Robinson dived from 12,900 feet towards the monster:

> I saw shells bursting and night tracer flying around it. When I drew closer I noticed that the anti-aircraft aim was too high or too low; also some 800 ft behind. I could hear the bursts when I was about 3000 ft from the Zeppelin. I flew about 800 ft below it and from bow to stern distributed one drum [of ammunition] along it. It seemed to have no effect; I therefore moved to one side and gave it another drum

– without apparent effect. I then got behind it. By this time I was very close – 500 ft or less and concentrated one drum on the underneath rear. I hardly finished the drum before I saw the part I fired at, glow. In a few seconds the whole rear part was blazing. I quickly got out of the way of the falling, blazing Zeppelin and being very excited, fired off a few red Very lights.[330]

For the airship commander, Hauptmann Wilhelm Schramm and his fifteen-man crew, there was no escape, as the wood-framed airship fell in flames. Londoners cheered as *SL.13* crashed in a fireball behind The Plough Inn at Cuffley, and then burned for several hours. She was the first airship shot down on British soil and Lieutenant Robinson was awarded the Victoria Cross for his outstanding bravery.[331]

Such tales of heroism were not the sort of copy that Repington supplied. He was a journalist who prided himself on his opinion columns and articles on the prosecution of the war. And his reputation as the most well informed military correspondent in London had to be constantly nurtured by good quality intelligence and importantly, gossip. Consequently, he regularly dined with senior officers at the Carlton, and often brightened the occasion by introducing pretty young women to the table. As the champagne flowed and good food was in abundance, Repington might receive a torrent of news from his unguarded guests. Alternatively, Repington and Emilie hosted dinners at Brook Street, when Emilie could display her cooking skills. Although she employed a good cook, she loved to indulge her love of food and often prepared soups or exotic seafood herself. For although the war had restricted commercial fishing around the coast of Britain, inshore fishing still hauled in large quantities of lobster and shellfish. Emilie could wheel in her contacts, such as Sir Lawrence and Lady Jenkins and Major-General Aylmer Haldane, who not only enjoyed her splendid dinners but provided inches of column fodder for Repington's pen. All the while, it seemed that the libidinous journalist had an open-ended pass from Molly for his evening activities. She continued to excuse Repington's behaviour, or at least found a way to rationalise it:

> Even in wartime, however, people must lunch and dine somewhere, and as time went on it was inevitable that Charley should go about a good deal without me. His work and his travels brought him into contact with everyone of note in an ever-widening circle, and it would have been quite impossible for me to keep up with it.[332]

Molly was well aware that to mix regularly and entertain in the lavish scale that Emilie could handle would require a very expensive and ever-changing wardrobe. Molly admitted she was happy in a narrow social circle that included the Hamiltons, Protheros and Haldanes; but her knowledge of Repington's other mistresses, especially Emilie, must have been wounding:

> I was content that he should recreate himself in this way as an offset to the strenuous and exhausting brain-work which was his real life. I dealt with all his correspondence,

so that it was impossible for me not to be aware of the way in which he was run after, and of the persistence with which the modern society woman pursues the man who has captured her momentary interest. He would have been more than human – or perhaps less than human – if he had not enjoyed it and occasionally caught fire himself.[333]

Molly found increasing comfort in her Catholic religion, a faith she shared with Emilie. Although Repington was an agnostic, he never attempted to derail her devotion and was happy for their only daughter, Laetitia, to be baptised into the Catholic Church. Cynics might argue that he could do little else, since Laetitia was, most probably, the product of one of Repington's pre-war affairs. Nonetheless, Molly gamely consented to help bring up the child, who gave her much pleasure and companionship.[334]

Emilie remained on good terms with her former lover Sir John Cowans and kept up with news of his social activities, for he was still much in demand at house parties. However, even he could not lift the spirits at one particular gathering on 17 September 1916. It was the occasion of a party given by Margot Asquith and her husband, and Cowans was brought in as a reliably lively guest. The Prime Minister was in a relaxed mood since he had just returned from a visit to France, where military operations seemed to be progressing well; and on the political front, he was pleased that for once, his Cabinet seemed fairly united. On the Sunday, Cowans took on the other house guests at tennis, while Margot organised other games in the house. The harmony was suddenly shattered that evening after dinner, when Margot took a telephone call from 10 Downing Street. A secretary announced to Margot that her stepson Raymond had been shot dead on the Somme as he rose out of the trenches to lead an attack. The ghastly news enveloped everyone, including Cowans, who promised his sobbing Premier that he would do all he could to find out the circumstances of Raymond's death.[335]

By Sept 1916, Emilie's torrid affair with Charles Repington seemed to be over, but the two remained on good terms, drifting into a platonic friendship. Emilie was careful not to lose such a valuable connection to the Northcliffe camp. In fact, 80 Brook Street again became a useful stop off point for further political intrigue – but this time, Asquith's enemies swore to finish off his political career. Since the beginning of the year, Northcliffe had campaigned for the extension of conscription to married men and following several visits to GHQ in France, he began actively supporting the 'brass hats' against the 'frock coats'. He persisted in lobbying for the removal of Asquith, whom he saw as a master of indecision. Writing a memo to his editor at *The Daily Mail*, Northcliffe demanded a leader containing a smiling picture of Lloyd George, with the caption underneath, 'Do it now.' The worst photograph of Asquith was also to be included with the caption 'Wait and see.'[336]

Emilie made herself useful by providing her Mayfair property as a 'safe house' or meeting place for Northcliffe and his associates. While 80 Brook Street was the scene of plotting to remove Asquith, it had also become a base for those working to remove the Commander-in-Chief, Sir Douglas Haig, who had only been in his post for nine months. Jean Hamilton noted in her diary:

> Everyone is talking of the Cabal against Haig, by French, Winston, Carson & Co. I don't know who they all are, but I believe Miss Grigsby, Colonel Repington's cast-off mistress, holds a sort of Salon for them.[337]

It might seem that Sir Edward Carson, Attorney-General and leader of Ulster Unionism, had more than enough to occupy himself working to undermine Asquith, without attacking Haig. Emilie would not have found Carson physically attractive. 'His chin was too long,' a colleague remembered, 'the bones of his strong jaw too palpable beneath the skin, but there was grandeur in his forceful masculine looks.' Indeed, it was his aura of power and his ability to broker political deals that enamoured the 'Kentucky Belle' – she loved a 'fixer' better than anyone. In a bid to further weaken Asquith's position, Carson resigned from the government in October, which put him temporarily outside the centre of power, together with Winston Churchill. This was an ideal perch from where the Ulsterman could snipe at other enemies, such as Haig, and Lloyd George would later concede that it was much better to have Carson 'inside the tent pissing out than outside the tent pissing in'.[338] However, by the autumn of 1916, there were a host of other aggrieved politicians and redundant generals – all queuing up to make trouble for Haig. French was still smouldering about his successor as Commander-in-Chief, and his office in Horse Guards was a clearing-house for gossip from generals whom Haig had removed. The King had warned Haig about the 'cabal' and General Robertson felt compelled to warn his chief that 'Winston, French and various degommed people are trying to make mischief.' It was certainly wanton troublemaking and Emilie relished every minute of it.[339]

The 'cabal' did not have long to wait before they claimed a scalp – a big one. At the beginning of December, Asquith was forced to resign as Prime Minister. On 9 December 1916 a new coalition Cabinet was formed with Lloyd George as Prime Minister, but the existing Cabinet members made it a condition that they would only continue to serve if Winston Churchill was excluded. While Lloyd George was prepared to sacrifice Churchill, he was determined to bring on board the other maverick, Northcliffe, so he could keep an eye on him. The wily newsman declined the offer, preferring to keep his independent voice. There was also another, less publicised casualty of Asquith's fall and ironically, he lived just across the road from Emilie. Lewis Harcourt, or 'Loulou' as he was known to his friends, lived at no. 69 Brook Street. He had married the fabulously wealthy American, Mary Burns, a niece of the banker Pierpoint Morgan. She had brought to the marriage the superb house in Brook Street, which she had decorated in the French Empire style, so popular in her native New York. But it was not to bring her happiness. Harcourt was Secretary of

State for the Colonies and was therefore a senior member of the Asquith government – he regularly sat next to Asquith at Cabinet meetings, muttering comments to his leader, rather than addressing the gathering. Most cabinet colleagues were less than impressed. Charles Hobhouse thought Loulou was 'subtle, secretive, adroit and not very reliable'.[340] But he proved loyal to Asquith and resigned at the same time, much to the relief of those who knew about his private life. For he was also a paedophile, whose rampant activities knew no bounds. Yet, astonishingly, he had retained an influential office of state and a conspiracy of silence surrounded his private life. For some of his friends who covered for him, such as Lord Esher, the conspiracy would rebound – the unchecked Harcourt even attempted to rape Esher's young daughter.[341]

Emilie had become friendly with another American exile, who had also been driven out of New York by scandal. Jean Brandt was, like Emilie, a beautiful redhead, and a wealthy Southerner from Georgia who had fled New York in 1897 after it was found out that she had been secretly married for five years to a New York socialite. She secured a divorce and fled to London to escape the ensuing press interest. She subsequently married Augustus Brandt, the wealthy chairman of a London merchant bank, and re-established herself as a wife and chatelaine of the Castle Hill estate at Bletchingly, Surrey. With a new life in England, she hardly looked back to the New York days except, like Emilie, she had a burning desire to show those she left behind, that she could be accepted by London society, the one society that really mattered.[342]

The American refugees were not the only ones trying to escape scandal. During late 1916, General Sir John Cowans, who as Quartermaster-General was battling heroically to feed and clothe the British Army, was also in danger of being dragged down by a tawdry drama. Emilie's ex-lover had made the mistake of 'knowing' Mrs William Cornwallis-West, or 'Patsy' as she was known. Patsy was extremely well connected, having once been a member of King Edward VII's 'loose box', along with Lady Randolph Churchill, and was now more well known as the mother of George (second husband of Lady Randolph Churchill) and mother of Mary, Princess of Pless.

Although she was the wife of Colonel William Cornwallis-West, Honorary Colonel of 4th Battalion, Royal Welsh Fusiliers (RWF), she set her cap at one of the young battalion officers, Lieutenant Patrick Barrett. He resisted her questionable charms but she persisted, became distraught and persuaded her husband to have Barrett transferred to another battalion. All might have remained quiet, except that the local land agent's wife appeared to have a few scores to settle with Patsy and complained to the authorities about her conduct. The scandal erupted. Patsy had boasted of the power she wielded at the War Office, which was shown not to be an exaggeration when it was discovered that Barrett's transfer was, at the very least, facilitated by General Cowans. It was also alleged that he blocked an inquiry into the events. During the hearing, it became apparent that Patsy was in the habit of calling in other favours from officials at the War Office, and Field-Marshal Lord French was also criticised for condoning the removal of one Brigadier-General who had fallen foul of Patsy.[343] Cowans was summoned to an Army Court of Enquiry, and pending the outcome, he was suspended from the Army Council. On 3 January 1917, a Court of Inquiry severely censured both Patsy and Cowans.

Newspaper editors loved the story, building speculation and feverishly reporting the details of Patsy's intriguing. The fact that she was confirmed as a former lover of the late King added spice to the story and at the same time ensured she would receive no help from influential circles. 'The Wicked Woman of Wales' was roundly condemned. Although Cowans denied in court that he had ever had sex with Patsy, his obligations to her seemed all-consuming and he was censured for his part in the scandal. The War Office sought to mitigate his role by feeding the press with a number of pro-Cowans appreciations and he was able to continue his vital work. But the effect on the Cornwallis-West family was disastrous. Colonel Cornwallis-West, who stood by his wife throughout, died shortly after the case was heard and the Denbigh estate passed to their son George. Clueless with money, George had massive debts and as soon as he inherited everything the bailiffs took it all. Patsy was evicted and went to live with her sister at 'Clouds' in Wiltshire.

Fortunately for Cowans, he was thrown a lifeline when Charles Repington, his old comrade from the Rifle Brigade and brother-in-Emilie's-arms, rushed to his aid. He wrote an article in *The Times* proclaiming the valuable work of the Quartermaster-General's Department and the personal qualities of its chief. Most newspapers loved the scandal but London society definitely did not, especially those who knew Sir John Cowans. Jean Hamilton was horrified and contemptuous:

> Scurrilous rags of newspapers everywhere spreading slander and lies – at present they blow the big bassoon over the courageous and chivalrous conduct of the Prime Minister over this Jack Cowans and Mrs Cornwallis West affair, shrieking on the King to remove Sir John Cowans, and painting the wicked woman of Wales in the blackest colours. I suppose it is a political move – Mrs Beach, the Agent's wife whom Mrs West did not invite to her parties, in her desire for revenge only setting a match to the trail, but the howling down of the upper class may go too far even for Mr Lloyd George's benefit.[344]

Lloyd George, despite endless affairs with secretaries, Liberal Party apparatchiks and a regular mistress in the shape of Frances Stevenson, sensed a political opportunity in this sexual scandal. For one thing, siding with the Welsh people of Denbighshire who were supporting the young officer, Barrett, would stress his Welsh sympathies. He could also make political capital out of Prime Minister Asquith's discomfort over the case, especially if it meant the removal of Cowans, one of the most prominent generals in the British Army. To remove the Quartermaster-General at such a critical stage in the war however, when the US was finally tipping in favour of entry, would be political suicide; especially since Cowans was also involved in delicate negotiations with the Americans for them to loan materials and vehicles to Britain.[345] Expediency won the day and Cowans survived.

Even by the spring of 1917, it was by no means inevitable that America would come into the War. There were still plenty of Emilie's countrymen who felt that America should stay out of what they considered 'a European affair'. Such isolationism was further boosted by radicals and socialists who claimed that banks and big businesses would profit from the war, while it would be the poor that sacrificed their sons. The executions after the Irish Easter Rising hardly helped the Allied cause in America. Nonetheless, there were also powerful arguments for ditching America's neutral stance. Mindful of the sinking of the *Lusitania* in 1915, there was alarm in January 1917 over the German declaration of unrestricted submarine warfare, which would jeopardise US passenger and merchant ships. There were also events closer to America's backyard. American-Mexican relations had plummeted to an all-time low and there were fears of German assistance to Mexico.[346]

In April, President Woodrow Wilson finally made the decision and brought America into the War, as an 'Associated Power' on the side of the Allies. It took this event to bring Emilie's friend, 'Klondike Joe' Boyle, actively into the war. Using his membership of the American Committee of Engineers, he was now able to assemble a mission to travel to Russia to improve their grossly inefficient railway system, which regularly trapped large quantities of supplies and troops in sidings and railheads. With a fond farewell from Emilie, 'Klondike Joe' set off for Russia in June 1917 and embarked on an extraordinary adventure that would see him caught up in the Russian Revolution. Ultimately, his activities would take him across the border into Romania, where a lasting relationship with Queen Marie would seal his place in history.[347] While Colonel Joe Boyle was in Russia, Emilie kept in contact with his operations via his secretary, John Kennalley. When Kennalley was staying at the Savoy in September 1917, Emilie arranged a dinner there and called Repington over to join them so he could be apprised first hand of the deteriorating events on the Eastern Front. It transpired that Boyle had just been moved to the Romanian front to try and sort out the transportation mess in Moldavia, the last part of the country still in Allied hands. Repington thoroughly enjoyed himself, garnering this credible intelligence and he was surprised to hear that in Romania 'Kennalley does not find that bribing is needed.'[348]

While Emilie had managed to tilt her relationship with Repington towards pure friendship, she had not given up on sex with other men. During 1917, she resurrected a relationship with 47-year-old Lieutenant-Colonel Mackay from Edinburgh.[349] Mackay Mackay (sic) had originally met Emilie when he visited New York in 1912. The friendship was rekindled when he bumped into her in 1915 in London, but at the time Emilie was cultivating more influential officers and Mackay had to wait his turn. However, by early 1917, he was Assistant Provost Marshal of Western Command and called to see her in Brook Street. Their relationship soon deepened and before long, he was accepting invitations to her cottage in West Drayton. During one such weekend, he met Emilie's elderly gardener who admitted that looking after the rose garden as well as the vegetable garden and lawns was too much for him.

Labour during the war was scarce but Mackay said he could help. Within weeks, a Private Barton, serving in Chester with the Military Foot Police, appeared at Old Meadows with instructions to help Emilie with gardening on a permanent basis. She was delighted, but Mackay had a further surprise in store. The following week, a Lance-Corporal Fraser arrived at the cottage, ready and able to dig in the garden. With two servicemen at her disposal, Emilie's only remaining qualms concerned her chickens, which were feeling rather unhappy. No sooner had she told Mackay about her fowls, than a Private Leach appeared, hotfoot from Chester, who was something of a 'chicken fancier', and proceeded to remedy the problem.

Mackay had impressed Emilie so much that she told her American friend Jean Brandt about the seemingly endless supply of labour. This was indeed fortunate, for Brandt happened to be in need of a chauffeur, as well as a cleaner. As soon as news of this vacancy was conveyed to Mackay, Mrs Brandt was miraculously offered the services of Lance-Corporal Harry Edwards as a cleaner, and Private Tomlin as a chauffeur. Like the other men, Tomlin was still a serving soldier but it was not long before he was in a chauffeur's uniform, installed in an apartment above Brandt's garage and driving her around London. Tomlin was also on hand to drive up to Chester to collect Mackay and bring him down to London to see Emilie. Mackay could be seen in the back of the motor car with Emilie and Jean beside him, being driven on jaunts around the capital, or for days out to the cottage at West Drayton. With nearly half a million cars on the roads, such trips were never quite the idyllic outings of popular imagination, but were still more than agreeable. Despite his duties in Chester, Mackay found himself in London every other weekend, staying with Emilie at either West Drayton or Brook Street. Eyebrows were raised at the frequency that papers requiring Mackay's attention, had to be brought to London by dispatch rider, questions were increasingly asked in Western Command about the disappearance of servicemen to London. But for the moment, Mackay managed to cover up his schemes and Emilie's beloved garden never looked better.[350]

It may have been a tranquil summer in West Drayton, but the centre of London was about to experience a dramatic onslaught. 7 July was a beautiful, warm day. Families were out in the parks enjoying the fine weather, while others promenaded in the latest summer fashions. Although it was a Saturday morning, there were plenty of office and shop workers crossing the bridges into the City district. Michael MacDonagh, a journalist working for *The Times* was on his way to his office:

> I was due at *The Times* office at eleven o'clock and my tram from Clapham had begun to cross Blackfriars Bridge when a woman on the upper deck of the tram, where she and I were the only passengers on the upper deck, called out, 'what a lot of aeroplanes.' I looked up and saw the fleet approaching from a north-easterly direction. 'Are they Germans?' the woman asked me. 'Oh no', I replied, 'If they were Germans we should hear our guns firing at them. I am sure they are our own airman.'[351]

Moments later the Central Telegraph Office received a direct hit, followed by explosions near St Bartholomew's Hospital, which scarred the exterior walls. The 'friendly' formation was, in fact, 22 G. IV Gotha bombers, which went on to blast their way across the East End, causing 54 deaths and injuring 190. Many of the casualties resulted from curious civilians who stood out in the streets, watching the German bombers and leaving themselves exposed. Others were injured by falling shrapnel from anti-aircraft shells. Attempts were made to engage the raiders and over 100 sorties were flown against the formation. The British fighters climbed too slowly and only managed to shoot down one Gotha for the loss of two of their own aircraft. The 'Apron Screens' that skirted the capital failed to catch the enemy; this network of steel cables hanging from stationary balloons at 8000 feet was designed to slice through the wings of the Gothas but the cables were too few and too far apart to do any damage.

As soon as the anti-aircraft guns stopped, Charles Repington noted how quickly everyone started going about their business, and he was no exception.[352] Before long, he was off to see Emilie at Old Meadows to catch up on gossip. Since their relationship had become platonic, he had visited Emilie at her cottage several times, even coming away with a large bunch of roses for Molly.[353] This time he brought Emilie's friend Doris Keane with him for Sunday lunch. Doris regaled them with stories about the theatre and the exciting news that she had been offered a huge sum to act her role of Margherita Cavallini in the movie version of *Romance*. The play was a love story concerning a beautiful opera singer who gives up her love for a young priest so that he can pursue his vocation. Doris's connection to the production was not just professional. She had been involved firstly with the writer, Ned Sheldon, and then the financial backer of the play, Howard Gould. She became pregnant by Gould and gave birth to a daughter Ronda in February 1915, cutting short the play's successful run in America. Drawing on her renowned stamina, she then brought *Romance* over to London the same year.[354] It was a breathless tale, and one with which Emilie could easily identify.

Emilie returned to Brook Street and organised another party on Friday 27 July, which included a high-spirited Doris Keane, Repington and Jacob Epstein, who was sculpting a bust of Doris. The party started at the actress's new house at 34 Chapel Street and then moved on to the Grosvenor Gallery to see the latest exhibition of portraits by Philip de László and Ambrose McEvoy.[355] Emilie believed she knew about art. As previously noted, in her New York past, she had once possessed paintings by Monet and Pissarro and had herself been the subject of several portraits by Anders Zorn. So as she moved along the gallery, she was able to study the exquisite works by de László with an experienced eye. The portrait of an austere Lord Carnock was hung next to a dark and sombre picture of the ageing socialite, Mrs Arthur Wilson, but the third de László portrait, on loan from its owner, Emilie failed to recognise. The sitter was tall and statuesque, with a luminous quality and as the rest of the party caught up with Emilie, she crouched to read the sitter's name. Coming closer,

Repington knew straightaway who it was – she was a friend of his old friend, Lord French. All agreed it was a beautiful picture. It was probably the only time Emilie ever came face to face with Winifred Bennett, 'Wendy'.

There were more outings during the summer of 1917 involving Emilie, Repington and assorted girlfriends. Even Molly Repington was occasionally invited to dine at 80 Brook Street. A popular trip involved leaving London by train and stopping at Marlow to enjoy a leisurely lunch, followed by a dreamy trip back along the Thames in a motor-launch to a dinner-date at Skindle's in Maidenhead. It was an area Emilie knew well from the days before the war, when she rented 'The Chalet' at Taplow.[356] The summer ended with a glorious week in Cornwall, when Doris took time off from the West End to join Emilie in a motor tour of the north coast. Fuel, of course was restricted, but the pair knew how to secure a steady source and hurtled around the narrow Cornish lanes from one hotel to the next.

The motoring ladies returned to London, to tell Repington about Doris Keane's real life 'romance'. It transpired that she was becoming extremely close to her theatrical leading man, Basil Sydney. However, another philandering friend of Repington's appeared to be in a spot of bother. General Sir John Cowans was still enjoying regular sex with the ever compliant Mrs Dennistoun; but such was the regularity of their affair that it could no longer be kept a secret. Repington was well aware that his friend and fellow 'swordsman' was becoming hemmed in by the increasing demands of Dennistoun and her husband. Looking for moral support, Cowans was now calling on Repington to join him for lunch dates with the married woman.[357]

For Emilie 1918 started on a happy note, when her great friend Doris married Basil Sydney. Shortly before the wedding, *Romance* had closed at The Lyric after a run of 1049 performances, and Doris was now free to pursue other theatrical projects. However, for Emilie's other friends, the year would prove extremely testing. Repington left his position as Military Correspondent with *The Times* in January, after a furious row with the editor. The following month, through the medium of the ultra-conservative *Morning Post,* he fiercely attacked the Prime Minister, Lloyd George, over his government's failure to maintain the strength of the British Army. Repington was seething about not only the manpower shortage but also Lloyd George's cherished restrictions on the British General Staff. Repington, in turn, now came under attack from the government and its supporters. Fred Oliver, the prolific correspondent and stalwart of the Department of Information, alleged that Repington might even be a spy.[358] The Police and the Security Service were also now on Repington's case. On the morning of 13 February, two Scotland Yard detectives arrived at his home, Maryon Hall, and questioned him in connection with a breach of The Defence of the Realm Act (DORA), concerning his article. He was visibly shaken and when friends saw him later for lunch, he talked wildly about being shot for treason.[359] He and his newspaper proprietor soon found themselves in the dock at Bow Street Magistrates Court on charges that the article had exposed secret plans for military operations. The courtroom was packed, mainly with women, who had come to see the old philanderer defend himself. The air was heady with their powerful scent and sighs, as Repington gave a bravura performance. The proceedings ended with him receiving a heavy fine for the technical offence of 'disobeying the Censor'. Emilie left the courtroom with a phalanx of other women supporters and returned to Old Meadows, where another drama was unfolding.

Arriving at the cottage, Emilie was alarmed to discover that her gardener had been arrested. He had been working for her ever since her old friend Lieutenant-Colonel Mackay had arranged for some of his men to help her with her gardening. Mackay, of course, had become a regular visitor to Old Meadows and he gave no indication to Emilie that there was a problem with using his men, though she was well aware that they were servicemen. Fraser, the gardener in question, had been working at the cottage one afternoon when he was interrupted by the arrival of two plain-clothes policemen. He was arrested straightaway and taken to New Scotland Yard, questioned and taken into custody. Several days later, Mackay received a telegram saying an officer from Western Command needed to meet him urgently in London. Mackay quickly left his base in Chester and caught a train down to Euston station. As he stepped off the train, he was arrested by detectives. As other military policemen blocked potential escape routes, Mackay was swiftly taken to a secure room, his shoe laces removed and he was searched. Forcing their way through the large crowd that had gathered, the police marched him off to Scotland Yard for questioning. In a bizarre turn of events, he was incarcerated in the Tower of London for a month, enduring solitary confinement.

On 6 May 1918, Mackay appeared before a District Court Martial at Westminster Guildhall, on 25 charges of improperly using soldiers under his command and making false expenses claims. Emilie was called as a witness and underwent a vigorous cross-examination about the employment of servicemen in her garden. She wavered, but took cover behind the excuse that a recent severe illness had caused her to lose her memory. It was a weak ruse that seemed to be accepted by the presiding officer. She attempted to further distance herself from the case by writing to the court, stating that she was dismayed that her name had been dragged into the scandal. Mackay denied the charges, which also involved the improper use of servicemen at Mrs Brandt's house, and the further accusation that he might have borrowed money from 'the ladies' to make good any financial losses from his actions. 'I am not in the habit,' he angrily replied, 'of borrowing money from ladies, Sir.' Clearly this was an allegation that he could not countenance for a moment. He denied that the reason for his repeated visits to Old Meadows was to pursue his 'intimate relationship' with Emilie and denied that he regularly visited the cottage to see her every two weeks. Mackay's defence argued that this was an unjustified slur on an unmarried woman. When Emilie took the witness stand, she lamely argued that Mackay's men were only planting vegetables for the war effort, and because of a recent illness, she had a very poor recollection of anything else. The prosecution seemed to be enfeebled by the notion of a pretty, unmarried woman in the witness stand and the notion that her reputation might be sullied by association was enough to make them cease questioning. Mackay was convicted and Emilie went home to her vegetables.

Generally, the public took a very dim view of anyone trying to profit out of the armed services and the Mackay case was no exception. It was particularly galling for many that a wealthy American should also be involved. Although there was some grumbling that the national sacrifice was not shouldered equally by all classes, there could be no suggestion that the loss of sons was not shared equally. Most gentry and aristocratic families had suffered casualties in the war; in some cases those losses were multiple. Ettie Desborough, the bright and engaging socialite, had lost both her sons by the end of 1915. By 1918, Jean Hamilton's aunt, Nora Anderson, had already lost two sons – Charlie at Festubert, Ronnie at Givençy – then in the March 1918 she learned that a third son Teddy was killed in a flying accident. Seven days later, her fourth and last son, Bertie, was killed during the German Spring Offensive. It was an inconceivable sacrifice.[360]

After the embarrassing court case, Emilie spent the remaining months of the war keeping a low profile. She occasionally met Charles Repington for lunch but their exchanges were no longer the highly charged encounters of previous years. It seems that Emilie spent many happy days dallying with the 'Georgian' poets, or at least with those who survived. Most of them lived near each other in the Leatherhead district of Surrey, which was not far for her to travel. Their poetry style was already becoming eclipsed by the harsher, modernist work of T.S. Eliot, Aldous Huxley and Herbert Read, men who reflected post-war rather than pre-war spirit. Yet, the 'lark-loving' and 'sheep smitten' Georgian coterie still held a dreamy grip on Emilie. Perhaps she still identified with them because their style reminded her of her glorious early years in the war, when her beauty and sexual allure could captivate powerful and influential men.[361]

On 11 November, Emilie attended a small party and as she and the guests poured out into the streets to join the throng, the eleventh hour struck. All over London, the bells rang out. Henry Havelock Ellis, who had sold Old Meadows to Emilie before the war, was visiting a friend in Bloomsbury Square that morning. Seeing the crowds made him realise that some things had changed forever:

> When I went in, the streets were as usual. When I came out an hour later, they were transformed, flags flying everywhere, shouting and gesticulating crowds, and vehicles of all kinds, laden with youths and girls, dashing along to nowhere in particular. I felt sad, for peace does not bring back what war took away, and the ending of the war only makes the difference clearer.[362]

8

Reputations

There were many single women when the war ended; wives who had lost husbands, sweethearts who had lost boyfriends, or women who were simply told that their loved one was missing, believed killed and with no known grave. Gentle letters to the bereaved from a platoon or company commander usually masked the ghastly end that the soldier had suffered. A report of a hero's death was far more palatable than the reality of being blown to pieces, drowning in a shell-hole or being buried alive in a dug-out. For those relatives without the comfort of a known grave, there were a host of spiritualists on hand to feed their desperation – seeking to finish unfinished lives was a profitable business. There were other, less cruel legacies from the conflict. Social customs had changed. Church attendance declined, while service life had spread both cigarette smoking and a tolerance of sexual liberty. Skirts had risen to unprecedented heights and the rather flaccid pre-war European light music had been pepped up by jazz and the exuberant Charleston.[363]

Most people just had an overriding sense of relief that it was all over. They didn't want to look back but only forwards to a new world that must be worth the sacrifice. In 1918, women had achieved a limited franchise and had also made inroads into traditional male work. For the first time in their lives, young people had experienced a different life, either in the services or in the wartime factories, which gave them a freedom from parental control. Marie Stopes' 1918 book on sexual awareness was much talked about and sexologists found a ready audience, believing that now was the time for women to discover their repressed desires. There were bizarre calls to ban 'non-orgasmic' women from politics, lest they try to keep down other more progressive women. Sex was coming out from under the counter. 'When I left England in 1911,' observed Sir Robert Bruce Lockhart, 'contraceptives were hard to buy outside London or other large cities. By 1919 every village chemist was selling them.'[364]

The war had not changed Emilie. She had used the conflict to her own advantage and showcased her sexual allure to gain access to powerful and influential men. But peacetime had a much more limited role for the likes of Charles Repington or Jack Cowans and they soon exited the stage. The only returning warrior that Emilie greeted was her old friend 'Klondike Joe' Boyle, who returned to London in December 1918, after eighteen months protecting Romania's interests. He had defended the vulnerable state, firstly against German and then Bolshevik plots. In the process, the super-energetic Canadian became the lover and confidant of Queen Marie of Romania. Now he had come to the British capital to lobby for aid for Romania and to gain British support for the integrity of Romania's borders at the forthcoming Paris Peace Conference. Emilie was in contact with Boyle at some stage before his premature death in 1923 and it was claimed that she had acquired his bundle of love letters written by Queen Marie. This appears unlikely, since according to Boyle's biographer these love letters were retained by his son and daughter after his death and later destroyed at the request of the Queen. However, Boyle's medals, and possibly some other letters and gifts from the Queen, were believed to pass into other hands. Their whereabouts are still unknown.[365]

Emilie left 80 Brook Street in 1919, selling her long leasehold to a Mrs Aitcheson, who probably had little idea that the house had witnessed such intrigues and sexual adventures. Emilie then went on an extended tour of India, where, as one admirer recalled, she was known as 'the Undressed Salad'. She returned to London to live at 15 Hanover Square, but it was a different city with new priorities and there was little demand for Emilie's salons, attended by the great and the not so good. Charles Repington was still about town and although he remained with Molly, he had spent most of their savings and their home, Maryon Hall in Hampstead, had to be sold. He briefly maintained a flat in Shepherd's Market, which caused much amusement to those who were aware of the area's red light activities. The couple then moved to Hove. By coincidence, Repington's old friend, Lord French, languished in a nursing-home nearby. French died in 1925 and Repington wrote his obituary in the *Daily Telegraph*. It was Repington's last piece of journalism – on the day it was published, he died at his desk, pen in hand.[366] Cyril Falls, an authoritative historian of the First World War, conceded that Repington could be accused of 'living in the greatest comfort, dining and wining with all the prettiest and most charming ladies of London, and from the vantage of Hampstead, continually calling for more sacrifices'. Nevertheless, Falls praised the publication of Repington's diaries for their value as a record of 'a well-informed observer's view of the First World War events – as they happened'. Emilie had been a valuable friend to him in his bid to influence military policy. And in the old thruster's large field of mistresses, she was always his most fancied filly.[367]

General Sir John Cowans died prematurely on 16 April 1921, while at Menton on the French Riviera. He had been made a full general in 1919 and retired from the army shortly after, taking up an appointment in 1921 as Managing Director of a company set up to exploit the Mesopotamian oil fields. Much to Emilie's delight, he converted to Catholicism just before his death in 1921 and lay in state at Westminster Cathedral before his funeral. The packed congregation included Emilie and a great many other female admirers. Patsy Cornwallis-West, who had dragged Cowans into her scandal, pre-deceased him by nine months. Disgraced and written out of private and public life, her grave in the churchyard at Milford in the New

Forest was marked by a simple cross, devoid of any loving inscription.[368] Despite Cowan's elaborate funeral, his own reputation failed to rest in peace. In March 1925, his name came to the fore when Dorothy Dennistoun brought a civil action against ex-husband, Ian, whom she had divorced four years earlier. An informal maintenance provision had broken down and she wanted recompense from her husband who had since re-married Almina, Countess of Carnarvon. It was a bloody and well-publicised courtroom wrangle, which became known as 'The Dustbin Case', with tales of exotic lovers, a hidden pregnancy and a weak husband who connived in his wife's sexual excesses. Cowan's role in their domestic affairs was dissected and it was reported that he had enjoyed four years of 'appointments' with Dorothy in exchange for helping Ian Dennistoun's career. It was a wretched blight on Cowan's justly earned reputation as one of the most capable generals of the First World War.[369]

During the following years Emilie kept her base in Hanover Square in London. But she was determined not to miss out on the roaring twenties, and New York was the place to be. Picking up her old artistic contacts in the city, she befriended the American writer and photographer, Carl Van Vechten, who was a patron of the Harlem Renaissance and other black artistic ventures. He moved in bohemian circles and a constant stream of artists, writers and actors passed through his house. He photographed many in his circle, including Emilie, wearing as she often did a clinging animal print crêpe dress – a fashion later made popular by the Tarzan films.[370] She teamed up again with Gladys Unger, who was enjoying moderate success on Broadway with her adaptation of *The Love Habit*. Others in Emilie's New York circle included Blanche Knopf, the silent film actor Charles Meredith and Fania Marinoff (Van Vechten's wife). There was a party every night and the group seemed to stumble through a constant alcoholic haze, a lifestyle Van Vechten labelled 'The Splendid Drunken Twenties'. Sometimes the group would decamp to London, take in a few plays, parties and bars in the West End and then take the train out to Emilie's cottage at West Drayton. There, Emilie would entertain in lavish style, while her friend Dwight Fiske, the nightclub entertainer, would deliver his hilarious narratives while playing the piano. Fiske specialised in verbal dexterity and delighted his audience with risqué offerings, usually involving sexually needy women – a subject that Emilie found extremely amusing.[371] While in America, Emilie also became attracted to another exotic character, known as Chief Buffalo Child Long Lance. He enjoyed celebrity status in the 1920s. Long Lance was a journalist who adopted the Native Indian cause and became their spokesman, even appearing in a feature film. However, he was later exposed as a fraud, and rather than being the charismatic son of a Blackfoot Chief, it was confirmed that he was, in fact, the son of a school caretaker. Lance was promptly dropped by Emilie, but not before he had helped her spend some of her dwindling fortune.

During the 1930s, Emilie spent more time back in London. In 1932, she took a lease on 49 Park Street and became involved with the mainstream arts scene, becoming a patron and supporter of such bodies as the British Women's Symphony

Orchestra. Emilie was now in her fifties, but still displaying that beautiful alabaster skin that had made both men and women stare in awe. She continued to adore the party scene and regularly hosted a table at charity balls. She also remained loyal to old friends, such as the playwright and inspiration behind *Romance,* Ned Sheldon, who was increasingly crippled with arthritis. His former lover and the star of the play, Doris Keane, never rekindled her fame. She went on to perform in the less successful play *Roxana.* Immediately after the war, she was seen in a New York run of *Romance,* and in 1926 she again played the role of Margherita Cavallini when the play was revived in London. Doris then attempted a new role in the play *Starlight,* written by her old friend Gladys Unger, but it was not a success. Emilie, Doris and Gladys were re-united for the last time at the wedding of Doris's daughter Ronda in 1936. Gladys Unger had enjoyed better fortunes after the First World War, and co-scripted Cecil B. De Mille's first two 'talkies' in the late 1920s. She died on 25 May 1940 in Manhattan. Like Emilie, she never married. On 25 November 1945, Doris died aged 63.[372]

During the 1930s, Emilie had established some new relationships that would see her through to old age, but rather than the wild and passionate affairs she had enjoyed in her youth, these were platonic friendships. Men like Sir Winston Churchill's cousin, Sir Shane Leslie, became part of her circle and probably her greatest supporter in later life. She moved to an apartment in Curzon Place, a short distance from the home of her old lover, Jack Cowans. In 1934, she employed Willena Chisholm, who acted first as a maid and secretary, and later as a companion.[373] After the Second World War, Emilie continued to divide her time between an apartment in Mayfair and her beloved cottage at West Drayton. 'I have devoted many years of my life caring for and beautifying the property as an island of beauty and peace in the middle of the suburban development which has grown up around it.' She employed the well-known garden designer Percy Cane to redesign the grounds, incorporating her beloved rose garden.[374]

However, Emilie's low profile during the late 1940s did not last; 1947 saw the publication of the novel *The Stoic,* the third and last book in the trilogy by Theodore Dreiser, depicting the life of a corrupt financier and his exotic mistress. In the novels, the fictitious Frank Cowperwood is thinly disguised as Charles Yerkes, while the heroine, Berenice Fleming, is based on Emilie. Dreiser lived in New York in the early 1900s, at the same time as the couple and he avidly followed their real life saga. His first two books were *The Financier,* which concentrated on Yerkes' life, and was published seven years after the 'Traction King's' death, and *The Titan,* which was published in 1914. However, it was *The Stoic,* published in 1947 that contained far more details of Emilie's life. Dreiser was a serial womaniser and had moved in the same New York artistic milieu as Emilie. He knew her friends and ex-lovers and it was rumoured that they put pressure on him not to publish the novel. Dreiser died suddenly in 1945 and it was left to his wife, Helen, to persuade a publisher to take on the potentially libellous project. Two years later she succeeded, and an edition

of *The Stoic,* with the original real-life characters heavily disguised, was published.
Everyone knew the real identity of the manipulating heroine in Dreiser's book, but
by now Emilie was beyond caring.[375]

By the 1950s, Emilie was drinking heavily and had withdrawn from public gaze.
Her increasingly eccentric behaviour was driving her remaining friends away and she
sought solace with her companions Willina and her brother, Hugh Chisholm. In her
eighties she was overtaken by dementia and was moved to the Regent's Park Nursing
Home in St Edmunds Terrace, opposite the Park.[376] On 11 February 1964 she died
of bronchopneumonia. She was 88 years old and had outlived all her contemporaries.
and the vast wealth that she had accumulated had all but disappeared.[377] Once estate
duty tax of £134,809 (equivalent to over £2 million today) was paid, there was
very little left for her executor, Lord Southborough, to administer. She left both Old
Meadows and its adjacent cottage, 'The Poplars' to the National Trust, directing that
Willina Chisholm should inhabit 'The Poplars' until her death. Given Emilie's love of
Old Meadows, it was surprising that she stipulated that the name be changed on her
death and all reference to her association with it be eradicated. She had instructed
that her fabulous collection of couture gowns was to be offered to her maid but as she
had no use for them, Lord Southborough offered the best examples to the Victoria
& Albert Museum in London. The curator had to admit that it was 'an unusually
interesting and charming collection'. Her jewellery, the gifts of so many lovers, went
to auction at Sotheby's.[378]

It was left to Emilie's old friend, Sir Shane Leslie, to pen her obituary. 'The passing
of an Edwardian hostess may be unnoticed but deserves memory in any record of
Mayfair in its most brilliant phase.' Leslie was right about Emilie's flair as a hostess, but
he was too easily seduced by the Grigsby enigma. He was not alone. The normally
acute observer, novelist Ford Maddox Ford, believed that Emilie really did move in
royal circles and that she could even influence ambassadorial appointments. That was
far from the truth. During the First World War however, she did manage to breach
both the walls of the War Council and the bastions of Fleet Street. To do so, she
employed the oldest weapon in a woman's armoury – 'the blue beast'. In her own
words she became 'the mascot of High Command'.[379]

The Youell sisters in Galatz, Christmas 1904. From left: Gladys, Winifred and Sybil. (Bennett Papers, Camilla Shivarg)

A Romanian scene in 1905. (Bennett Papers, Camilla Shivarg)

Winifred Bennett wearing
Romanian fashions. (Bennett Papers,
Camilla Shivarg)

Winifred (sitting) with friends beside
A-503, one of the first London reg-
istrations. (Bennett Papers, Camilla
Shivarg)

Percy Bennett depicted as a 'Servant of Empire'. (Bennett Papers, Camilla Shivarg)

The Russian battleship *Potemkin* from Percy Bennett's album. (Bennett Papers, Camilla Shivarg)

September Marien

Winifred in Marienbad. (Bennett Papers, Camilla Shivarg)

'Life with Percy could be fun,' Italy 1906. Standing from left: Percy, Princess Demidoff and Raymond. Sitting from left: Jeanette, Prince Demidoff and Winifred. (Bennett Papers, Camilla Shivarg)

The elegant Mrs Bennett. (Bennett Papers, Camilla Shivarg)

Winifred. 'Those dark, magnetic eyes'. (Bennett Papers, Camilla Shivarg)

Piccadilly Circus before the First World War. (Moffett Studio, (Library of Congress # LC–USZ62-136309)

Field Marshal Sir John French, Paris 1914. ((Bain News Service, Library of Congress # LC-DIG-ggbain-17041)

'The Lady of the Lake'. (Bennett Papers, Camilla Shivarg)

Lancaster Gate. From the Park.

Scene of the 'Dances of Death'. 94 Lancaster Gate is in the foreground at the end of the terrace. (Images of London)

George Gordon Moore. (Julian P. Graham/Loon Hill Studios)

Suffragettes advertising a meeting in London. Sir John French's sister, Lottie Despard, tops the bill. (Bain News Service, Library of Congress # LC–DIG–ggbain–00111)

Winifred in the silver *lamé* dress which inspired Sir John French to christen her his 'Silver Girl'. (Bennett Papers, Camilla Shivarg)

Lady Diana Manners. (Bain News Service, Library of Congress # LC-DIG-ggbain- 32924)

Sir John French reviewing the troops. (Imperial War Museum # Q 70032)

'Landing the big one.' Winifred and friends in Scotland. (Bennett Papers, Camilla Shivarg)

Winifred 'Wendy' Bennett reclining. (Bennett Papers, Camilla Shivarg)

The Paris Opera House in 1919, where Iris Bennett danced with a French soldier (a *poilu*). (Bennett Papers, Camilla Shivarg)

Sybil, Winifred and Iris in Paris. (Bennett Papers, Camilla Shivarg)

Emilie Grigsby. 'The Poem Girl' (Bain News Service, Library of Congress # LC-DIG-ggbain-26961.

Emilie's 'House of Mystery', 660 Park Avenue, New York. (Bain News Service, Library of Congress # LC-DIG-ggbain-01707)

'Miss Grigsby', by Anders Zorn, painted in 1907. (Sotheby's Picture Library)

Emilie's balcony view of the coronation of George V, 22 June 1911. (Bain News Service, Library of Congress # LC-DIG-ggbain-09602)

Emilie's Poiret mantle, 1913. (Victoria & Albert Museum # 2006BD5591-01)

The arrest of a suffragette, (Bain News Service, Library of Congress # LC-DIG-ggbain-10397)

Crowds outside Downing Street, August 1914. The towers of the War Office can be seen in the distance. (Bain News Service, Library of Congress # LC-DIG-ggbain-16881)

80 Brook Street, Mayfair, which Emilie purchased in 1913. (Author's collection)

Emilie in her prime. (Library of Congress # LC-USZ62-105441)

Lieutenant–General Sir John Cowans (right). (National Library of Scotland (119) L.718)

Old Meadows, West Drayton in 1948, photographed while Emilie lived there. (English Heritage NMR #BB48/00533)

Basil Sydney and Doris Keane appearing in the play 'Romance'. (Bain News Service, Library of Congress # LC-DIG-ggbain-28993)

Above left: Gladys Unger. (Bain News Service, Library of Congress # LC-DIG-ggbain-12541)

Above: Paul Poiret, the couturier favoured by Emilie. (Library of Congress # LC-USZ62-100840)

Left: Lieutenant-Colonel Charles à Court Repington. (Mary Repington)

Lady Randolph (Jennie) Churchill.
(Bain News Service, Library of
Congress # LC-DIG-ggbain-05642)

Sir John Cowans, who was appointed
Quartermaster-General in 1912.
(Bain News Service, Library of
Congress # LC-DIG-ggbain-18647)

Emilie Grigsby in 1934. (Carl Van Vechten, Library of Congress # Lot 12735)

Alderley Park, Cheshire. (Picture Cheshire)

Sylvia (with a broken arm) and her bridesmaids, 1906. Also present are Venetia Stanley (seated left), Clementine Hozier (standing left) and Blanche Stanley (seated right). (Anthony Pitt-Rivers)

Sylvia helps pull Venetia in the snow. (Anthony Pitt-Rivers)

Sylvia's horse is steadied by Blanche before joining the hunt. (Anthony Pitt-Rivers)

Sylvia and Blanche raid the kitchens. (Anthony Pitt-Rivers)

Captain Hon. Anthony Henley, Private Secretary to the Secretary of State for War. (Anthony Pitt–Rivers)

Sylvia in Italy. (Anthony Pitt–Rivers)

Penrhos — Holyhead

Left: Penrhôs in Anglesey, the Stanley family home. (Archives and Special Collections, Bangor University # BM37539)

Below left: Herbert Henry Asquith. (Bain News Service, Library of Congress # LC-DIG-ggbain-20102)

Below: A picnic at Holy Island. From left: Sylvia, Venetia Stanley, Violet Asquith, H.H. Asquith, Edwin Montagu and Maurice (Bongie) Bonham-Carter. (Anthony Pitt-Rivers)

Above: Party tricks at Alderley. (Anthony Pitt-Rivers)

Above left: Count Zeppelin watches his creation prepare for action. (Library of Congress # LC-USZ62-44993)

Left: Sylvia and Blanche tackle estate management. (Anthony Pitt-Rivers)

Blanche Stanley, Winston and Clementine Churchill on the Anglesey coast. (Anthony Pitt-Rivers)

Winston Churchill and Venetia Stanley on Penrhôs beach. (Anthony Pitt-Rivers)

'Digging for Victory'. From left: unidentified, Venetia Stanley and Winston Churchill. (Anthony Pitt-Rivers)

Behind the ha-ha from right: Lyulph second; Anthony fourth; Sylvia seventh. (Anthony Pitt-Rivers)

Venetia (mounted), Sylvia (walking behind) and Anthony Henley. (Anthony Pitt-Rivers)

Lyulph Lord Sheffield, Sylvia, Rosalind and Kitty. (Anthony Pitt-Rivers)

18 Mansfield Street, the Stanley's London townhouse. (Anthony Pitt-Rivers)

Margot Asquith
and Sylvia
at Penrhôs.
(Anthony Pitt–
Rivers)

H.H. Asquith and Sylvia. (Anthony Pitt–Rivers)

Brigadier-General Hon. Anthony Henley leaving Buckingham Palace. (Anthony Pitt-Rivers)

Sylvia and Skiff. (Anthony Pitt-Rivers)

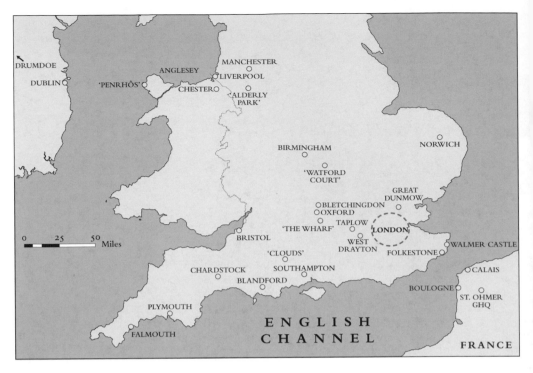

England and Wales, 1914.

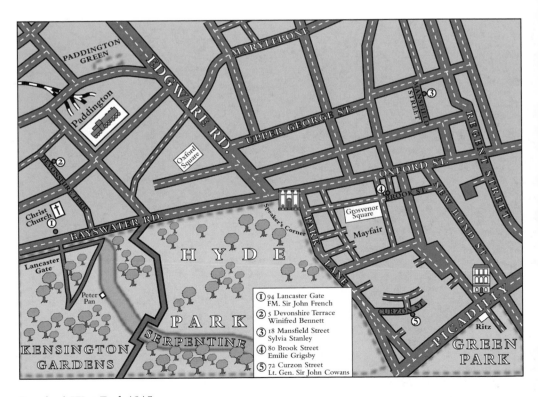

① 94 Lancaster Gate
FM. Sir John French

② 5 Devonshire Terrace
Winifred Bennett

③ 18 Mansfield Street
Sylvia Stanley

④ 80 Brook Street
Emilie Grigsby

⑤ 72 Curzon Street
Lt. Gen. Sir John Cowans

London's West End, 1915

SYLVIA HENLEY

9

A Liberal Heritage

Off the west coast of Anglesey, lies Holy Island, so-called because of its historic burial chambers and standing stones. The island is reached via the Stanley Causeway and although it is now home to a largely redundant smelting works, it contains a beautiful secret. Overlooking the cobalt blue water of Beddmanarch Bay, lie the remains of the old Penrhôs estate, once owned by the important and influential Stanley family. It is now a nature reserve, but few of the visitors who pass the isolated and overgrown ruins of the old house realise that it was once the backdrop to a drama of power and passion. Its ghosts are still there perhaps, and those who walk past the old boathouse might sometimes hear the faint voice of Prime Minister Asquith regaling his young friends with tales from the 'bear-pit', or see the shadowy image of Winston Churchill digging for sand eels at low tide. This place was once a haven for a political class that is now extinct. It was also a refuge for a remarkable woman, the Hon. Sylvia Henley, who became an indispensable part of that world.

Sylvia was born on 19 March 1882, into a wealthy and privileged family. The fifth child of Lyulph Stanley and Mary Bell, she joined a dynasty that had enjoyed centuries of mixed fortunes.[380] The Stanleys of Alderley could claim a direct lineage back to the Norman Conquest and were descended from a junior branch of the Stanleys of Knowsley – a line that included Sir Thomas Stanley and Sir William Stanley, both famous for their roles in deciding the outcome of the Battle of Bosworth in 1485. Sir Thomas was rewarded with the Earldom of Derby and fathered the senior branch of the family, while his brother, Sir William, became careless and lost his head. Since those violent days, the Stanleys had produced a succession of more circumspect Members of Parliament, deans and bishops.

With such close connections to the state, it was not surprising that the family had prospered over the centuries. The Stanleys of Alderley had been rewarded with a baronetcy in 1660 and a peerage in 1829. Sylvia's father, Lyulph, was the third son of the 3rd Lord Stanley of Alderley. On her mother's side, Sylvia inherited not only 169 first and second cousins, but also numerous formidable aunts. Amongst the latter were Alice, who married Colonel (later General) Augustus Pitt-Rivers and Kate, Lady Amberley, who was the mother of Bertrand Russell. Other aunts included the Countess of Carlisle, who became the chatelaine of Castle Howard in Yorkshire, and Blanche, Countess of Airlie, the grandmother of Clementine Hozier, who would later marry Winston Churchill and become one of Sylvia's closest friends.[381]

Home for Sylvia and her siblings was Alderley Park, a rambling early nineteenth-century house, deep inside the Alderley Estate near Macclesfield, Cheshire. The house had replaced an earlier hall and mansion on the same site, but this more recent edifice was on a much grander scale. Alderley Park had over 50 bedrooms, as well as drawing rooms, morning rooms, great hall, libraries and the honeycomb of the servants' world of laundries, kitchens and pantries. However, the house was no architectural gem, being 'built of grey stone, its frigid neo-classical façade facing north', though the coach house, stables and 'Tenants Hall' were handsome buildings, set amidst a glorious landscape. Indeed, it was this vista that left the biggest impression on guests, with its lakes and park flanked with massive, mature beech woods as well as the more unusual mulberry and tulip trees. There were innovations on the estate, including underground coal-fired flues that heated the soil to enable the culture of peaches, figs and apricots. To support the house and family, the 4500-acre estate included a home farm and rent from over 80 properties and smaller farms. Furthermore, a succession of opportune marriages had endowed the Stanleys with further wealth and an estate at Penrhôs, on Holyhead Island, off the Anglesey coast, as well as a London town house in Mansfield Street.[382]

As a daughter in such a household, Sylvia grew up in a crowd. Her governess and the servants of the house were always in attendance and her immediate family was growing. By the time she was five, she had acquired two more sisters; her hordes of cousins were forever invading the nurseries and playrooms at Alderley. While her brothers were sent away at six years old to their boarding prep schools, Sylvia's schooling followed the normal upper class convention for girls – education at home, followed possibly by a girls' boarding school in the teenage years. So after a spell in the nursery at Alderley, Sylvia progressed to the family schoolroom, where she learned the basics of reading and writing, piano, singing and needlework, as well as modern foreign languages.

She enjoyed a charmed upbringing, with all the opportunities such an estate could offer. Apart from her studies, supervised by a governess, she became a capable and robust rider and excelled at tennis and swimming. All the Stanley girls were fond of outdoor activities and Sylvia, in particular, was always to the fore when there was larking around on the estate. The sisters were in on every escapade alongside the boys. Perhaps it was their radical liberal heritage, but Lyulph also taught his children to be heard as well as seen. As a teenager, Sylvia was encouraged to join in the robust family discussions. The vociferous younger end of the family always provided lively and sometimes wild input to the family gatherings. While neither Sylvia nor her sisters, Blanche and Venetia, were destined to become university 'Girton Girls', they could nevertheless offer their friends and guests intelligent and stimulating conversation and in Sylvia's case, a frighteningly direct manner of interrogation.[383]

As a teenager, Sylvia was in awe of her brightest eldest brother, Arthur, who was destined to follow Lyulph's career path, attending Balliol College, Oxford, becoming a barrister and sitting as a Liberal MP – for the seat of Eddisbury in Cheshire.[384] It was at Balliol that Arthur first met the Hon. Anthony Morton Henley, who would later join him in a legal career at the bar. Their friendship extended to visits to Alderley Park, where Anthony and his younger, racier brother, Francis, would be invited for Saturday-to-Monday house parties. The brothers soon met the sixteen-year-old Sylvia and although there was an initial attraction between Francis Henley and Sylvia, she soon gravitated towards his dark, moustachioed older brother, Anthony. The Old Etonian captivated Sylvia with his tales of derring-do while at Balliol, and his legendary stamina – he had just teamed up with his friend, Hilaire Belloc, to walk from Oxford to London in under twelve hours.

'Old Honks', as Anthony was known at university, was an eminently suitable escort for Sylvia, being the younger son of the 3rd Lord Henley and his wife, Clare Jekyll. Their backgrounds were even more compatible, for Anthony's family was steeped in Liberal politics and his father had once been Liberal MP for Northampton. When the 3rd Lord Henley died in 1898, Anthony's elder half-brother Frederic inherited the title, but since it was an Irish creation, it did not allow the holder an automatic seat in the House of Lords.[385] The Henley estate did not quite match the Stanley acres and while the family seat, Watford Court, near Rugby, was a substantial Elizabethan house, the family wealth did not percolate down to the son of a second marriage. The family's second estate at Chardstock on the Devon/Dorset border was supposed to support the later siblings, but it was not a productive investment.[386] Nevertheless, when Anthony began courting Sylvia, his prospects as a barrister looked bright and he was more than capable of holding his own in the intellectually testing arena of the Stanley gatherings. For Anthony, it would be an effortless transition from Balliol to the Inner Temple, with its quadrangles, gothic halls and cramped staircases. For the moment, however, the prospect of a new war for a young and adventurous man was too much to ignore.

The first stirring tales of the Boer War in 1899 were attracting young men to the colours whose families were not known for their martial traditions. Anthony, who was a competent rider and certainly fit enough for army service, was encouraged by one of Sylvia's cousins who was recruiting for replacements for a mounted volunteer unit, to join the 28th (Bedfordshire) Company, known as Compton's Horse. It was part of the Imperial Yeomanry, formed to provide mounted escort and policing support to the regulars. When Lance Corporal Henley arrived in South Africa in May 1900, he found a chaotic organisation. Rather than taking part in gallant cavalry charges or tactical sweeps across the veldt, he was shunted into mundane duties in support of actions near Johannesburg and Pretoria. He was bound to a unit whose numbers were constantly depleted by Boer snipers or the poaching of other regular units. So, when the opportunity came to see more action with the 2nd Dragoons (Royal Scots Greys), he immediately accepted and was commissioned as a Second Lieutenant within the month. He spent the next year in operations in the Transvaal, rising to the rank of Lieutenant by the end of the war in 1902.[387]

The men in Sylvia's life were disappearing from Alderley. Her older brother Oliver, who had served in the Boer War, was now carving out a career in the Royal Artillery, while another brother, Edward, had embarked on a promising vocation in the Colonial Service and was posted to Nigeria, only to die prematurely at the age of 26.[388]

When Sylvia was 21, her father inherited the Barony of Stanley. Lyulph Stanley had never expected to become Lord Stanley. His eccentric elder brother, the 3rd Lord Stanley, had converted to Islam and married a Spanish bigamist. 'Squat, fat and swarthy with a heavy black moustache' – and that was just his wife – the union failed to produce any children. Another elder brother, John, who had fought in the Crimean War, had also predeceased him. So Lyulph became the 4th Lord Stanley and used his new position as a platform to argue his twin passions of educational reform and agnosticism. A Fellow of Balliol, he was also a one-time Liberal MP for Oldham. Whenever the family congregated, there was spirited debate. Although the family were strong supporters of the Liberal Party, Lyulph was very much a free thinker and encouraged robust political debate amongst his inner circle as well as his house guests. Bertrand Russell, a cousin of Sylvia's, remembered Sunday lunches being fertile ground for religious or political argument as Sylvia's uncle, Algernon, a Catholic priest and Papal Chamberlain, would take on various sons-in-law who fought the Protestant cause, while Lyulph would use any excuse to attack the Anglican Church. Rather than accept, as most of society did, that Christianity was 'a faith held by inheritance', the Stanleys insisted that faith should be held only by conviction.[389]

Such combative hospitality could be very daunting to guests or would-be suitors of the Stanley children. Adelaide, one of Lyulph's grandchildren, recalled him firing tough and obscure questions at guests around the dining table, who would then have to answer in front of the whole family. 'Now tell me,' he would say, fixing one suddenly with his Jovian bright-blue eye, 'What do you know about the Marian Heresy?' It was enough to finish off all but the most resilient, though such a fierce environment did breed questioning and independent children. Lyulph's wife, Mary, known as Maisie, was a softer character who compensated for Lyulph's lack of empathy and promised a warm sanctuary to any guest who found the intellectual duelling too much to handle. Her tactile personality also attracted the artistic George

Howard, 9th Earl of Carlisle, with whom she was reported to have had an affair, resulting in the birth of Venetia Stanley.[390]

Sylvia had inherited many of her father's characteristics. A friend admitted, 'she could be caustic; she was nearly always astringent; for she thought it false to disguise her feelings and she was unflinchingly truthful.' Meanwhile, Anthony's mien was a good balance to her rather testing and wilful personality. For he was known to be 'a boon companion, out-of-doors, or in' and always ready to inject light-hearted banter into the sometimes overheated Stanley family gatherings.[391] While Anthony may have been good company, Lyulph Stanley was not hugely impressed with his career prospects, especially as he was keen to marry Sylvia. Anthony had dumped his once promising legal career in favour of the Army, where, at the age of 30 he found himself adjutant of the Scots Greys. However, when his appointment came to an end in early 1906, he married Sylvia. On her wedding day on 24 April, the resilient bride stood for the photographs with her arm in plaster, having broken it several days earlier while trying to break in a horse – everyone joked that she was obviously the tougher of the two and she should be the one in the army uniform. Shortly after the wedding, Captain Anthony Henley was transferred to the 5th (Royal Irish) Lancers, a cavalry regiment that felt more comfortable with titled families than Balliol men, as intellectual capacity was considered a very dubious characteristic in an Edwardian cavalry officer.[392]

Anthony's regiment was based at their depot near Dublin, which was very convenient for the Stanley estate at Penrhôs, just off the island of Anglesey and easily reached by boat from Dublin. It was at Penrhôs that Sylvia spent many idyllic holidays with her family and it was a house that was adored by adults and children alike. Sylvia's niece, Adelaide, recalled:

> The rambling grey stone mansion with its adjoining farm buildings enclosed by battlemented granite walls looked over a narrow strait to the green fields of Anglesey. Eastwards, the mountains of Snowdonia rose on the horizon beyond the Menai Straits. To the west and south, a belt of woods – gnarled sycamores and ancient beech trees – encircled the house and grounds, sheltering them from the frequent gales ... It was but a step from the garden through the woods to the sea with its little shell-strewn beaches curving between the rocky points where the oyster-catcher hides her eggs to this day, and the white sea birds walk upon the shining ribbed sand at low tide and the lonely cry of the curlew echoes over the water.[393]

Penrhôs was certainly a retreat, and about as far away from London as you could wish.

The estate was reached by crossing Anglesey and passing over a causeway in the north-west to Holyhead Island. This causeway, known as the 'Stanley Embankment', carried a road and rail link to the seaport of Holyhead, several miles beyond Penrhôs. The estate looked back to the mainland over Beddmanarch Bay and the gardens had all the mystery and adventure that children or romantics would relish – rock pools, ferneries, hot-houses, beehives and walled gardens, all tended by a regiment of eighteen gardeners. The one drawback to this glorious estate was the freezing, dark Penrhôs House. There were open fires, but the plumbing and sanitary ware was basic in the extreme. There was no electric light, so oil lamps and candles spluttered everywhere, and no telephone until the 1920s. The children were wary about visiting the older parts of the house, where the warren of stone-flagged passageways led to dark recesses and twisting, rickety staircases. Yet, despite a haunted feel, Penrhôs generated genuine affection and perhaps it was such splendid isolation, enhanced by the smells of beeswax, old leather books and summer flowers, that entranced all who came to visit the house.[394]

Indeed, any number of the powerful and influential came to stay at Penrhôs. Winston Churchill, who married Sylvia's cousin Clementine Hozier in 1908, was a regular guest and was never happier than when digging for shells or prawning on the Penrhôs beach. As well as being cousins, Clementine formed a close friendship with Sylvia, especially following the tragedy of her sister Kitty's death some years before. Typhoid, no respecter of class, had claimed Kitty when she was barely seventeen, and her swift, cruel death had rocked the Hozier and Stanley families. As they grew older, Sylvia proved a true friend to her cousin but she still found Clementine 'very uneven' in temperament and inclined to be approachable one day, remote the next. Still, they met regularly, especially when Sylvia discovered she was pregnant.[395]

Just a year after their marriage, Sylvia and Anthony were blessed with a child. On 4 March 1907, Sylvia gave birth to a daughter, Rosalind. She was born at Alderley and the christening took place in the local church shortly afterwards. It was not a solemn affair and, as usual, Sylvia's sister Venetia led the irreverent behaviour as the christening party neared the font. As the baby bawled, she called out that 'the young gorilla should be drowned'.[396] Not to everyone's taste, Venetia's remarks were typical of the raucous Stanley style, which also ran to a range of practical jokes. Again it would be Venetia who instigated the mayhem, often employing her exotic menagerie of wild animals, including Pluto the monkey, Lancelot the bear, as well as a fox and a penguin. Clementine Hozier, who often stayed at Alderley, enjoyed the chaos and company of her female cousins, or the 'Alderney [sic] cows', as she christened them. Writing to Winston, she delighted in the chaos caused by the three-foot tall bear, when he was stung trying to prize honey out of the beehives. Another party trick employed by the girls was to release the animals onto unsuspecting visitors, and on occasions the wives of Liberal Party worthies could be seen running shrieking into the house. In the end, it all got out of hand and Lyulph banished the animals to London Zoo.[397]

Although Anthony spent long periods away with his regiment, punctuated with short leave, Sylvia was fulfilling the duties of an Edwardian wife and producing babies and, hopefully, an heir. Barely ten months after the birth of her first daughter, Sylvia produced a second daughter. Mary Katherine, known as 'Kitty', was born on 30 January 1908 and joined the swelling ranks of children at Alderley. Nannies and maids took care of much of the work in the nursery, leaving Sylvia time to engage in the hectic social activities that Alderley offered. In the season, there were shooting parties and Sylvia and Venetia were also daring riders and although they would comply with the more sedate side-saddle for hunting, at other times they were 'ride-astriders'. According to Lawrence Jones, Venetia in particular, 'rode like an Amazon'.[398]

While her husband was away on military duties, Sylvia and the children remained at Alderley for much of the time. The vast house, though, was constantly buzzing with activity, especially with the regular round of house parties. Alderley, like other great houses before the war, had an abundance of staff and servants. There were over 40 members of staff indoors and even more outside, employed in farming the estate, pest control and maintaining the shoot. When a house party was arranged, the guests would bring their own valets and maids and the servants quarters would be filled to bursting point. Below stairs the chaos in the staff quarters was no doubt controlled by Alderley's butler and housekeeper, but even these stalwarts were tested by the extraordinary workload during bath time. Before running hot water was installed at the house, baths for the Stanleys and their guests had to be filled by a chain of servants running up and down flights of stairs carrying pails of hot water from the kitchens. Each bath – and there were probably over 20 baths to fill after a day's hunting or shooting – required a maid to make 25 round trips from kitchen to bedroom. Newspapers, which in a Liberal supporting family such as the Stanleys would be the *Daily Chronicle, Daily News* and *Westminster Gazette,* had to be ironed before the family could read them. This was not to iron out the creases, as is commonly thought, but to make the print stay on the newspaper rather than transfer to the reader's hands. The Stanleys were benevolent employers but even so, most servants worked from 6.30am to 10.00pm, with half a day off each week and one full day per month. Yet, despite the long hours, most servants remained discreet about what they saw and heard, especially during house parties or 'Saturdays-to-Mondays'.[399]

For such house parties – and Alderley was no exception – guests' names were inserted into small brass frames on bedroom doors. However, the hostess would discreetly place established lovers in adjacent or nearby bedrooms and this usually had the desired effect as the lights went off late at night. There were mistakes though, as Lord Charles Beresford found to his cost. In the early hours of the morning the lusty peer crept into what he thought was his mistress's bedroom. Taking a run onto the bed, he leaped onto the warm heap in the middle, shouting 'Cock-a-doodle-doo', only to discover he had landed on the Bishop of Chester and his wife.[400]

Sylvia and her younger sister Venetia did not want for a hectic social life, either in Alderley or down in London. They mixed in a whirl, whose shining light was the beautiful Lady Diana Manners, most probably the daughter of Harry Cust but brought up as the daughter of the Duke of Rutland. She was a key member of a social group known as 'The Corrupt Coterie', who tended to be the sons and daughters of an older exclusive group branded 'The Souls'. The Coterie comprised younger members from such families as the Asquiths, Grenfells, Horners and Listers, and increasingly the group invited Venetia Stanley to join them. However, it was the

Asquith family who would become closest to the Stanleys and it was the embrace of H.H. Asquith in particular that would prove most dangerous.

Violet, the daughter of the powerful Liberal politician H.H. Asquith, had met Arthur Stanley as early as 1905, at a party on the River Thames and thought him 'a delightful man'. Arthur not only launched himself onto the river but also onto the highly charged Violet, who was much taken with his talk of 'eschatology and subjective idealism', not to mention 'the relative position of 'the pre-Socratics'. If Violet was possessed of an inquiring and precocious mind, she was certainly eclipsed by the intellect of her whirlwind stepmother, Margot.[401]

Margot Tennant had been the epitome of the Edwardian 'new woman'. She was the daughter of the wealthy Glasgow bleach magnate, Sir Charles Tennant, and had prided herself as a holder of political and literary 'salons', as well as becoming a leading figure in the 'Souls'. She married the rising political star Herbert Asquith in 1894, and later became a regular visitor to Alderley. However, the Asquiths were not welcomed by all the Stanley family. Sylvia's aunt, Blanche Airlie 'loathed' Violet Asquith, while others gave Margot a wide berth – especially when she started elaborating on her problems with her narrow hips and childbirth.[402] Her husband H.H. Asquith was another matter and after his first visit to Alderley, he was genuinely welcomed by all, for he could contribute to any discussion and talk, with some authority, on a wealth of subjects. He became a firm friend of Lyulph as they had much in common. They had both been at Balliol, followed by election as Liberal MPs, though Lyulph had retired as Asquith started in the House of Commons. By now, Asquith was Chancellor of the Exchequer in the Liberal Government, which had won a landslide victory in the 1906 general election, and was poised to gain the Premiership. For Liberal grandees like the Stanleys, such a connection was vital to maintain if their voice was to be heard. The fact that Asquith's own background was solidly middle class was surmountable. An Oxford University education, a successful career at the bar and a glittering political vocation had gradually ensured his entry into the smartest houses in the country. Variously known as 'Squiffy' (from his supposed fondness for drink), or 'Old Block', Asquith's second marriage to Margot Tennant had also introduced him to some more exclusive sets in the hunting world as well as those 'Souls' who indulged in philosophical debate.[403]

For all the outward appearance of a talented and united family, there were undercurrents in the Asquith family. While Margot had 'star' quality, she nevertheless failed to supply Asquith with his need to be constantly reassured. She was too absorbed with sharpening her own wit to deal with pampering her politician husband. She regularly clashed with the other *grandes dames* on the circuit and became well-known for the icy put-down. Lady Colefax, who assumed that she was at the centre of all activities, did not impress Margot, who quipped that in the presence of Sibyl Colefax, 'one could not talk about the birth of Christ without she would claim to have been there in the manger.'[404] Margot tolerated HH's 'harem' of female admirers – indeed she had her own worshippers – and was happy for them to spend time massaging his ego. She would save her energy for combating Asquith's favourite daughter, Violet, who had first claim on her father. However, Margot was also occupied with a new obsession, a new face in town.

The object of Margot's fascination was a rising star of the stage, who combined artistry with the thrill and shock of an apparently naked body. Canadian-born Maud Allan was an Edwardian sex goddess who performed a 20-minute dance routine titled 'The Vision of Salome', which re-enacted the biblical story of the seductress who demanded the head of John the Baptist as the price for performing the exotic dance. Her dance had come to the notice of King Edward VII, and in September 1907 she was summoned to appear before him while he was staying in Marienbad. After dinner one evening, he settled down with a small group of friends and courtiers to enjoy the entertainment and despite the misgivings of his private secretary that Maud danced wearing only 'two oyster shells and a five franc piece', the King was clearly delighted with what he saw. His approval soon percolated down through the arts establishment and it was not long before Maud found that society hostesses as well as theatre producers were falling over themselves to book her 'Vision of Salome'. In London, hostesses would arrange all-women evenings and book Maud to appear in her stage costume consisting of only a tiny bra and a miniscule G-string of diamonds, with various layers of wafting silk veils. Women, who were only just emerging from their tight corsets, were fascinated by Maud's liberated style and freedom of movement. Refreshed and emboldened by her performance, they too would attempt the steps in front of their friends and embrace their own sexuality. This certainly seemed to be the case with Margot Asquith and her friends who, after attending her professional engagements, were rumoured to visit Maud in her dressing room to take a closer look at this daring creature.

Margot formed a close bond with Maud and introduced her to her husband and through him, the curvaceous dancer was also invited to a number of official dinners. Margot became so infatuated that she paid for the lease on Maud's apartment in Regent's Park and continued to do so for the next eighteen years. It was an enduring friendship, which would survive the coming storm over the dancer's own private life.[405]

In April 1908 Asquith succeeded Sir Henry Campbell-Bannerman as Prime Minister. The following year, Sylvia's father, Lyulph, succeeded to his second barony on the death of his grandmother. His newly acquired title of Lord Sheffield soon became his preferred designation and he used this in his increasing appearances in the House of Lords. When he attended debates, he would stay at the Stanley's London house at 18 Mansfield Street and he would often be joined by Sylvia. They were both in the capital shortly after the death of the King in 1910 and witnessed the aftermath. There was widespread mourning and streets were sometimes thick with black shrouded figures observing the official mourning period. In fact it became so *de rigeur* to be seen in mourning attire that it almost prompted a fashion, though too many of the general public, hoping to be thought of as court insiders, sported the 'garments of woe' long after the appointed mourning period.[406] The streets of central London were still full of horse-drawn cabs and broughams, despite the emergence of the motor car, and at busy thoroughfares such as Marble Arch and Oxford Circus the dung and rubbish mounted up. The age of the 'Crossing Sweepers' seemed a distant memory.

In 1909, Anthony was sent to Staff College, Camberley, to train as a staff officer and Sylvia joined him with their two girls, in a house in the town. Their rather stilted social life revolved around the College and Sylvia had to make do with hearing stories and gossip from her sister Venetia about their family and friends in Alderley or down in London. Not all news was good; during one of her frequent visits to the family house in Mansfield Street, Venetia heard that her friend, Violet Asquith, had suffered a tragic loss. Violet's admirer, Archie Gordon, was killed in a motoring accident and Venetia was quick to comfort her. The two became very close companions and it was during this period that Venetia came into contact with Violet's father, H.H. Asquith. The Prime Minister wrote the first of his letters to her in 1910, and in January 1912, Venetia joined Violet on holiday in Sicily with Asquith and Edwin Montagu, Under-Secretary of State for India and a member of Asquith's Liberal Government. Montagu was pursuing Venetia and had even asked her to marry him – a proposal that at first she accepted and then later declined. He was no Adonis but he was persistent and was clearly besotted with Venetia. Meanwhile, Asquith remained oblivious to his colleague's amorous ambitions and following their return from holiday, he invited Venetia to a house party, following this up with invitations to 10 Downing Street. During 1913, he kept up his correspondence with her; but there were no signs yet of his obsessive love of later years. Venetia was no conventional beauty but as a friend, Lawrence Jones, observed, she had 'aquiline good looks and a masculine intellect'. Despite her limited education, as befitted an aristocratic lady, 'she carried the Anthologies in her head and walked the high garden walls of Alderley with the casual stride of a boy.'[407]

Asquith, with or without passion in his life, was always focussed on the political battle of the time. With support from Lloyd George and Winston Churchill, Asquith attacked the power of the House of Lords in retaliation for their suppression of his party's 'People's Budget' in 1909. With much lobbying and arm-twisting, Asquith managed to push through the 1911 Parliament Act, which prevented the Lords from vetoing any legislation that had originated in the Commons. It was heady stuff, and while Lyulph Sheffield would be personally hit by the new Liberal land taxes, his loyalty remained with the party. Nonetheless, he was relieved that Asquith's threat to flood the Lords with 100 new Liberal peers did not materialise. However, both Lyulph and Asquith did share common ground over the increasingly violent debate on women's suffrage. Both argued forcibly against votes for women and Asquith had been physically attacked and had his windows smashed, while Lyulph argued for penal servitude and hard labour for the offenders.[408]

In 1911 Anthony was appointed General Staff Officer Grade 3 (GSO3). This meant that he and Sylvia could be together in London and they leased a house at 83 Queen's Gate, near Kensington Gardens. Two years later Anthony celebrated his appointment as Brigade Major, 2nd Cavalry Brigade, under the polo fanatic Brigadier-General

Beavoir de Lisle. And it was not long before he and Sylvia received further good news. Not only was she pregnant but Anthony's younger brother, Francis, became engaged to Lady Dorothy Howard. She was yet another of Sylvia's cousins. The irony was that while Francis was a brewer, Lady Dorothy's mother was a well-known campaigner for teetotalism.

On 18 December 1913, Sylvia gave birth to another daughter Elizabeth, but her joy was cruelly cut short by the baby's death several weeks later. While Sylvia mourned the loss of her daughter, she received regular visits from Venetia, who lightened the mood with tales of her love life and in particular, her two admirers, Edwin Montagu and H.H. Asquith. Asquith was writing regularly to his adored Venetia telling her of constant lobbying from the suffragist movement and his harassment by the more militant suffragettes. But Asquith's Liberal Government faced a more immediate threat. As a price for the support, several years before, of Irish MPs for the 1911 Parliament Act, Asquith was now under pressure to establish Home Rule for Ireland. However, his introduction of the Third Irish Home Rule Bill in 1912 had merely inflamed an already nervous Protestant population, including a number of prominent soldiers. Tension was mounting and while Asquith was playing bridge late one evening in March 1914 with the Stanleys, he was alerted by telegram that Brigadier-General Hubert Gough, GOC 3rd Cavalry Brigade, together with other officers in the brigade quartered near Dublin, threatened to resign their commissions as a protest. They objected to the possibility that they would be sent in to quell Ulster's opposition to Home Rule. The 'Curragh Incident', as it became known, had the whiff of mutiny about it and highlighted the very real possibility of civil war. Concessions were made at the last minute and the cavalry officers backed down. But Asquith was furious when he learnt that extra concessions were added without Cabinet sanction. He wrote about the full details of the drama to Venetia, presumably aware that her brother-in-law Anthony Henley held a commission in the 5th Lancers, the regiment that contained most of the belligerents. Indeed, Asquith was very anxious to keep Anthony close to him and when the PM took on the role of Secretary of State for War in April, one of his first appointments was Captain Anthony Henley as his Private Secretary. Asquith attempted to run the War Office at the same time as carrying out his duties as Prime Minister – a state of affairs that continued until the outbreak of war in August. It was not as if Asquith had a clear desk, for domestic controversies were raging all around him. Sir Edward Carson and his Unionists were trying to derail the Irish Home Rule Bill, while the findings of the select committee on the Marconi scandal reverberated through Westminster. Yet despite these undoubted problems, Asquith kept up a fast and furious correspondence with Venetia, firing off 236 letters during 1914 alone.

Anthony Henley, as Private Secretary, played a secondary role to Sir Herbert Creedy, the professional civil servant who was the Principal Private Secretary in the War Office. Nonetheless, it was a plum job and his appointment probably owed more to Venetia's influence with Asquith than personal merit. Venetia was, after all, extremely fond of her brother-in-law. Perhaps, too fond.

'One Half of a Pair of Scissors'

As soon as war was declared on 4 August, Captain Anthony Henley extricated himself from his administration job at the War Office and joined his regiment, the 5th (Royal Irish) Lancers. The bulk of the cavalry regiment were mobilising at their depot at Marlborough Barracks, Dublin, to form part of the 3rd Cavalry Brigade bound for France. All the cavalry regiments were short of horses, which had to be rapidly purchased from all over Ireland. As the mixture of officers' chargers, troop horses and heavier artillery horses arrived, they all had to be checked by veterinary surgeons, re-shod and groomed. The cavalrymen had to check their swords, lances, Lee-Enfield rifles as well as their uniforms, bandoliers and personal kit. Finally, on 15 August, the flotilla steamed out of Dublin on the two-day voyage to Le Havre, where the 9000 men and horses of the 1st Cavalry Division were assembling. When the 5th Lancers arrived, Anthony marshalled his troopers in 'C' Squadron and they marched and entrained up to the front, saving the horses. But no sooner had the 5th Lancers arrived at the outskirts of Mons and taken up positions on the flanks of the British Expeditionary Force, than the call went out to retire, and the Retreat from Mons began. Anthony and his men acted as the rearguard covering the brigade withdrawal, skirmishing with the enemy as they fell back.[409]

As the opposing armies wheeled and tilted in a bid to outflank each other, the civilian population in Britain saw the first tangible results of the fighting. Increasing numbers of casualties were arriving at hospitals in London and the south-east. Asquith toured some of the hospitals, encountering the wounded from Anthony's regiment, the 5th Lancers, including their Commanding Officer, Lieutenant-Colonel Parker, who was felled in one of the first engagements.[410] The sight of the prostrate cavalry officer alarmed Asquith, reminding him that his old friend Anthony might be amongst the dead or wounded. He checked the casualty reports, found he was safe and telegrammed Sylvia without delay. Asquith was still feeling guilty about Anthony. He had pulled him away from a previously comfortable job to become his Private Secretary at the War Office. Anthony had proved 'most useful and helpful' in his role, but Asquith had now relinquished his role as Secretary of State for War, to concentrate on the Premiership, and had installed Lord Kitchener in his place. When the war was over, and it seemed that might not be too long, Anthony would be left working with the taciturn and formidable 'K'. Asquith had a word with the

Commander-in-Chief, Field Marshal Sir John French, and Anthony soon found himself transferred, much to his dismay, away from the front and on to French's Staff as a GSO2.[411] Anthony was keen to see action, unlike some of his older colleagues, who came in for criticism:

Dug-out officers, more particularly senior ones, welcomed war. To them came power and pay without any danger. Unhappy husbands and miserable wives welcomed war as a way out and even courted death. Munitions makers and caterers, clothiers and countless other people welcomed war.[412]

Women were apprehensive about the war, but supportive of their men. For those pressing for women's rights, the outbreak of hostilities presented a quandary. Mrs Emmeline Pankhurst realised that those behind the cause of women's suffrage had to be seen to be helping a nation in need. 'I who have been against the Government,' she declared, 'am now for it. Our country's war shall be our war.' But while Emmeline swung her Women's Social and Political Union to the right, her daughter Sylvia Pankhurst became more radical and adopted a rigid anti-war stance. Even for those women willing to help, there were immediate obstacles to their involvement. The eminent Scot, Dr Elsie Inglis, attempted to raise a women's ambulance unit, but received a rebuff from the War Office. 'My good lady,' she was told, 'go home and sit still.' Her reply was unprintable, but in these early days before the war had sapped the nation, entrenched attitudes held sway. [413] And as the first winter of the war approached, some soldiers were disparaging of women's attempts to help:

There are thousands of worthy people in the old country who hardly have an idea the war is on, or what it means. Others run hospitals, great and small because it is the thing to do; others trot off to war-work gaily and make splints and bandages for the broken, as if they were selling programmes at a society matinee. They use the work centres as gas and gossip clubs and talk over the scandals of society … Remember many of the men and women at home are having the time of their lives; only the war victims themselves, personally hurt through the death of their nearest and dearest, really know what war is.[414]

Such feelings demonstrated the gulf between those who had experienced combat and those who had not. It was an age-old difference, but made starker in the First World War by the sheer proximity of London to the battlefront in France. To be fair, many on the Home Front such as women or older men had little choice but to help raise funds for Belgian refugees or make bandages on 'mules' for the wounded. One person, though, who could not be accused of lethargy, was the Prime Minister. H.H. Asquith started the war with a huge workload and his capacity for dealing with paperwork and administration was legendary. His output of correspondence was extraordinary and a good many of the letters he wrote every day included social mail. The principal object of his affection remained Venetia Stanley, with whom he was devastatingly smitten, even though the age difference – he was 62 and she was 27 – made the relationship more than questionable. He wrote to her, sometimes two or three times a day, while in the House of Commons or when he was conducting Cabinet meetings. He was so consumed with passion that he appeared oblivious to his Cabinet colleague Edwin Montagu and his desire for the same woman. Nevertheless, he was still in possession of sharp mental faculties and his ability to organise and administer the business of government did not seem to be impaired by the distraction of Venetia. Physically, he was not in great shape but off-duty, he was far from stuffy and was good company, as Winston Churchill found on many occasions:

> He [Asquith] frequently set the whole party competing who could write down in five minutes, the most Generals beginning with L, or poets beginning with a T, or historians with some other initial. He had innumerable varieties of these games and always excelled in them.[415]

While Venetia may not have been available to compete with Asquith's appetite for Greek texts, she nevertheless had a keen wit and intellect and was in her sexual prime. Ultimately, it was her passion and energy that Asquith needed and demanded. In the same way that Field Marshal Sir John French required his mistress, Winifred Bennett, to confide in and to act as his safety valve, so Asquith needed Venetia as a sounding board and to confirm that he was still intellectually alive. She had little dress sense and she was no classical beauty, with one friend describing her as 'a splendid, virginal, comradely creature'. But that is precisely what Asquith required, for he probably did not have the physical stamina to keep up with a highly-strung beauty, preferring a mistress who could stimulate his intellect and massage his ego. When he later confessed all to Sylvia, he claimed that Venetia had never even kissed him, though such limited physical contact seemed unavoidable.[416] Asquith was content to adore her, rather than physically possess her and he was unequivocal about his love, even if it was not consummated. 'Darling, I love you: how much I cannot put into words, but *some day* you will know.' Perhaps he was in love with love, with the idea of romance, for such passion did not preclude him from enjoying the company of other women, particularly Lady Scott, widow of the polar explorer. He was also much taken with Mrs Hilda Harrison, whom he first met when staying with his sister-in-law at Easton Grey, near Malmesbury, Wiltshire. It was a friendship that was to last until his death.[417]

Despite his political commitments during the war, Asquith found time to visit both Alderley and Penrhôs, with or without Margot, but his visits always coincided with Venetia's. Sylvia was also a fixture at any party as she remained based at Alderley with the children for most of the war years. Rosalind, Kitty and Juliet grew up under the watchful eye of the Stanley grandparents, in the rambling and 'unbeautiful' Alderley Park, which was also home to any number of their cousins, all safely corralled together away from the danger of Zeppelin attacks around London. With the girls dressed in white muslin and the boys kitted out in sailor suits, the children were taught, until they were thirteen, by a French governess and old Stanley retainer, Mademoiselle Marie-Leczinka Dombe, and enjoyed all the advantages of life on a country estate. They saw little of their father, who only made infrequent visits to Alderley and according to one cousin, the Henley children evinced 'terror' in the presence of their strict parents. Rather like Winston Churchill, who said of his socialite mother, Jenny, 'I loved her dearly, but at a distance,' so Sylvia may have seemed a remote figure to her children. However, in the holidays at Penrhôs, she would take them bathing or arrange picnic trips, joining with the inexhaustible supply of cousins and aunts. Or when they were brought down to London with their nanny to stay at Mansfield Street, Sylvia would take them on expeditions to the Natural History Museum, Madame Tussaud's, or the Tower of London. Summer months were often spent at Penrhôs in Anglesey, which was still the remote sanctuary that it had been before the war. Sylvia would take her children for picnics on Mill Island, a small outcrop that boasted a 'Stanley Windmill', or there would be outings farther along the coast where a Stanley folly, Twr Ellin, towered above the cliffs. The children missed their father and their letters to him during the war betray a love and touching innocence. However, through lack of time or inclination, he rarely seemed to respond. Nonetheless, despite their emotional and sometimes geographical distance, Sylvia and Anthony instilled in the children from a young age a capacity for hard work and industry. Above all, the Henley children continued to exude a spirited self-confidence that was a trademark of the Stanley inheritance.[418]

In January 1915 Sylvia admonished Asquith over his dominating influence over Venetia. In her customary direct manner, she told the 'Prime' that he was both a good and bad influence on her sister. He, of course, was totally surprised to be accused of exerting influence, as he argued that all power lay with Venetia. He didn't realise how right he was, for unknown to him, she had embarked on a dangerous game of balancing Asquith's obsession with the passionate designs of Edwin Montagu. Sylvia was aware of this double game, and this may have accelerated her correspondence with Asquith, pitting herself against her sister for the ear of the PM. She wrote to Asquith, warning him about stories circulating that he had initially rejected the idea of dispatching an expeditionary force to France and Belgium in 1914; he was therefore seen as lukewarm about defending 'plucky Belgium'. There was also increasing disquiet in some military quarters that shell production was flagging.[419]

Conscious that he had to be seen promoting the industrial muscle behind the war effort, on 20 April 1915 Asquith travelled north to Newcastle to witness munitions manufacture and to address the workers. He went armed with Lord Kitchener's assurance that all was well with the supply of shells and that contrary to stories about troops being let down by shortages, there was no cause for concern. But all was not well. Kitchener was keen to grasp any hint of optimism from his C-in-C, Field Marshal Sir John French that his troops were ready and confident of success in the forthcoming operations. Kitchener wrote to Asquith on 14 April, assuring the Prime Minister that ammunition supplies were not a problem. But there was a chronic shortage of high explosive (HE) shells, and the Battle of Aubers Ridge on 9 May reinforced this desperate truth.[420]

At this time, Asquith was writing to Venetia daily; although he was aware that she had another suitor, he was oblivious to the fact that she had reignited a relationship with Edwin Montagu, a member of his own cabinet. Worse still, he had no idea that Venetia was even showing his love letters to Montagu.[421] While Venetia played a duplicitous game with her suitors, Sylvia looked on. Her own marriage seemed to be sound, though she felt Anthony, or 'Chunky' as he was now known, could always write more often. But then, he was very busy in France and his career prospects had improved with his recent promotion to GSO1. Most families of regular officers felt proud of the role that their husbands were playing in the war, but they were also mindful that the conflict could make or break their careers. With a transfer from French's staff to the staff of the 49th Division and the temporary rank of Lieutenant-Colonel, Anthony's rise looked assured. Sylvia and Anthony exchanged very loving letters on 22 April and the following day, a contented Sylvia was able to report on the latest house party at Alderley, which included Asquith and Montagu. Both the politicians seemed to have monopolised Lady Sheffield, telling her that according to the French and British C-in-Cs, the war would 'not last beyond August'. Sylvia thought Venetia was in good spirits and not in the 'low dampish mood' of recent weeks. It was no coincidence that several days later, Venetia decided secretly to accept Montagu's proposal of marriage, which may have accounted for her lighter spirits. Tellingly, Sylvia also observed that Montagu was in a chipper mood and 'not the morose man he can be'.[422]

Days later, on 24 April, while at his divisional headquarters in France, Anthony wrote lovingly to his wife about their ninth wedding anniversary. For some reason, Sylvia failed to respond with the same enthusiasm. 'What a curiously cold creature I am at times,' she confessed to him. Having had three daughters, one of whom had died prematurely, it seems that her failure to produce a son was haunting her and she was consumed with the prospect that at 33, time was running out. She busied herself with helping out in the temporary military hospital set up in the Tenants Hall, a splendid annexe to Alderley Park, named for its use for the annual tenants' dinner. She did much of the auxiliary nursing work that a VAD would do; sterilizing equipment, preparing and rolling bandages but the work of removing dressings required a more trained hand. The 'morning straffe' as it was known from the screams of the wounded, meant the removal of blood-sodden bandages from festering wounds – a most unpleasant experience for the nurse and an even worse one for any of the 23 patients.[423]

Sylvia came down to the Stanley's London house at 18 Mansfield Street on 3 May to catch up with friends in town. In May of each year, the families with country houses tended to decamp to their London houses for the three-month season of art exhibitions, racing, balls and grand dinners. The war had curtailed many of these activities and although Lyulph and Maisie Sheffield were never followers of the herd, their children had tended to support the events. Sylvia also intended to visit Lady Dorothy Henley, wife of Anthony's brother, Francis, who was serving with the Royal Naval Division in the Dardanelles. They lived at nearby Montagu Square, and there were enough other friends to ensure a busy fortnight for Sylvia. She also met Venetia at the house, who was preparing for her forthcoming trip to France where she would work as a nurse in a stationary hospital. Asquith believed her motives for going were not entirely patriotic, since she was tired of the strictures of country house life during the War and anticipated that 'hospital drudgery' might somehow give her a new zest for 'the pleasures of the world'. Asquith had arranged a party at his home for 8 May but Venetia had already accepted an invitation to stay with Winston and Clementine Churchill at Hoe Farm in Surrey, so declined. However, it was the first time Asquith had invited Sylvia to 'The Wharf' to join Lloyd George, the Chief Justice, Violet Asquith and Maurice ('Bongie') Bonham Carter. She would train up to Oxford and be collected by Asquith's motor for the short drive down to the house, set back from the River Thames at Sutton Courtenay, near Abingdon. Venetia was always a little condescending about the size and style of the house, which was built in handsome red brick, originally eighteenth century, but converted more recently by Walter Cave. Still, despite its lack of pretension, it could comfortably accommodate a good house party; and Asquith was intent that weekend on adding to his 'harem'.

The Prime Minister had the capacity to love several women at the same time and he was becoming increasingly absorbed by Sylvia. Margot Asquith was keen for this relationship to develop, as it drew her husband away from Venetia, whom she saw as the real threat. But Violet Asquith, who was incredibly possessive of her father, sensed a new, more dangerous challenge to her father's affections, from Sylvia. Violet spent most of the weekend house party at The Wharf trying to freeze out Sylvia, but failed. Sylvia was flattered by the PM's attention, though wary of his motives, as she insisted on telling her husband:

> As we went to bed, the PM said he must show me his room. I was rather against this, as his affectionate nature gets the better of his wisdom, as you know. But there was no gainsaying him. We were standing talking, his arm around me, of books. French novelists like David and Balzac, a branch of literature, which I know better than any other, so I was not at so complete a disadvantage as on most other topics. When Violet came in, she hoped to break up the party – the arm slipped away a bit – but she looked just like a nettle. She says the PM was not going to be disturbed, tho' I would have welcomed being able to get away without paying the toll, which I knew would be inevitable … I knew for certain he would exact a kiss from me, and knowing this I was glad it should be one of sympathy for that part of his life that I know about. And I told him how much love and sympathy I felt for him and kissed him – he can't do without affection … To me it is always a blot that the PM

cannot like one without the physical side coming in so much. I should like him so much better if he held my hand and did not paw so much.[424]

The following morning, as the house party reassembled in the morning room to write their customary letters to friends and family, Asquith composed a letter to Venetia with news of their activities, mentioning that of course this was Sylvia's first visit. He declared his fondness for Sylvia and confirmed that he was taking her for a drive in his motor around the countryside – a joy previously confined to Venetia, and which had happened on over 100 previous occasions. While exhibiting the usual devotion to Venetia in his letter, Asquith was trying to make Venetia jealous of her sister; but it was completely futile. Venetia was about to tell him, after months of vacillating, that she planned to marry Montagu.[425]

After Asquith's house party, Sylvia returned to Mansfield Street to find Venetia ill in bed with a high fever. Prior to leaving for France, she had to receive the usual inoculations but suffered a bad reaction and fell ill. Edwin visited but instead of attending the bedside, spent more time downstairs with Sylvia, lamenting the lack of love from Venetia. Suddenly, the doorbell rang and Sylvia quickly dispatched him upstairs while she received the next visitor. The situation soon degenerated into farce when she realised it was Asquith at the door. He was shown into the drawing room, unaware of his rival upstairs. Sylvia told him that Venetia was too ill to see anyone and proceeded to occupy the PM downstairs, though there was the usual prospect of some fumbling. 'I must say, honestly,' she wrote to her husband, 'his hand holding bores me very much. To begin with, he ceases to talk normally and is rather a silly old man.' Nonetheless, Asquith seemed keen to give Sylvia an update on the recent fall-out between Sir John French and one of his Army Commanders, General Horace Smith-Dorrien. Even if the PM's pawing proved a bore, Sylvia was flattered to be taken into his confidence.[426]

Venetia wrote to Asquith at midnight on 11 May and dropped her bombshell. During the morning of 12 May, Asquith received her letter announcing her engagement to Edwin Montagu. Although stunned by the news, he continued his lunch appointment with Prince Paul of Serbia, followed by a raucous Prime Minister's Question Time in the House of Commons. Despite his undoubted emotional turmoil, he had the ability to compartmentalise his mind; to split his thoughts between the business of state and heart. While still in the House, he summoned a few short sentences and despatched what amounted to a confirmation of receipt to Venetia. Shortly afterwards, he rushed off another letter, but this time it was addressed to Sylvia. Several hours later, he addressed a second letter to Sylvia, in which he agonised over Venetia's choice of Montagu and the fact that he could not cope with being thrown over in favour of a man he considered his physical and emotional inferior. Though there was much anguish and wounded pride, he turned surprisingly quickly to Sylvia for support, asking and then demanding to know why Venetia had betrayed him. Sylvia attempted to soothe the PM's heartache but she could do little to temper his outrage over another issue – Venetia's decision to convert to Judaism, as a condition of the marriage.[427]

Although Montagu had pressure from his brother and sister not to marry a Christian – 'they are all so totally unlike the Jews' he was told – it was the influence of his father Lord Swaythling that ultimately decided the issue. He would not pass on his inheritance to Edwin unless he married a Jewess. Sylvia was aware that for her sister, conversion was not a seismic leap, since she had no faith at all, but the prospect of being poor was far more terrifying. Sylvia thought that Venetia was 'fond' of Montagu and found him 'companionable' but did not love him. After all, she could hardly even bare to kiss him. And if she was not in love with him, what would happen if she really fell in love with someone else?[428]

The English upper class had an ambivalent attitude to the Jews. While men like Sir Ernest Cassel, Philip Sassoon or Alfred de Rothschild were fêted for their financial acumen and generosity, and regularly appeared at court and in the great aristocratic houses, there remained suspicion behind their backs. George V, unlike his father, had little time for the Jewish race and a modern reader might be shocked at the number of anti-Semitic remarks contained in some of the diaries of hostesses of the day. Amongst senior military commanders there was a feeling that the Jews were a race apart. Sir John French was happy to record, 'We dined at the Carlton. Such an awful crowd – mostly Jews by the look of them.' Sir Douglas Haig might comment: 'Mr Montagu, Minister of Munitions, came to see me … I thought him a capable and agreeable man. (He is apparently a Jew).' No doubt it was ignorance, fear or jealousy that motivated such remarks, but for men like Edwin Montague, seemingly at the centre of power, it was a wounding reminder that however talented or artistic a Jew might be, he would never quite enter the inner sanctum of London society. Neither was being a Jew in academia or the legal profession free of such stigma. A Balliol man, L.E. Jones, recalled a Junior Counsel who shared his barristers' chambe, describing a Jewish colleague as 'a bottle-shouldered, flat-footed Jew, who had been to neither public school nor university, who had never played a game or walked a mile in his life.' The intolerance was mindless, in the way that people might be condemned for their accents, hairstyles or shoes, and this suspicion amongst the upper classes was not just confined to Britain. Amongst the wealthy and educated Protestant circles of America's east coast, Jews found they were on the outside, a position reinforced by Harvard University's restricted admission quotas for Jewish students.[429]

On 13 May, Sylvia was acting as gatekeeper at Mansfield Street. Montagu appeared and went up to see Venetia in her bedroom where there was more mutual agonising and wailing – Venetia over the PM and Montagu over her lack of love for him. Meanwhile, Sylvia received another three letters from Asquith, discussing the emotional turmoil – but he was rapidly regaining control of his love life and steering Sylvia into the now vacant position of head confidante. 'But whom have I but you to turn to?' he reasoned and proceeded to flatter her. 'You are wise and loving and know everything.'[430] It was intoxicating language, particularly since it was Venetia who had always laid claim to scholarship in the past. It was no secret to those around them that Sylvia had rapidly replaced Venetia in Asquith's affections. Maurice Bonham Carter, private secretary to the PM and shortly to marry Violet, closely observed his master. 'I do not quite know what are his hobbies now, Sylvia to some extent I think.' He was careful to add, 'My impression is that he is not unhappy.'[431] Indeed, Asquith, in between his laments about Venetia's fate, was finding contentment in his relationship with Sylvia. He met her on the evening of 13 May after dinner with mutual friends and insisted that she partner him for a game of bridge. The following day Asquith asked her to dine with him, but not before she had accompanied him for a two-hour drive, when the PM was able once again to vent his anger at the union between Venetia and Montagu. Venetia's decision to convert to Judaism had caused him much grief and though it was of little consequence to the agnostic Venetia, to the PM it smacked of betrayal of her class and clan. One of the most vehement opponents of the match was Violet Asquith, Venetia's old friend. 'The whole thing simply revolts me,' she wrote to her brother Arthur, 'both in its physical & spiritual aspect.'

In fact, the union, or at least the physical side of it, also repelled Venetia. She repeatedly told Montagu that sex would only take place on her terms, should she want it, but that she should also be free to seek it elsewhere. With Asquith, there had been 'correspondence sex', but it is most probable that he and Venetia barely kissed and petted and it stopped there, the grand affair was never physically consummated. Furthermore, Sylvia, as a confidante of both the parties, believed that Venetia and Asquith never slept together. Venetia's sexuality remained a mystery, for although she later engaged in plenty of extra-marital affairs, it seems her attraction to men was perhaps analytical or detached. She could still remain emotionally aloof, a state of affairs that had both frustrated and intrigued Asquith. (Ironically, he shared the same fate as the victim in La Belle Dame sans Merci, a ballad by his favourite poet, Keats.) She even admitted to Montagu, 'I'm completely cold-blooded' and the only love she could offer a man was 'thin and meagre'. Raymond Asquith believed that Venetia had lesbian tendencies, a judgement reinforced when she told him of a 'Sapphic dinner' she enjoyed with Diana Manners, just months after her marriage to Montagu. While such activities may have been just 'larky experiments' for Diana, for Venetia they indicated a wider agenda and may explain her willingness to conduct long affairs with two men who were satisfied with very limited sexual contact. For his part, Asquith was hardly in the peak of physical condition, and although he generated some fumbling advances towards his 'harem', it seems his sexual demands on Venetia were very limited.[432]

While superficially, Margot initially supported the idea of the Montagu/Stanley marriage, especially since it removed such an intimate of her husband, in private she could become hysterical about the way she had been treated. After a Howard family wedding on 15 May, Margot quickly retreated from the Henry VII Chapel, taking Sylvia with her. As they sat in private, Margot 'began by incoherent spasms' and then, according to Sylvia, launched into a torrent of abuse about how badly she was treated

by Sylvia and her friends while Asquith had continued his relationship with Venetia.
[433] Sylvia made her retract her 'vilest accusations' and Margot became more subdued but the climate of intrigue continued.[434]

Sylvia then went back to Alderley together with Venetia and Montagu, but it was hardly a warm welcome. Despite his advancing years, Lyulph Sheffield was still determined to be heard on the subject of the marriage. His bearded, ruddy face and twinkling eyes belied his trenchant opinions and he lost no time in voicing his opposition. He was 'fearfully disappointed', viewing the prospect of the marriage 'with deep distaste', while Lady Sheffield was rather depressed and proceeded to rant at Sylvia. After a while, Sylvia tired of her mother's criticism that she had spent too much time in London and disappeared with Montagu in tow, to help him choose some pearls as an engagement present for Venetia. Writing to her husband that night, Sylvia was in desperate need of support. 'I want for your companionship and your advice,' she pleaded, but it was a mixed message to Anthony. On the one hand, she wanted to show him how the PM now needed her and it was her duty to console him, but on the other she genuinely claimed she needed her husband. The idea of 'duty' shown by women to men engaged in war, or the prosecution of war, was not as strange as it seems. There was a campaign in Britain and to a greater extent in France to encourage women to write to soldiers they had never met, in an effort to boost morale. It was seen as a woman's patriotic duty and even if the correspondence led to passion, it was not seen as immoral behaviour. Yet, duty or not, Anthony was unlikely to see Asquith's repeated approaches to his wife and her reaction as patriotic. Sylvia delighted in the attention and even enjoyed the fact that her younger sister, who was always the star, was no longer in the limelight. 'I am certain it cuts her to see the PM is fond of me,' she wrote. There were more car drives around Richmond Park, Esher and Woking, with Asquith behind the wheel and Sylvia, her hat suitably anchored with a silk scarf, listening, laughing and cajoling the PM out of his sullen mood. He loved it. She wrote, 'He is now very fond of me in just the most wonderfully nice way. I hope our relations will never change.'[435]

Asquith was also facing his most potent political challenge at this very time. He and his Liberal Government were heavily criticised for their seemingly weak prosecution of the war. This was compounded by the 'Shell Scandal' which had erupted on 9 May, but it was the conscription issue, and the Liberal Government's failure to prepare for the inevitable compulsory call-up, that sealed its fate. The increasingly erratic First Sea Lord, Lord Fisher, resigned on 14 May – yet again – because of his inability to work with Winston Churchill and went into hiding at the Charing Cross Hotel. Admiral 'Jacky' Fisher's resignation caused a major headache for Asquith. The increasingly wild First Sea Lord had already tried to resign in January when his proposal to shoot all German prisoners-of-war held in Britain, in reprisal for the German Zeppelin raids, was vetoed by the First Lord of the Admiralty, Winston Churchill.[436] Asquith would later look back at this month of anguish and recall that there were compensations. 'One of my most valued and intimate correspondents at this time was Mrs Henley.'[437] Indeed, not only was Sylvia becoming a correspondent, she was also on hand to calm the Prime Minister in his anxious state. He wrote daily, sometimes twice a day, to Sylvia during the turmoil and although he claimed the loss of Venetia made him feel like 'one half of a pair of scissors', he now pursued Sylvia with the same energy and urgency that he had employed with her sister. His letters were followed up with late-night personal visits to Mansfield Street and if he found Sylvia out, he would leave petulant messages – 'I suppose you will be at your damned Red Cross.'[438] Being the confidante of the PM was becoming a full-time occupation, though the receipt of daily missives from Downing Street with the red seal over the envelope flap was still exhilarating.

With so many political factions developing, as well as a concerted press campaign and an increasingly hostile Conservative opposition, the Liberal Cabinet finally split on 25 May. Asquith, despite his private emotional turmoil, deftly welded together a coalition government with the Conservatives and Unionists, but there were casualties. As a price for joining the coalition, the Conservatives demanded the removal of Churchill from the Admiralty and Lord Haldane was also sacrificed, while Montagu lost his Cabinet place but maintained influence as Financial Secretary at the Treasury. The upheaval was critical for another reason. Lord Kitchener remained as head of the War Office but lost responsibility for munitions productions and David Lloyd George was brought in as the new Minister of Munitions, a move that would invigorate the arms industry and yoke British industry to the war effort.

It was Sylvia's steady and empathetic friendship that saw Asquith through this turbulent political and emotional sea. He loved his wife Margot but she was exhausting and her judgements erratic. Violet was too close to her father to render dispassionate advice but Sylvia knew the system and the personalities. 'He has such confidence in me,' she wrote, 'that I can act as a safety valve – he can say exactly what he thinks and feels.' And he said it all. In fact, far too much about his colleagues, his enemies and his fears for the future, so that Sylvia felt her knowledge was a liability. 'I will tell you one day,' she wrote to Anthony, 'something he told me. I dare not put it down, as it really would matter so terribly if anybody else by accident opened this letter.'[439] Intimacy was becoming a problem. The day after the collapse of the last Gladstonian Liberal Government, Asquith took Sylvia for another long car drive and used her as a sounding board for his promotions and demotions to the new coalition Cabinet. When they parted, Asquith kissed her. He always kissed her if they parted in private and this worried her. When his mind had been in turmoil over Venetia, a kiss for compassion had been acceptable to her, in the manner of a kiss she would give her father. But now she didn't consider it necessary. She also knew that Asquith was 'very, very fond' of her, as she repeatedly told Anthony who was fully occupied on the Western Front and was helpless to respond. Perhaps she wanted to make him jealous because she sensed in his letters to her that he was not giving her the attention or the passion she desired. However, she did not tell Anthony that barely two weeks after the news of Venetia's betrothal, Asquith had in fact confessed to Sylvia, 'You are my anchor and I love you and need you.'[440]

While her children remained at Alderley, Sylvia spent more time at the Stanley town house in Mansfield Street. She was finding dinner parties in town were livelier, but travelling to them could be an ordeal – an early experience with drunks, as well as a proposition from a Glaswegian on the 'Tube' convinced her that cabs were a much safer mode of transport. She was available to accompany the PM at a moment's notice, but the downside entailed having to mediate in the perpetual dramas between Venetia and Montagu. They were due to be married on 26 July 1915 and although Venetia was preparing to be received into the Jewish faith, their relationship was decidedly unstable. They would take it in turns to appear at Mansfield Street in tears. Sylvia would have to listen to tantrums and weeping followed by remorse, which was extremely wearying. The cycle was only broken by Venetia leaving for a short trip to France on 24 May, where she was to work as a nursing auxiliary for a month in a small hospital at Wimereux. When she came back, there would be further angst. Asquith, by comparison, was easier for Sylvia to handle and his mortification over Venetia appeared to recede by the day, though Sylvia was constantly on the lookout for the 'blue beast' emerging.[441] After a long evening at The Wharf with Asquith and others, she wrote to Anthony:

> After dinner the PM said he'd like a little talk with me later. It was already after 11 – and tho' I love being with him – I rather wanted to go to bed (and talks late at night have an element of danger). He did not come for me till nearly midnight and we went and sat in his bedroom on either side of the fire. I won't sit next to him, as too much 'close quarters' comes in and I think he realises that. We talked of the war and how appallingly he felt the responsibility at times ... and then we talked of our relations. I wanted to first tell him that so long as it remained platonic there was nothing I wanted more, but as soon as I felt there was a danger of that form of love giving place to the other – it must be all over.[442]

She repeatedly fended off his rather weak physical approaches, such as kissing or enveloping arms, and when she reproached him for his gestures, he wrote startled apologies to her, disclaiming all thoughts of sex. Yet, his letters gush with superlatives as he explained that his love for her was set on a higher frequency and that it was an idealised love. 'An erotic adventure,' he protested, 'was never my idea.'[443]

Sylvia's 'no-nonsense' attitude to life also infused her ideas on sexual relations. She was married and took her vows seriously, and although she relished the company of men, she seemed naive about what they expected. This was similar to many of her social class, in marked contrast to the more experienced working-class women. One candid docker's wife was heard warning a new young wife, whose husband was departing for the front:

> You don't know what you're up agen yet. But you wait till you've been to bed over three thousand nights with the same man, like me, and had to put up with everything, then you'd be bloomin' glad the old Kaiser went potty.[444]

Potty or not, the Kaiser was keeping the pressure on the British and French lines. At the end of May, Asquith was compelled to visit the front and witness British operations and talk to generals about supplies and logistics. While staying at GHQ with Sir John French, he sent Sylvia daily bulletins about the military operations. He was clearly impressed with the elaborate trench systems in place and some of his observations to Sylvia would have been useful if they had fallen into enemy hands. However, he was less inspired by an evening with the Commander of the 7th Division, Major-General Hubert Gough. The Irishman had been a thorn in Asquith's side during the 'Curragh Incident' the previous year, and Asquith thought it ironic that both he and French should now be guests of the 'fecund' general.[445]

Even while he was on vital business in France, Asquith was persuaded by Venetia to visit her at the hospital. She was still keen that their relationship could flourish, even after she became married to Montagu, but Asquith was not so sure. He wrote a letter to her on 11 June, elegising over what might have been and signing off as 'broken-hearted and ever-devoted', but behind the mask of remorse, he had moved on. He was consumed with Sylvia, but she, too, was playing a dangerous game. While she believed that 'it is manifestly my duty to do all I can' to relax the PM, and Asquith himself was keen to point out that Margot was 'delighted' about their relationship, there would come a time when Asquith would become obsessive about his new conquest. Sylvia also tried to allay Anthony's fears by reminding him that 'I have not the component parts to hold his affection like Venetia.' It was quite a balancing act both to inform and placate all the players in Sylvia's life, and at times it must have proved complicated to remember who had been told what. In common with other women of her class, a good deal of the day would be taken up with letter writing to relatives and friends. She wrote daily to Anthony and regularly to her mother, her siblings Venetia and Oliver, her older daughters, Rosalind and Kitty, as well as a host of friends. Then there was her incoming mail to deal with each day and a number of house calls to be made and calls to be received. Knowing that she had the ear of the PM, she began receiving house calls from irate wives of politicians axed in Asquith's Cabinet reshuffle, including her cousin Clementine Churchill. However, 'Clemmie's desire to dance on his [Asquith's] grave' because of Winston's removal from the Admiralty, was tempered both by Sylvia and by an invitation to lunch at 10 Downing Street.[446]

Asquith kept up his rate of correspondence with Sylvia, even coming out of the Chamber of the House during a break in business to write to her. Writing in pencil as usual, he implored her to 'go on loving me dearest, it makes so much difference.' He began to become more demanding, entreating her to write to him every day, 'with a proper beginning and a proper ending' and warning her to end each letter as 'S'. Sometimes he didn't even wait to reach a writing desk, and scrawled letters off to her while being transported by motor to meetings. Travelling at the scandalously high speed of 30mph, Asquith's jerky, barely decipherable letters would announce his love and trust for her, while at the same time expressing his sympathy for her 'black dog' days. Such mild depression seemed to haunt Sylvia and her letters often refer to it, though the condition was usually very transient. She was a fortunate sufferer who seemed to shake off her dark moods fairly quickly, though while they lasted, she was unapproachable and withdrawn.[447]

Although Asquith was consumed with rapture for Sylvia, he nevertheless insured himself against rejection. Maintaining his 'harem' was always important to him, especially when Sylvia had thrown a bucket of cold water over him. He always maintained affection for Lady Diana Manners – and she for him – ever since their first encounter in Venice. Not long after his rift with Venetia, Asquith had called to see Diana, who was ill in bed. She was left in no doubt about the Prime Minister's quest, for the following day a letter arrived for her, marked 'Personal.' 'This letter' as her lover Duff Cooper recalled, 'seemed practically to be an offer to Diana to fill the vacated situation.' According to Cooper, Diana declined the invitation, which must have pleased Asquith's wife, Margot, who felt that Sylvia was far more suitable company for her husband.[448] Yet, for all the posturing, Asquith maintained a love for his wife. She was hard to ignore. She was no conventional beauty, but she had a star quality and left a huge impression (not always positive) on anyone who met her. Her great friend and admirer, E.F. Benson, immortalised her in his book *Dodo*:

> She is almost always picturesque. She seems to say and do anything that comes into her head, but all she says and does is rather striking. She can accommodate herself to nearly any circumstances. She is never colourless; and she is not quite like anybody else I have ever met. She has an immense amount of vitality, and she is almost always doing something. She is beautiful, unscrupulous, dramatic, warm-hearted, cold-blooded, and a hundred other things.[449]

She was also very indiscreet. She had personally experienced childbirth problems in the past and was only too keen to advise other mothers to protect against becoming pregnant. 'Henry always withdrew in time,' she enthused, 'such a noble man.'[450]

On 2 June, Sylvia heard that Anthony was able to snatch a few days leave. 'How wonderful to think that in a week you will be here and that I shall feel the touch of your hands and lips. I am tortured by anxiety that you have to cross the Channel.' Anthony safely returned and the pair were briefly united for a few days. While she was with Anthony, Sylvia did not write to Asquith in France – a state of affairs that clearly upset the PM, who was 'counting the hours' before her next letter. Demanding to know why not even one letter came from Mansfield Street, he reminded her he needed something from her 'every day.'

Asquith was delighted therefore to receive his first letter from Sylvia for a week and it made him jubilant. 'Why have I come to love you so much?' he gushed, while asking her to 'think of me always, every day, if possible at all hours of the day.' In his all-consuming passion, he visualised her constantly. 'How clearly I have before me now your face,' he wrote, 'I only hope and pray that it may come to me in my dreams.'[451]

Sylvia responded to the PM with warmth, but was still wary of his physical approaches and warned him about his suffocating advances. He reacted with boyish enthusiasm to her attempts to calm him down:

> My dearest. What a heavenly team we are together: despite your criticisms (about writing letters at War Councils) and your warnings (about limits!), I can't tell you what a supreme delight it is to me, to come to you & sit beside you and confide things to you: and to feel that the wisest of women is near me – and really loves me! I believe you do; and you don't know or imagine how much I love you.[452]

The barely chastened politician promised that he would never write her love letters from a Cabinet meeting again (a habit he had acquired during his relationship with Venetia) but he did send her a ticket for the Visitors' Gallery in the House, so that she could witness his next speech. She was becoming adept at critically appraising his speeches and he constantly sought her advice over whether he should be quiet, tense, dignified or outspoken when delivering his ovations. She also had to dampen the PM's private declarations and dowse his flaming love prose. When he overdid the passion, she soon told him to behave himself, so that the proud orator of the House was instantly reduced to a quivering apologist:

> It gave me a twinge of pain that you could <u>ever</u> have suspected that I should be tempted to convert our wonderful relations of love & confidence into – what shall we call it? – an erotic adventure? But after a little reflection I put it down to my clumsiness of expression.[453]

Writing to Anthony, Sylvia was keen to tell him all about her adventures in London, and in particular, how attractive to men she had become. At a dinner one evening, she was placed next to General Sir Leslie Rundle, who thought her 'very nearly divine'. Clearly the old Zulu War veteran failed to come up to the mark for she was quick to describe him as 'a stupid old boy'. But other admirers were lurking in the drawing room and once a few rubbers of bridge were played, the party broke up and one of the other male guests offered to escort her home to Mansfield Street. She accepted his gallant offer, but as soon as they arrived home and Sylvia opened the front door, he suddenly leapt on her. She pushed him off and still shaking, proceeded to give him a dressing down. The startled escort spluttered an apology and made a hasty retreat. Sylvia was quick to report the incident to both Anthony and Asquith, but her reaction was more one of surprise and fascination as to why men found her attractive. 'I couldn't have believed it possible,' she wrote, 'to make anybody lose their head like that – I must be looking very attractive otherwise it really is too extraordinary. I don't in any way ask for it.' Telling Asquith about the incident only served to excite him even more and bring out the protective spirit in him.[454]

The discovery of her charisma had come late to Sylvia and her ability to charm and captivate men gave her a new confidence. With her star in the ascendant, she made the most of her new influence and political intimacies and used the occasion of a car drive with Major-General Sir William 'Wullie' Robertson to argue Anthony's case for obtaining an active field command. The talk had gone well and Sylvia now waited to hear news from Anthony of his promotion. In the meantime, Asquith's letters to Sylvia continued to arrive daily at Mansfield Street. Venetia was away in France, escaping the storm surrounding her engagement and did not return until after 10 July. She landed at Folkestone and a day later was picked up by a relieved Montagu and returned to London. She still had to undergo her Jewish conversion before the wedding and she had spent some time 'mugging up all about the Paschal Lamb'. She abided by Lord Swaythling's stipulation of 'no Judaism, no money', coolly confiding to Montagu, 'I think one is happier rich than poor.' On 12 July she was received into the Jewish faith.[455]

Venetia spent the next few days preparing for her wedding. She returned to Mansfield Street to stay with Sylvia but her elated mood did not last for long. Every day she witnessed letters arriving addressed to Sylvia from the PM. It was too much for Venetia to bear. As far as she was concerned, Sylvia was the sister who had grown up in her shadow and who had always lacked her own success with men. It was Venetia who had always been the centre of attention in the family and growing up, felt herself the more enigmatic sibling. Venetia had, until recently, had first call on the most powerful man in the land. She had controlled the emotions of a man she had not even deigned properly to kiss. Now Sylvia had usurped her position. It was time to act.

During the afternoon of 15 July, Venetia left an opened envelope in the sitting room at Mansfield Street. Sylvia happened to glance at it and to her astonishment, recognised the handwriting. It was addressed to 'Miss Venetia Stanley' and had been posted from overseas. There was no obvious censor's mark on it, but she knew at once who had sent the letter. She was devastated.

Betrayal

Anthony Henley had never been a great letter writer. His correspondence with Sylvia did not match the moving collections of some officers from the First World War.[456] Neither was he in the habit of sending frequent letters to his children, so although Sylvia was worried that his recent dispatches had been brief and rather remote, she put this down to his pressure of work on the divisional staff. However, his recent letter to Venetia would take some explaining. Sylvia knew that Anthony had always been very fond of Venetia. He had known her for over ten years and enjoyed her wit and wisdom; but on one occasion the previous year, when he was home on leave, their playful banter had gone beyond the usual limits. Sylvia feared that the pair had become even closer and the following morning, when Venetia had returned home after a walk, Sylvia confronted her and asked to see Anthony's letter. Venetia refused and went out again. Left alone and fearing the worst, Sylvia decided to write to Anthony:

> It is entirely your fault that I am suspicious. I never should have been suspicious but for last Nov. and that was not in oblivion, as I promised you. Now this is why I am sure it is all beginning again ... I could not help seeing that you had written to Venetia. I made up my mind I would ask her to show me your letter and I was not surprised she would not. I realise with deep sorrow that my love for you cannot survive, while you do not tend it ... it is so cutting to me that perhaps the 11th July was nothing to you, when it meant so much to me, but the person you report having is not me & I minded your [sic] going so much.[457]

Sylvia was stonewalled by both Venetia and Anthony. He failed to reply to Sylvia's searching letter, so she sent another, the following day:

> I nearly asked for advice of the PM ... Venetia came in to me last night and said she would show me your letter. But I saw she could not bring herself to give you away and she began lying. I did not tax her with lying this morning, and implored her to show me what you had written. Why should there be such impossibly secret things that you must say – more lies – and now I give up. It is getting worse rather than better as I see you're so false, telling me I am everything to you. And now I know

that as you said it, you were longing to be with her and not me. I see now why you were anxious that I should drive with the PM. I little suspected it. I am going to say nothing to the PM till I hear from you and God knows I don't want to talk of this bitter thing.[458]

Sylvia was in a state of shock. She had extracted from Venetia some details about Anthony's letter. The words 'I long to be with you' cut her deeply, as she tried to recall hints about the pair's behaviour that she had missed. Despite her passionate nature, had her 'Stanley trait' of sudden cold moods driven him away? She was alone in the house and Venetia had disappeared. But what was it about her sister, the volatile and earthy Venetia, that drove men to such distraction? She collected her thoughts and wrote to Anthony that night. It was a cool, detached letter in which she bluntly spelled out her fears. 'You realise that my love for you cannot survive.' It was a theme she returned to in her letters to him over the next few, endless days. 'I am still young enough to begin again,' and more defiantly, 'I have a strong will and by God I will overcome my love for you.' Her handwriting had become shaky. She implored Anthony to come clean about his love for her sister, but he still failed to reply. Her normally strong constitution was not helped by her reaction to recent inoculations, and she suddenly collapsed. Her mother rushed down from Alderley and called the doctor, who diagnosed blood poisoning. She was dangerously ill for 24 hours but came through the physical crisis. The emotional crisis would take longer to mend, though help came from an unlikely source. Edwin Montagu was the only person in whom Sylvia confided and it transpired that the man who had been derided by her family and friends for his religion and his looks was, indeed, a true friend. He had his own suspicions and had confronted Venetia about her relationship with Anthony. With only weeks until his marriage, Montagu found himself challenged not only by the ghost of Asquith but by the current threat from Anthony Henley.[459]

Meanwhile, Asquith was concerned about Sylvia's state of health and particularly her mental distraction. He knew something had devastated her and despite her excuses about depression, he persisted in trying to find out what had happened. On Sunday 20 July 1915, Sylvia visited Asquith and his family at 'The Wharf' and was clearly drawing closer towards him. 'A rudderless ship is so easily blown onto a sea shore,' she warned her husband. Asquith, with his barrister's mentality, pursued Sylvia over the reasons for her withdrawal, yet she stubbornly refused to discuss her marital problems, except with Montagu. Bizarrely, Asquith then changed tack, and attempted to woo her with jewellery of a most intimate kind. He presented his married friend with a ring and tried to persuade her to wear it on the little finger of her right hand. Coaxing her out of her sadness, he reminded her how much she meant to him. 'You lift loads,' he repeated to her, 'and turn twilight into sunshine.' He also recalled their 'mad-cap' drives together, hurtling like some 'Toad of Toad Hall' through all the quiet country lanes. Despite his jollity, Asquith was under considerable pressure himself. There was a continuing rift with Churchill, exacerbated by Clementine's visits to

Downing Street, when she berated Asquith over his decision to exclude her husband from the Cabinet. 'Damn Clementine and her little spiteful tongue,' Asquith wrote of Sylvia's cousin. 'I brush aside the Clementines and all that petty tribe.'[460] And the PM was not the only one to find Clementine difficult to handle. Jean Hamilton found her tricky and unpredictable. 'I can't like Clemmie Churchill,' she wrote, 'she is like glancing cold water to me. Very shallow.' Yet several days later, she found Clementine 'nicer and sweeter'.[461] However, Clementine was not going to let up on her attacks on Asquith and even he was beginning to question whether Winston's removal was worthwhile. After all, things were no easier with the coalition government and Asquith's heart was never really committed to this particular piece of political fixing. In his letters to Sylvia, he despaired at having to work with opposition party members. She continued to offer him sound advice and dismissed his doubts about the wisdom of working with the Conservative First Lord of the Admiralty, Arthur Balfour. On military matters, Asquith happily passed on to Sylvia news about senior commanders – who was 'in' and who was 'out'. 'Hamilton has sacked 2 more generals in the 9th Corps,' he reported, 'Lindley and Sitwell (do you know them?) – for incompetence' … Like Lord North, our Generals "make me tremble".'[462]

After the devastating news on 12 May that Venetia was to marry Montagu, Asquith had sent her some further painful and remorseful letters. There had also been the meeting in France. But he had now switched allegiance to Sylvia and her calm, soothing correspondence with him seemed to have a cathartic effect. He still felt wretched over Venetia's choice of groom and the decision to change her religion, so he kept out of her way. He did not see Venetia again, except by mistake on 15 July at 10 Downing Street, when he walked into Margot's bedroom and there she was, standing talking to his wife. In a letter to Sylvia, he reported that he was startled at the meeting and made a quick exit from the bedroom. Asquith's last communication to Venetia was a letter accompanying his wedding present of two silver boxes (chosen by Sylvia). In return he received a letter from Venetia on her wedding day, 26 July 1915, and which he chose to show immediately to Sylvia, as if to confirm that his previous relationship was definitely over.[463]

Throughout the summer of 1915, Sylvia and Anthony's correspondence remained polite, even civilized. Anthony's remorse for his affair with Venetia went into pages, yet Sylvia could not forget and not yet, forgive. Between trips back to Alderley or Penrhôs to see her children, she threw herself into voluntary work in London, becoming a nursing auxiliary at a baby and children's clinic in the West End of London. Her official job description was 'VAD' (Voluntary Aid Detachment), which meant that despite her background, she had to undergo a rigid selection procedure, including a character reference, confirmation of her parents' nationality, school references and production of either St John's Ambulance or Red Cross First Aid certificates. All these checks were designed to make sure that the Voluntary Aid Detachments recruited the 'right sort' of girl and the authorities could count on obedience and a degree of sexual probity.

Nursing, or at least auxiliary nursing, was a popular option for middle and upper class women wanting to help the war effort. At the very beginning of the war, Lady Sarah Wilson, the redoubtable sister of the Duke of Marlborough, had helped set up a hospital in Étaples, in northern France and had enlisted the help of such socialites as Alice Keppel. Since then, there had been a number of small hospitals set up by private subscription and staffed by a steady flow of volunteers. Many girls joined as VADs to assist in hospitals at home, while many more were required to serve overseas in military base hospitals and dressing stations. Sometimes it could be grim work. One young VAD working at St George's Hospital remembered a ward 'full of men with part of their faces blown away' and spoke of 'the difficulty of feeding those who had no jaws, by means of cup and tubes'.[464] Sylvia was spared these horrors for the moment and because of her young family, she was excused from service abroad, though she had secured her large A3 size passport in December 1914, in case of emergencies. She enjoyed her work, assisting Dr Fren in the baby unit at King's, especially when she was brought in to listen to consultations. Yet at times, she yearned for more variety than the constant round of baby weighing, checking dressings and preparing circumcisions.[465]

'The Prime', as the Stanley family christened Asquith, was very supportive of the work of the nursing services but it was not just the vocation that he admired. He was also rather partial to a nursing outfit. During his 'affair' with Venetia, she worked as a nursing auxiliary and on one occasion informed Asquith that she was wearing her uniform, while writing to him. He responded that he could not wait to see her. 'I *must* have a glimpse of you in it,' he purred.[466] Yet the allure appeared to have worn off by late 1915. By then, he was very close to Sylvia and after declaring 'I love you and miss you,' he summoned her for lunch at 10 Downing Street. She had to come straight from her work at the clinic, but she was disappointed at his reaction:

> It was a lunchtime party, but no one minded my appearing in my uniform except the PM, who manifested a good deal of disgust. He thought it a repulsive get up. I was quite surprised what a difference it made to him.[467]

Sylvia's working uniform was drab and Asquith always preferred 'a dash of colour' on his women. Yet the war had changed attitudes to fashion and dress. 'Dressing down', at least in public, was *de rigeur*. The American-born society beauty, Adèle Essex, had some firm views on the matter:

> As for dressing, one simply hasn't the time to be bothered with dress. One feels one must wear something dark, and generally, at dinner, one is wearing the same gown everywhere until it is almost a joke. On the street, too, we wear about the same clothes, generally black or dark blue serge. I would not say that we are shabby; that would not be true; but we give no time and no money to clothes, and there is hardly such a thing as fashion. If one goes out to lunch, which probably means eggs

and something cold, one goes as she is, straight from work. Everybody is working, and is more or less 'grubby' in the middle of the day. For myself, I just slip off my big apron and the white cuffs I wear over my sleeves and go as I am.[468]

While such championing of the utilitarian style might be overstated, the war nevertheless generated a huge revolution in what was acceptable dress for women. But this change was not easily won. When it was first mooted that women could take over traditional male jobs, Edith Londonderry wrote to *The Times* advocating the employment of women in agriculture and received a welter of abusive letters. Not only did many men and women object to the 'erosion' of the traditional role model of mother and housewife but they were also against the idea of women wearing breeches instead of skirts. There was much talk of the seditious nature of 'the divided leg'.[469]

No uniform was required for Sylvia's other job at the Red Cross Enquiry Department at 31 St James Square. The unit comprised a massive clerical undertaking, which produced periodic lists of the wounded and missing for despairing relatives – a most valuable contribution to the Home Front. Unlike her sister's attitude to war work, Sylvia entered into her commitments with enthusiasm. There is no doubt that the war changed her. No longer was she an unworldly woman, cocooned in the safe upper class havens of Alderley and Penrhôs. Her separation from Anthony had forced her to see the lives of others close-up. Through her work at the children's clinic and the Red Cross, she had experienced other classes beyond her tight social set. Through her talks with the PM, she had heard the most intimate details of how the powerful operated and witnessed through the antics of her sister and husband the extraordinary weaving and unravelling of personal relationships and the capacity for betrayal. She had, she decided, become 'more formed, yet broader-minded'.[470] She needed to be if she was to come to terms with her own marital problems, for despite their denials, Venetia and Anthony continued their relationship. On 27 October, Venetia wrote to Anthony at his divisional headquarters in France:

My darling what can I have been up to. It's over a fortnight since I wrote a thing which I never meant to allow to happen again. But how it came about, I can't say except just general occupation of time in fussing about arranging looks and things. I am really almost ready for you to have come home now, that is as far as my house is concerned. I have been thinking since July 12th or whenever the exact date of that diversion at the hotel at Folkestone was. What ages ago, it seems. In one of your letters you suggest that I can't tell what earrings look like because I haven't got a looking glass, but I have now, and it's lovely, and if you think so too, you shall give it me back. If you don't like it then you shall have something else, but I should let you off a present. Which reminds me that at last you will be able to have a correspondence with someone, for I've been promised your box for the beginning of next week. I shall keep it here and probably use it till you come and claim it.[471]

When Venetia had returned from France just before her wedding the previous July, she arranged to be collected from Folkestone by Montagu. Venetia may have given an incorrect date in her letter to Anthony, but it would appear that there was an assignation between the two at a Folkestone hotel, just before Montagu appeared. It was not an isolated incident, for in early November, Venetia arranged to meet Anthony when he was next home on leave:

> Darling one line to say that Tuesday week, no Tuesday fortnight, is the very day I long to see you, and of course I shall come to Alderley over the Sunday (it's Mother's birthday incidentally). Capel is an excellent plan, we shall be introduced to this admirable and select Night Club when we'll win his money at bridge. How <u>fearfully</u> glad I shall be to see you. I really can think of nothing else. I go to Alderley for a lunch with Nol on Thursday. I'll write from there, but this is only a hasty line to clinch you for the week after next.

Sylvia appeared unaware that the affair between her sister and her husband was still carrying on. However, she continued to believe that her own relationship with Asquith was entirely innocent. Because she successfully parried his physical advances, she convinced herself that their private conversations or intimate drives together were purely platonic. She also believed that their very close friendship was somehow altruistic and that she was only doing her duty, both in relieving the PM's stress and acting as a sounding board. All Asquith knew was that he couldn't do without Sylvia and he was aggrieved if one of his letters to her took longer than twelve hours to reach her. If he failed to receive a daily letter from her, he would beg to see her 'as soon as possible, for as long as possible, as often as possible'.[472] Though Sylvia continued to deflect the PM's physical ambitions, he persisted in his overtures of love. He found the arrangements at Mansfield Street not to his liking, as invariably Stanley family members were present. 'When & where & how can I see you in anything like seclusion & *solitare*?' Asquith pleaded. 'I long for the time when you will have a pied-à-terre of your own.'[473] She warned him, as she had done before, that she was 'an unusual person' and that she had an 'odious and cold exterior', yet her quixotic nature only served to fuel Asquith's passion. It was as if the PM needed to role play, with Sylvia as the scolding mistress and himself as the naughty boy, in constant need of correction and grateful for any verbal punishment that she cared to dispense.[474] Yet, even with Sylvia's almost undivided attention, Asquith still craved the company of other women. He was adept at playing off his female companions against each other and continued to spread his favours amongst his 'harem', many of whom were old admirers. Pamela McKenna (née Jekyll), wife of the Chancellor of the Exchequer, and Viola Parsons (née Tree) were two regular correspondents.

The idea that a powerful and intellectual man, such as Asquith, could conduct a series of 'affairs' without actually consummating them was not without precedent. The feminist novelist Olive Schreiner enjoyed a passionate and intimate relationship with the sex psychologist, Havelock Ellis for over a year, but they did not have sex. There was much talk between them of a 'pure' and 'mental' fusion that transcended their physical differences. And Duff Cooper, never a man to miss a sexual opportunity, nevertheless found in Diana Manners someone who could satisfy his desire for intimacy, without consummation:

> She is the only person who is worth making love to, who understands the game and how to play it. She is the only woman with whom excessive intimacy never breeds the faintest shadow of contempt or disgust, and this is, I think, not only because we never proceed to extremes. There is a great deal to be said for the love-making that sends one away hungry, exasperating though it is. With most women, the further one goes the more one is disillusioned, but with her exactly the opposite happens.[475]

Sylvia allowed no sexual contact with Asquith and physical closeness seemed to go no further than holding hands and embracing, yet the pair maintained an extraordinary closeness. Despite Margot Asquith's preference for 'divide and rule', she thought Sylvia 'perfectly true and straight and a fine creature'.[476] Sylvia was certainly all of this, but what helped, of course, was the fact that she was married and therefore convention allowed close friendships to flourish with the opposite sex. Had Margot realised the state of Sylvia's marriage, and the depth of Asquith's obsession with her, she might have formed a different view.

Amidst all this emotional drama, there was one event that brightened the darker November days. Violet Asquith married her father's private secretary, Maurice 'Bongie' Bonham Carter. It appeared that the long-time enmity between Violet and Margot might recede, especially if Bongie could take Violet's attention away from her father. On the morning of the wedding, Margot, with her husband's infidelity foremost in her mind, became dramatic and declared that she would see off any woman who ever threatened to 'cast even a shadow' between Bongie and Violet. Yet Margot was not entirely without extramarital attention herself. While she was undoubtedly still in love with Asquith, she had other admirers, such as the energetic octogenarian Wilfred Blunt, at whose home she spent several nights[477]

The week before Christmas, Sylvia returned to Alderley to spend time with her family. Asquith found he was bereft without his regular contact with her. 'I have got so much into the habit,' he moaned, 'of relying on your judgement & finding strength as well as repose in your companionship.' The Stanley festivities in Cheshire were punctuated by rumours that the German Zeppelins could now even bomb nearby Manchester and Liverpool. This gossip was not wide of the mark, for the following month one airship actually passed directly over the family estate after an abortive mission to attack Liverpool.[478] During the winter of 1915, the Zeppelin attacks were concentrated against cities in the Midlands and the east coast and after a year of airship attacks, 277 civilians had been killed and 645 wounded. Although wireless interception warned the authorities of an impending raid, little was done to capitalise on the intelligence. Searchlights were often badly spaced and even though Zeppelins were over 170 metres long, the searchlights failed to illuminate them for long enough to enable fighter pilots to zero in. Moving at an average speed of 60 mph, these airships were largely impervious to shell punctures in their fabric, because of their gas pressures, and it was only the development of incendiary rounds that caused the airships to ignite. Night flying was also still in its infancy and not only was take off and landing extremely hazardous, visibility in the night sky was often appalling. One pilot reported that he had been flying directly above a Zeppelin for some time, without realising it.

The Government had been slow to appreciate the extent to which morale could be sapped by the Zeppelin threat and they were also dragging their feet over another, more emotive issue – conscription. Unlike most countries on the continent, Britain had no history of compulsive military service. She had always prided herself on maintaining a small regular army supported by a voluntary militia or Territorial Army. Even with the huge manpower losses from the early battles of the war, talk of conscription always proved an anathema. Yet by December 1915, the stark fact was that there were insufficient volunteers coming forward. Asquith had swallowed his personal distaste for the move and supported a compromise deal for conscripting only unmarried men, but he was facing a crisis amongst his erstwhile Liberal supporters. Reginald McKenna and three other front bench stalwarts opposed the draft and despite Asquith's friendship with Pamela McKenna, persisted in stirring up the debate. Lloyd George had also begun to make trouble and was actively plotting the downfall of the PM. Jean Hamilton noted that LG wrote a letter to Bonar Law to the effect that 'he and Northcliffe would be strong enough between them to turn out Asquith.'[479]

Sylvia would see changes in the New Year. She was still receiving regular letters from Asquith. Though he had given up writing to her during Cabinet meetings, he was now sending his dispatches during interruptions in the business of the House, from of all places, the Divisional Lobby. She reduced her hours at the clinic and the Red Cross to embark on a new, if unglamorous, venture with canteens. In January 1916, after some lobbying by Clementine Churchill, Sylvia agreed to help run the Hendon District Canteen for the growing numbers of men and women working in the local munitions factories. Clementine was a member of the national committee that ran a network of similar canteens throughout the northern suburbs of London, catering for over 1000 men and women at each sitting. The canteens fulfilled a valuable service and some co-ordination was now creeping in, but there had been endless friction between the canteen committees and other voluntary bodies. Some of the formidable women charging about London so frightened one observer she declared that 'the problem of saving the working-class from the Relief Committees has got to be faced.'[480] At the end of the month, Sylvia acquired some time off from her new regime to greet Anthony who had come home on leave. It was a testing time

for the couple. Leaving aside the question of Anthony's affair, their estrangement was
not that unusual in marriages where the husband had gone off to war. For many
servicemen found they felt an increasing distance from those at home who had not
shared their experiences and who could never understand the fierce bonds that
combat forged. There was a great camaraderie amongst men who had seen active
service, and indeed, there were some men who felt a greater sense of solidarity with
their enemy sitting opposite them in their trench, than with those at home. For those
on the Home Front, no amount of hospital, charity or war work would earn the
same respect as someone who had been under fire. A remote and difficult soldier
husband on leave, such as Anthony, was all too common. And the leave was brief. As
soon as Anthony had returned to France, Sylvia was again nagged by doubts, which
she quickly conveyed to her husband:

> I have taken the children to St Paul's. They seemed to enjoy it surprisingly. I
> sometimes like the complete isolation one can enjoy while one is in a great
> crowded church, and I allowed my thoughts to wander back to what is behind
> and to speculate as to what is to come to us. It will always be a sorrow to me to
> give you up as my intimate lover. To give up the entire possession of you, but I am,
> I think, sensible enough to realise that it isn't a relationship which can be eternal,
> and I am now prepared to accept a compromise. I have showed you how deeply
> and passionately I can love you, and how you can be so much the centre of my life,
> that all else is eclipsed. But such a love must be exacting and that makes life rather
> difficult, especially to a man of your temperament. You describe yourself as '*volage*',
> the exact translation is 'fickle'. I don't take you to mean it literally, but more that
> you want liberty to fly off without question – and return at will. I mean to try and
> develop a like tendency.[481]

While Sylvia might talk of independence, she was still some way from a separation, let
alone a divorce. Yet, she was keen to tell Anthony about the latest gossip concerning
Henry 'Sommie' Somerset and his wife Kitty. It was a domestic mess. Somerset
was deeply in love with Lord Freddy Blackwood's wife, while Kitty had fallen for
Brigadier Billy Lambton. The discord was so advanced that Sylvia was convinced
they would all shortly divorce, using a 'stalking horse' in the courts, to avoid further
embarrassing publicity.[482]

In February 1916, Sylvia joined a 'Saturday-to-Monday' at Walmer Castle on the
Kent coast. It was a freezing house that had been lent to the PM and his family as
a weekend retreat. Being so close to the Channel Ports, it was the scene of regular
meetings between politicians and senior commanders. It was also a suitable place
for Asquith and Margot to host parties for friends, such as Sir John Cowans, the
Quartermaster-General, whom Sylvia had met before. 'I rather like Cowans,' she
taunted her husband, 'he has so much personal charm that when you are with him,
one cannot help coming under it.'[483] Cowans' legendary charm must have been

rubbing off on his colleagues, for as Asquith observed, formerly taciturn military commanders were suddenly opening up. 'I have just had a long talk with Sir Douglas Haig,' he confided to Sylvia, 'who is on capital form and much improved in articulateness [sic] since he took over command.'[484] Articulate and sharp performers were also outshining the old guard on the political stage. On 7 March Leo Amery attended the House of Commons to hear 'A.J.B. [Balfour] deliver a dreary rambling disquisition without life or purpose, followed by Winston, very much alive, full of purpose and self-assertion'.[485] While several weeks later, Duff Cooper witnessed the Prime Minister and his entourage leave for France. 'They looked an odd lot,' he noticed. 'The PM wearing a very light brown leather overcoat, the collar turned up, his long white hair sticking out behind and his red face.' Asquith had a comfortable, if rumpled appearance, while his rival Lloyd George seemed a sharper dresser, always with an eye to his public image. He was always protesting against the 'odious' photographers, noted Charles Hobhouse, 'and then smoothing his hair and adjusting his collar and stopping at a convenient corner to allow them to catch him'.[486] Both Lloyd George and Winston Churchill outshone Asquith and despite the PM's undoubted political acumen, he lacked panache and 'star quality'. Leo Amery, sitting in the House of Commons during a debate on 25 April, was distinctly unimpressed with the Prime Minister and noted in his diary, 'Asquith, what might have been expected. No real grip or life in it.'[487]

Some weeks before the launch of the Battle of the Somme on 1 July, Anthony managed to extract some leave and returned home. His relations with Sylvia had improved in recent weeks and they had spent a happy and intimate week in London. The deprivation and horrors of the Western Front were left behind, as was the emotional turmoil of the previous year. While Sylvia enjoyed a respite from her marital problems, her sister Venetia was barely into the first year of her marriage and was already showing signs of a hedonistic streak. Her social life became wilder and more extravagant as she entertained her dwindling band of 'Coterie' members. Many of this exclusive set had already perished. The two Grenfell brothers, Julian and Billy, fell within two months of each other, then Charles Lister, from wounds he received at Gallipoli. George Vernon and Ego Charteris were also amongst the dead. Raymond Asquith would not last out the year, and would be followed in 1917 by Edward Horner and Patrick Shaw-Stewart. A grim tally, but one that Venetia and her friend Diana Manners were determined to put to the back of their minds. Venetia now dressed in the latest fashions and had abandoned her previously frumpy style. Her passionless marriage to Edwin, who was consumed with his return to the Cabinet, was enlivened by entertaining on a lavish scale. She also employed her boundless energy in renovating their house at 24 Queen Anne's Gate. She also engaged in less innocent pursuits. Some of her set indulged in drug-taking – chloroform or morphia were favourites – and although none appeared to become addicted, the thought of such society beauties as Lady Diana Manners or Katherine Asquith injecting themselves failed to trouble their friends. However, while Diana was happy to confide to Raymond Asquith that she was on occasions 'drugged in very deed by my hand with Morphia', she was determined to keep it from her mother. Dining one evening with Edwin and Venetia Montagu, Diana had ordered supplies of chloroform to be delivered to her at their house. Her mother found out, interrupted the party in Queen Anne's Gate and demanded to know what her daughter was doing. Edwin gallantly covered for Diana, claiming the chloroform was for his hay fever, but probably failed to convince the Duchess. There were occasions when others took part. Duff Cooper, who had a promising job with the Foreign Office, recorded in his diary that he and Patrick Shaw-Stewart joined Diana Manners and Katherine Asquith in a drug-fuelled evening. In Cooper's case, Diana was only too happy to inject him.[488]

Diana Manners was quite a handful. On one occasion before the war, Sylvia was asked to chaperone her to a ball in London, but it was an impossible task. They both arrived together but as the evening wore on Sylvia started to tire by 2.30am, whilst Diana was just revving up. Sylvia soon had had enough and retired to bed but Diana partied on until 4.30am and was escorted home by someone, quite who, she couldn't remember. It was all heady stuff for the time. The war had changed the stiff formalities of chaperoning, although single women were still careful not to be seen dining in public with just one man.[489] A correct façade was still maintained but in private everyone could relax. Diana could be even more provocative. She made it her mission to shock the more staid members of her circle; sometimes her efforts were trumped:

> At dinner with the Horners the conversation at one end of the table turned to sodomy and someone told the story of the officer who had buggered his batman in a shell hole between the British and German lines. Old and deaf Sir John Horner called down the table to ask what was causing the laughter. His son Edward tried to turn the conversation, but Diana insisted on repeating the anecdote. Sir John thought for a moment. 'He must have been an uncommonly handy feller,' he grunted.[490]

These intimate dinner parties were the lifeblood of London society, where great events could be touched upon but earnest or intellectual argument was to be kept to a minimum. The mental duelling that took place at Alderley Park between the Stanley family and their guests was quite the exception in smart society. Certainly in London, gossip was the driving force. Venetia excelled at good anecdotes and her parties at Queen Anne's Gate could be riotous affairs, particularly without the presence of her censorious husband, Edwin, now occupied as the new Minister of Munitions.[491] Sylvia was often present at these gatherings when she was in London; any reference to Anthony by either sister was studiously avoided. However, while Sylvia earnestly hoped that Anthony's affair with Venetia was over, she did not bargain on the pair's duplicity. They were still in contact and writing to each other, with various assignations arranged during the summer of 1916, or whenever Anthony might steal over to London. Venetia's schemes did not always go according to plan:

> My darling do you really like me to write to you. I will of course if you do, tho' as you may have noticed, letters are not just my thing right now. The Claudines wrote to you today. Rather a delay I fear. I went to Capel but now just as I was counting on you for certain, the whole plan seemed to have fallen through owing to the Russian not turning up. I'm very sad about it as it looks as tho' I should have to call a solitary dinner in London on the 29th. Solitary at any rate in spirit ... I went 2 see Sylvia this afternoon, who was in bed with a bad throat. If I were you I should try 2 make her give up those ghastly canteens. She works far too hard at them. At any rate she should go away for all August and most of September. I must stop. Write again. You are the only person who ever does.
>
> Much love always.
> V[492]

While Anthony kept up his correspondence with Venetia, Sylvia still wrote religiously to Anthony at the front. She rarely mentioned Asquith in her letters, but gave Anthony news of their children or other family members, as well as gossip about her committee work. After all, there was not much war news to discuss in her letters. During June, the newspapers had few dramatic stories and Sylvia found her military contacts quite reticent. Like everyone else, she had heard rumours of some big 'push' coming, which would lift the fortunes of the British and French armies, but there was nothing specific. On 1 July 1916, she was staying at Alderley and in the early afternoon took her children to see 'Puss in Boots' at the Royal Exchange in Manchester, a matinee in aid of the Soldiers' Fund. She then returned to Alderley to make up a parcel of cakes and looked out some of Anthony's favourite cigars. It was then that one of the maids came in to see Sylvia with news of the start of a massive British offensive on the Somme. She sat down and wrote to Anthony immediately. In the following days, she heard nothing from him. Five days later, a letter arrived. It was a huge relief, for it was confirmation that his unit, the 49th Division, was fortunately on the flank of the main operations and for the moment he was safe. However, Sylvia's brother, Lieutenant-Colonel Oliver Stanley, serving with the Royal Field Artillery (RFA), was not so lucky and was wounded in the shoulder. After two days in a Rouen hospital, he was invalided home to recuperate at Mansfield Street.[493]

Sylvia came down to London and stayed some time at Mansfield Street to help nurse her brother and then returned to Alderley for the August holidays, or as Asquith put it, 'on the train that carries you back to maternal duties.' Shortly after she arrived, she took the children to stay at Penrhôs, joining the vast Stanley baggage train that moved *en masse* each summer to Holy Island, off Anglesey. The Penrhôs estate fared well during the war, as farming was taxed lightly compared to other industries and there were lucrative military contracts for products such as horse fodder. While some of the valets and footmen had joined up for the war, there was no shortage of female servants, especially as there were limited employment opportunities on the island. So the household carried on much as before. On arrival at Penrhôs, Sylvia and the children were welcomed by the housekeeper and once the maids had unpacked all the cases, the children with their nanny made off for the beach. Whatever the weather, and it was usually blustery, there were regular picnic expeditions to Helen's Tower, 'Caligula's Arch' or Mill Island. Occasionally, Asquith would join a house party at Penrhôs but the travelling time usually prohibited this and he had to remain in London, musing upon Sylvia's role – as a mother and as his companion. Asquith rarely mentioned Anthony in his letters to Sylvia and did not seem to consider him part of the equation, only marvelling at Sylvia's ability to 'dualise' her responsibilities.[494]

There was also some good news for Sylvia during the hot summer – she discovered she was pregnant. At first, her spirits were buoyed because she had another chance to produce a son – a development that might help to heal the rifts in her marriage. But not everyone was delighted for her. While Margot Asquith rejoiced at the news and told her husband, he was not so pleased. Asquith felt indignant, for despite their closeness, Sylvia had not told him the news first and, in a fit of pique, he thought that a new child might also divert her attention away from him.[495] Meanwhile, Anthony was delighted with the prospect of an heir and the good news bucked his spirits. The recent operations on the Somme had boosted his career and his administrative skills had been employed to great effect in the 49th Division HQ. Not only was he awarded the Distinguished Service Order (DSO) but he was twice Mentioned in Dispatches (MiD) during the campaign. He now appeared keen to mend the damage done to his private life and was anxious to declare his love for Sylvia and to seek forgiveness for his past wanderings. But she was still wounded and vulnerable after the exposure of his passion for Venetia. She tried to forget and convince herself that they could return to their former relationship, but she could not banish the dark thoughts. She put them at the back of her mind, yet just when she thought she had control of her emotions, the demons would loom larger than ever. She blamed herself for her predicament:

> What a cold hearted person I was to suggest that you did not feel what you wrote. There must have been a black devil with me on that occasion. I want to believe you love me as truly and deeply as it is possible but I don't go about it the best way.[496]

Anthony returned home on leave in late August and joined Sylvia and the children at a rented house in Gloucester Place, London. Sylvia organised a celebration for the returning decorated soldier, but again their moods failed to chime. He was preoccupied and distant. He soon disappeared to his tailors, George Winter & Son in Conduit Street, to be measured for new army breeches, followed by a trip to his club, Brooks's, in St James's Street. When he returned to the house, his time seemed to be taken up with handling the sale of a family estate, which he and his brothers had put in hand. He had hoped that his straitened financial circumstances might be relieved by the sale of the Henley acres at Chardstock, in Dorset, but he was to be disappointed. The estate, which consisted of over 20 farms, two villages and various sporting rights – 3500 acres in all – was already heavily mortgaged. Farm prices had barely increased since the Henleys had purchased the estate the previous century, and after the bank was discharged, there was only a small sum to distribute amongst Anthony and his two brothers.[497]

The Battle of the Somme raged on during the summer of 1916 and into the autumn. Gains were few and the casualties mounted. Field-Marshal Haig's 'bite-and-hold' operations were not always applied by his generals, often because of fierce and determined German resistance. The fact that Britain was a junior partner to the French was often overlooked. It meant that British troops had often to fight over terrain and in conditions not of their choosing, at the bidding of the French High Command. Neither Asquith nor his government ministers could afford to use this as an excuse to defend the high casualty rate – on 1 July British forces suffered two casualties for every metre of frontage attacked – as Asquith did not wish to appear to be the poodle of the French, especially as he was determined to enforce British sovereignty in Ireland. There, the problems were mounting. The Irish situation was as intractable as ever and Asquith confided to Sylvia that there was 'a lot of agitation' at the eleventh hour from both Ireland and America to reprieve Sir Roger Casement, on trial for treason. Those petitions were ignored by the British Government.[498]

Other domestic issues dogged Asquith and criticism of his private life was coming to the fore, especially amongst the women's movement. Even though the vociferous campaign for votes for women was tempered by the war, the activists still attacked the Prime Minister for his personal lifestyle. The suffragette Ethel Smyth was horrified at the antics of the Prime Minister. 'It is disgraceful,' she wrote to the Archbishop of Canterbury, 'that millions of women shall be trampled underfoot because of the "convictions" of an old man who notoriously can't be left alone in a room with a young girl after dinner.'[499] And it wasn't only women who were tiring of Asquith's behaviour. Duff Cooper, who had designs on Diana Manners, was fed up with the PM's company, noting that he was 'oblivious of young men and lecherous of young women'.[500]

Asquith seemed to be flagging, though he kept up his round of social engagements. On 12 August, he organised a party at 'The Wharf', driving Sylvia down to the house to meet the other guests who included Nancy Cunard and her fiancé, a young guardsman, related to the Tennants. It was not a great success, with Violet Asquith still proving to be 'a prickly thorn' in Sylvia's presence. The drive back to London for Sylvia was depressing:

I motored up with the PM but he was almost completely silent. I can't quite understand him. He obviously likes me as a companion, as everyday I have driven with him alone & he might have asked Diana Manners. Otherwise I might easily have thought he was fond. I suppose he is getting rag tired.[501]

Tired he might be, but Asquith was due to receive a terrible shock. In the early hours of 14 September, while the Prime Minister was still asleep, over in France his son Raymond had been awake for hours. He was at 'stand to' position in a grim and desolate fire trench on the Somme. He was steadying himself before taking his company of Grenadier Guards over the top and into an attack towards the village of Lesboeufs. Raymond knew it was an operation fraught with difficulties, yet kept up the customary optimism in front of his men. His recent gilded civilian life now seemed far away. He had been the finest scholar in his year at Oxford, and was raised, like so many, 'to believe in manly, chivalric values'.[502] He had little opportunity to test those values. As he clambered out of the trench with his men and through the gaps in his own wire, he staggered forward into a hail of shrapnel and bullets. He was immediately struck by a round in his chest and fell. Although Raymond was carted off the field, he died soon afterwards. The awful news took several days to reach his family. His father was distraught with grief and could only bring himself to send off a short telegram to Sylvia, confirming his loss. Raymond's wife, Katherine was inconsolable, as were close friends such as Diana Cooper and other members of the 'Coterie', in which Raymond had been the shining star. Despite his loss, Asquith continued to be roundly criticised in the press for his war leadership; after a short respite, his political opponents re-grouped for a final assault against him.

So far 1916 had been a bad year for Asquith. Despite the coalition, some Conservatives were pushing Lloyd George's case for a tougher and more vigorous prosecution of the war, as well as lobbying for the opening up of an effective eastern front. Ireland had heated up considerably since the Easter Rising and the executions of fourteen rebels had merely served to inflame the situation. Lord Kitchener's death had removed a stubborn but loyal ally of Asquith's and his supporters were thinning out. To make matters worse, Sir Max Aitken, proprietor of the *Daily Express*, was working behind the scenes to bring Bonar Law, the Conservative Leader, into an unlikely alliance with Lloyd George against Asquith. Indeed, Lloyd George did not want for press support and his protectors within the newspaper industry were always on guard. The Chairman of the Newspaper Proprietors Association, George Riddell, forcefully warned Lloyd George's mistress, Frances Stevenson,' be very careful, as D's [David's] enemies are always on the watch … they would put poison in his cup.'[503]

Lloyd George decided to strike first. On 1 December, he proposed that a small hand-picked War Committee should take day-to-day decisions without reference to the Cabinet. This group would include Andrew Bonar Law, the Conservative Leader in the Coalition, together with Sir Edward Carson, but would pointedly exclude Asquith. Unsurprisingly, the Prime Minister rejected the plan on 4 December. The following day Lloyd George resigned, informing Asquith that 'vigour and vision are the supreme needs at this time.' His resignation was followed by Bonar Law and the remaining Conservative Cabinet members, which finished the government. With a large Liberal majority behind him, Asquith could have appealed to the House under a Secret Session, but privately he knew the game was up.[504]

Writing to Sylvia the day after his resignation, Asquith confessed 'to feeling a certain sense of relief'. In his letter he poured out his feelings to his 'angel of goodness and understanding', for he was obviously exhausted by the political battles of the last month and even for such an experienced politician, he had found it a 'hellish' experience.[505] While Asquith was a close friend of the Stanley family, there were some members who were pleased to see him go. 'I am sorry for the downfall of our dear old PM,' wrote Margaret Stanley, 'but I do feel that a change will be for the good.'[506] Leaving 10 Downing Street was still traumatic for Asquith and his family, and the swiftness of his departure caused domestic problems. Sonia Keppel, whose mother Alice was a fervent Liberal, recalled how her family came to the rescue:

> The implications of his resignation were immediately felt at 16 Grosvenor Street as, homeless from 10 Downing Street, he and his family came here. Mamma moved out of her own bedroom for Mrs Asquith, and moved into Papa's room; Mr Asquith went into the spare room: and their son Anthony (aged fourteen) was accommodated in a vacant maid's room. (Their daughter, Elizabeth, went to some other friends).[507]

Asquith retained the support of a minority group of Liberal MPs but his days of power and influence were ebbing away.

While his talents for pursuing war had never been very apparent, Asquith had nevertheless 'laid the foundations for the machinery for a government to wage war'. He also achieved the Herculean task of holding together a divisive Liberal party and later the coalition government against all odds. When measured against his considerable peace-time successes as Premier, it is extraordinary that he had both the stamina and the will to pursue his love affairs with such intensity.[508]

Sylvia continued to be a sounding board for Asquith, though as she became heavily pregnant his interest appeared to wane. On 29 January 1917, Sylvia gave birth to a 'small and very plump Juliet'. 'Of course I feel a little disappointed,' Sylvia confessed to Anthony. 'At last I know I am not able to lift myself as if Monday's efforts had produced a boy. It is no good moping and I only hope next time will bring us what we want so much.'[509] In the weeks following the birth, Sylvia wrote regularly to Anthony, who had still not seen the baby, letting him know how she was developing; but transmitting very few details about her contacts with Asquith. Despite the arrival of a beautiful baby daughter, she could not be consoled. 'I feel sadness that I have not had the joy of giving you a son. I realise how complete our happiness at meeting would have been if it had been a little boy who lay between us.' While Sylvia waited for Anthony to finalise his leave, she travelled to Penrhôs with her nurse and maid in attendance. When she arrived she caught up with family gossip, including the news that 'Venetia is rather in love with Scatters.' By this time it was unlikely that Venetia was sleeping with her husband and it was widely rumoured that Sir Mathew 'Scatters' Wilson, a well-known libertine, was spending too much time in Venetia's company. This was encouraging news for Sylvia, who desperately hoped that Anthony's infatuation with her sister had been exhausted.[510]

Venetia cared little for what Edwin did, as long as he funded her increasingly extravagant lifestyle. For all the grief in his private life, Edwin was coming out of the political wilderness. He had initially turned down a Cabinet post from Lloyd George through loyalty to his former colleague, Asquith, but in June 1917 he capitulated and accepted the post of Secretary of State for India. Asquith was outraged and branded Montagu a traitor; but Montagu was ambitious and felt he had served his former master for long enough. A Cabinet colleague, Charles Hobhouse, summed up the new Indian supremo:

> Clever, even brilliant; he will probably not desert his party, but always attach himself to its most conspicuous men, and is determined to achieve a career, which he will probably do. He will probably swallow a good deal of boot blacking on the way. He has no courage, but some violence and bears malice and gossip.[511]

Montagu was not the only one whose career was lifting off. In May 1917, as the Battle of Arras petered out, Anthony Henley was appointed to his first active field command. As a Temporary Brigadier-General, he became General Officer Commanding (GOC) 127th Infantry Brigade, part of the 42nd Division. He joined them at Epéhy as they were re-fitting after a gruelling tour of duty in Gallipoli and Egypt. When the brigade moved forward into their frontline positions, one of Anthony's first tasks was to organise the digging of a new fire-trench – a mile long and 500 yards in advance of the existing line. The drawback was that it was half-way across No Man's Land. The fact that the operation was achieved with minimal casualties was a tribute to the skill and bravery of his engineers and men, as well as his own organisational abilities, which were recognised by several more MiDs during the year.[512] His family were delighted that, at last, he was seeing some action. His widowed mother Clare wrote to him regularly and they were warm letters, with the usual family news, but they still had a formality – she signed them 'your loving mother, C.C.L. Henley'. It was a formality completely at odds with the letters he received from his mother-in-law, 'Maisie' Stanley, who joked and teased him in her correspondence.[513]

Sylvia's close relationship with Asquith had now lasted for over two years and she was still a regular guest at 'The Wharf', where she was always placed next to the 'Ex PM' as she now referred to him. He called her 'my angel' and loved to have her hand on his, but as always that was as far as she let him advance and he seemed content with that limit, whatever passion poured out in his letters. When he could not meet her in London or at one of the regular house parties in the Home Counties, he longed for 'the vanished hand'. She was becoming increasingly busy and unavailable. Her success in setting up and administering workers' canteens in Hendon and Cricklewood had attracted the interest of King's College Hospital. This growing institution was now located in Camberwell and provided medical care south of the river, with over 550 military and civilian beds. Large numbers of auxiliaries and other workers from the area had to be fed and Sylvia was tasked with setting up a new canteen in the hospital.[514] Her newly acquired independence did not suit Asquith, who always liked to set the agenda, and although he remained devoted to her he continued to test his charms on other women. His antics earned the disapproval of socialites such as Jean Hamilton: 'I hear the Asquith lot disgraced themselves last night. Mr Asquith openly flirting.'[515] One particular favourite was Hilda Harrison, an old acquaintance who had moved to Boar's Hill, not far from 'The Wharf'. She had lost her husband, Major Roland Harrison, on 16 September 1917, almost on the anniversary of Raymond Asquith's death. Grief seemed to unite the PM and Hilda and a shared love of Shakespeare and the classics heightened their interest in each other. During one house party at 'The Wharf', Lady Cynthia Asquith, one of Asquith's daughters-in-law, observed 'the Pip-Emma [Asquith] and the little war widow [Hilda Harrison] sat out reading their own books in two cheek-by-jowl chairs.' It was hardly Antony and Cleopatra, and in his correspondence with her, Asquith rarely resorted to the intimate musings that he offered Sylvia. Hilda had a real love of scholarship – an attribute that Sylvia found hard to match.[516]

The end of the year brought the Asquith family further bad news. A younger son, Brigadier-General Arthur 'Oc' Asquith, was shot by a sniper on 20 December and shortly afterwards had to have the lower part of his leg amputated. Days later, Patrick Shaw-Stewart, one of the last standard bearers of the brilliant and witty set that surrounded Raymond Asquith, was blown to pieces. The New Year brought little respite, with depressing conditions at home, including further shortages of food and fuel. Rail transport was constantly disrupted and petrol rationed, while the government brought in more and more restrictive regulations. The military situation seemed similarly dire. It was true that the British Army itself was in good shape, especially after the limited tactical success of the Battle of Cambrai the previous November, but the strategic position for the Allies was ominous. Russia was convulsed by revolution and had withdrawn from the war, allowing the Germans to transfer large numbers of their troops from the Eastern to the Western Front. America had already entered the war but it would be months before her troops and equipment could bolster the Allies on the battlefield. So, in a desperate bid to crush the British and French armies before the Americans could intervene, the Germans launched a massive surprise offensive at dawn on 21 March 1918.

Anthony's 127th Brigade was part of the 42nd (East Lancashire) Division, a territorial unit that was held in reserve for several days as the German onslaught forced a 40-mile-deep salient into the British lines. The enemy were particularly successful in pushing back units in General Gough's Fifth Army sector, but fared less well against those in the British Third Army sector. And it was here that Anthony's brigade repelled repeated attacks at Ervillers and later at Bucquoy. Similar British actions along the front prevented a complete disaster and gradually the enemy's *Michael* offensive ran out of steam. It had failed to split the British and French armies to enable a much feared breakthrough. While Anthony survived the crisis, others in the Stanley family were less fortunate. Sylvia's brother Oliver, already wounded twice, had his leg shattered by an explosion. A DSO, Croix de Guerre and three MiDs were small compensation for his crippling injury.[517]

While British forces struggled on in France and Flanders, the Home Front was gripped by a resurgence of 'spy fever'. Captain Harold Spencer of the *Imperialist* magazine alleged that a German Prince had compiled a list of 47,000 British citizens whose depraved activities, carried out under German influence, were undermining military resolve. A 'Black Book' was supposed to contain not only the names of actors, dancers and chorus girls, but certain senior politicians and their wives, most notably H.H. Asquith and Margot Asquith. The latter had invited suspicion by her fondness for the bohemian or *avant garde* set. One dancer in particular had attracted Margot's attention and such was her fascination for this lithe trouper that she regularly paid for her accommodation. Margot's new best friend was Maud 'Salome' Allan, who had enjoyed such extraordinary success with her Salome dance in Edwardian London revues before the war. She had attempted to repeat the recipe abroad. It was not a success. So, in early 1918 she was trying to rekindle her relationship with the British public and accepted an invitation to play the temptress in a revival of Oscar Wilde's interpretation of the classic story. Because of its salacious content, Wilde's *Salome* could only be shown to private audiences and invited subscribers. The play was advertised in *The Times* on 10 February 1918, with an opening date the following April.

However, when the *Salome* advert appeared, one zealot promptly advised the *Imperialist Magazine*, now re-named the *Vigilante,* and its columnist Spencer was quick to pounce. On 16 February, with the connivance of the magazine owner, Noel Pemberton Billing MP, Spencer's short article appeared. It was outrageous and beyond bizarre. Titled 'The Cult of the Clitoris', it suggested that Maud Allan was responsible for encouraging many of the 47,000 undesirables. Using the perceived sexual 'science' of the time, Spencer inferred that because Maud was sexually aware, she must be a lesbian and consequently in possession of an impossibly large clitoris – a threat to one and all. While putting together his short article, Spencer had decided on the provocative title after telephoning a village doctor for help with suitable terminology. He was told that the term 'clitoris' defined 'a superficial organ that, when unduly excited or overdeveloped, possessed the most dreadful influence on any woman, that she would do the most extraordinary things.'[518]

Pemberton-Billing wanted a wide audience for his extraordinary theories and the best way was to invoke a court case. An appalled Maud took the bait and despite advice from friends to ignore the accusations in the article, she sued the publisher for libel. The case came to court at the Old Bailey in May 1918. The timing could not have been worse, with Britain and her Allies with their 'backs to the wall' after the recent German *Michael* offensive. The enemy had only been stopped ten miles outside Amiens and had inflicted terrible losses on the British – casualties were estimated at 160,000. The British had looked defeat in the face and they felt vulnerable.[519] Anyone who appeared to dent the morale of the nation or undermine the Home Front would not be tolerated, and this was the line of Pemberton-Billing's defence. Maud was deemed to be the instigator of a degenerate plot to undermine the national resolve and she was aided by her friends, H.H. and Margot Asquith. Maud later wrote that Pemberton-Billing's defence was really 'part of a campaign to get rid of Asquith' and that the 'venom manifested against his wife' resulted from the belief in some quarters that Margot had fraternized with German prisoners of war and surrounded herself with 'anti-British influences'. The public mood verged on hysteria and people remembered Margot's earlier court case concerning alleged pro-German tendencies.[520]

Pemberton-Billing, conducting his own defence, out-manoeuvred Maud at every turn. There were gasps from the public gallery when Pemberton-Billing pressured Maud to confess that her brother was a convicted murderer. Her personal credibility was further crushed when she admitted that she knew what a clitoris was and, as virtually no-one in the population then knew what (or where) it was, she was deemed to possess dark and dangerous knowledge. She was thereby accused of promoting 'the cult of the clitoris'. An inference of lesbian activity between Maud and Margot Asquith was also thrown in, and the spy hysteria was further stoked up by the accusation in court that Alice Keppel had conveyed German messages to England. False witnesses were produced who claimed to have seen the 'Black Book' of degenerates, so that everyone, it seemed, could be sucked into the vortex. In his summing up, the judge suggested to the jury that it was Wilde's play *Salome* that was also on trial and consequently the jury had little difficulty in finding Pemberton-Billing innocent of all charges. Maud Allan's reputation was ruined.

The furore over the 'Black Book' subsided as the good news came in of a reversal of British fortunes on the Western Front. Military advances were actually made in the summer and public interest in 'treasonable activities' started to wane. Maud, though, remained isolated. One of her few friends to remain loyal was Margot Asquith, who undertook to pay for Maud's accommodation for another ten years[521]

With the Maud Allan affair receding from the public eye, the summer of 1918 saw a number of British successes on the battlefront. Anthony's 127th Brigade was in the van of the British advance, progress made possible by the co-ordination of all-arms, including tanks, aircraft and artillery. On 21 August the brigade distinguished itself in operations to the west of Miraumont and several days later it participated in the capture of Pys. This new mobile war meant brigade headquarters were constantly on the move and letters between Anthony and Sylvia were no longer delivered on time. That was of little concern to Sylvia, who spent much of August at Glenconner, the Tennant's family seat near Berwick, and originally the family home of Margot Asquith. Asquith was also invited and took the opportunity to drive up from London, so that he would have a motor available to spend some private time with Sylvia.

Anthony spent the last months of the war fully occupied with planning his brigade's advance towards the vast German defensive position known as the Hindenburg Line. On 27 September the unit took part in the breakthrough of the line and the brigade continued fighting almost up to the Armistice. Anthony finished the war having been Mentioned in Dispatches eight times. It was a record of which he could be justifiably proud. Like most returning soldiers, he looked forward to returning to a domestic world that he remembered before 1914, and that included women in their traditional roles. But lives had not stood still at home and the war had fostered a new independence in women. Sylvia would make sure her marriage was on very different terms.

A Changing World

Just a few weeks after the end of the war, a General Election was held – the first election in which women over the age of 30 were allowed to vote. The rider to this development was the condition that these women had to be ratepayers or married to a ratepayer. Consequently, six million out of eleven million adult women were eligible to vote, but such limitations had allowed former opponents of women's suffrage, such as Asquith, to be steadily won over. 'Let the women work out their own salvation,' he had previously exhorted, yet now he proclaimed, 'they have worked it out during this war. How could we have carried on the war without them?' Sylvia and her sisters were of course eligible and duly voted in their first election, when Lloyd George's coalition government was returned. Asquith and his supporters were now just a minority within the Liberal Parliamentary Party, securing only 26 seats but remaining in opposition to the coalition, alongside the Labour Party. With the coalition in power, there was every hope that the female franchise would be extended, but the war had not seen a huge and irreversible shift in the status of women. Upper class women were in a better position to defend their new-found independence, but those from the working class would soon see the erosion of their immediate gains in employment or status.[522]

The large country estates would stagger on after the war, some lucky enough to have an heir coming back from the conflict and a large and productive acreage to see off the threats of recession and death duties. But for many other estates, the war was the final straw. Domestic servants would no longer be available in the quantity and at a price that could be afforded and many of the erstwhile powerful and influential families had to sell their central London townhouses to staunch the haemorrhage of funds. It signalled the end of the dominance by the old families of London political life. For Sylvia, the war did not necessarily break the chain of domesticity and child rearing – that was largely removed from her anyway by the availability of servants and nannies – but it did enable her to see life outside her social bubble. Her work in the hospital and canteens brought her into regular contact with other classes and for the first time in her life she had experienced that intoxicating feeling of independence. New opportunities surfaced and her administrative skills were recognised in 1920, when she was recruited to the Board of Governors of King's College Hospital, a post she was to hold until 1973.[523]

Anthony returned from the war unscathed. He was fortunate, for even though his family might have considered him safe as a Brigadier-General, 232 generals were killed, wounded or captured. He was also a lucky statistic amongst his old school friends, for over half of all Old Etonians serving overseas became casualties.[524] He was appointed a CMG (Companion of the Order of St Michael and St George) in 1919 and retired with the rank of Honorary Brigadier-General in the Reserve of Officers. The Stanleys of Alderley were also fortunate that they suffered no deaths, and only one son, Oliver was wounded, albeit three times. For the aristocracy as a whole though, it was a disastrous war, with nearly 20 per cent of serving peers under 50 years of age being killed in action.[525]

The war scythed through families, rich or poor, and the grief was the same for the aristocracy as it was for the wretched, desperate poor in the city slums. The conflict had also destroyed old certainties and social conventions, such as marriage, took a battering. However, some unions did not need a war to undermine them; in the case of Edwin and Venetia Montagu, it was almost over before it had begun. Duff Cooper certainly thought so and wasted no time in declaring it finished. 'The relations of Edwin and Venetia are very distressing,' he wrote. 'She seems hardly to be able to bear him – she cannot help showing it and he cannot help seeing it.'[526] Cooper had little sympathy for the man who had really helped Sylvia in her darkest hours during the war:

> Alas, I no longer like and cannot pity him … He is a man incapable of inspiring trust, confidence or lasting love. He has no friends or followers either in politics or in private life. He has great qualities of charm and intellect but they are all warped by something, which I believe to be a mixture of cowardice, jealousy and suspicion.[527]

The Montagus continued their tortured relationship only on Venetia's terms – she choosing who she slept with and Montagu pining over her. Her conversion to Judaism still rankled with society hostesses, for it seemed to some as if she had deserted her class and it was this apparent 'disloyalty' that caused continued sniping behind her back. She might be spied at a dinner party and described unkindly as 'large and fleshy' but she could still hook and reel in some of the most influential men in the country. While Montagu, as Secretary of State for India, headed off to the Paris Peace Conference in 1919, Venetia decided to attend – but not in the capacity her husband would have hoped. While Montagu stayed alone at the Majestic Hotel, his wife reclined at the more luxurious Ritz, in an adjacent bedroom to Lord Beaverbrook. It was common knowledge that she was one of Beaverbrook's mistresses. It was sad to see the Montagus dining together with Beaverbrook at the Ritz Grill and afterwards Montagu retiring tactfully to his lonely room. He was not the only man to spend his nights alone. George Clemenceau, the veteran French Prime Minister also found himself out of the running. 'I am like those little charms that the ladies put on their breasts,' he confided to Lloyd George. 'They have no hesitation in putting me there nowadays. At my age I am not dangerous!'[528] Montagu's political career ended in 1922, when he resigned following a fall-out with Lord Curzon. The birth of a daughter, Judith in 1923, did little to bolster his spirits. He gamely took the baby as his own, though it was later revealed that she was most probably the result of Venetia's relationship with Eric Dudley. Montagu, the devoted lover of Venetia and truest of friends to Sylvia, died the following year.[529]

Immediately after the war temporary ranks were rescinded and those who had enjoyed elevation to the rank of general for the duration of the war now found themselves reduced to their substantive regimental ranks for pay purposes. In Anthony's case this meant reverting to the pay of a Captain, so he retired from the Army and sought other employment, becoming a director of the shipowners Arthur Capel & Co. The family moved to 9 Oxford Square and became near neighbours to Katherine Asquith, Raymond's widow. Anthony was spending more time working abroad, particularly in Romania, where his company was involved in the post-war shipping boom. Sylvia stayed in London and looked after the three girls, employing a governess to help teach the younger ones, while the eldest, Rosalind, attended Notting Hill High School. For a time, when Sylvia's brother Arthur was ill, Sylvia also took in his eldest child, Adelaide. Her other brother, Oliver, whom she had nursed during the war, married in 1919. Athough Sylvia remained close to him, she clashed constantly with his new, strong-willed wife, Kathleen. It was a situation made worse when Oliver and his family moved to nearby Cambridge Square.[530]

In 1922, Margot Asquith, who now seemed to inhabit an international set, published her autobiography, prompting Dorothy Parker to jibe, 'the affair between Margot Asquith and Margot Asquith is one of the prettiest love stories in literature.' Still, Margot herself was no stranger to acidic putdowns. When she met the American actress, Jean Harlow, no quarter was reportedly given. Harlow asked 'Are you Margot Asquith?' mispronouncing her Christian name with a hard 't.' 'My dear, the "t" is silent,' replied Margot, 'as in Harlow.' While Margot could easily defend herself, it was more than could be said for her vulnerable friend, the dancer Maud Allan. Her career was in tatters after the sensational 1918 court case and she spent much of her time in America, trying unsuccessfully to re-ignite her dancing and acting career. She returned to England in the late 1920s and, having once denied her Sapphic preferences in the courtroom, began a ten-year lesbian relationship with Margot Asquith's secretary. That affair ended in bitterness and recrimination and Maud died in 1956, almost forgotten and in near poverty.[531]

In the immediate years after the war, Asquith slid towards the margins of British politics, but that wily operator Lloyd George was not immune to changes in fortune. Conservative pressure within the coalition eventually ejected him from 10 Downing Street in 1922. Faced with a new Conservative Prime Minister, Stanley Baldwin, the Lloyd George Liberals and Asquith Liberals decided to call a truce in order to fight the 1924 election. The Liberal grandees were wheeled out for the cause, whatever their age. Lyulph Sheffield and his brother-in-law, Sir Hugh Bell, both in their eighties, found they were addressing two or three meetings a day in support of

Arthur Stanley, who was standing for Parliament. Despite his optimism, Asquith lost his seat in the October election, when the Liberal Party haemorrhaged seats. The following year he was elevated to the peerage, as Earl of Oxford and Asquith, his own surname being attached to the title at the insistence of the existing peer, the Earl of Oxford. Although he remained close to Sylvia after the war, his passion was largely spent. He no longer needed her regular reassurance and advice, as he had in the days when he was besieged by political opponents, and the frequency of their letters declined. However, he did maintain a steady correspondence with Hilda Harrison. His letters, lacking the passion and intimacy he once showered on Sylvia, reflected more his delight in a shared interest in art and literature. As his physical health deteriorated, Asquith's appetite for quotations in Greek, Latin and Italian showed no sign of abating. In 1927 he suffered a stroke but recovered sufficiently to pay one last visit to Venetia Montagu, to whom he had become reconciled. The following winter he succumbed to a chill and died on 15 February 1928. He was buried in the churchyard at Sutton Courtenay, near his treasured sanctuary 'The Wharf.' The years were kinder to Margot who lived to see her step-daughter Violet embark on a political career, notably supporting Winston Churchill in his fight against Nazi appeasement in the 1930s. Margot died in 1945, aged 81, within months of her young daughter, Elizabeth.

In 1923, Anthony's eldest half-brother, the 4th Lord Henley died and the title passed to another older brother. At this stage, Anthony became heir to the barony and the following year, he and the family left London to live at the old Henley family seat at Watford Court in Northamptonshire. It was to be a brief stay. In 1925, Anthony was in Romania on business when he died suddenly, reportedly while 'playing cricket'. He was only 51.[532] It was a terrible shock for Sylvia, made more miserable by the fact that their last years together had not been their happiest. Her sadness was compounded by the death, within months, of her beloved father Lyulph. The old warhorse was beset with arthritis and deafness, and suddenly was overtaken by senility. It was tragic for the family to see that supreme, combative intellect fade away in his last days at Alderley Park. His eldest son, Arthur, succeeded to the Stanley title and took over the running of both Alderley and Penrhôs. But the gloss had been rubbed away from these great houses and they no longer played host to large house parties or the intellectual and political giants of the day. Economies were put in place. The hunters were sold, furniture dispatched to the auction house and many of the domestic servants were dismissed.

Following the deaths of her husband and father, Sylvia decided to take a complete break from her normal life. In October 1925, she accompanied her famous cousin, the writer and traveller Gertrude Bell, on her last visit to Baghdad. Bell was hugely influential in the creation of a new Iraq after the collapse of the old Ottoman Empire and she was delighted to show Sylvia the sights and introduce her to the people of this extraordinary place. After an adventurous journey the pair eventually arrived, but Sylvia suffered an infected eye, made worse by the prodding of a local doctor.

She returned to Britain, leaving her cousin in Iraq. Bell never returned home, dying tragically the following year from an apparent overdose of sleeping pills.[533]

In 1931, there were two events that caused Sylvia some concern. One was the marriage of her daughter Rosalind to her cousin, Captain George Pitt-Rivers, a man whom Sylvia found most difficult – he was reported to be too similar to his eccentric grandfather, who had established the Pitt-Rivers Museum in Oxford. Despite the birth of a son, Anthony, the couple split after a few years.[534] For Sylvia the other alarming incident of 1931 was a fire at her old family home, Alderley Park. The destruction was not quite complete but most of the mansion, save a few sitting-rooms, bedrooms and the Tennant's Hall, had to be demolished two years later. The disaster heralded the end of the Stanley estate and their 500-year association with Cheshire. After three divorces, crippling estate duties and an extravagant gambling lifestyle, the 6th Lord Stanley sold the entire Alderley Estate in 1938. The sale of the 4500-acre estate was not a happy one and the mood of the tenants, who had enjoyed a previously good relationship with the Stanleys, turned to passive hostility. The whole transaction realised less than £500,000 and many of the farm lots and parcels of land remained unsold at the auction, so the sale limped on for several years. The heart of the estate where the house once stood was a ruin. The beautiful beech wood that had flanked the mansion was felled during the Second World War and the walled gardens and grounds degenerated into scrubland. It was a desperate end to a once glorious estate. In the 1950s, ICI purchased the remains of the estate, erected a large complex and replanted the woods.[535]

Penrhôs was used by Arthur, the 5th Lord Stanley and his family in the 1920s and 1930s, but it was a shadow of its former self. Other family members congregated from time to time, but it had been passed to a new generation who did not have the influential connections and the house was no longer host to the great political figures of the day. Large sections of the house became uninhabitable and the Second World War saw the billeting of troops in its haunted rooms. The interior was wrecked and the best of its architectural features were removed. It became a ruin after the war and was sold in 1948. Between them, the dissolute 6th and 7th Lord Stanleys managed to destroy the family inheritance and by 1971 there was precious little for the 8th Lord Stanley to administer. Nonetheless, through his personal probity and competent political skills, he restored the good name of the family. The land and beach of the old Penrhôs Estate on Holy Island has since become a nature reserve and today most ramblers who stumble across the ivy enveloped ruins of the old house have little idea of the dramas that once unfolded there.[536]

When Winston Churchill became Prime Minister in 1940, his old friend Sylvia Stanley was on hand to lend moral support. During the war, she also gave practical support to causes such as the Polish Army in exile and was personally awarded a brooch for her work by the C-in-C, General Sikorski. She was a regular visitor to Downing Street and became a close friend of Churchill's Assistant Private Secretary, Jock Colville. His wartime diaries refer to numerous lunch and dinner dates with

Sylvia, often accompanied by her daughter Juliet, who was working as a Principal in the nearby Treasury.[537] Sylvia also tried to maintain her friendship with Churchill's wife, Clementine, though it was not always easy. Much to Sylvia's disquiet, Clementine often rebuffed her. Such coolness may have arisen because Clementine feared intimate conversations, in which she might mistakenly give away confidential information. Or it may just have been the Hozier blood, which prompted mood swings from friendly to glacial. [538] There was also the less charitable view that Clementine knew Sylvia's penchant for the company of Prime Ministers in crisis and may have feared a repeat of the Asquith years. She need not have worried, for Sylvia was a true friend to both of them, during the war and after. There were holidays together, such as a motoring vacation in post-war France, when Clementine joined Sylvia, her daughter Rosalind and grandson Anthony in a jaunt around the west coast. Sylvia also joined Clementine for a two-month trip to Ceylon. According to Clementine, 'We set out two old crocks & have returned quite set up.'[539] Still living in Oxford Square, Sylvia remained a regular companion in Clementine's life. They met regularly at small lunch or dinner parties, played backgammon, or enjoyed trips to concerts or exhibitions. Churchill, too, enjoyed Sylvia's company, for she still retained that spark and interest in life, as well as the ability to play a devilish hand of bezique, a talent that the ex-PM always admired.

Sylvia's children remained a great source of pride to her. One daughter was an accomplished artist, another worked for the Board of Trade, while her eldest daughter, Rosalind, pursued a career in medical research, successfully identifying the thyroid hormone, triiodothyronine, and achieving worldwide recognition. The accolades were crowned by Rosalind's becoming one of the first women Fellows of the Royal Society. Sylvia's own post-war accomplishments were also notable. She continued to be involved with the administration of King's College Hospital, London, as well as the Regional Hospital Board. In recognition of her tireless work, she was awarded the OBE in 1962 and six years later the hospital opened the 'Sylvia Henley Ward', which is still in use.

Through the 1960s and 1970s, 'she marched on, ramrod straight, defying time.' A friend wrote that 'One reward of her energetic life was a face that under snow white hair grew better looking as every year passed.' In fact she was still so slim that in the 1970s she could still appear in an haute couture dress that was made for her by Paquin in 1913. In 1977, her incredible stamina started to fail her and after her personal nurse died, she was admitted to St George's Nursing Home in Westminster. Sylvia Henley died of a heart attack on 18 May 1980, aged 98, remaining lucid and in command until the end. She was almost the last member of a Liberal generation that operated at the very centre of power. Indeed, for a time, through her extremely close relationship with the Prime Minister, she was privy to the nation's greatest secrets and remained the wisest of counsellors. She created in her mentor, H.H. Asquith, a passion certainly equal to that aroused by her sister and yet she remained loyal to those close to her. She tamed 'the blue beast' but never championed it.

Afterword: 'The Human Soul on Fire'

This story has not been a tale of faint hearts and martyred women – at least not where the main characters are concerned. Winifred, Emilie and Sylvia were no pawns of the great and powerful and they were certainly not invisible members of a society that prided itself on virtue and duty. They were feisty and very visible ladies. But leaving aside for a moment the morality of their illicit relationships, did they herald the age of the new independent woman or were they merely products of their late Edwardian age?

Certainly, their wealth and comfortable backgrounds meant they could afford to be independent. Emilie's enormous dollar legacy dwarfed anything that Sylvia or Winifred could boast but they all enjoyed a financial security unavailable to the vast majority of Edwardian women. Nonetheless, they represented a spirit and desire amongst the female population for more freedom, an aspiration that gained momentum as the War ended. Such hopes would be partly satisfied by the extension of the franchise, reform of the divorce laws and a growing understanding about birth control. Though these three women were no suffragette 'heroines', they enjoyed and made the most of their male-dominated society, using sexual allure to captivate their suitors; and it was the Great War itself that catapulted them into the very centre of power.

What of their effect on their military and political lovers during the War? Winifred Bennett seemed to cast a soothing and moderating influence on the emotional and at times self-combusting Field Marshal Lord French. This was particularly evident during the 1915 'Shell Scandal', and later that year when forces (not just the German enemy) were ranged against French after the Battle of Loos. The wise counsel she gave her lover eased his anguish about his resignation, enabling his successor, Field Marshal Haig, to take over as Commander-in-Chief in December 1915. For Emilie Grigsby, the War brought great dividends. She was able, via her relationships with such military heavyweights as General Cowans and such well-informed military gossips as Colonel Charles Repington, to reach the inner sanctum of power. From there, she could indulge her real love of intrigue by promoting herself as a political 'fixer', whose salons at 80 Brook Street were designed to allow influential figures such as Lord Northcliffe and Lord Carson to conspire at will. A mistress of invention, she probably never loved anyone except herself. This could not be said of Sylvia Henley, that steadfast confidante of Prime Minister Asquith, who provided him with unflinching support during the May 1915 political crisis as well as during his tenure as Prime Minister of the Coalition Government, until his downfall in December 1916. In the light of his clumsy physical advances towards her, her readiness to accept his intense mental intimacy might seem bizarre today. Furthermore, it is hard to see her denial of her own sexuality as anything but naïve – all the more surprising in a woman of such intellectual maturity. Even so, the combined betrayal by Sylvia's sister, Venetia, and her own husband at the very height of Asquith's obsessive demands would have destroyed a lesser woman.

All this illicit passion among Britain's elite could not have developed without the compliance of the press. The closeness of the press and senior politicians and military figures during the Great War was astonishing. Contemporary allegations against modern politicians appear trifling in the light of what could have been exposed at the time. Northcliffe, the media giant of his day, had much to conceal about his own complicated private life, yet he made it his business to hear about the sexual peccadillos of his political enemies. That he chose to conceal their affairs only served to strengthen his hand; and with such a promise of immunity, men such as French, Cowans and Asquith became almost reckless about their affairs. Their prodigious output of love letters meant that there was every chance that their correspondence could fall into the wrong hands and even give succour to the enemy, whilst in French's case, he was fortunate that his main courier, George Gordon Moore, remained silent on the subject. Occasionally, some scandal did leak into the press. One of French's earlier affairs landed him with a mention in a divorce case, whilst the Asquiths were dragged into the Maud Allan tragedy. Cowans was severely rebuked over the 'Patsy Cornwallis Affair' and the later Dennistoun scandal, and even Emilie Grigsby had to make a court appearance during the Mackay Trial.

Wartime, with its excuses for absence from the marital home, made affairs easier for both sexes. Travel also allowed these women to spend time with their suitors. Winifred could waft in and out of European cities owing to the postings of her diplomat husband. Emilie could travel more easily between countries, at least in the early years of the War, since she was a citizen of a neutral country. Sylvia, in the time-honoured traditions of her class, would travel between the family seat, other estates and the London town house. It all made secret assignations far easier.

There would come a time when the passion began to fade and the illicit affairs petered out. As the War drew to a close, the three women no longer found themselves at the centre of power and they would never again experience such influence. Even Sylvia, who continued to enjoy a lively and stimulating social life for the rest of her days, would never re-live the drama and stimulus of the war years.

Each of these women's stories is unique but their collective experience highlights the strong bond between power and passion. That ebullient old warhorse and Allied Commander-in-Chief, Field Marshal Ferdinand Foch, once said that 'the most powerful weapon on earth is the human soul on fire' – a *bon mot* that Winifred, Emilie and Sylvia understood only too well.

Notes

Chapter 1

1 Ellen Holtzman, 'The Pursuit of Married Love: Women's Attitudes Toward Sexuality and Marriage in Great Britain 1918–1939', in *Journal of Social History*, 16:2 (1982: Winter). At the outbreak of war in 1914, life expectancy was 55 years for women and 52 years for men.

2 Lady Hamilton, wife of Sir Ian Hamilton was one who was appalled that the subject of 'the blue beast' should be aired by other women. See Lady Hamilton Diary, 4 August 1916, Sir Ian Hamilton Papers, Liddell Hart Centre for Military Archives, King's College, London (hereafter LHCMA).

3 Quoted in Jonathan Walker, 'Breaking the Rules: Officers' Memoirs Published 1920–1935', in *Stand To!* 2002.

4 George Curnock of the *Daily Mail* heard the soldiers of the BEF singing the classic lyrics of *Tipperary* as they disembarked at Boulogne, and published it in his newspaper. The song, which was barely known, became famous overnight, but these words were rarely sung. The tune was usually sung to the words shown here. 2nd Lieutenant F.T. Nettleingham, *Tommy's Tunes* (Erskine Macdonald, London 1917).

5 Clare Makepeace, 'Punters and their prostitutes. British soldiers, masculinity and *maisons tolérées* in the First World War', in J.H. Arnold and S. Brady (Eds.), *What is Masculinity?* (Palgrave Macmillan, London 2011).

6 Trevor Fisher, 'Britain's Unpermissive Society', in *History Today*, Vol. 42, August 1992.

7 For a study of Lloyd George's complicated love life, see Ffion Hague, *The Pain and the Privilege. The Women in Lloyd George's Life* (HarperPress, London 2008). Frances Stevenson eventually married Lloyd George in 1943.

8 Pétain was discovered by his ADC at the Hotel Terminus in the Gard du Nord. See William Martin, *Verdun 1916* (Osprey, Oxford 2001), p.44. Pershing was already a widower, having lost his wife and most of their children in a house fire in 1915. He had first become acquainted with Resco when she painted his portrait.

9 Arthur Marwick, *The Deluge. British Society and the First World War* (Palgrave Macmillan, London 2006), p.62.

10 *The Diaries of Lady Cynthia Asquith 1915–18* (Century, London 1987), p.70.

11 Not only had French's writing deteriorated since the days of the Boer War diary, but during the First World War period he often put the wrong dates on his letters, which can further confuse the reader.

12 Interview with Roderick Suddaby, 13 January 1976, IWM Sound Archive ref. 6987. *The Milwaukee Journal* of 2 January 1976 reported that the collection was sold at Sotheby's auction for $9800 in December 1975.

13 Quoted in Gerard DeGroot, *Blighty. British Society in the Era of the Great War* (Longman, London 1996), pp.76–7.

14   In 1903, Sylvia went on a holiday to Homburg with friends including her sister Blanche.
      It was a spa town made famous by visits from King Edward VII, and after returning from
      one jaunt, the Monarch sported a hat, which was christened the Homburg.
15   Joan Wyndham, *Dawn Chorus* (Virago Press, London 2004), p.22.
16   Galatz featured in Bram Stoker's novel *Dracula*.
17   Ethel Pantazzi, *Roumania in Light & Shadow* (Fisher Unwin, London 1921), pp.80–1. Also,
      Princess Anne-Marie Callimachi, *Yesterday was Mine* (Falcon Press, London 1952), pp.72–3.
      The old quarter of Galatz was substantially destroyed by bombing in the Second World
      War.
18   After the country's formation, she was still subject to restrictions by the major powers. Full
      independence came in 1877.
19   Quoted in Hannah Pakula, *Queen of Roumania: The Life of Princess Marie, Granddaughter
      of Queen Victoria* (Weidenfeld & Nicolson, London 1984), pp.59, 88–9. Also James
      Pope-Hennessy, *Queen Mary 1867–1953* (George Allen & Unwin, London 1959), p.251.
      The Prince of Wales was angry at this match, hoping that Marie could have married his
      son Prince George (later George V).
20   The Youell sisters also spoke Romanian, but this language was not used in court circles.
      The Romanian language is unusual in that it has barely any regional dialects. Any
      Romanian speaker can be understood throughout the country.
21   Greek influence in Romania had steadily increased since the seventeenth century. Greeks
      dominated commercial life as well as the Orthodox Church, and Greek became the
      language of the inner court; see R. Seton-Watson, *A History of the Roumanians* (Cambridge
      University Press, London 1934), pp.78–81.
22   Pantazzi, op. cit., pp.76–7.
23   *The Hong Kong Guide 1893* (OUP, Oxford 1982). Also *The West Australian*, 16 July 1981.
      And Percy Bennett photograph album, Camilla Shivarg Papers. When not engaged
      on government business, Bennett entertained himself by being carted about in chairs,
      Jinrikisha or Sampans, or with trips on the Peak Tramway. Other diversions included
      visits to Deep Bay, Quarry Bay, Shau-ki Wan or the climb up 4000 feet to the summit of
      Taimoshan.
24   From Manila, Bennett travelled regularly to Yokohama to help supervise the 1894 British
      trade and territory agreement.
25   De Lazlo's output was prolific. It is estimated that by the end of his career, he had
      executed over 3500 paintings.
26   Bennett kept the hat band pinned to his photograph of the battleship and placed it in an
      album. It is still kept in the family. Einstein's legendary film depicts the mutiny on the
      battleship *Potemkin*. Propaganda ensured that an exaggerated slaughter took place on the
      Richelieu Steps. Alexander Shivarg to Author 23 September 2010.
27   See Neal Bascombe, *Red Mutiny: Mutiny, Revolution and Revenge on the Battleship Potemkin*
      (Weidenfeld & Nicolson, London 2007).
28   Ethel Pantazzi, op. cit., p.68.
29   H. Pakula, op. cit., pp.114–5. Also Pantazzi, op. cit., pp.80–1.
30   The London Exhibition was held near the Shepherd's Bush area of West London, which
      due to the large number of white exhibition buildings, was renamed 'White City.' The site
      is today occupied by BBC Television Centre and the Westfield Shopping Centre.
31   A photographic portrait of 'Andrew Percy Bennett' is held by the National Portrait
      Gallery, London.
32   Comyn-Platt eventually married Henriette in 1917. He was knighted in 1922. See
      Michael Munn, *David Niven: The Man Behind the Balloon* (J.R. Brooks, London 2009).
33   Maureen Waller, *The English Marriage: Tales of Love, Money and Adultery* (John Murray,
      London 2009), pp.330–1.
34   Born in 1880, Jack Annesley received his first commission from the Militia in 1900, just
      in time to see service in the Boer War alongside his father in the 10th Hussars. Annesley

distinguished himself in South Africa, returning with the Queen's Medal (3 clasps) and the King's Medal (2 clasps).

35   The name 'Hussars' had been borrowed from the Hungarians.

36   Stephen Badsey, *Doctrine and the Cavalry 1880–1918* (Ashgate, Vermont US 2008), pp.8–9.

37   The title had not been proved since 1844. Debrett's claimed the title to be dormant and it was not proved again until 1959, when Brigadier Francis Annesley won a court case. Arthur Annesley, 11th Viscount Valentia was also created 1st Baron Annesley in 1917.

38   One sister, Lettice, married Geoffrey Bowlby, and one of their daughters, Kitty would become Lady Trenchard, whilst Eva later married Admiral Sir Roger Keyes. After Jack Annesley's death, Caryl became heir and eventually succeeded to the title as the 12th Viscount Valentia. When he died in 1949, the estate was sold to the Astor family. In 1994 Dr Michael Peagram bought the estate and extensively renovated the house and parkland as well as establishing an archive of the estate's history.

39   Field Marshal Sir John French (J.F.) to Mrs Winifred Bennett (W.B.), 22 April 1915. 'Bennett Correspondence' microfiche PP/MCR/C33 roll 1, Sir John French Papers, Imperial War Museum, London (hereafter IWM).

40   L.E. Jones, *An Edwardian Youth* (Macmillan, London 1956), pp.207–8.

41   Philip Ziegler, *Diana Cooper* (Hamish Hamilton, London 1981), pp.22, 39.

42   Peter Upton, *The Tenth* (King's Royal Hussar Museum, Winchester 1999).

43   Viscountess Byng of Vimy, *Up the Stream of Time* (Macmillan, Toronto 1945), pp.85–6. Also Jeffery Williams, *Byng of Vimy* (Leo Cooper, London 1983), pp.53–7.

44   The Force came under General Sir Ian Hamilton's Mediterranean Command.

45   Viscountess Byng, op. cit., p.88.

46   Jeffery Williams, op. cit., pp.58–9.

47   The higher appointments were KCMG ('Kindly Call Me God') and GCMG ('God Calls Me God').

48   94 Lancaster Gate was part of two terraces built in 1856. The house was demolished in 1936 and replaced with a red brick block of flats, named 'Barrie House'. These flats, together with a similar replacement block in the second terrace ruined the symmetry of one of London's most elegant colonnaded terraces. See Westminster Archive Centre, London.

49   George H. Cassar, *The Tragedy of Sir John French* (Associated University Presses, Newark 1985), p.181.

50   *New York Times* 5 December 1912. It was on one of his transatlantic cruises in 1910 that Moore first met French. See George Cassar op. cit., p.181.

51   George G. Moore to Stuyvesant Fish, 12 February 1963, Monterey County Historical Society, and www.bigsurlandtrust.org.

52   A set that included many of the sons and daughters of an earlier intellectual circle known as 'The Souls.'

53   J.F. to W.B. 24 February 1915, 11 December 1915, French Papers, IWM.

54   Roberson lived at nearby Westbourne Terrace.

55   His wife was one of eight daughters, known as the 'Eight Belles' of the wealthy landowner, Richard Selby-Lowndes. For an excellent study of French's life and career, see Professor Richard Holmes, *The Little Field Marshal* (Weidenfeld & Nicolson, London 2004).

56   J.F. to W.B., 24 February 1915, French Papers, IWM.

57   Philip Ziegler, op. cit., pp.8, 26. Even if she rejected a man, as Ziegler points out, 'she always hated to let any man pass out of her life.'

Chapter 2

58   Adrian Gregory, *The Last Great War. British Society and the First World War* (CUP, Cambridge 2008), pp.13–16, 294.

59   Bilborough, quoted in Angela K. Smith, *The Second Battlefield. Women, Modernism and the First World War* (Manchester University Press, Manchester 2000), p.23. For Brittain, see Alan Bishop & Terry Smart (Eds.), *Vera Brittain. War Diary 1913–1917. Chronicle of Youth.* (Victor Gollancz, London 1981), p.85. For Nielson, see, Joyce Marlow (Ed.), *The Virago Book of Women and the Great War* (Virago Press, London 1998), p.21.

60   Lady Hamilton Diary, 1 March 1916, LHCMA, King's College, London.

61   Lieutenant-Colonel L.A. Strange, *Recollections of an Airman* (John Hamilton, London 1933), p.109.

62   Lieutenant-Colonel F. Whitmore, *10th PWO Royal Hussars and the Essex Yeomanry During the European War 1914–1918* (Benham, Colchester 1920), p.7. Annesley's Divisional Commander (3rd Cavalry Division) was Major-General Sir Julian Byng, who had been his C-in-C in Egypt.

63   *The Tatler*, 15 December 1915. Lieutenant Edward Leatham, 12th Lancers, was killed in action, 31 October 1914. Major Victor Brooke DSO, 9th Lancers, was killed in action 29 August 1914.

64   He was later re-buried in Ypres Town Cemetery.

65   *The Oxford Times*, 28 November 1914.

66   Richard Holmes, op. cit., p.278. From October 1914 to March 1916, GHQ was based at St Omer, some 20 miles from Calais.

67   J.F. to W.B, 19 November 1914, French Papers. This referred to her letter, some months earlier, wishing the C-in-C good fortune.

68   Lord Valentia to Messrs Maud & Tunicliffe, 24 February 1915, 33L/193 Annesley Papers, Oxfordshire County Archives, Oxford.

69   Mrs C.S. Peel, *How We Lived Then* (John Lane, London 1929), p.55.

70   Lieutenant W.B.P. Spencer, ref. GS1515, Liddle Collection, Leeds University.

71   Quoted in Stanley Weintraub, *Stillness Heard Around the World* (OUP, Oxford 1985), p.5.

72   Original members were Britain, France, Belgium, Serbia and Russia. The US joined the Allies in 1917, but was only ever an 'Associated Power.'

73   J.F. to W.B. 18 January 1915, French Papers. Also Frederic Coleman, *From Mons to Ypres with French* (Sampson, Low, Marston, London 1916).

74   J.F. to W.B., 26 January 1915, French Papers. Also *The Times*, 2, 4, 5, 7, 13, 16 January 1915. French assiduously destroyed all his lover's letters.

75   J.F. to W.B., 14 February 1915, French Papers.

76   J.F. to W.B., 14, 18 February 1915, French Papers.

77   Winston Churchill, *Great Contemporaries* (Macmillan, London 1942), pp.68–9.

78   J.F. to W.B., 3 June 1915, French Papers.

79   J.F. to W.B. 4 February 1915, French Papers.

80   Gough was Sir Douglas Haig's Chief of Staff and was one of the ablest soldiers in the BEF. Although the Irishman had fallen out with French over the issue of Home Rule for Ireland just before the outbreak of war, he still maintained the confidence of his C-in-C and the pair had met only the week before to discuss Gough's future divisional command. He was killed on 20 February 1915 while reconnoitring the ground for an attack on Neuve Chapelle. For Gough's life, see Ian Beckett, *Johnnie Gough VC. A Biography of Brigadier-General Sir John Edmond Gough VC, KCB* (Tom Donovan, London 1989).

81   J.F. to W.B., 24 February 1915, French Papers.

82   For Stopes, see Ruth Hall (Ed.), *Dear Dr Stopes* (André Deutsch, London 1978), p.148.

83   Susie Steinbach, *Women in England 1760–1914. A Social History* (Weidenfeld & Nicolson, London 2003), p.132.

84   Adam Hochschild, 'John French and Charlotte Despard: The Odd Couple' in *History Today*, Vol. 61, issue 6, 2011.

85   C.D. Baker-Carr, *From Chauffeur to Brigadier* (Ernest Benn, London 1930), op. cit., p.27.

86   J.F. to W.B., 24 February 1915, French Papers.

87   C.S. Peel, op. cit., p.79.

88   Officers ditched their uniforms and donned black tie before entering the clubs.

89   Philip Ziegler, *Diana Cooper* (Hamish Hamilton, London), pp.62–3. Also, Diana Cooper, *Autobiography* (Carroll & Graf, New York 1985), op. cit., pp.96–7.

90   Diana Cooper, op. cit., pp.95–6, 142–3.

91   Ziegler, op. cit., p.94. Also Diana Cooper, op. cit., pp.144–5.

92   J.F. to W.B., 27 February, 2 March 1915, French Papers.

93   Ibid.

94   J.F. to W.B. 9 March 1915, French Papers.

95   J.F. to W.B., 15 March 1915, French Papers.

96   Clause 1696 of King's Regulations, concerning facial hair, was repealed in October 1916, and allowed the upper lip to be shaved. *The Times* 17 October 1916.

97   Major-General Sir Edward Spears, ref. 4231, Imperial War Museum Sound Archive, London.

98   J.F. to W.B., 8 April 1915, French Papers.

99   J.F. to W.B., 2 May 1915, French Papers.

100   One of Moore's contacts was Colonel Isaac Lewis, whose Lewis machine-gun would be adopted by the British Army the following October. The Lewis Gun was already in service with the Belgian Army. See Field-Marshal Viscount French of Ypres, *1914* (Constable, London 1919), p.354.

101   Lord Haldane, speaking in the House of Lords, 16 November 1915. See *Hansard,* H.L. Deb, 16 November 1915 Vol. 20, cc372.

102   J.F. to W.B., 2 May 1915, French Papers.

103   J.F. to W.B., 22 April 1915, French Papers.

104   J.F. to W.B., 2 May 1915, French Papers.

105   J.F. to W.B., 12 June 1915, French Papers.

106   *1914,* op. cit., p.357.

107   Charles Repington, *The First World War 1914–1918 Vol. I* (Constable, London 1920), pp.36–7.

108   Robinson changed his name to Dawson in 1917; S.J. Taylor, *The Great Outsiders. Northcliffe, Rothermere and The Daily Mail* (Phoenix, London 1998), p.157; According to Charles Hobhouse, it was O'Connor and Marlowe who orchestrated the attacks, see Edward David (Ed.), *Inside Asquith's Cabinet. From the Diaries of Charles Hobhouse* (John Murray, London 1977), op. cit., p.249.

109   A.J.P. Taylor, *Lloyd George: A Diary of Frances Stevenson* (Hutchinson, London 1971), p.142.

110   Paget was badly gassed. The son of Sir Arthur Paget and his American wife Minnie, Bertie was to suffer an agonising two years of gas-induced decline before his death in 1917. It was a squalid end for such a bright and debonnaire character and many more casualties would be suffered before its limitations would render gas warfare redundant.

111   J.F. to W.B., 21 May 1915, French Papers. See also Richard Holmes, op. cit., p.290.

112   J.F. to W.B., 21 May 1915, French Papers. For Kitchener's attributes and failings, see Dominick Graham & Shelford Bidwell, *Coalitions, Politicians and Generals* (Brassey's, London 1993), p.70.

113   Alan Bishop, Terry Smart (Eds.), *Vera Brittain, Chronicle of Youth* (Victor Gollancz, London 1981), p.215. Also *Inside Asquith,* op. cit., p.231.

114   Caroline Playne, op. cit., p.108.

115   The feud had deepened in the early days of the First World War. Smith-Dorrien was commanding II Corps, and made a decision to stand and fight at Le Cateau, against the 'alleged' orders of his C-in-C.

116   The Prince was apt to change his opinion of commanders. When Haig replaced French in December 1915, the Prince commented about Haig 'I can't stand the man myself, so hard and unsympathetic.' By 1918 he had completely revised his opinion. Quoted in Philip Ziegler, *King Edward VIII* (Collins, London 1990), pp.61, 63, 67. See also HRH Prince Edward to French, 31 December 1914, ref 873, Misc. Corres., French Papers, IWM.

117   *The New York Times,* 4 July 1915. The origin of this feud was thought to be the defeat of the Boer commander, Cronje. Credit for this defeat was given to Smith-Dorrien and his superior, Kitchener. French, with some justification felt that the victory was his.

118   Charles Hobhouse was visiting the Coldstream Guards. *Inside Asquith,* op. cit., p.221.

119   There were other catastrophes on the Home Front. On 22 May 1915, a wooden troop train and a passenger train collided at Gretna Green, killing 227 soldiers and civilians.

120   J.F. to W.B., 24 May 1915, French Papers.

121   J.F. to W.B., 25 June 1915, French Papers.

122   *New York Times,* 10 March 1916.

123   *New York Times,* 27 June, 18 August 1915.

124   *The Diaries of Lady Cynthia Asquith 1915–18* (Century Hutchinson, London 1987), p.24.

125   Michael and Eleanor Brock (Eds.), *H.H. Asquith Letters to Venetia Stanley* (OUP, Oxford 1982), p.343.

126   Diana Cooper, op. cit., p.141.

127   J.F. to W.B., 22 August 1915, French Papers.

128   J.F. to W.B. 13 September 1915, French Papers.

129   J.F. to W.B. 13–15 September 1915, French Papers. The 'hospital' was later converted to military training school; see Diana Cooper, op. cit., 133–5.

130   J.F. to W.B. 10 November 1915, French Papers.

131   J.F. to W.B. 29 October 1915, French Papers.

132   Michael MacDonagh, *In London During The Great War. The Diary of a Journalist* (Eyre and Spottiswoode, London 1935), pp.82–4.

133   Caroline Playne, *Society at War 1914–1916* (George Allen & Unwin, London 1931), p.81.

134   J.F. to W.B. 8 November 1915, French Papers.

135   Mark Bonham-Carter (Ed.), *The Autobiography of Margot Asquith* (Weidenfeld & Nicolson, London 1995), pp.302–3. This extract is contained in MSS Eng.d.3198-3218, Bodleian Library, Oxford University. After the war, the Imperial War Graves Commission was tasked with the huge undertaking of creating new cemeteries with Portland headstones.

Chapter 3

136   Gary Sheffield, & John Bourne, (Eds.), *Douglas Haig. War Diaries and Letters 1914–1918* (Weidenfeld & Nicolson, London 2005), 21 November 1914, 6 November 1915.

137   Dominick Graham, op. cit., pp.70–1.

138   *Hansard.* House of Lords Debate, 16 November 1915, vol 20, cc359–86. *The Tatler,* no. 752, 24 November 1915. Just months before his speech, John Philipps, 1st Viscount St Davids had suffered the loss of his political activist wife, Leonora, as well as his elder son. His surviving son was killed in 1916. See also, Jonathan Walker, 'Thruster Repington and the Great Shell Scandal' in *The Douglas Haig Fellowship's Journal,* No. 14, November 2010.

139   Hob house, op. cit., pp.253–4.

140   J.F. to W.B., 14 November 1915, French Papers. Also Colin Clifford, *The Asquiths* (John Murray, London 2002), p.242.

141   J.F. to W.B., 8 November 1915, 13–15 November 1915, French Papers.

142   Jennifer Ellis (Ed.), *Thatched with Gold. The Memoirs of Mabell Countess of Airlie* (Hutchinson, London 1962), p.137.

143   Lord Esher to Lord Stamfordham, 3 December 1916, in Oliver, Viscount Esher, *Journals and Letters of Reginald Viscount Esher, Vol. IV* (Ivor Nicholson & Watson, London 1938).

144   Quoted in Charles Repington, *The First World War 1914–1918, Vol. I* (Constable, London 1920), p.111. Also J.F. to W.B., 1 January 1915. The three peers who excluded Alice Keppel were the Duke of Norfolk, the Duke of Portland and Lord Salisbury.

145   Lady Hamilton Diary, 1 March 1916, LHCMA.

146   J.F. to W.B., 6 January 1916, French Papers.

147   J.F. to W.B., 1 January 1916, French Papers.

148   J.F. to W.B., 3 January 1916, French Papers.

149   The Gardens were famous for their 'Forsythia', so named after William Forsyth, an earlier Superintendent of Kensington Gardens.

150   The character also gave her name to the child's playhouse, or 'Wendy House.' Barrie, whose secretary was Lady Cynthia Asquith, lived near Sir John French, opposite Kensington Gardens. Before his death he gave the rights to *Peter Pan* to the Great Ormond Street Hospital.

151   Superintendents' Reports, Metpol 2/1720, National Archives, Kew, London. Also DeGroot, op. cit., p.142.

152   E.S. Turner, *Dear Old Blighty* (Michael Joseph, London 1980), p.205–8.

153   French was subsequently created Earl of Ypres in 1922. Lady Hamilton Diary, 1 March 1916, LHCMA.

154   Sir Thomas Beecham received a knighthood in the New Years Honours List of 1916. Later that year he inherited a baronetcy.

155   She later divorced Prince Dimitri Soutzo and married her lover Paul Morand. Morand would later disgrace himself by accepting the post of Vichy Ambassador in Bucharest during WWII. See Callimachi, op. cit., p.126.

156   *New York Times* 10 March 1916.

157   Sheffield & Bourne, *Haig Diaries*, op. cit., 10 October 1916.

158   Oliver Esher, op. cit., Esher to Lady Brett, 12 August 1916. See also Charles Repington, *Vol I*, op. cit., p.127, 205, 342.

159   Lady Hamilton Diary, 24 April 1916, LHCMA.

160   Lady Hamilton Diary, 4 August 1916, LHCMA.

161   Francis Wyndham, *The Other Garden* (Jonathan Cape, London 1988), p.142.

162   Richard Holmes, op. cit., pp.46–7.

163   Sir Francis Jeune, Judge and President of the Division had retired as Lord St Helier in 1905 and died the same year. In 1920, there were still only 1629 divorces registered in England and Wales; see Arthur Marwick, op. cit., p.151.

164   Richard Holmes, op. cit., p.135. For his study of Sir John French, Professor Holmes was able to carry out numerous interviews with the French family.

165   Gail Savage, 'Erotic Stories and Public Decency: Newspaper Reporting of Divorce Proceedings in England' in *The Historical Journal*, 41, 2 (1998) (Cambridge University Press).

166   It was alleged that the typhus epidemic arrived via Mongolian trench diggers, serving with the nearby Russian troops.

167   Pantazzi, op. cit., p.109. See also Glen E. Torrey, 'The Romanian Campaign of 1916: Its Impact on the Belligerents', in *Slavic Review*, Vol. 39, No. 1 (March, 1980), pp.27–43.

168   Ibid, Also Lord Hankey, *The Supreme Command 1914–1918 Vol. 2* (Constable, London 1961), p.555. After his resignation, Asquith remained Leader of the Liberal Party.

169   'Question of Undue Influence', WO 141/63, National Archives, London. See also *The New York Times*, 4 January 1917.

170   R.W. Seton-Watson, op. cit., pp.516–18.

171   A series of letters exist within French's 'Official Correspondence File' in the IWM that are addressed to a 'Mrs Hood' in Woking. These are French's thank-you letters to Gladys, who acted as his courier in 1918. See French Papers, IWM.

172   Conrad Rushing, 'The English Players Incident: What really Happened', in *James Joyce Quarterly*, Vol. 37, No. 3, 2000. See also Gordon Bowker, *James Joyce. A Biography* (Weidenfeld & Nicolson, London 2011), pp.246–8, 253–5.

173   J. Lawrence Mitchell, 'Joyce and Boxing', in *James Joyce Quarterly*, Vol. 31, No. 2, 1994. Percy Bennett was also depicted in Tom Stoppard's 1974 play, 'Travesties.'

174   B. Goff to Reta Jacomb Hood, 5 October 1918, Author's Collection.

175   B. Goff to Reta Jacomb Hood, 6 April 1918, Author's Collection.

176   Arthur Marwick, op. cit., p.297. Worldwide, it is estimated that the pandemic killed in excess of 50 million people.

177   C.S. Peel, op. cit., pp.179–80.

Chapter 4

178 Iris Bennett Diary, 26 March 1919, Bennett Papers, Camilla Shivarg.

179 Lady Hamilton Diary, 2 June 1919, LHCMA. City weddings during the First World War and inter-war period were usually held on weekdays. Duff Cooper later became Winston Churchill's wartime Minister for Information. He was great-great uncle to the British Prime Minister, David Cameron.

180 John Colville, *The Fringes of Power. Downing Street Diaries 1939–1955* (Hodder and Stoughton, London 1985), pp.464–5.

181 Iris Bennett Diary 4 August 1919, Bennett Papers.

182 Iris Bennett Diary, 14 August 1919, Bennett Papers.

183 For details of the attack, see T. Ryle Dwyer, *The Squad and the Intelligence Operations of Michael Collins* (Mercier Press, Cork 2005), pp.70–3. Also *The New York Times*, 20 December 1919.

184 *Dawn Chorus*, op. cit., p.37.

185 *Dawn Chorus*, op. cit., p.49.

186 *Dawn Chorus*, op. cit., p.50.

187 The Earldom became extinct in 1988, on the death of John, the 3rd Earl of Ypres.

188 Richard Holmes, op. cit., p.363.

189 The Rancho San Carlos was sold to the Oppenheimers in 1939, and was subsequently developed into the Santa Lucia Preserve. For the history of the estate see Barbara Briggs-Anderson's text in Loon Hill Studios, www.julianpgraham.com.

190 J.F. to W.B., 27 July 1922, French Papers.

191 Gail Savage, 'Erotic Stories and Public Decency: Newspaper Reporting of Divorce Proceedings in England', in *The Historical Journal*, 41, 2 (1998), pp.511–528.

192 *Dawn Chorus*, op. cit., pp.66, 70.

193 Joan Wyndham Obituary, 14 April 2007, *The Daily Telegraph*. This obituary was more accurate than many, such as *The Guardian,* which claimed that Iris (born in 1900) was Lord French's illegitimate daughter (16 April 2007). This was impossible as Winifred and French did not meet until January 1914.

194 In the 1930s, Winifred lived at 1 Elm Park Gardens, then 7 Milborne Grove, The Boltons, London. See will dated 14 October 1930 and codicil dated 28 February 1938. Her place of death is recorded at 63 Fitzjohn's Avenue, Hampstead. In *Dawn Chorus,* Joan Wyndham accepted the relationship between her mother, Iris, and 'Sid' Houselander was unusual. Houselander was probably sexually ambiguous but had enjoyed a previous relationship with the famous 'Ace of Spies', Sydney Reilly; see *Dawn Chorus*, op. cit., pp.66–8.

195 Francis Wyndham, *The Other Garden* (Jonathan Cape, London 1988), pp.141–2. Francis Wyndham used his recollections of Winifred Bennett as the basis for the character 'Mrs Dodo Bassett' who is the mistress of a distinguished general. Francis Wyndham to Author, 22 November 2011.

196 *Dawn Chorus,* op. cit., p.117.

197 *Dawn Chorus,* op. cit., p.117.

198 *Dawn Chorus,* op. cit., p.121.

199 *Dawn Chorus,* op. cit., p.123.

Chapter 5

200 *The Chicago Sunday Tribune*, 31 December 1905, *The Guthrie Daily Leader*, 5 January 1906. There were numerous witnesses to the incident, who wasted no time in informing the press. The author Theodore Dreiser used the story of Emilie Grigsby and Charles Yerkes as the basis for his trilogy of novels, *The Financier* (1912), *The Titan* (1914) and *The Stoic* (1947). See also, Wesley Towner, *The Elegant Auctioneers* (Victor Gollancz, London 1971), p.216.

201   Her death certificate, registered 13 February 1964, gives her age 'about 83' indicating a
      birth date of 1880. Other sources place her birth in 1876 (*New York Times*, 2 July 1911;
      Victoria & Albert Museum accession records, London; John Franch, *Robber Baron. The
      Life of Charles Tyson Yerkes* (University of Illinois Press, Chicago 2008). The immigration
      records for her numerous transatlantic voyages give a birth date of 23 April 1880 and her
      birthplace as Manchester, Kentucky.
202   When she left the convent, the nuns presented Emilie with a volume on the history of the
      institution.
203   Franch, op. cit., pp.251–3.
204   For van Beers and Yerkes, see John Franch op. cit., pp.207–8.
205   The 1912 sale particulars of 'The House of Mystery' show much detail of the interior of
      660 Fifth Avenue. The concealed lift was discovered when curious buyers looked through
      the house. See also the *New York Times*, 14 December 1911; Wesley Towner, op. cit.,
      pp.210–16; Franch, op. cit., pp.303–10.
206   For the seven years that Emilie lived as his mistress, Yerkes insisted on keeping his public
      distance. When they travelled to London or Paris, he would always book a solo ticket, or
      travel with his wife, while Emilie would follow, discreetly, a week later. He continued to
      lavish luxuries and property on her, seemingly unperturbed when she sold them. In 1900
      he funded a carriage house for her at 123 East 77th Street, where she could keep her
      brougham, together with stabling for horses at the rear, and servants' quarters above. But
      two years later, she had sold the 'Brinckerhoff Carriage House.'
207   Philip Gerber, 'The Alabaster Protégé: Dreiser and Berenice Fleming' in *American Literature*
      Vol. 43, No. 2 (May 1971).
208   For an excellent study of Yerkes' life and relationships, especially his London connections,
      see Tim Sherwood, *Charles Tyson Yerkes: The Traction King of London* (The History Press,
      Stroud 2008). See also Robert Forrey, 'Charles Tyson Yerkes: Philadelphia-born Robber
      Barron' in *The Pennsylvania Magazine of History and Biography*, Vol. 99, No. 2 (April 1975),
      pp.226–41. Also the exhaustive biography by John Franch, op. cit.
209   Mrs Ellen Dunlap Hopkins first met Emilie when they were both having their portraits
      painted by Wilhelm Funk in 1901. Hopkins was later embroiled in a fraud court case in
      1910. She escaped prosecution and died in 1939.
210   Eric Homberger, *Mrs Astor's New York: Money and Social Power in a Gilded Age* (Yale
      University Press, New York 2002), op. cit., p.5.
211   Sherwood, op. cit., p.31.
212   Howard Marten recollections in *The Poppy and the Owl*, October 1996.
213   Extensive UK passenger lists are available through www.ancestry.co.uk
214   Anonymous, *I: In Which A Woman Tells The Truth About Herself* (D. Appleton, New York
      1904), p. 31–3.
215   Brian Masters, *The Life of E.F. Benson* (Pimlico, London 1993), pp.178–9.
216   Quoted in Celia Lee, *Jean, Lady Hamilton 1861–1941: A Soldier's Wife* (Celia Lee, London
      2001), p.97.
217   Leon Edel, *The Life of Henry James, Vol. 2* (Penguin, London 1977), pp.502–7.
218   *The Minneapolis Journal,* 1 January 1906. Also Towner, op. cit., p.218.
219   *The Chicago Daily Tribune,* 3 January 1906.
220   *The Times Dispatch,* 3 January 1906.
221   *The Washington Times,* 20 June 1907. Yerkes provided a large sum in his will to maintain
      the Yerkes Observatory in the University of Chicago. In 1910, Yerkes' widow died, having
      dissipated most of her wealth in fruitless legal battles against his estate.
222   *The Chicago Sunday Tribune,* 31 December 1905. See also Philip Gerber, *op. cit.*
223   *The Reading Eagle,* 7 January 1906.
224   The House of Worth was actually established by a British designer, Charles Worth who
      died in 1895, leaving behind a very successful label.
225   Emilie continued to visit Poiret; in 1913 she commissioned him to create a startling short
      evening coat in silk and velvet with metallic embroidery. At her death, this creation as well

as the rest of her couture collection was bequeathed to the Victoria & Albert Museum, London. For individual pieces see Blythe House section records, e.g. T.162–1967.

226 Yerkes had already purchased two Zorn paintings, which hung in Emilie's house in Park Avenue, New York. Her portrait by Funk had enjoyed some attention when it was included in an exhibition at the Knoedler Gallery in New York. See *The New York Times*, 5 January 1902.

227 Zorn's portrait of Emilie was auctioned by Sotheby's of London in 2003, fetching in excess of £200,000.

228 Homberger, op. cit., pp.20–1.

229 The *New York Times*, 9 January 1906. Also Bryson, op. cit., pp.234–5.

230 Homberger, op. cit., pp.273–7.

231 The *New York Times*, 2 July 1911.

232 The *New York Times*, 28 June 1909. The *New York Times* regularly printed the names of prominent passengers leaving on steamships from the home port. For example, on 11 May 1911, the German registered SS *Amerika* left on a transatlantic voyage bound for England, with the *New York Times* announcing that the ship carried amongst others, 'Miss E.B. Grigsby'.

233 Most of Edith Lees' papers and diaries were destroyed after her death. For Paris, see Toni Bentley, *Sisters of Salome* (Yale University Press, New Haven 2002), p.183.

234 Helena Wojtczak, *Notable Sussex Women* (The Hastings Press, Hastings 2008), p.9.

235 Heidi Ardizzone, *An Illuminated Life: Belle da Costa Greene's Journey from Prejudice to Privilege* (W.W. Norton, New York 2007), p.159.

236 Heidi Ardizzone, op. cit. pp.198–9.

237 Belle da Costa Greene (B.G.) to Bernard Berenson (B.B.), 17 October 1910, Berenson Archive, The Harvard University Center for Italian Renaissance Studies, Villa I Tatti, Florence. The author is indebted to Ilaria Della Monica for her assistance at the Berenson Archives. See also, Wesley Towner, op. cit., pp.272–9, and Heidi Ardizzone, op. cit., p.204.

238 Henry Havelock Ellis wrote a number of groundbreaking studies of sexuality, including *Sexual Inversion* (1896) and six volumes of *Studies in the Psychology of Sex* (1897–1910). In his private life he pursued the idea of a 'pure' rather than physical relationship with former loves such as the feminist Olive Schreiner.

239 John Stewart Collis, *Havelock Ellis: Artist of Life* (William Sloane, New York 1959), pp.138–9. Also Phyllis Grosskurth, *Havelock Ellis: A Biography* (Alfred Knopf, New York 1980), pp.236–7.

240 Draft for 'My Life' autobiography, Henry Havelock Ellis, MSS 70559, British Library Manuscript Collection.

241 B.G. to B.B., 21 March 1911, Berenson Archive.

242 Leslie, op. cit., p.230. Also *The New York Times* 4 June 1911. Emilie is not listed amongst the official Delhi Durbar attendees.

243 *The New York Times*, 2, 9 July 1911.

244 *The New York Times*, 4 July, 11 July 1911

245 *The New York Times* 6, 7 September 1911. RMS *Olympic* took five days to cross the Atlantic and carried 1931 passengers.

246 The Pissarro was titled 'Les Coteaux de Thierceville.' It was sold recently (2009) for $1,426,500. After obtaining the commission for Emilie's profitable sale, Kennerley earned the presidency of Anderson Galleries several years later. For reports of the sale, see *The New York Times*, 30 January 1912; for Kennerley and Emilie see Mathew Bruccoli, *The Fortunes of Mitchell Kennerley* (Harcourt Brace Jovan, San Diego 1986), p.57–8, 75–6. In 1930, Kennerley bequeathed the bronze of Emilie's head to Vassar College, New York.

247 Copies of the 'Illustrated Catalogue of the Art and Literary Collections of Miss Emilie Grigsby of New York City' are still widely available. The catalogue, which was published by The Anderson Auction Co., shows not only details of the lots, but illustrations of many of the rooms in 'The House of Mystery.'

248 *New York Tribune*, 24 December 1911.

249   For a splendid description of the bidding at the sale, see Towner, op. cit., pp.283–7. Also
      The New York Times, 26, 28, 30 January, 9 February 1912. See also *New York Tribune*, 24
      December 1911.
250   For Colvin and Meredith, see E.V. Lucas, *The Colvins and Their Friends* (Methuen, London
      1928), pp.201–7. Also Heidi Ardizzone op. cit. and Leslie, op. cit., p.230.
251   She had an extensive private collection of Native American outfits and weapons. See also
      The New York Times, 28 April 1912.
252   Shane Leslie, *Long Shadows* (John Murray, London 1966), p.230.
253   Gerber op. cit.
254   French's regiment, the 19th Hussars had indeed moved to Hounslow in June 1874, but
      at that stage, he was only a subaltern. The following year he married his first wife Isabella
      Soundy and in 1876, the 19th left for Ireland, so it is likely that he was courting Isabella at
      this time. See also Leslie, op. cit., p.231.
255   Quoted in Gerber, op. cit.
256   B.G. to B.B., 20 September 1913. Berenson Archive. Berenson's great-great niece is the
      actress Marisa Berenson. Another niece, Berry was the wife of actor Anthony Perkins, and
      was killed in the terrorist attack on the Twin Towers in New York.
257   80 Brook Street comprised a corner mansion block, described as a 'competent piece of
      Francophile classicism', and was built by Mathews, Rogers and Co. between 1910–13 at
      the request of the 2nd Duke of Westminster.
258   F.H.W. Sheppard, *Survey of London: Volume 40: The Grosvenor Estate in Mayfair, Part 2, The
      Buildings* (English Heritage, London 1980).

Chapter 6

259   The states of Alaska and Hawaii did not join the US until 1959.
260   Jones, op. cit., p.392. For a literary review of the 'Georgian Poets', see Robert H. Ross,
      The Georgian Revolt: Rise and fall of a Poetic Ideal 1910–22 (Faber & Faber, London 1967).
261   *The Times*, 12 February 1964; *The New York Times*, 14 February 1964; Jones, op. cit.,
      pp.404–24; Colin Clifford, *The Asquiths* (John Murray, London 2002), pp.246–9.
262   *The New York Times*, 8 May 1915.
263   Shane Leslie, *op. cit.*, pp.176–7. See also Ernest May, *The World War and American Isolation
      1914–1917* (Harvard University Press, Cambridge, Mass., 1959).
264   Quoted in Richard Davenport-Hines, *Ettie: The Intimate Life and Dauntless Spirit of Lady
      Desborough* (Weidenfeld & Nicolson, London 2008), pp.140, 235, 241.
265   Quoted in Stella Margetson, *Victorian High Society* (B.T. Batsford, London 1980), p.119.
266   Major D. Chapman-Huston, *General Sir John Cowans: The Quartermaster-General of the
      Great War, Vol. 1* (Hutchinson & Co, London 1924), p.246. Cowans entered the army
      in 1881, as a young officer in the Rifle Brigade. He later served on Kitchener's staff as
      Director-General of Military Education. During the Boer War, he was Deputy Assistant
      Quartermaster-General, in charge of the vast and complicated transport operations
      between Britain and South Africa. Promoted Brigadier-General in 1908, he was made
      Director-General of Territorial Forces from 1910 to 1912. He was promoted Lieutenant-
      General in 1915. Despite the fact that his name was mentioned in various scandals, he was
      still appointed full General in 1919.
267   Major D. Chapman-Huston, op. cit., pp.228–30. For an example of Cowans 'can do'
      philosophy, see Brigadier-General C.D. Baker-Carr, *From Chauffeur to Brigadier* (Ernest
      Benn, London 1930), pp.12–13.
268   Even in 1918, the Bishop of Southwark was advocating that sexual intercourse was not for
      enjoyment but only for pro-creation.
269   Nigel Jones, *Rupert Brooke: Life, Death & Myth* (Richard Cohen, London 1999), pp.239–40.
      See also Paul Ferris, *Sex and the British. A Twentieth Century History* (Michael Joseph, London
      1993), pp.84–9; Hera Cook, *The Long Sexual Revolution* (OUP, Oxford 2004), pp.112–5.

270   Patricia Knight, 'Women and Abortion in Victorian and Edwardian England' in *History Workshop* no. 4, Autumn 1977. Also Hera Cook op. cit., p.127.

271   Lucy Bland, *Banishing the Beast: English Feminism and Sexual Morality 1885–1914* (Penguin, London 1995), p.245.

272   Anne Hanley, 'The S Word: The spectre of syphilis within middle-class marriage in late Victorian & Edwardian Britain.' Thesis, Dept. of History, University of Sydney, Australia, October 2009. Also Ferris, op. cit., pp.64–70. The problem of sex and the soldier is examined by Clare Makepeace, 'Punters and their prostitutes. British soldiers, masculinity and maisons tolérées in the First World War' in John Arnold and Sean Brady (Eds.), *What is Masculinity?* (Palgrave Macmillan, London 2011).

273   John Julius Norwich, op. cit., p.38. Quoted in Ziegler, op. cit., p.71.

274   Helen Long, op. cit., p.10. *The Times,* 7 October 1916 recorded that an Army Order of 6 October 1916 finally rescinded the restriction on shaving the upper lip. After that date, many officers still retained their moustaches, but equally younger officers were relieved to remove their lacklustre growths.

275   Lady Hamilton Diary, Sunday 23 January 1916, LHCMA. Also Chapman-Huston op. cit., p.231.

276   Sir E. Denison Ross, *Both Ends of the Candle* (Faber & Faber, London 1943), p.176.

277   Cowans military correspondence was profuse. His letters are to be found in The Imperial War Museum, London (Sir John Cowans Papers, Sir Henry Wilson Papers); The Bodleian Library, Oxford University (MSS Asquith); National Archives (Stewart papers).

278   Anne de Courcy, *Society's Queen. The Life of Edith, Marchioness of Londonderry* (Phoenix, London 2004), pp.132–5. The original title, 'Women's Corps' was dropped when it was realised that the initials 'WC' were rather unfortunate.

279   De Courcy, op. cit., pp.141–4.

280   Ruth Hall (Ed.), *Dear Dr Stopes. Sex in the 1920s* (Andre Deutsch, London 1978), p.176.

281   Quoted in Ellen Holtzman, 'The Pursuit of Married Love: Women's Attitudes Toward Sexuality and Marriage in Great Britain, 1918–1939', in *Journal of Social History*, 16:2. Winter 1982.

282   Ruth Hall, op. cit., p.175. Stopes' first marriage in 1911 was annulled on the grounds on non-consummation. See also Ferris, op. cit., pp.79–80, and Mary Lynn Stewart, 'Science is Always Chaste: Sex Education and Sexual Initiation in France, 1880s–1930s', in *Journal of Contemporary History*, Vol. 32, No. 3, July 1977.

283   A.N. Wilson, *After the Victorians* (Hutchinson, London 2005), pp.75, 267. Childbirth itself was a risky venture; By 1920 approximately 39,000 women a year still died giving birth. For Lutyens, see also Maureen Waller, *The English Marriage* (John Murray, London 2009), pp.334–6.

284   Lucy Bland, op. cit., pp.267–73.

285   Michael and Eleanor Brock, *Letters to Venetia Stanley* (Oxford University Press, Oxford 1985), p.100.

286   For a life of Lord Northcliffe, see S.J. Taylor, *The Great Outsiders. Northcliffe, Rothermere and The Daily Mail* (Weidenfeld & Nicolson, London 1996).

287   For a study of Repington's controversial life, see Jonathan Walker, 'Thruster Repington and the Great Shell Scandal' in *The Journal of The Douglas Haig Fellowship,* No. 14, November 2010. For his military career, see A.J.A. Morris (Ed.), *The Letters of Lieutenant-Colonel Charles à Court Repington CMG, Military Correspondent of The Times 1903–1918* (Sutton Publishing, Stroud 1999).

288   Although Molly is sometimes referred to as 'Mrs Repington' in contemporary letters or diaries, there is no evidence that Charles Repington ever married her. Neither of their spouses would accept divorce, and in Molly's case, it was her devout religious observance that forbade such a step.

289   Lieutenant-Colonel Charles à Court, Repington, *The First World War 1914–1918 Vol. I & II* (Constable & Co., London 1920), 8, 18 November, 4 December 1915, 15 April 1916.

290   *I: In Which a Woman,* op. cit., pp.38–9.

291   Leslie op. cit., p.231.

292   Lady Hamilton Diary, 11 January 1916, Sir Ian Hamilton Papers, Liddell Hart Centre for Military Archives (hereafter LHCMA), King's College, London.

293   *The Tatler*, 1 December 1915.

294   B.G. to B.B., 20 September 1913, Berenson Archive. Also Ardizzone op. cit., p.301.

295   *The Tatler*, 9 February 1916.

296   *The New York Times*, 2 January 1916. Adèle Essex also supervised charitable working parties and underwrote a 'Lady Essex Charity Matinee' at the Gaiety Theatre, using professional actors mixed with society volunteers, such as Lady Diana Manners and Lady Cynthia Asquith.

297   Gerard Degroot, *Blighty. British Society in the Era of the Great War* (Longman, London 1996), pp.201–9, 226–7. Also, Mrs C.S. Peel, op. cit., pp.51–3.

298   Jennie eventually married Montagu Porch on 1 June 1918. For studies of her eventful life, see Anne Sebba, *Jennie Churchill. Winston's American Mother* (John Murray, London 2007); Celia Lee & John Lee, *The Churchills: A Family Portrait* (Palgrave Macmillan, London 2010); Charles Higham, *Dark Lady. Winston Churchill's Mother and Her World* (Virgin Books, London 2006).

299   See also Lady Hamilton Diary, 19 May 1919, LHCMA. HMS *Maine* also served during the Boxer Rebellion in 1900 and was finally sunk off the coast of Ireland during the First World War.

300   The organisation later moved to 41 Hertford Street, changed its name to the American Women's Club and expanded its membership. The American Women's Club is now based at 68 Old Brompton Road and continues to thrive. The author is indebted to Madeline Morrow, AWC Historian, for her assistance.

301   L.E. Jones, op. cit., p.207.

302   *I: In Which a Woman*, op. cit., pp.135–6.

303   Arthur Marwick, *War and Social Change in the Twentieth Century* (Macmillan, London 1974), p.150.

304   Stephen Haden Guest (Trans.), *King of Fashion. The Autobiography of Paul Poiret* (V&A Publishing, London 2009), pp.112–122.

305   By comparison with the French casualties, the British Empire had suffered approximately 950,000 men killed, wounded or missing by the end of 1915. See *Statistics of the Military Effort of the British Empire during the Great War 1914–1920* (War Office, London 1922).

306   *I: In Which a Woman*, op. cit., p.167.

307   After Emilie's death the V&A were offered 98 items, many of which were couture items by Italian, French and Japanese designers. Included, were sets of beautiful underwear made by 'The White House' of Paris, with 'Emilie' embroidered on the side. See Lord Southborough file, P/1966/2686, V&A Archives, Blythe House, London.

308   By 1918 conscription was extended to include all men under 51. Rates of pay for domestic staff were pitifully low. A butler might earn £45 p.a. and a ladies' maid, £32 p.a.

309   Lady Hamilton Diary, 11 January 1916, LHCMA.

310   Lady Hamilton Diary, 24 April 1916, LHCMA.

311   Mary Repington, *Thanks for the Memory* (Constable & Co, London 1938), p.272.

312   Lady Hamilton Diary, Tuesday 11 January 1916, LHCMA.

313   When it came to matrimonial disputes, Australian newspapers were far less deferential than their British counterparts. See *The West Australian*, Perth, 20 March 1925. Also *The Argus*, Melbourne, 18 March 1925 and *The Sydney Morning Herald*, 7, 13 March 1925 and *The Brisbane Courier*, 6 March 1925.

Chapter 7

314   The flower show closed for 1917 and 1918, but re-opened after the war.

315   Leslie, op. cit., p.231. Also Charles Repington, op. cit., 23 May 1916.

316   Hulton founded the famous Hulton-Getty Picture Archive.

317   Sonia Keppel, *Edwardian Daughter* (Hamish Hamilton, London 1958), p.119.

318   Violet would engage in a brief marriage to Major Denys Trefusis before returning
      to her old love, Vita Sackville-West. See Diana Souhami, *Mrs Keppel and her Daughter*
      (HarperCollins, London 1996).

319   Although the freehold of 80 Brook Street was, like most houses in Mayfair, still held by
      the Grosvenor Estate, it was common practice in Edwardian Britain to rent your home. At
      the outbreak of war in 1914, over 90 per cent of the housing stock was rented. See Helen
      Long, *The Edwardian House* (Manchester University Press, Manchester 1982), p.8.

320   Helen Long, op. cit., p.90.

321   Lady Hamilton Diary, Sunday 20 June 1915, LHCMA.

322   At the time that Emilie lived at 80 Brook Street, the basement was quiet, save for the
      rumbling of motor cars in the street above. The stretch of the Jubilee Underground Line
      that now runs directly beneath, was only opened in 1977.

323   80 Brook Street was used by the Government during the Second World War to house
      Canadian Air Force nurses. It was acquired in 1947 by the firm of solicitors, Gordon
      Dadds, who practice in the building today. The author is indebted to Andrew Whittaker of
      Gordon Dadds for his help and hospitality.

324   At this time, over 16 per cent of the population was engaged in domestic service.

325   Leslie, op. cit., p.230. The six attic figures represent 'History, Drama, Poetry, Religion,
      Romance and Philosophy – all fields of knowledge held within the library.

326   *The Sketch*, 12 January 1916, 18 September 1918, *Tatler,* 12 January 1916, 14 August 1918.
      Also Franch, op. cit., p.302.

327   The *New York Times* obituary, 26 May 1940. Library of Congress (Prints and Photographs
      Division) LC-B2-2638-3. Also Franch, op. cit., pp.301–2, and Sherwood, op. cit., pp.108–9.

328   Quoted in Ferris, op. cit., p.64.

329   E.S. Turner, op. cit., pp.206–7.

330   H.A. Jones, *The War In the Air, Vol. III* (Oxford at the Clarendon Press, London 1931),
      pp.224–5. The 'L' designation stood for *Lutschiff* or airship.

331   Robinson was later shot down and made a POW. He died of Spanish Flue on 31
      December 1918. Raymond Rimell, *Zeppelin: A Battle for Air Supremacy in World War I*
      (Conway, London 1984).

332   Mary Repington, *Thanks for the Memory* (Constable, London 1938), p.272.

333   Mary Repington, op. cit., pp.272–3.

334   See Laetitia Stapleton, 'Lieut.-Colonel Charles à Court Repington' in *The Army Quarterly*,
      Vol. 105, No. 2, April 1975. Molly died in 1953.

335   Bonham Carter, op. cit., pp.316–7; Clifford, op. cit., pp.366–9. An appalling slander was
      circulated by Lloyd George's Private Secretary, 'that Raymond Asquith was so disliked by
      his own men that it was one of their own bombs which accounted for his end', see Colin
      Clifford, op. cit., p.459.

336   J. Lee Thompson, 'Fleet Street Colossus: The Rise and Fall of Northcliffe, 1896–1922',
      in *Parliamentary History*, Vol. 25, Part 1, 2006, pp.115–38. Northcliffe's animosity towards
      Asquith's conduct of the war was further stoked by the news of the death of his nephew,
      Vere, at the Battle of the Ancre on 13 November 1916.

337   Lady Hamilton Diary, 8 October 1916, Vol. X Reel 3 (6 July 1916–20 November 1917),
      LHCMA. See also A.J.A. Morris (Ed.), *op. cit.*, p.287.

338   For Carson, see J.M. Bourne, *Who's Who in World War One* (Routledge, London 2001)

339   Richard Holmes, *The Little Field Marshal* (Weidenfeld & Nicolson, London 1981),
      pp.327–8; Peter Fraser, *Lord Esher. A Political Biography* (Hart-Davis MacGibbon, London
      1973), pp.332–6; Gary Sheffield & John Bourne (Eds.), *Douglas Haig. War Diaries and
      Letters 1914–18* (Phoenix, London 2006), 17 September, 10 October 1916. L.E. Jones, *An
      Edwardian Youth* (Macmillan, London 1958), p.184. The word 'degommed' was slang for
      sacked or sent home (from the French word *dégomme*, meaning 'to come unstuck').

340   Edward David (Ed.), *Inside Asquith's Cabinet. From the Diaries of Charles Hobhouse* (John
      Murray, London 1977), p.229.

341 Harcourt (later Lord Harcourt) preyed on both sexes, even assaulting the daughter of his good friend Lord Esher. On 24 February 1921, Harcourt was found dead in his bedroom at 69 Brook Street, having consumed a whole bottle of Bromidia. See Mathew Parris, *Great Parliamentary Scandals* (Robson Books, London 1995), pp.83–5.

342 Jean had been secretly married to the son of Ward McAllister who coined the idea of the 'Four Hundred' at the head of New York society. She subsequently married Augustus Brandt on 4 May 1898 in Savannah, US.

343 Courts of Inquiry Records 1918, WO 33/3282, National Archives, London. See also *The New York Times*, 4 January 1917. See also Lady Hamilton Diary, 18 September 1916, and Chapman-Huston Vol. II, op. cit., pp.146–55. The story of the Cornwallis-West scandal is told by Tim Coates in *Patsy* (Bloomsbury, London 2003).

344 Lady Hamilton Diary 14 January 1917, LHCMA.

345 Tim Coates, *op. cit.*, p.195, 228.

346 These concerns were aggravated by revelations in the 'Zimmermann Note', which purported to show evidence of German meddling. The US, however did not enter the war as an 'Allied' state, but rather as an 'associated power.' For the full astonishing story of the Zimmerman telegram and its exploitation by British Intelligence, see David Ramsay, *Blinker Hall: Spymaster* (Spellmount 2009).

347 For a life of this extraordinary man, see Leonard Taylor, *The Sourdough & The Queen. The Many Lives of Klondike Joe Boyle* (Methuen, Toronto 1983).

348 Hannah Pakula, *Queen of Roumania. The Life of Princess Marie, Grand-daughter of Queen Victoria* (Weidenfeld & Nicolson, London 1984), pp.240–2. Also, Charles Repington, op. cit., 13 September 1917.

349 Mackay had joined the Army at sixteen, served in the Loyal North Lancashire Regiment and was Mentioned in Despatches during the Boer War. He later became Chief of the Uganda Police and Commandant and Inspector-General of the Liberian Frontier Force. He volunteered for service in November 1914 and was appointed a Railway Transport Officer after being rejected for service abroad. His service records are confusing, due to his change of name in 1909 from Mackay Cadell to Mackay Mackay.

350 *The Times*, 7, 8, 9 May 1918. Also Leslie, op. cit., p.231.

351 Michael MacDonagh, Michael, *In London During The Great War. The Diary of a Journalist* (Eyre and Spottiswoode, London 1935), p.198.

352 Repington diary, 7 July 1917.

353 Repington, 16 June 1917.

354 For the story of Sheldon's doomed affair with Keane, see Eric Barnes, *The Man Who Lived Twice* (Charles Scribner, New York 1956), p.62, 83–93. *Romance* was a 'must see' and continued to be the subject of much excitement amongst London's theatre community. Even Doris Keane's hairstyle appears to have created a fashion. See Jean Hamilton Diary, 26 January 1916, LHCMA.

355 Charles Repington, 27 July 1917.

356 Charles Repington, 26 August 1917.

357 For dates see Charles Repington diary, including 20 November 1917.

358 Lady Hamilton Diary, 17 February 1918, LHCMA.

359 Lady Hamilton Diary 13 February 1918, LHCMA.

360 Lady Hamilton Diary, 15 April 1918, LHCMA.

361 Robert Ross, *The Georgian Revolt: Rise and Fall of a Poetic Ideal 1910–22* (Faber & Faber, London 1967), p.195.

362 Henry Havelock Ellis to Margaret Sanger, 19 November 1918, Box 4, Reel 4 Personal Correspondence 1915–20, MSS 38919, Margaret Sanger Papers, Library of Congress, Washington DC.

Chapter 8

363   For the immediate post war world, see Michael Sherborne, *H.G. Wells. Another Kind of Life* (Peter Owen, London 2010), pp.245–50.

364   Arthur Marwick, op. cit., p.147. Also De Groot, op. cit., p.307.

365   Taylor, op. cit., pp.370–1. Sir Shane Leslie, *Long Shadows* (John Murray, London 1966), pp.229–30.

366   Mary Repington, op. cit., p.311. Charles Repington died on 25 May 1925. 28 years later, Molly was buried alongside him in a cemetery in Hove.

367   A.E. Sullivan, 'Colonel Repington', in *The Army Quarterly and Defence Journal*, Vol. XCVII, No. 1, October 1968. Also Cyril Falls, *War Books. A Critical Guide* (Peter Davies, London 1930).

368   Tim Coates, op. cit., p.259.

369   In 1923, Lord Carnarvon died from a mosquito bite after famously discovering the tomb of Tutankhamen. His widow, Almina married Ian Dennistoun in the same year. See The Earl of Carnarvon, *No Regrets* (Weidenfeld and Nicolson, London 1976), pp.136–7.

370   See Van Vechten's portrait, which he also complemented with a picture of Emilie's back. Her leopard print Busvine dress is now in the V&A couture collection in London.

371   For Van Vechten's diary of the period, see Bruce Kellner (Ed.), *The Splendid Drunken Twenties* (University of Illinois, Chicago 2003).

372   *The Times*, 19 December 1936, 21 April, 22 June 1937, 8 December 1964. *The New York Times*, 26 November 1945.

373   Barnes, op. cit., p.286. Also *The Times*, 12 February 1964. Leslie toyed with the idea of writing Emilie's life story, but the project never developed. His short biography of her is contained in his papers held in the University of Georgetown. See, Folder 2, Box 46, Sir Shane Leslie Papers, Special Collections, Georgetown University Library, Washington DC, US.

374   Will dated 8 March 1951.

375   Gerber, 'The Alabaster Protégé', op. cit. Dreiser kept extensive notes in the preparation of his novels and these are still held in the University of Pennsylvania's Annenberg Rare Book & Manuscript Library, USA. For extracts of Dreiser's prodigious correspondence, see Thomas Riggio (Ed.), *Letters to Women: New Letters Volume 2. Theodore Dreiser* (University of Illinois Press, Chicago 2009).

376   Tim Sherwood, op. cit., p.106.

377   Her death certificate states an 'approximate age of 83.'

378   Lord Southborough to Mrs Ginsberg, 13 October, 13 December 1966, File PP/1966/2686, V&A Museum Archives, London. Also see *The Times*, 8 December 1964, regarding Sotheby's sale.

379   Leslie wrote her obituary in *The Times*, 12 February 1964. For Ford, see Ford Maddox Ford, *Portraits from Life* (Houghton Mifflin, Boston 1980), p.177.

Chapter 9

380   The size of the Stanley family was the norm. At the turn of the century, 80 per cent of families had more than four children. A.N. Wilson, *After the Victorians* (Hutchinson, London 2005), p.269.

381   Rosalind Venetia Pitt-Rivers, *Biographical Memoirs of Fellows of the Royal Society*, Vol. 39, February 1994. Through Sylvia's mother, Mary Bell, another cousin was Gertrude Bell, the traveller and archaeologist.

382   'The Stanleys of Alderley', in *Cheshire Life*, July 1936. Also Adelaide Lubbock, *People in Glass Houses. Growing up at Government House* (Hamish Hamilton, London 1977), p.21.

383   Physically fit and keen cyclists, 'Girton Girls' were sporty university-educated women, who typified the Edwardian 'New Woman.' The first all-female colleges were Girton, Newnham

and Lady Margaret Hall, See Angelique Richardson and Chris Willis (Eds.), *The New Woman in Fiction and in Fact* (Palgrave Macmillan, London 2002).

384   He won the seat of Eddisbury in 1906 and lost it in the 1910 General Election.

385   Irish peerages were granted to allow the holder the prestige of a peerage, while still allowing them to contest a seat in the House of Commons. Quite often the holder or his title had no Irish connection. A later English creation of the Barony of Northington (1885), a UK peerage, was bestowed on the 3rd Lord Henley, allowing him a seat in the House of Lords. The family continued to use the title 'Henley' (1799), due to its seniority. They were also part of the Eden family, a surname that the later lords adopted.

386   Watford Court was demolished in 1977, to make way for a housing estate.

387   For a comprehensive study of the Imperial Yeomanry in South Africa, see K. Asplin, *The Roll of the Imperial Yeomanry, Scottish Horse & Lovat's Scouts. 2nd Boer War 1899–1902* (DP & G Publishing, London 2006). See also Michael and Eleanor Brock, (Eds.), *H.H. Asquith. Letters to Venetia Stanley* (Oxford University Press, Oxford 1982), p.66. For Anthony Henley's army service record, see *Quarterly Army List,* January 1918 (HMSO, London 1918). The January issues of this mammoth tome contain details of all regular army officers' service records.

388   Oliver Stanley, DSO, became a Lieutenant-Colonel during the First World War. The current Lord Stanley is descended from his line. See Peter Stanley, *The House of Stanley* (The Pentland Press, Edinburgh 1998), p.408–10.

389   Bertrand Russell, *The Autobiography* (Routledge, London 2000), p.600.

390   Adelaide Lubbock, op. cit., pp.10–11. For Lord Carlisle, see *Lady Cynthia Asquith Diaries 1915–18* (Century, London 1987), p.283.

391   *The Times,* 22 May 1980.

392   Anthony Henley joined the 5th Lancers in November 1907, see *Army List* July 1914. Also *A Complete Record of the Recipients of the Distinguished Service Order 1886–1923* (J.B. Hayward, London 1923). Mary Soames, *Clementine Churchill. The Biography of a Marriage* (Houghton Mifflin, Boston 2003), p.37. Also Sylvia Henley (S.H.) to Anthony Henley (A.H.), 13 November 1915, Sylvia Henley Papers, MSS.Eng.lett.c.643, *Special Collections,* Bodleian Library, Oxford University.

393   Adelaide Lubbock, op. cit., pp.24–5.

394   *The Stanleys,* op. cit.

395   Mary Soames, *Speaking for Themselves. The Personal Letters of Winston and Clementine Churchill* (Doubleday, London 1998), p.107.

396   Adelaide Lubbock, op. cit., p.12.

397   Adelaide Lubbock, op. cit., p.14. Also Clementine Churchill to Winston Churchill, 11 September 1909, Mary Soames, op. cit.

398   Quoted in Philip Ziegler, *Diana Cooper* (Hamish Hamilton, London 1981), p.58.

399   Bill Bryson, *At Home. A Short History of Private Life* (Doubleday, London 2010), op. cit., p.98.

400   Bill Bryson, op. cit., p.97.

401   Violet Asquith Diary, 12 July 1905, Mark Bonham Carter & Mark Pottle (Eds.), *Lantern Slides. The Diaries and Letters of Violet Bonham Carter 1904–1914* (Weidenfeld & Nicolson, London 1996). In 1914 Arthur Stanley left for Australia to become the Governor of Victoria, a post he would hold for five years.

402   L.E. Jones, *An Edwardian Youth* (Macmillan, London 1956), p.218. Adelaide Lubbock, op. cit., p.13.

403   For Asquith, see Michael Brock, op. cit., p.24. The children of Asquith's first marriage to Helen were Raymond, Herbert, Arthur, Violet and Cyril. Following her death he married Margot, who produced Elizabeth and Anthony.

404   Brian Masters, *The Life of E.F. Benson* (Chatto & Windus, London 1991).op. cit., p.239.

405   Toni Bentley, *Sisters of Salome* (Yale University Press, New Haven 2002), pp.57–72. Also Judith Hanna, *Dance, Sex and Gender* (University of Chicago Press, Chicago 1988), pp.183–4, and *The New York Times,* 23 August 1908.

406   *The Tatler,* 7 December 1912.

407   Michael Brock, op. cit., pp.1–2. Also L.E. Jones, op. cit., p.214.

408   Clementine Churchill to Winston Churchill, 11 September 1909, Mary Soames, op. cit.

Chapter 10

409   Ciaran Byrne, *The Harp and Crown. The History of the 5th (Royal Irish) Lancers 1902–1922* (Lulu Books, Dublin 2010).

410   Ironically, Lieutenant-Colonel Parker was one of the main protagonists in 'The Curragh Incident'.

411   Asquith to Venetia Stanley, 5, 10, 31 August 1914, Brock op. cit., p.157, 163, 208. Anthony Henley was promoted GSO2 on 10 October 1914.

412   A 'dug-out' officer was one who had seen service, probably in India or Africa and retired before 1914. He then volunteered for service in the war and was 'dug-out' of retirement. Brigadier-General F.P. Crozier, *A Brass Hat in No Man's Land* (Jonathan Cape, London 1930), p.156.

413   Caroline Playne, op. cit., p.124. Also, Arthur Marwick, *The Deluge. British Society and the First World War* (Palgrave Macmillan, London 2006), p.128–9.

414   Crozier, op. cit., p.161.

415   Winston Churchill, *Great Contemporaries* (Macmillan, London 1942), p.105.

416   (S.H.) to (A.H.), 14 May 1915, ref MSS.Eng.lett.c.641-7.

417   For Asquith's correspondence with Hilda Harrison, see Desmond MacCarthy, (Ed.), *H.H.A. Letters of the Earl of Oxford and Asquith to a Friend. First Series 1915–1922* (1933) and *Second Series 1922–1927* (1934) both (Geoffrey Bles, London). Also, L.E. Jones, op. cit., p.214.

418   The Royal Society op. cit., p.329. A number of the letters written by the children to their father have survived and are to be found in the Sylvia Henley Papers, MSS.Eng. lett.c.641–9, Bodleian Library, Oxford.

419   H.H. Asquith to Venetia Stanley, 14 January 1915, Brock, op. cit., p.379.

420   The pressure from the French Army and the desire of the C-in-C to engage the enemy may have overridden his reservations before Aubers Ridge. After the battle he was quite clear about the problem. See also, B. McGill, 'Asquith's Predicament 1914–1918' in *Journal of Modern History*, Vol. 39 No. 3, September 1967.

421   Michael Hart, review of *H.H. Asquith. Letters to Venetia Stanley*, in English Historical Review, Vol. 99, no. 392, July 1984, pp.580–4.

422   S.H. to A.H., 23 April, 25 April 1915, Sylvia Henley Papers.

423   S.H. to A.H., 24 April 1915, Sylvia Henley Papers.

424   S.H. to A.H., 9 May 1915, Sylvia Henley Papers.

425   H.H.A. to Venetia Stanley, 9 May 1915, Brock, op. cit., p.588.

426   S.H. to A.H., 11 May 1915, Sylvia Henley Papers.

427   H.H.A. to S.H., 13 May 1915, ref MSS.Eng.lett.c. 541/1-5, Sylvia Henley Papers.

428   S.H. to A.H., 7, 8 May 1915, Sylvia Henley Papers.

429   Sir John French to Winifred Bennett, 1 January 1916, French Papers, IWM. For US Jews, see Heidi Ardizzone, op. cit., p.108. Also Ziegler, op. cit., p.29. For Haig, see Gary Sheffield and John Bourne (Eds.), *Douglas Haig. War Diaries and Letters 1914–18* (Phoenix, London 2006), 7 September 1916. Also, L.E. Jones, *An Edwardian Youth* (Macmillan, London 1958), p.178.

430   H.H.A. to S.H., 12 May 1915, Sylvia Henley Papers.

431   Maurice Bonham Carter (later Sir Maurice) to Violet Asquith, 22 June 1915. Quoted in Mark Pottle (Ed.), *Champion Redoubtable: The Diaries and Letters of Violet Bonham Carter 1914–1945* (Weidenfeld & Nicolson, London 1998).

432   This theory is explored by Naomi Levine in her study, *Politics, Religion & Love* (New York University Press, New York 1991), pp.271–2.

433   Margot would later turn against Montagu. See Christopher Page, *Command in the Royal*

Naval Division (Spellmount, Staplehurst 1998), p.50. For Margot's abuse, S.H. to A.H., 16 May 1915, Sylvia Henley Papers.

434 S.H. to A.H., 16 May 1915, Sylvia Henley Papers.

435 S.H. to A.H., 21 May 1915, Sylvia Henley Papers. For 'duty' correspondence see H.G. Cocks, 'Sporty Girls and Artistic Boys: Friendship, Illicit Sex and the British Companionship Advertisement 1913–1928', in *Journal of the History of Sexuality*, Vol. 11 No. 3, July 2002, p.466.

436 H.H.A. to Venetia Stanley, 5 January 1915, Brock op. cit., p.359.

437 The Earl of Oxford and Asquith, *Memories and Reflections 1852–1927*, 2 Vols. (Cassell, London 1928).

438 H.H.A. to S.H., 17 May 1915, Sylvia Henley Papers.

439 S.H. to A.H. 16 May 1915, Sylvia Henley Papers.

440 S.H. to A.H. 26, 27 May, Sylvia Henley Papers; H.H.A. to S.H., 31 May, 2 June 1915, Sylvia Henley Papers.

441 H.H.A. to S.H., 17 May 1915, Sylvia Henley Papers.

442 S.H. to A.H., 29 May 1915, Sylvia Henley Papers.

443 H.H.A. to S.H., 18 June 1915, Sylvia Asquith Papers.

444 Ferris, op. cit., p.82.

445 H.H.A. to S.H., 31 May 1915, Sylvia Henley Papers.

446 H.H.A. to S.H., 27 May 1915, Sylvia Henley Papers; S.H. to A.H., 5, 15 June 1915, Sylvia Henley Papers.

447 H.H.A. to S.H., 1, 5, 8, 12 June 1915, Sylvia Henley Papers. Sylvia's lifelong friend, Winston Churchill was similarly afflicted with days when he could not shrug off 'the black dog.' Regarding Asquith's driving, a speed limit of 20mph had been in force since 1903 and was not revised until 1930.

448 Quoted in Ziegler, op. cit., p.60–1.

449 Quoted in Brian Masters, op. cit., p.102.

450 Martin Pugh, *We Danced All Night* (The Bodley Head, London 2008), p.97.

451 H.H.A. to S.H., 8 June 1915, Sylvia Henley Papers.

452 H.H.A. to S.H., 14 June 1915, Sylvia Henley Papers.

453 H.H.A. to S.H., 19 June 1915, Sylvia Henley Papers.

454 S.H. to A.H., 16 June 1915, Sylvia Henley Papers.

455 Venetia Stanley to Edwin Montagu, 6 June 1915, Brock, op. cit., p.604.

Chapter 11

456 Amongst the finest of these collections of letters to a wife and children were those written by Lieutenant-Colonel Rowland Feilding. See Jonathan Walker (Ed.), *War Letters to a Wife* (Spellmount, Staplehurst 2000).

457 S.H. to A.H., 15 July 1915, Sylvia Henley Papers.

458 S.H. to A.H., 16 July 1915, Sylvia Henley Papers.

459 S.H. to A.H., 15, 16, 19, 20, 21, 23 July 1915, Sylvia Henley Papers.

460 H.H.A. to S.H., 18, 19, 20, 22, 26, 28 July 1915, Sylvia Henley Papers.

461 Clementine was pregnant with her fourth child and was extremely concerned that she and Winston lacked the income to support a large family according to Lady Hamilton. In June 1918, she considered that if she had twins, perhaps the childless Jean would like to adopt one. Jean declined the generous offer but it was an unusual and bizarre approach. The author is indebted to Celia Lee for discovering this surprising entry in Lady Hamilton's diary. The Churchill's fourth child, Marigold, was born in 1918 but was not adopted. She subsequently died in August 1921. See *The Daily Telegraph*, 25 March 2001. Also Lady Hamilton Diary, 21 June 1918, Liddell Hart Centre for Military Archives (hereafter LHCMA), King's College London.

462   H.H.A. to S.H., 28 August 1915, Sylvia Henley Papers.
463   H.H.A. to S.H., 15 July 1915, Sylvia Henley Papers.
464   Caroline Playne, op. cit., p.128.
465   In pre-NHS hospitals and nursing homes, circumcision was a routine neonatal procedure amongst most middle and upper class families. S.H. to A.H., 4, 10 November 1915, Sylvia Henley Papers.
466   H.H.A. to Venetia Stanley, 22 February 1915, Sylvia Henley Papers.
467   S.H. to A.H., 3 November 1915, Sylvia Henley Papers. For Walmer, see Colin Clifford, *The Asquiths* (John Murray, London 2002), p.244.
468   *The New York Times*, 2 January 1916.
469   De Courcy, op. cit., p.133.
470   There was a limit to social intercourse in the wartime workplace. See Gail Braybon & Penny Summerfield, *Out of the Cage* (Pandora, London 1987), pp.75–7.
471   Venetia Stanley to Anthony Henley, 27 October 1915, MS.Eng.lett.c.647, Sylvia Henley Papers, Special Collections, Bodleian Library, Oxford University.
472   H.H.A. to S.H., 15 November 1915, Sylvia Henley Papers.
473   H.H.A. to S.H., 29 November 1915, Sylvia Henley Papers.
474   H.H.A. to S.H., 16 November 1915, Sylvia Henley Papers.
475   John Julius Norwich, op. cit., p.14–15.
476   Margot Asquith, diary, d. 3215, quoted in Colin Clifford, op. cit.
477   H.H.A. to S.H., 10 December 1915, Sylvia Henley Papers. Also Colin Clifford, op. cit., pp.333–4
478   H.H.A. to S.H., 19 December 1915, Sylvia Henley Papers. For Zeppelin activity in the Peak District, see H.A. Jones, *The War in the Air, Vol. III* (OUP, Oxford 1931), pp.137–140.
479   Lady Hamilton Diary, Monday 10 January 1916, LHCMA. Also Clifford, op. cit., pp.329–33. For Asquith's problems over the conscription issue, see R.J.Q. Adams, 'Asquith's Choice: The May Coalition and the Coming of Conscription 1915–1916' in *Journal of British Studies* 25 (1986).
480   See also Mary Soames, *Speaking for Themselves. The Personal Letters of Winston and Clementine Churchill* (Doubleday, London 1998), pp.114, 121, 131. For committees, see Carolyne Playne, op. cit., p.103.
481   S.H. to A.H., 23 January 1916, Sylvia Henley Papers.
482   S.H. to A.H., 15 January 1916, Sylvia Henley Papers. Henry and Kitty Somerset did eventually divorce in 1920 and subsequently remarried their respective lovers.
483   S.H. to A.H., 20 February 1916, Sylvia Henley Papers.
484   H.H.A. to S.H., 26 February 1916, Sylvia Henley Papers. Field-Marshal Sir Douglas Haig had taken over as C-in-C after the resignation of Field-Marshal Sir John French in December 1915.
485   Leo Amery, *Diaries Volume I. 1896–1929* (Hutchinson, London 1980), 7 March 1916.
486   Edward David (Ed.), *Inside Asquith's Cabinet: From the Diaries of Charles Hobhouse* (John Murray, London 1977), pp.250–1.
487   Leo Amery Diaries, op. cit., 25 April 1916.
488   John Julius Norwich, *The Duff Cooper Diaries 1915–1951* (Phoenix, London 2006), pp.24, 27. Also Ziegler, op. cit., pp.54–5.
489   Philip Ziegler, *Diana Cooper* (Hamish Hamilton, London 1981), p.39. Also C.S. Peel, op. cit., p.70.
490   Ziegler, op. cit., p.56. This story must have been relayed at a later date, since the term 'batman' was not used until after the First World War.
491   Edwin Montagu replaced Lloyd George as Minister of Munitions on 1 July 1916.
492   Venetia Montagu to Anthony Henley, 22 June 1916, MS.Eng.lett.c.647, Special Collections, Bodleian Library, Oxford University.
493   S.H. to A.H., 18 July 1916, Sylvia Henley Papers.
494   H.H.A. to S.H., 10 August 1917, Sylvia Henley Papers. For farming, see Bernard Waites, *A Class Society at War. England 1914–1918* (Berg, Leamington Spa 1987), p.95.

495   H.H.A. to S.H., 4 July 1916, Sylvia Henley Papers.
496   S.H. to A.H., 8 August 1916, Sylvia Henley Papers.
497   The sale of the various lots took three years to complete. Anthony's mother, Clare, kept
      him informed of the progress of the sale. See Lady Henley to A.H., ref. 36, MSS.Eng.
      lett.c.541, Bodleian Library, Oxford University.
498   For casualties, see Peter Barton, *The Somme* (Constable, London 2006), pp.302–5.
499   Cate Haste, *Rules of Desire. Sex in Britain World War I to the Present* (Chatto & Windus,
      London 1992), p.2. See also S.H. to A.H., 4 August 1916, Sylvia Henley Papers.
500   John Julius Norwich, op. cit., p.35, 22 August 1916.
501   S.H. to A.H., 14 August 1916, Sylvia Henley Papers.
502   Gerard DeGroot, *Blighty. British Society in the Era of the Great War* (Longman, London
      1996), p.44.
503   A.J.P. Taylor (Ed.), *Lloyd George: A Diary of Frances Stevenson* (Hutchinson, London 1971),
      p.110. Also Arthur Marwick, op. cit., pp.222–3.
504   D. Lloyd George to H.H. Asquith, 5 December 1916, 31 fols. 37, Asquith Papers, Special
      Collections, Bodleian Library, Oxford University. For Lloyd George's role in Asquith's
      removal, see Michael Fry, 'Political Change in Britain, August 1914 to December 1916:
      Lloyd George Replaces Asquith. The Issues Underlying the Facts', in *The Historical Journal*,
      Vol. 31, No. 3 (September 1988).
505   H.H.A. to S.H., 6 December 1916, Sylvia Henley Papers.
506   Quoted in Adelaide Lubbock, op. cit., p.112.
507   Sonia Keppel, *Edwardian Daughter* (Hamish Hamilton, London 1958), p.144. See also Giles
      St Aubyn, *Edward VII. Prince and King* (Collins, London 1979), p.379.
508   For an assessment of the political achievements of Asquith, compared to Lloyd George, see
      Gary Sheffield, *Forgotten Victory. The First World War: Myths and Realities* (Headline, London
      2001), pp.80–3.
509   S.H. to A.H., 30 January 1917, Sylvia Henley Papers.
510   S.H. to A.H., 1 February 1917, Sylvia Henley Papers. Also Levine, op. cit. pp.486–7.
      Wilson had also recently embarked on an affair with Lady Curzon.
511   *Inside Asquith,* ibid., p.229.
512   'Tribute to the 7th Manchesters', op. cit.
513   Some of their letters have survived and are held in the Sylvia Henley Papers.
514   *King's View*, February 1978, ref KH/OB/29, King's College Archives, London.
515   Jean Hamilton Diary, 6 December 1917, LHCMA.
516   Major R.D. Harrison, DSO, served in the Royal Field Artillery. His death meant Hilda had
      to bring up her young son and daughter on her own. For Cynthia Asquith, see *The Diaries
      of Lady Cynthia Asquith 1915–18* (Century, London 1987), p.458. After Asquith's death,
      his many letters to Hilda Harrison were edited into two volumes; see *H.H.A. Letters to a
      Friend. First Series 1915–1922* (1933) and *Second Series 1922–1927* (1934), both (Geoffrey
      Bles, London); see also 'Mr Asquith Unbends to a Woman Friend' in *The Courier-Mail*, 20
      January 1934, Bisbane, Australia.
517   Thomas, Lord Stanley, *The Stanleys of Alderley 1927–2001* (AMCD Publishers, Anglesey
      2004), p.11.
518   'As I See It – The First 47,000' in *Imperialist*, 26 January 1918. See also Judith Walkowitz,
      'The Vision of Salome: Cosmopolitanism and Exotic Dancing in London 1908–1918', in
      The American Historical Review, Vol. 108, no. 2, April 2003; Jodie Medd, 'The Cult of the
      Clitoris: Anatomy of a National Scandal' in *Modernism/Modernity*, Vol. 9, No.1 January
      2002.
519   Martin Middlebrook, *The Kaiser's Battle* (Allen Lane, London 1978), p.347. It is highly
      likely that the infamous 'Black Book' never existed, as it was not produced as evidence in
      the case.
520   Walkowitz, op. cit. Also Colin Clifford, *The Asquiths* (John Murray, London 2002), p.456–8.
      Also Caroline Playne, op. cit., pp.248–9 and Adrian Gregory, op. cit., pp.241–2.

521 Toni Bentley, op. cit., pp.72–84. See also Deborah Cohler, 'Sapphism and Sedition:
     Producing Female Homosexuality in Great War Britain', in *Journal of the History of
     Sexuality*, Vol. 16, #1, January 2007, pp.82–94. Margot ceased supporting Maud Allan when
     H.H. Asquith died in 1928.

Chapter 12

522 Susan Kent, 'The Politics of Sexual Difference: World War I and the Demise of British
     Feminism' in *Journal of British Studies,* 27. July 1988. (The University of Chicago Press).
     Also Arthur Marwick, op. cit., p.136.

523 *King's View*, February 1978, op. cit.. Pre NHS hospitals, including King's were largely
     funded by private subscribers, legacies, fundraising and voluntary contributions from
     patients, and were governed by a Board of Governors. The third and present King's
     College Hospital was built on land donated by Viscount Hambleden. See also, Arthur
     Marwick, op. cit., p.341.

524 For generals, see Frank Davies and Graham Maddocks, *Bloody Red Tabs* (Leo Cooper,
     London 1995). For Etonians, see *List of Etonians Who Fought in the Great War 1914–1919*
     (The Medici Society, London 1921), p.280. A total of 1157 died, 1467 were wounded and
     130 captured out of 4852 who served overseas.

525 Keith Simpson, 'The Officers' in Ian Beckett and Keith Simpson (Eds.), *A Nation in Arms*
     (MUP, Manchester 1985).

526 John Julius Norwich, op. cit., p.85.

527 John Julius Norwich, op. cit., p.97.

528 *Lord Riddell's Intimate Diary of the Peace Conference and after 1918–1923* (Victor Galancz,
     London 1933), p.152.

529 James Reginato, 'A Six-Decade Roman Holiday' in *Vanity Fair,* November 2011. Also
     Ziegler, op. cit., p.106; Levine op. cit., p.530, 670–4. Venetia remained one of Lord
     Beaverbrook's lovers for over ten years. In 1962, the gregarious Judith married the art
     historian Milton Gendel. She had been a friend of Princess Margaret since the Second
     World War, and her close friendship with the Princess was captured in the iconic
     photograph of the 'PM set' on a Mustique beach.

530 Lord Stanley, op. cit., p.10. Lady Kathleen Thynne was the daughter of the 5th Marquess
     of Bath.

531 Toni Bentley, op. cit., p.82–3.

532 Hon. Anthony Morton Henley died on 17 May 1925 and he narrowly missed succeeding
     to the title, since his step-brother, the 5th Lord Henley died on 23 October 1925.

533 For letters relating to this trip, see The Gertrude Bell Archive, Newcastle University
     Library.

534 Royal Society, op. cit.

535 Radnor Mere has also been turned into a nature reserve. For full details of the rescue of
     the former estate, see Family History Society of Cheshire, *Volume 2, The Stanleys of Alderley*
     (CD, www.fhsc.org.uk)

536 Thomas, Lord Stanley, op. cit., pp.182–5.

537 See John Colville, *The Fringes of Power. Downing Street Diaries 1939–1955* (Hodder and
     Stoughton, London 1985), pp.120, 165, 421, 440, 468, 592.

538 Mary Soames, *Clementine Churchill. The Biography*, op. cit., pp.107, 330.

539 Mary Soames, ibid., p.500.

Bibliography

Unpublished Sources

The Bodleian Library, Oxford, holds an extensive collection of letters written by Sylvia Henley to her husband, Anthony Henley, as well as a number of letters from Venetia Stanley to Anthony Henley. The Library also holds a considerable number of letters written by H.H. Asquith to Sylvia Henley. The bulk of this correspondence was purchased at auction by the Bodleian in 1983. It appears that Asquith destroyed all his letters from Sylvia Henley.

Lord French's love letters to Winifred Bennett were kept by her, while it seems that he destroyed all her correspondence. The Imperial War Museum purchased the collection of 99 letters at auction in December 1975.

Archives, Libraries and Private Collections

American Women's Club
Records of the AMC during the First World War

University of Bangor Special Collections
Records of the Stanley family and Penrhôs, GB 0222/Bangor72

Berenson Archive, the Harvard University Center for Italian Renaissance Studies (Italy)
Correspondence between Bernard Berenson and Belle da Costa Greene

Oxford University, Bodleian Library, Special Collections & Western Manuscripts (temp held RSL)
Sylvia Henley Papers, including:

> Letters from Hon. Sylvia Henley to Hon. Anthony Morton Henley 1915–18 and letters from their children (MSS.Eng.lett.c.641-7)
> Letters between Anthony Henley and his mother, together with letters from the Stanley family (MSS.Eng.lett.c.648)

Letters to Sylvia Henley from the Stanley family (MSS.Eng.lett.c.649)
Miscellaneous items relating to Anthony and Sylvia Henley (MSS.Eng.hist.c.1071)
Letters from H.H.Asquith to Sylvia Henley, 1915–1919 (MSS.Eng.lett.c. 542/1-5)

H.H.Asquith Papers (microfiched), ref. MSS.Asquith 1-152

British Library
Copies of *The Tatler & Bystander* 1908–1920
Henry Havelock Ellis, correspondence & papers MSS 70524-89

Camilla Shivarg
Private papers of the Bennett family
    Iris Bennett's diary
    Percy Bennett photograph albums
    Winifred Bennett news cuttings and ephemera

Georgetown University Special Collections (US)
Sir Shane Leslie Papers (Box 46, Folder 2 – Miss Emilie Grigsby)

Guildhall Library, London
Records of London street directories 1890–1920

Imperial War Museum
Department of Documents:
    Papers of Sir John Cowans 1916–20
    Diaries and correspondence of Field-Marshal Lord French, including letters from
        Mrs Winifred Bennett (1914–1922), PP/MCR/C33

Sound Archive:
    Major-General Sir Edward Spears
    Roderick Suddaby

Library of Congress (US)
Margaret Sanger Papers (MSS 38919), correspondence with Henry Havelock Ellis
Digital Photographic Archives

Liddle Collection
Memoirs and ephemera of various First World War combatants

Liddell Hart Centre for Military Archives, King's College, London
Sir Ian Hamilton Papers, diaries of his wife, Lady Hamilton (microfiche) ref. 20/1/3.Vol
    X, reel 3. 1915–19

Liddell Hart Papers (correspondence regarding Charles Repington)
Records relating to the history of King's College Hospital (KH/OB/29)

The Mary Evans Picture Library
   The Graphic, 1910–20
   The London Illustrated News 1898–22
   The Sphere, 1908–18

National Archives
'Report on Women's War Work' (TNA KU 1/50)
'Superintendents' Reports (Metpol 2/1720) (WO 141/63)
'Courts of Inquiry Records' (WO 33/3282)

Oxfordshire Record Office
Annesley Estate Papers

Robinson Library, Newcastle University
The Gertrude Bell Archive

Cambridge University, Trinity College Library, Modern Manuscript Collections
Papers of Edwin Samuel Montagu ref. GBR/0016/Montagu
Correspondence with Venetia Montagu, 1909–19

Victoria & Albert Museum Archives
Accession records of Emilie Grigsby's couture collection

Westminster City Archive Centre
House and street histories – Mayfair, Marylebone, Paddington

The Women's Library, London Metropolitan University
Papers of prominent Edwardian women, including Charlotte Despard (7CFD) and Sylvia
Pankhurst (7ESP)

Published Sources

Abbott, Elizabeth, *A History of Mistresses* (Duckworth Overlook, London 2010)
Amery, Leo, *Diaries Volume I. 1896–1929* (Hutchinson, London 1980)
Anonymous, *I: In Which a Woman Tells the Truth About Herself* (D. Appleton & Co.,
   New York 1904)

Ardizzone, Heidi, *An Illuminated Life. Belle da Costa Greene's Journey from Prejudice to Privilege* (W.W. Norton & Co., New York 2007)

Arnold, John, and Sean Brady (Eds.), *What is Masculinity?* (Palgrave Macmillan, London 2011)

Arthur, Max, *Lost Voices of the Edwardians* (Harper Press, London 2006)

Asplin, K, *The Roll of the Imperial Yeomanry, Scottish Horse & Lovat's Scouts. 2nd Boer War 1899–1902* (DP & G Publishing, London 2006)

Asquith, The Earl of Oxford and, *Memories & Reflections 1852–1927, Vol. I & II* (Cassell, London 1928)

Asquith, Lady Cynthia, *Diaries 1915–18* (Century, London 1987)

Badsey, Stephen, *Doctrine and the Cavalry 1880–1918* (Ashgate, Vermont, US 2008)

Baker-Carr, Brigadier-General C.D., *From Chauffeur to Brigadier* (Ernest Benn, London 1930)

Barnes, Eric, *The Man Who Lived Twice* (Charles Scribner, New York 1956)

Barton, Peter, *The Somme* (Constable, London 2006)

Bascombe, Neal, *Red Mutiny: Mutiny, Revolution and Revenge on the Battleship Potemkin* (Weidenfeld & Nicolson, London 2007)

Beckett, Ian, *Johnnie Gough VC. A Biography of Brigadier-General Sir John Edmond Gough VC, KCB* (Tom Donovan, London 1989)

Beckett, Ian & Keith Simpson (Eds.), *A Nation in Arms. A Social Study of the British Army in the First World War* (Manchester University Press, Manchester 1985)

Bentley, Toni, *Sisters of Salome* (Yale University Press, New Haven 2002)

Bishop, Alan & Terry Smart (Eds.), *Vera Brittain. War Diary 1913–1917. Chronicle of Youth* (Victor Gollancz, London 1981)

Bland, Lucy, *Banishing the Beast: English Feminism and Sexual Morality, 1885–1914* (Penguin, London 1995)

Bonham Carter, Mark, & Mark Pottle, *Lantern Slides. The Diaries and Letters of Violet Bonham Carter 1904–1914* (Weidenfeld & Nicolson, London 1996)

Bonham Carter, Mark, (Ed.), *The Autobiography of Margot Asquith* (Weidenfeld & Nicolson, London 1995)

Bowker, Gordon, *James Joyce. A Biography* (Weidenfeld & Nicolson, London 2011)

Braybon, Gail, & Summerfield, Penny, *Out of the Cage. Women's Experiences in Two World Wars* (Pandora, London 1987)

Brock, Michael and Eleanor (Eds.), *H.H. Asquith. Letters to Venetia Stanley* (Oxford University Press, Oxford 1982 & 1985)

Bourne, J.M., *Britain and the Great War 1914–1918* (Edward Arnold, London 1989)

_____ *Who's Who in World War One* (Routledge, London 2001)

Bowker, Gordon, *James Joyce. A Biography* (Weidenfeld & Nicolson, London 2011)

Bruccoli, Mathew, *The Fortunes of Mitchell Kennerley, Bookman* (Harcourt Brace Jovanovich, San Diego 1986)

Brook-Shepherd, *Uncle of Europe. The Social and Diplomatic Life of Edward VII* (Collins, London 1975)

Bryson, Bill, *At Home. A Short History of Private Life* (Doubleday, London 2010)

Byng of Vimy, Viscountess, *Up the Stream of Time* (Macmillan, Toronto 1945)

Byrne, Ciaran, *The Harp and the Crown. The History of the 5th (Royal Irish) Lancers 1902–1922* (Lulu Books, Dublin 2010)

Callimachi, Princess Anne-Marie, *Yesterday Was Mine* (The Falcon Press, London 1952)

Carnarvon, Earl of, *No Regrets* (Weidenfeld & Nicolson, London 1976)

Cassar, George H., *Asquith As War Leader* (Hambledon Press, London 1994)

The Tragedy of Sir John French (Associated University Presses, New Jersey 1985)

Cecil, Robert, *Life in Edwardian England* (B.T. Batsford, London 1972)

Chapman-Huston, Major D., *General Sir John Cowans. The Quartermaster-General of the Great War Vol. I & II* (Hutchinson, London 1923)

Charteris, Brigadier-General John, *At GHQ* (Cassell, London 1931)

Churchill, Winston, *Great Contemporaries* (Macmillan, London 1942)

Clifford, Colin, *The Asquiths* (John Murray, London 2002)

Coates, Tim, *Patsy. The Story of Mary Cornwallis West* (Bloomsbury, London 2003)

Coleman, Frederic, *From Mons to Ypres with French* (Sampson, Low, Marston, London 1916)

Collis, John, *Havelock Ellis: Artist of Life* (William Sloane, New York 1959)

Cook, Hera, *The Long Sexual Revolution. English Women, Sex, and Contraception 1800–1975* (Oxford University Press, Oxford 2004)

Cooper, Diana, *Diana Cooper. Autobiography* (Carroll & Graf, New York 1985)

Crozier, Brigadier-General F.P., *A Brass Hat in No Man's Land* (Jonathan Cape, London 1930)

de Courcy, Anne, *The Viceroy's Daughters. The Lives of the Curzon Sisters* (Weidenfeld & Nicolson, London 2000)

_____ *Society's Queen. The Life of Edith, Marchioness of Londonderry* (Phoenix, London 2004)

Crutwell, C.R.M.F., *A History of the Great War 1914–1918* (OUP, Oxford 1936)

Davenport-Hines, Richard, *Ettie. The Intimate Life and Dauntless Spirit of Lady Desborough* (Weidenfeld & Nicolson, London 2008)

David, Edward (Ed.), *Inside Asquith's Cabinet. From the Diaries of Charles Hobhouse* (John Murray, London 1977)

Davies, Frank, & Graham Maddocks, *Bloody Red Tabs* (Leo Cooper, London 1995)

Degroot, Gerard, *Blighty. British Society in the Era of the Great War* (Longman, London 1996)

Delany, Paul, *The Neo-Pagans. Friendship and Love in the Rupert Brooke Circle* (Macmillan, London 1987)

Denison Ross, Sir Edward, *Both Ends of the Candle* (Faber & Faber, London)

Dollard, Catherine, *The Surplus Woman. Unmarried in Imperial Germany 1871–1918* (Berghahn Books, New York 2009)

Dreiser, Theodore, *The Financier* (Harper & Bros, New York 1912)

_____ *The Titan* (John Lane, New York 1914)

_____ *The Stoic* (Doubleday, New York 1947)

Dwyer, T. Ryle, *The Squad. And the Intelligence Operations of Michael Collins* (Mercier Press, Cork 2005)

Edel, Leon, *The Life of Henry James. Vol. II* (Penguin, London 1977)

Eksteins, Modris, *Rites of Spring. The Great War and the Birth of the Modern Age* (Bantam Press, London 1989)

Ellis, Jennifer, (Ed.), *Thatched with Gold. The Memoirs of Mabell Countess of Airlie* (Hutchinson, London 1962)

Esher, Oliver Viscount, *Journals and Letters of Reginald Viscount Esher, Vol. IV* (Ivor Nicolson & Watson, London 1938)

Eton College, *List of Etonians Who Fought in the Great War 1914–1919* (The Medici Society, London 1921)

Falls, Cyril, *War Books. A Critical Guide* (Peter Davies, London 1930)

Family History Society of Cheshire, *Parish History Series. Vol. 2. The Stanleys of Alderley.*

Ferris, Paul, *Sex and the British: A Twentieth Century History* (Michael Joseph, London 1993)

Fielding, Daphne, *Emerald & Nancy. Lady Cunard and her Daughter* (Eyre & Spottiswoode, London 1968)

Flower, Newman, (Ed.), *The Journals of Arnold Bennett 1911–1921* (Cassell, London 1932)

Ford Maddox Ford, *Portraits from Life* (Houghton Miflin, Boston 1980)

Franch, John, *Robber Baron. The Life of Charles Tyson Yerkes* (University of Illinois, Chicago 2006)

Fraser, Peter, *Lord Esher. A Political Biography* (Hart Davis MacGibbon, London 1973)

French, Major Hon. Gerald, *The Life of Field-Marshal Sir John French* (Cassell, London 1931)

French, Field-Marshal Viscount French of Ypres, *1914* (Constable, London 1919)

Graham, Dominick, and Shelford Bidwell, *Coalitions, Politicians and Generals. Some Aspects of Command in Two World Wars* (Brassey's, London 1993)

Grayzel, Susan, *Women's Identities at War: Gender, Motherhood, and Politics in Britain and France During the First World War* (University of North Carolina Press, North Carolina US 1999)

Green, Martin, *Children of the Sun. A Narrative of Decadence in England After 1918* (Pimlico, London 1992)

Gregory, Adrian, *The Last Great War. British Society and the First World War* (Cambridge University Press, Cambridge 2008)

Grosskurth, Phyllis, *Havelock Ellis. A Biography* (Alfred A Knopf, New York 1980)

Hague, Ffion, *The Pain and the Privilege: The Women in Lloyd George's Life* (Harper Perennial, London 2009)

Hall, Lesley, *Sex, Gender and Social Change in Britain Since 1880* (Macmillan, London 2000)

Hall, Ruth, (Ed.), *Dear Dr Stopes* (André Deutsch, London 1978)

Hankey, Lord, *The Supreme Command 1914–1918, Vol. 2* (Constable, London 1921)

Hanna, Judith, *Dance, Sex and Gender* (University of Chicago Press, Chicago 1988)

Haste, Cate, *Rules of Desire. Sex in Britain: World War I to the Present* (Chatto & Windus, London 1992)

Hirschfeld, Magnus, *The Sexual History of the World War* (Cadillac Publishing Co., New York 1946)

Holmes, Richard, *The Little Field Marshal. A Life of Sir John French* (Weidenfeld & Nicolson, London 1981)

Homberger, Eric, *Mrs Astor's New York. Money and Social Power in a Gilded Age*, (Yale University Press, New Haven 2002)

Horsler, Val, *All for Love. Seven Centuries of Illicit Liaison* (The National Archives, London 2006)

Jones, HA, *The War in the Air, Vol. III* (Oxford University Press, London 1931)

Jones, LE, *An Edwardian Youth* (Macmillan, London 1956)

Jones, Nigel, *Rupert Brooke. Life, Death & Myth* (Richard Cohen Books, London 1999)

Jenkins, Roy, *Asquith: Portrait of a Man and an Era* (Collins, London 1964)

Kellner, Bruce, (Ed.), *The Splendid Drunken Twenties* (University of Illinois, Chicago 2003)

Keppel, Sonia, *Edwardian Daughter* (Hamish Hamilton, London 1958)

Kettle, Michael, *Salome's Last Veil: The Libel Case of the Century* (HarperCollins, London 1977)

Lamont-Brown, Raymond, *Edward VII's Last Loves. Alice Keppel & Agnes Keyser* (Sutton Publishing, Stroud 1998)

Lee, Celia, *Jean, Lady Hamilton 1861–1941* (Celia Lee, London 2001)

Leslie, Shane, *Long Shadows* (John Murray, London 1966)

_____ *The End of a Chapter* (Heinemann, London 1916).

Levine, Naomi, *Politics, Religion & Love* (New York University Press, New York 1991)

Long, Helen, *The Edwardian House* (Manchester University Press, Manchester 2002)

Lubbock, Adelaide, *People in Glass Houses. Growing up at Government House* (Hamish Hamilton, London 1978)

Lucas, E.V., *The Colvins and Their Friends* (Methuen, London 1928)

MacDonagh, Michael, *In London During The Great War. The Diary of a Journalist* (Eyre and Spottiswoode, London 1935)

MacCarthy, Desmond, (Ed.), *H.H.A. Letters of the Earl of Oxford and Asquith to a Friend. First Series 1915–1922* (1933) and *Second Series 1922–1927* (1934) both (Geoffrey Bles, London)

Magnus, Philip, *King Edward the Seventh* (John Murray, London 1964)

Margetson, Stella, *Victorian High Society* (B.T. Batsford, London 1980)

Marlow, Joyce (Ed.), *The Virago Book of Women and the Great War* (Virago Press, London 1998)

Martin, William, *Verdun 1916* (Osprey, Oxford 1916)

Marwick, Arthur, *The Deluge. British Society and the First World War* (Palgrave Macmillan, London 2006)

_____ *War and Social Change in the Twentieth Century* (Macmillan, London 1974)

Masters, Brian, *The Life of E. F. Benson* (Chatto & Windus, London 1991)

May, Ernest, *The World War and American Isolation 1914–1917* (Harvard University Press, Cambridge, Mass., 1959)

Middlebrook, Martin, *The Kaiser's Battle* (Allen Lane, London 1978)

Mitford, Nancy, *The Ladies of Alderley* (Hamish Hamilton, London 1967)

Moncrieff, A.R. Hope, *London* (A & C Black, London 1916)

Morris, A.J.A. (Ed.), *The Letters of Lieutenant-Colonel Charles à Court Repington CMG, Military Correspondent of The Times 1903–1918* (Sutton Publishing, Stroud 1999)

Munn, Michael, *David Niven: The Man Behind the Balloon* (J.R. Books, London 2009)

Nicolson, Juliet, *The Perfect Summer. Dancing into Shadow* in 1911, (John Murray, London 2006)

Norwich, John Julius, (Ed.), *The Duff Cooper Diaries 1915–1951* (Weidenfeld & Nicolson, London 2005)

Page, Christopher, *Command in the Royal Naval Division* (Spellmount, Staplehurst 1998)

Pakula, Hannah, *Queen of Roumania. The Life of Princess Marie, Grand-daughter of Queen Victoria* (Weidenfeld & Nicolson, London 1984)

Pankhurst, Christabel, *The Great Scourge and How to End It* (E. Pankhurst, London 1913)

Pantazzi, Ethel Greening, *Roumania in Light & Shadow* (T. Fisher Unwin, London 1921)

Parris, Mathew, *Great Parliamentary Scandals* (Robson Books, 1997)

Peel, Mrs C.S., *How We Lived Then* (John Lane, London 1929)

Playne, Caroline, *Society at War 1914–1916* (George Allen & Unwin, London 1931)

Poiret, Paul, (Stephen Haden Guest, trans.), *King of Fashion. The Autobiography of Paul Poiret* (V&A Publishing, London 2009)

Pope-Hennessy, James, *Queen Mary. 1867–1953* (George Allen & Unwin, London 1959)

Pottle, Mark, (Ed.), *Champion Redoubtable. The Diaries and Letters of Violet Bonham Carter 1914–1945* (Weidenfeld & Nicolson, London 1998)

Pugh, Martin, *We Danced All Night. A Social History of Britain Between the Wars* (The Bodley Head, London 2008)

Repington, Lieutenant-Colonel Charles à Court, *The First World War 1914–1918 Vol. I & II* (Constable & Co., London 1920)

Repington, Mary, *Thanks for the Memory* (Constable, London 1938)

Richardson, Angelique, & Willis, Chris (Eds.), *The New Woman in Fiction and in Fact. Fin-de-Siècle Feminisms* (Palgrave Macmillan, London 2002)

Riddell, Lord, *Intimate Diary of the Peace Conference and After 1918–1923* (Victor Gollancz, London 1933)

Riggio, Thomas, *Women: New Letters Volume 2. Theodore Dreiser* (University of Illinois Press, Chicago 2009)

Rimmell, Raymond, *Zeppelin: A Battle for Air Supremacy in World War I* (Conway, London 1984)

Roiphe, Katie, *Uncommon Arrangements. Seven Portraits of Married Life in London Literary Circles 1910–1939* (The Dial Press, New York 2007)

Rose, Kenneth, *King George V* (Weidenfeld & Nicolson, London 1983)

Ross, Robert, *The Georgian Revolt: Rise and Fall of a Poetic Ideal 1910–22* (Faber & Faber, London 1967)

Russell, Bertrand, *The Autobiography* (Routledge, London 2000)

St Aubyn, Hon. Giles, *Edward VII. Prince and King* (Collins, London 1979)

Sackville-West, Vita, *The Edwardians* (Virago Press, London 1983)

Searle, George, *The Liberal Party: Triumph and Disintegration 1886–1929* (Palgrave Macmillan, London 1992)

Sebba, Anne, *Jennie Churchill. Winston's American Mother* (John Murray, London 2007)

Seton-Watson, R., *A History of the Roumanians* (Cambridge University Press, London 1934)

Sheffield, Gary, *Forgotten Victory. The First World War: Myths and Realities* (Headline, London 2001)

_____ *The Chief: Douglas Haig and the British Army* (Aurum Press, London 2011)

Sheffield, Gary, & John Bourne, (Eds.), *Douglas Haig. War Diaries and Letters 1914–1918* (Weidenfeld & Nicolson, London 2005)

Sheppard, FHW, *Survey of London: Volume 40: The Grosvenor Estate in Mayfair. Part 2: The Buildings* (English Heritage, London 1980)

Sherborne, Michael, *H. G. Wells. Another Kind of Life* (Peter Owen, London 2010)

Sherwood, Tim, *Charles Tyson Yerkes. The Traction King of London* (The History Press, Stroud 2008)

Souhami, Diana, *Mrs Keppel and Her Daughter* (HarperCollins, London 1996)

Sitwell, Osbert, *The Scarlet Tree* (Macmillan, London 1946)

Smith, Angela K., *The Second Battlefield. Women, Modernism and the First World War* (Manchester University Press, Manchester 2000)

Soames, Lady Mary, *Speaking for Themselves. The Personal Letters of Winston and Clementine Churchill* (Doubleday, London 1998)

_____ *Clementine Churchill. The Biography of a Marriage* (Houghton Mifflin, Boston 2003)

_____ *Clementine Churchill* (Cassell, London 1979)

Stanley, Peter, *The House of Stanley from the 12th Century* (Pentland Press, London 1998)

Stanley of Alderley, Thomas, Lord, *The Stanleys of Alderley 1927–2001* (AMCD Publishers, Anglesey 2004)

Steinbach, Susie, *Women in England 1760–1914. A Social History* (Weidenfeld & Nicolson, London 2003)

Stone, Lawrence, *Road to Divorce: England 1530–1987* (Oxford University Press, New York 1990)

Stopes, Marie, *Married Love* (Truth Publishing Co., New York 1918)

Strange, Lieutenant-Colonel L.A., *Recollections of an Airman* (John Hamilton, London 1933)

Taylor, Leonard, *The Sourdough and the Queen. The Many Lives of Klondike Joe Boyle* (Methuen, Toronto 1983)

Taylor, A.J.P. (Ed.), *Lloyd George: A Diary of Frances Stevenson* (Hutchinson, London 1971).

Taylor, S.J., *The Great Outsiders. Northcliffe, Rothermere and the Daily Mail* (Weidenfeld & Nicolson, London 1996)

Towner, Wesley, *The Elegant Auctioneers* (Victor Gollancz, London 1971)

Travers, Tim, *The Killing Ground. The British Army, the Western Front & the Emergence of Modern Warfare* (Routledge, London 1993)

Turner, E.S., *Gallant Gentlemen* (Michael Joseph, London 1956)

_____ *Dear Old Blighty* (Michael Joseph, London 1989)

Waites, Bernard, *A Class Society at War. 1914–1918* (Berg, Leamington Spa 1987)

Waley, Sir Sigismund, *Edwin Montagu: A Memoir and an Account of his Visits to India* (Asia Publishing House, 1964)

Walker, Jonathan, *The Blood Tub. General Gough and the Battle of Bullecourt, 1917* (Spellmount, Staplehurst 1998)

_____ as editor, *War Letters to a Wife* (Spellmount, Staplehurst 2000)

Waller, Maureen, *The English Marriage: Tales of Love, Money and Adultery* (John Murray, London 2009)

Weintraub, Stanley, *A Stillness Heard Around the World* (OUP, New York 1985)

Wheeler, Captain Owen, *The War Office Past and Present* (Methuen & Co, London 1914)

Whitmore, Lieutenant-Colonel F., *10th PWO Royal Hussars and the Essex Yeomanry During the European War 1914–1918* (Benham, Colchester 1920)

Williams, Jeffery, *Byng of Vimy* (Leo Cooper, London 1983)

Wilson, A.N., *After the Victorians* (Hutchinson, London 2005)

Wilson, Trevor, *The Myriad Faces of War* (Polity, Cambridge 1986)

Wojtczak, Helena, *Notable Sussex Women* (The Hastings Press, Hastings 2008)

Wyndham, Francis, *The Other Garden* (Jonathan Cape, London 1988)

Wyndham, Joan, *Dawn Chorus* (Virago, London 2004)

_____ *Anything Once* (Sinclair-Stevenson, London 1992)

_____ *Love is Blue* (Heinemann, London 1986)

Ziegler, Philip, *Diana Cooper* (Hamish Hamilton, London 1981)

Journals

American Literature

The American Historical Review

The Army Quarterly and Defence Journal

English Historical Review

European Journal of Women's Studies

The Historical Journal

Journal of the History of Sexuality

History Today

History Workshop

Hong Kong Guide

James Joyce Quarterly

Journal of British Studies
Journal of Contemporary History
Journal of Imperial and Commonwealth History
Journal of Military History
Journal of Modern History
Journal of the Royal Society
Journal of Social History
Parliamentary History
The Pennsylvania Magazine of History and Biography
The Poppy and the Owl
Records. The Journal of the Douglas Haig Fellowship
Slavic Review
War in History Journal
Women's History Review

Newspapers
The Argus (Australia)
The Brisbane Courier (Australia)
The Chicago Daily Tribune (US)
The Chicago Sunday Tribune (US)
The Courier-Mail (Australia)
The Daily Telegraph (UK)
The Guardian (UK)
The Guthrie Daily Leader (Australia)
Milwaukee Journal (US)
Minneapolis Journal (US)
The New York Times (US)
The Oxford Times (UK)
The Reading Eagle (US)
The Sydney Morning Herald (Australia)
The Times (UK)
The Times Dispatch (US)
The Washington Times (US)
The West Australian (Australia)

Official Histories and Publications
Hansard
House of Lords Debate, 16 November 1915 (Vol. 20 cc359–86)
Quarterly Army List January 1918, incorporating Army Service Records (HMSO, London 1918)
Kelly's Royal Blue Book: Fashionable Directory and Parliamentary Guide (B.W. Gardiner, London 1900–22)

Index

Airlie, Blanche, Countess of, 130
Airlie, Mabell, Countess of, 51
Aitken, Sir Max, 170
Allan, Maud, 137, 174–5, 184
Amberley, Lady Kate, 130
American Officers' Inn, 62
American Women's Hospital, 102
Amery, Leo, 165
Ancaster, Eloise, Countess of, 91
Anderson, Nora, 123
Anderson Auction Co., 87
Annesley, Captain Jack, background, 23; affair with
    Winifred, 23–4; in India, 24; as ADC, 25; in
    Cairo, 25–6; tastes, 28–9, 32; at war, 31; death,
    31; memorial, 32; possessions, 34; Winifred's grief
    over, 40, 49; memory of, 70
Asquith, Cynthia, 12, 46, 173
Asquith, Elizabeth, 180
Asquith, HH, background, 136, character
    and passion, 142, 148, 161, 165, 184; and
    cabinet colleagues, 11, 98, 115, 149–50, 152;
    correspondence, 12, 141, 152, 155, 161, 163; and
    Sylvia, 13, 143–162, 167–177, 180, 182, 184; and
    'harem', 13, 161, 169, 173, 184; and GG Moore,
    26–7, 46; and Romania, 42; 'Shell Scandal', 43,
    143–4, 149; and Sir John French, 52–3, 152; and
    Lloyd George, 59, 163, 165, 170; resignation of,
    59, 115; and 'Maud Allan Affair', 81, 174–5, 184;
    Irish problem, 91, 139, 169; political enemies
    of, 97, 114–5; against Northcliffe and press, 98,
    114, 163, 170; and Repington, 99; and Patsy
    Cornwallis-West, 117; at Penrhôs, 129, 142, 168;
    with Stanley family, 136, 139, 144, 171, 179;
    and Margot Asquith, 136, 152–3; at Alderley,
    136, 142; political career, 136–8, 171, 177–80;
    and Venetia Stanley, 138–49, 152, 158–9; and
    Edwin Montagu, 138, 172; women's suffrage,
    138, 177; Anthony Henley, 139–40, 149, 157;
    tours hospitals, 140; and Lord Kitchener, 140; at
    'The Wharf', 145, 151, 157, 169; at GHQ, 152;
    Admiral Fisher's resignation, 149; in Coalition
    Government, 150, 158, 170; and 'Curragh
    Incident', 139, 152; and Clementine Churchill,
    152, 157–8; and Diana Manners, 153, 169;
    conscription debate, 163; and Pamela McKenna,
    161, 163; at Walmer Castle, 164; and Haig, 165;
    Winston Churchill, 165; casualty rates, 169;

Raymond Asquith's death, 170, 173; resignation
    as PM, 171; with Alice Keppel, 171; with Hilda
    Harrison, 173; as Earl of Oxford, 180; death, 180
Asquith, Herbert (son), 12
Asquith, Katherine, 165–6, 179
Asquith, Margot, background, 136, 176, character
    and wit, 136, 179; and GG Moore, 26; and Sir
    John French, 30–1; visit to Ypres, 49; at GHQ,
    51; with the 'Souls', 68, 136; and Paul Poiret, 81;
    death of Raymond, 114; and Maud Allan, 137,
    174–5, 179; with Stanley family, 142, 148–9; and
    Sylvia, 145, 152–3, 162, 168; and HH Asquith,
    150, 162; and Violet Asquith, 162; and Wilfred
    Blunt, 162; and Sir John Cowans, 164; with
    Venetia Stanley, 145, 149; death, 180
Asquith, 'Oc', 91, 173
Asquith, Raymond, 12, 26, 148, 166, 173
Asquith, Violet, 90, 136, 138, 145, 148, 169
Astor, Lady Nancy, 102
Aubers Ridge, 43, 144
Balfour, Arthur, 41, 96, 158, 165
Baker-Carr, Christopher, 37–8
Barrett, Lieutenant Patrick, 116–7
Barrie, JM, 54
Bartlett, Paul, 110
Beatty, Admiral, 11
Beaverbrook, Lord, 178
Beecham, Sir Thomas, 55
Bell, Gertrude, 180–1
Bell, Sir Hugh, 179–80
Belloc, Hilaire, 131
Bennett, Percy, marriage, 18; background, 18–19;
    as Vice-Consul, 19; as father, 19; in Vienna,
    20; and Potemkin, 20–1; in Romania, 21; as
    Royal Commissioner, 22; character, 22; buys 5
    Devonshire Terr., 22; appointed CMG, 26; and
    GG Moore, 26; and passion, 37; and Winifred,
    52; divorce, 58, 68; in Zurich, 60; argues with
    Joyce, 61; as ambassador to Panama, 66; death, 69
Bennett, Winifred, correspondence with French,
    12, 29, 37; Fame as a beauty, 13, 19–20, 69; in
    Romania, 9, 15–18, 21, 33, 42, 58–60, 66, 70;
    birth, 15; sexuality, 9, 22–3, 36–7, 45, 67, 70–71;
    and Prince Ghika, 18; meets and marries Percy,
    18; travels with Percy, 19–20, 22; in tableaux,
    19; gives birth, 19; portrait painted, 20; meets
    Edward VII, 20; relations with Percy, 22, 24,

26–7, 32, 67–8; at 5 Devonshire Terrace, 22–3, 37; affair with Jack Annesley, 23–5, 28–9, 32, 70; meets GG Moore, 26; meets French, 26, 28, 32, 34; Jack's death, 31–2, 40, 49; destruction of letters, 34; French visits Devonshire Terrace, 34; sacred relationship, 35; sends French photo, 36; calming French, 37, 45, 47, 51, 142, 183; wooed by French, 37–40; as 'silver girl', 45; French's anger, 56; effect on French, 57; and GG Moore 37, 40, 42, 45–6; illness, 40; on holiday, 46; with Iris, 46, 48, 60, 64–7; and Gladys, 46; and Sybil, 64, 67; and society, 47, 55; trip to Panama, 66–7; at Bletchingdon, 49; in Ireland, 62, 65; travels to Egypt, 53; as 'Wendy', 54, 69, 121; cooling relations, 67; fund raising, 55, 60; with Sybil, 56; and divorce, 57, 68–9; in Zurich, 60–62; Gladys Hood, 60; Ireland, 62, 65; with Sybil, 64, 67; with Joan Wyndham, 70; death, 70–71
Berenson, Bernard, 84
Bernstorf, Count von, 56
Billing, Noel Pemberton, 174–5
Birth control, 93–5
Blackwood, Lord Frederick, 164
Bonar Law, Andrew, 170–1
Bonham-Carter, Maurice, 145, 162
Boyle, Joseph, 110–1, 118, 124–5
Brandt, Augustus, 116
Brandt, Jean, 116, 119
Braxton, Carter, 74
Brittain, Vera, 30
Brooke, Rupert, 90–1, 93
Bulldog Club, 111
Burbridge, General S., 74
Burns, Mary, 89, 115
Byng, General Sir Julian, 25, 29
Byng, Lady Evelyn, 25

Cadogan, Major Hon. Willie, 31
Cambrai, Battle of, 173
Campbell, Mrs Patrick, 112
Cane, Percy, 127
Cantacuzèe, Zizi, 17
Canteens, 163–4
Carlisle, Countess of, 130
Carlisle, George, Earl of, 133
Carnarvon, Almina Countess of, 126
Carnock, Lord, 120
Carol I, King of Romania, 16, 21
Carpenter, Edward, 83
Carrington, Charles, 10
Carson, Sir Edward, 115, 170, 184
Casement, Sir Roger, 169
Cave, Walter, 145
Cavendish Hotel, 54
Charing Cross Hospital, 62
Charteris family, 27
Charteris, Ego, 165
Chisholm, Hugh, 128
Chisholm, Willena, 127–8
Chrissoveloni, Dimitriu, 17
Chrissoveloni, Hélène, 17
Chrissoveloni, Sybil (née Youell), 16–18, 22, 42, 56, 64, 67, 187

Chrissoveloni, Zanni, 17, 22, 64, 67
Christmas Truce, 33
Churchill, Clementine (née Hozier), 130, 134, 145, 152, 157–8, 163, 182
Churchill, Lord Randolph, 102
Churchill, Lady Randolph (Jennie), 12, 89, 91, 101–2, 116
Churchill, Winston, 35, 39, 41, 45, 64, 96, 102, 115, 129–30, 134, 138, 142, 145, 149–50, 152, 157–8, 165, 180–2
Claridge's Hotel, 55, 108
Clemenceau, George, 178
Cleveland Street brothel raid, 10
Clifford, Lord and Lady, 86
Colefax, Lady Sibyl, 136
Coleville, Jock, 64, 181–2
Colvin, Sir Sidney, 87–8
Collins, Michael, 63, 65
Cooper, Duff, 64, 153, 162, 165–6, 169, 178
Cornwallis-West, George, 12, 102, 117
Cornwallis-West, Patsy, 12, 59, 116–7, 125–6, 184
Cornwallis-West, Colonel William, 116–7
'Corrupt Coterie', the, 27, 39, 96, 135, 165, 170
Cosgrave, Jack, 82–3, 85
Cowans, Lady Eva, 95
Cowans, General Sir John, character, 92–3, 95, 164; career, 11, 96, 106, 117; affairs, 92–3, 95, 184; and Emilie, 92, 96–7, 105, 124, 127, 183; the 'Ark', 96; and Dorothy Dennistoun, 106, 121; and Asquith family, 114, 164; and Patsy Cornwallis-West, 116–7, 124, 184; and Repington, 117, 121; death, 125
Cox, Kathleen, 90, 93
Cumbers, Yevonde, 55
Cunard, Maud, 105
Cunard, Nancy, 169
'Curragh Incident', 139, 152
Curzon, Lord, 11, 179

Dalziel, Sir James, 43–4
Dardanelles campaign, 45, 90, 98, 165
Delhi Durbar, 86
Dennistoun, Dorothy, 106, 121, 126, 184
Dennistoun, Colonel Ian, 106, 126
Desborough, Lord and Lady, 78, 91, 135
Desborough family (Grenfell), 165
Despard, Charlotte, 37, 66
Dessau, Mlle., 85–6
Dilke, Sir Charles, 10
Divorce, 57–8, 68–9
Dodge, Mabel, 100
Dombe, Mlle., 143
D.O.R.A., 121
Dreiser, Theodore, 127–8
Dudley, Eric, 179

Edward VII, King (earlier Prince of Wales), 11, 12, 20, 25, 53, 59, 77, 81, 137
Edward, Prince of Wales (later King Edward VIII and Duke of Windsor), 44, 64, 66, 83
Ellis, Edith Havelock, 83–5
Ellis, Henry Havelock, 83–4, 97, 123, 161–2
Epsom Derby, 107–8

Esher, Henry, Viscount, 11, 52, 57, 116
Essex, Adéle, Countess of, 91, 99, 101

Faber, Beryl, 84–5
Falls, Cyril, 125
Fashion, 80–1, 104
Ferdinand, King of Romania, 16–17, 33, 60
Festubert, Battle of, 42
Fish, Mrs Stuyvesant, 79
Fisher, Admiral Sir John, 149
Fitzwilliam, Earl and Countess of, 86
Foch, Marshal, 108, 185
Ford, Ford Maddox, 128
France, as coalition partner, 46–7
Frayne, Lord, 43
French, Lady Eleanora, 28, 57–8
French, Essex, 57
French, Lieutenant George, 43
French, Gerald, 57
French, Field Marshal Sir John (later Viscount
    French and Earl of Ypres), career, 11, 27–8;
    correspondence from, 11–12, 37, 60, 184; affair
    with Winifred, 12, 27–9, 32, 34–8, 40–42, 45,
    47, 49, 52–7, 65–7, 70–71, 142, 183; and GG
    Moore, 26–8, 36–42, 45–7, 52–3, 56–7, 68, 184;
    at 94 Lancaster Gate, 27, 32–3, 37–9, 52, 54,
    60; character, 27, 30, 40, 51–2; affairs, 28, 34,
    47, 184; relationship with Emilie, 88–9, 92, 99,
    107; and Margot Asquith, 30–31, 51; and Jack
    Annesley, 32, 34, 40, 49; at GHQ, St Omer, 32,
    34, 37, 40–42, 44–5, 50–51, 56; 1914 Christmas
    Truce, 33; belief in spirituality & religion, 35–6,
    42; opinion of other generals, 36; and Johnnie
    Gough, 36; passion, 36–7; at Bailleul, 36; and
    sister, Charlotte, 37, 66; as 'Peter Pan', 54, 70;
    Kensington Gardens, 54; and Lady Hamilton,
    55; heart attack, 50; and Patsy Cornwallis
    West, 59, 116; and Lord Granby, 39; with
    Diana Manners, 39, 47, 53; at Battle of Neuve
    Chapelle, 39; with Winston Churchill, 33, 39,
    41, 45; at Hazebrouck, 40; dealing with Haig,
    40, 45, 50–52, 56–7, 115; personal appearance,
    40; and General Sir Edward Spiers, 40; HH
    Asquith, 52, 152; resignation as C-in-C, 52;
    visiting wounded, 53; as Viscount, 55; and Lord
    Kitchener, 41, 43–6, 50, 53, 57, 59; and Arthur
    Balfour, 41; and Iris Bennett, 41; Battle of
    Festubert, 42; and Repington, 43, 53, 98, 105,
    107; creates 'Shell Scandal', 43–4, 143–4, 183;
    with George V, 44, 48; with Prince of Wales,
    44; and General Smith-Dorrien, 44, 146; and
    Anthony Henley, 141, 144; unpopularity, 45;
    and Northcliffe, 46; with Violet Asquith, 46; and
    Sir William Robertson, 47, 50; and Duchess of
    Rutland, 47; conduct at Battle of Loos, 50, 183;
    David Lloyd George, 50; Lord St Davids, 50–51;
    and General Joffre, 52; and Lord Esher, 52, 57;
    as Lord Lieutenant of Ireland, 62, 68; and Irish
    Troubles, 63–6; assassination attempt, 66; created
    Earl of Ypres, 67; as Captain of Deal Castle, 68;
    death, 68, 125
French, Lieut. Richard, 57
Frost, John, 37, 41

Funk, Wilhelm, 81

Galatz, 15–19, 21–2, 42, 59, 70, 187
George V, King, 17, 44, 48, 86, 115
Ghika, Prince, 18
GHQ, France 34, 37, 40–45, 50–51, 56, 114, 152,
    189, 212
'Glenconner', 176
Glyn, Elinor, 11
Godfrey-Faussett, Eugenie, 11
Gordon, Archie, 138
Gordon, General, 16
Gotha bombing raids, 120
Gough, Brigadier-General Hubert, 139, 152
Gough, Brigadier-General Johnnie, VC, 36
Gould, Howard 120
Granby, Lord John, 39
Great Dunmow, 25
Greene, Belle da Costa, 83–4, 89, 100, 102
Grigsby, Braxton 74–5, 87
Grigsby, Emilie, family history, 74; sexuality, 9, 81,
    84–4, 92–3, 100, 105; at Waldorf Astoria, 73–4;
    and Yerkes estate, 80, 100; visits art exhibition,
    13; converts to Catholicism, 74; relations with
    Yerkes, 75–6; commissions art, 75, 81, 87; arrives
    New York, 75; in 'House of Mystery' 75–6; sale
    of house, 87; failure on social circuit, 76; visits
    London, 77; as author, 77; at Taplow, 78–9, 121;
    with Henry James, 79; and Mrs Kernochan,
    79–80; pursues Henry Loomis, 80; beauty,
    80–81, 104; friendship with Paul Poiret, 81, 104;
    at the Opera House, 81–2; personal wealth, 82;
    and Thomas Mosher, 82; with Jack Cosgrave,
    82–3, 85; arrives in London, 83; meets Ward, 92;
    sets up salon for Northcliffe, 97–9, 114–5; and
    Edith and Henry Havelock Ellis, 83–5; close to
    Belle Greene, 83, 89; affair with Colvin, 87–8;
    affair with Cowans, 92, 96–7, 105–6, 114, 124–7;
    at 'Old Meadows', 84–5, 88–90, 99, 108, 119–20,
    126–8; meets Max Pam, 85; at Dehli Durbar,
    86; friend of Mlle. Dussau, 85–6; and Princess
    Mary and Royal family, 85–6; New York Times
    exposé, 86; and Mitchell Kennerley, 87 Georgian
    poetry, 123; and Sir John French, 88–9, 92, 107;
    travels to India, 88, 125; meets GG Moore, 88;
    affair with Repington, 98–9, 102, 104–5, 107,
    110–11, 113–15, 118, 124–5; at Brook Street, 89,
    92, 104, 108–9, 112–5, 119–22, 125; at outbreak
    of war, 90; relations with Rupert Brooke, 90–1,
    93; when Lusitania sinks, 91; hygiene of, 92; with
    bohemian set, 100, 126; and other Americans,
    101–2; couture clothes, 102–3, 128; friends
    with Gladys Unger, 111–12, 126–7; adventures
    with Doris Keane, 99, 111–12, 120–21, 127;
    servants, 104–5, 110; as hostess, 105; friend of
    Sir Shane Leslie, 110, 127–8; at RHS Show, 107;
    and Carson, 115, with Jean Brandt, 116, 119;
    sees Bennett portrait, 120–21; and Bartlett, 110;
    and Rodin, 110; friend of Joe Boyle, 110–11,
    118, 124–5; affair with Mackay, 118–9, 122–3;
    and Long Lance, 126; with Van Vechten, 125;
    in Dreiser novels, 127–8; and Chisholms, 128;
    death, 128

Grigsby, Colonel Lewis Braxton, 74–5
Grigsby, Susan 73–5

Haig, Field Marshal Sir Douglas, 13, 40, 45, 50–52,
    56–7, 115, 147, 165, 183
Haldane, Lord, 50, 150
Haldane, Major General Aylmer, 113
Hamilton, General Sir Ian 55, 78, 158,
Hamilton, Jean, Lady, 53, 55, 78, 98–9, 102, 105,
    117, 163, 173,
Hampshire, HMS, 107
Hankey, Maurice, 59
Harcourt, Lewis 'Loulou' (*later* Viscount) 11, 89,
    115–6
Hardon, Eugénie, 11
Harlow, Jean, 179
Harmsworth, St John, 98
Harrison, Hilda, 142, 173, 180
Harrison, Major Rowland, 173
Hazebrouck, 40
Henley, Hon. Anthony (*later* Brigadier-General),
    meets Stanley family, 131; background, 131–2;
    as husband 133; near Dublin,133; and birth of
    Rosalind and Kitty, 134; at Staff College, 138;
    as Brigade Major, 138; 'Curragh Incident',
    139; as Private Secretary, 139; with 3rd Cavalry
    Brigade, 140; at Mons, 140;in French's Staff, 141;
    as father, 143; letters, 144, 149; as Lieutenant-
    Colonel, 144; knowledge of Asquith, 150; on
    leave, 153; news of Asquith, 154; and 'Wullie'
    Robertson, 155; letter to Venetia, 155; betrayal,
    156–7; cool relations with Sylvia, 158; still with
    Venetia, 160–61; estrangement, 163–4; warmer
    to Sylvia, 165; sees Venetia, 166–7; and DSO,
    168; sells Chardstock estate, 169; Battle of the
    Somme, 169; birth of Juliet, 171; ends affair with
    Venetia, 172; as Brigadier-General, 172; German
    onslaught, 173–4; end of war, 176; return, 178;
    post-war career, 179; death, 180
Henley Lady Clare, 172
Henley, Lady Dorothy, 145
Henley, Anthony, 3rd Baron, 131
Henley, Hon. Francis, 131, 139, 145
Henley, Frederic (*later* 4th Baron),131
Henley, Juliet, 142–3, 171, 182
Henley, Kitty, 142–3, 152, 168
Henley, Rosalind, 142–3, 152, 168, 181–2
Henley, Hon. Sylvia, family background, 129–130,
    132; early years, 130; character, 133, 144, 157; at
    Penrhôs, 129, 133–4, 143, 167, 172; and Winston
    Churchill, 134, 181–2; relations with Clementine
    Churchill (née Hozier), 130, 134, 152, 158,
    163, 182; country house life with, 135; at
    Alderley, 130, 134–5, 143–4, 149, 162, 181; at
    18 Mansfield Street, 130, 137–8, 143–7, 150–51,
    154–5, 161, 167; and father, Lyulph, 130–3, 137;
    and brother, Arthur, 131; relations with husband,
    Anthony, 131–4, 138, 144, 149, 152–8, 163–172,
    175, 179–80; and sister, Blanche, 131; with sister,
    Venetia, 131, 134–5, 138–9, 145–149, 151–6,
    166, 172; and mother Mary ('Maisie'), 132, 149,
    157; and children, 134, 143, 152, 167–8, 171,
    179, 181–2; and Diana Manners, 135, 166; as

    confidante of HH Asquith, 143–151, 157–8,
    161, 168, 170–73, 180; friendship with Edwin
    Montagu, 143–4, 146–51, 157; work in nursing
    and VAD, 144, 158–9; and Margot Asquith, 145,
    148–9, 152, 162, 168; and Violet Asquith, 145,
    169; effect of 'the blue beast', 151, 154–5, 161–2,
    173, 184; discusses military operations, 152;
    and brother, Oliver, 152, 167, 174, 179; suffers
    depression, 153, 157; collapses, 157; and senior
    commanders, 155, 158; work with canteens,
    163, 173; visits St Paul's, 164; at Walmer Castle,
    164, 169, 172; at Royal Exchange, 167; visits
    'Glenconner', 176; women's suffrage, 177; joins
    Board of Governors, 177; travels with Gertrude
    Bell, 180–81; receives award, 181; friendship
    with Jock Colville, 181–2; and King's College
    Hospital, 182
Hobhouse, Charles, 51, 116, 165, 172
Hobson, Captain Richmond, 73, 76
Hood, Gladys, (née Youell), 16–17, 60–61, 187
Hoover, Mrs Herbert, 102
Hopkins, Ellen, 77
Horner family, 39, 135, 165–6
Hozier, Kitty, 134
'House of Mystery', 75–6, 87
Houselander, Sidonie, 69
Howard, Lady Dorothy, 139
Hulton, Sir Edward, 107

Indian Cavalry Corps, 34
Influenza epidemic, 63
Inglis, Dr Elsie, 141
IRA, 63, 65–6
Irish Easter Rising, 118, 170
Irish Home Rule, 139

James, Henry, 79, 87
Jenkins, Sir Lawrence & Lady, 113
Joffre, General, 52
Jones, Lawrence 138, 147
Joyce, James, 61
Judaism and Jews, 147, 151, 155

Keane, Ronda, 120, 127
Kennalley, John, 118
Kennerley, Mitchell, 87
Kensington Gardens, 22, 26, 33, 54, 69–71, 138,
    191–2
Keppel, Alice 53, 108–9, 159, 171, 175
Keppel, Sonya 108, 171
Kernochan, Katherine, 79–80
King's College Hospital, 173, 177, 182
Kitchener, Horatio, Lord, 13, 25–6, 44–5, 51, 57, 59,
    99, 107, 140, 150, 170
Knopf, Blanche 126

Lambton, Brig Billy 164
Lancaster Gate (94), 37–8, 57, 60, 67,
Lance, Chief Buffalo, 126
Lanvin, Jean-Marie 103
de László, Philip, 20, 120
Lawlor, Lillie, 84
Lesbian relationships, 83–4, 89, 100, 175, 179

Leslie, Sir Shane, 91, 99, 110, 127–8
Lewis, Sinclair, 91
Lister family, 135, 165
Lloyd George, David, 11, 50, 59, 115, 117, 138, 145, 150, 163, 165, 170–72, 177–8
Lockhart, Sir Robert Bruce, 124
Londonderry, Edith, Marchioness of, 96, 160
London Underground, 77
Loomis, Henry & Julia, 80
Loos, Battle of, 49–50,
Lusitania RMS, 91, 100, 118
Lutyens, Sir Edwin & Lady Emily, 97

Macdonagh, Michael, 119
Mackay, Lieutenant-Colonel Mackay, 118, 122–3, 184
McEvoy, Ambrose, 120
McKenna, Pamela, 161, 163
McKenna, Reginald, 163
Maine, Hospital Ship, 102
Manners, Lady Diana, 38–9, 45, 47, 53, 64, 84, 135, 153, 162, 165–6
Mansfield Street (18), 130, 138, 143–4, 146, 150, 167
Marriage, 9
Marbury, Bessie, 84
Marie, Princess (*later* Queen) of Romania, 17, 33, 64–5, 118, 125
Marienbad Golf Club, 20
Marinoff, Fania, 126
Marlborough, Duke and Duchess, 86, 91, 102
Marlowe, Thomas, 43
Mary, Princess, 83, 85–6
Meredith, Charles, 126
Meredith, George, 88
Metropolitan Opera House, 81–2
Milner, Lord Alfred, 11
Montagu, Edwin, pursuit of Venetia, 138; as cabinet member, 138, 147, 150, 172; in competition with Asquith, 139, 142, 144, 157; Sylvia's knowledge of, 143–4; proposes marriage, 144; as friend of Sylvia, 144, 157; and Venetia's conversion, 146–8, 155, 178; as Jew, 147; terms of marriage, 148, 178; and Margot, 148; and Stanley family, 149; marriage, 151; at Paris Conference, 178; death, 179

Moore, George Gordon, background, 26; friendship with French, 26; buys Lancaster Gate, 26; courts the Asquiths, 26, 46; invites Bennetts, 27; and Diana Manners, 28, 47; parties, 38; appearance, 39; at GHQ, 41–2; at GHQ, 43; visits US, 45; address to veterans 45–46; returns to Britain, 52; girlfriends 53; and French's dismissal, 53; rumours as spy, 56; court case, 56; leaves Britain, 60; help to the Duff Coopers, 64; leaves Britain, 68; ranching, 68; death, 68; meets Emily, 88; as courier, 36–7, 40, 184
Moran, Lord Charles, 64
Morand, Paul, 56
Morphine, 165–6
Mosher, Thomas, 77, 82
Murdoch, Keith, 98

Nesbitt, Cathleen, 90
Neuve Chapelle, Battle of, 39–40
New York City Public Library, 110
Niven, Henriette, 22
Night clubs, 24, 38–9, 60, 100
Northcliffe, Lord, 46, 97, 99, 114, 163, 184
Novello, Ivor, 62

O'Connor, TP, 43
'Old Meadows' (Woodpecker Farm), 84–5, 88, 90, 107–8, 118–22, 126–7
Olympic, RMS, 86, 88, 195
Orpen, William, 96
O'Shea, Kitty, 10

Paget, Lieutenant-Colonel, Bertie, 43
Pam, Max, 85
Pankhurst, Emmeline, 141
Pankhurst, Sylvia, 141
Pantazzi, Ethel, 18
Paris Peace Conference, 64–5, 125, 178
Paris, wartime, 102–4
Parker, Dorothy, 179
Parker, Lieutenant-Colonel, 140
Parnell, Charles, 10
Parsons, Viola 161
Paul, Prince of Serbia, 146
Penrhôs, 129, 133–4, 143, 168–9, 181
Pershing, General, 11
Petain, Marshal Philippe, 11
Philipps, Major-General Ivor, 50
Pitt-Rivers, Anthony, OBE, DL, 181–2
Pitt-Rivers, General Augustus and Alice, 130
Pitt- Rivers, Captain George, 181
Poets, 90, 123
Poiret, Paul, 81, 104
Polo players, 24, 31
Porch, Montagu, 102
Post-war society, 124
Postal service, 12
Potemkin, Battleship, 20–21
Proust, Marcel, 56

Queensbury, Marchioness of, 69

Repington, Lieutenant-Colonel Charles, and 'Shell Scandal', 43; and French, 53, 105, 107, 121, 125; and GG Moore, 53; relationship with Emilie, 98–9, 102–5, 107, 110–15, 118, 120, 123–4, 183; sexuality & affairs, 98, 105, 110, 114; and Northcliffe, 99; and Haig, 105; journalism & campaigns, 107, 109–11, 113, 121; and Kitchener, 107; friendship with Cowans, 117, 121; meets Kennalley, 118; and Joe Boyle, 111; with Doris Keane, 121; court case, 121–2; death, 125
Repington, Mary ('Molly'), 105, 113–4, 120–21, 125
Resco, Micheline, 11
Riddell, George, 170
Roberts, Lady Eileen, 56
Robertson, Sir William ('Wullie'), 27, 47, 59
Robinson, Geoffrey, 43

Robinson, James Fisher, 74
Robinson, Lieutenant, VC., 113
Rodin, Auguste, 110
Romania, history, 21; revolt, 22; war, 33; neutrality,
    42; enters war, 58–9; inter-allied conference,
    59; losing war, 60; Peace Conference, 65; and
    'Klondike Joe', 118
Roosevelt, Colonel and Mrs, 56
Ross, Sir Edward, 95
Rothermere, Lord Harold, 98
Rotterdam SS, 100
Russell, Bertram, 130, 132

Sassoon, Siegfried, 10
Schreiner, Olive, 83, 161
Scott, Lady, 101, 142
Selfridge, Mrs, 102
Sex, and soldiers, 10–11; and politicians, 11; 36–7,
    54, 97, 112, 124, 148, 151–2, 161–2, 174–5
Sexual diseases, 94
Shaw, G.B., 83
Shaw-Stewart, Patrick, 165–6, 173
Sheldon, Ned, 120, 127
'Shell Scandal', 43, 143–4, 183
Sigsbee, Admiral, 73
Sikorski, General, 181
Smith-Dorrien, General Sir Horace, 44, 112, 146
Smyth, Ethel, 169
Society of American Women in London, 102
Somerset, Lady Geraldine, 17
Somerset, Lord Henry, 164
Somerset, Lady Kitty, 164
Somme, Battle of the, 165, 170
'Souls', 65, 96, 135
Southborough, Lord, 128
Soutzo, Princess Hélène, 43
Spears, Major-General, Sir Edward, 40
Spencer, Captain Harold, 174
Spiritualism, 35–6
St. Davids, Lord, 50–51, 86
St. George's Hospital, 159
Stanfordham, Lord, 52
Stanley, 6th Lord, 181
Stanley, 7th Lord, 181
Stanley, 8th Lord, 181
Stanley, Adelaide, 132, 179
Stanley, Algernon, 132
Stanley ancestors, 129–30
Stanley Arthur, 131, 136, 148, 179, 180–1,
Stanley, Blanche, 131
Stanley, Edward, 132
Stanley, Lord Lyulph (also Lord Sheffield), 129,
    131–3, 136–7, 145, 149, 179–80
Stanley, Lady Mary ('Maisie', also Lady Sheffield),
    129, 132–3, 144–5, 149, 172
Stanley, Oliver 132, 152, 167, 174, 178–9
Stanley, Venetia, birth, 133; and Stanley family, 131,
    135, 138, 142; sexuality & character, 134–5, 138,
    142, 148, 157, 165; affair with HH Asquith, 98,
    138–9, 142–8, 150–55, 158–9, 180, 184; and
    'Corrupt Coterie', 135, 165; friendship with
    Violet Asquith, 138, 148; and Edwin Montagu,
    138–9, 143–9, 151, 155, 158, 161, 165–6, 172,

178–9; affair with Anthony Henley, 139, 155–7,
    160–61, 166–8, 184; as nurse, 145, 151–2;
    opinion of 'The Wharf', 145; and Margot
    Asquith, 145, 149; conversion to Judaism, 147–8,
    151, 155, 158; relations with Sylvia, 146–7, 150,
    152, 155–8; other affairs, 172, 179; affair with
    Beaverbrook, 178
Stevenson, Frances, 11, 117, 170
Stirby, Prince Barbo, 17, 33
Stopes, Dr Marie, 96–7, 124
Swaythling, Lord, 147, 155
Sydney, Basil, 121

Tableaux Vivants, 19
Taplow, 78–9, 121
Trask, Spencer, 76

United States, neutrality, 44, 90–91; journalists, 45;
    taxation, 82; Newport 'cottages', 82; heiresses, 91,
    101; East Coast sexuality, 93; Irish problem, 91;
    loans, 117; relations with Mexico, 118

Valentia, Viscount, 23, 31–2
Vechten, Carl van, 126
Verdun, Battle of, 11
Vernon, George, 165

Waldorf Astoria, 17, 73–4, 80
Walmer Castle, 164
Walpole, Hugh, 91
Walter, Babs, 95
Ward, Sir Edward & Lady, 86, 92
Warwick, Daisy, Countess of, 25
Watford Court, 131, 180
Wellesley, Lady Eileen, 90
Wells, H.G., 25
Wharf, The (house), 145, 151, 169, 172–3, 180
Wilde, Oscar, 10, 174
Wilson, Mrs Arthur, 120
Wilson, Sir Matthew, 172
Wilson, Lady Sarah, 159
Women's Patrols, 54
Women's suffrage, 141, 177
Wyndham, Captain Dick, 63, 65–7, 69
Wyndham, Francis, 69–70
Wyndham, Joan, 15, 67, 69–71,

Yerkes, Charles, background, 75; moves to New
    York, 75; supports Grigsby family, 75; at 5th
    Avenue, 76; fortune, 76–7; in London, 78; death,
    80; Will, 80; estate, 85, 87; mistresses, 111; in
    Dreiser novels, 127
Yerkes, Mara, 80
Yerkes Observatory, 75
Youell, Edward & Mary, 15–17, 59
Ypres Cemetery, 49

Zeppelin raids, 33–5, 46, 48–9, 101, 112–13, 149,
    162–3
Zorn, Anders, 81